I0753208

HISTORIC PHOTOS OF

DAYTONA BEACH

TEXT AND CAPTIONS BY

HAROLD D. CARDWELL, SR.

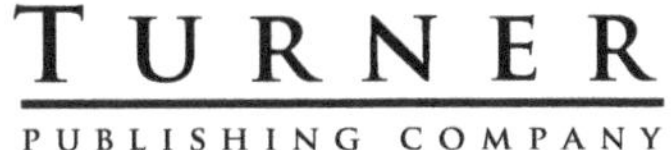

Road-beach racing resumed after a hiatus caused by World War II. The track was laid out for 3.5 miles (half the course was on the beach and half on the hard pavement) having a north turn and a south turn. The approach from the beach was hard-packed marl and shell.

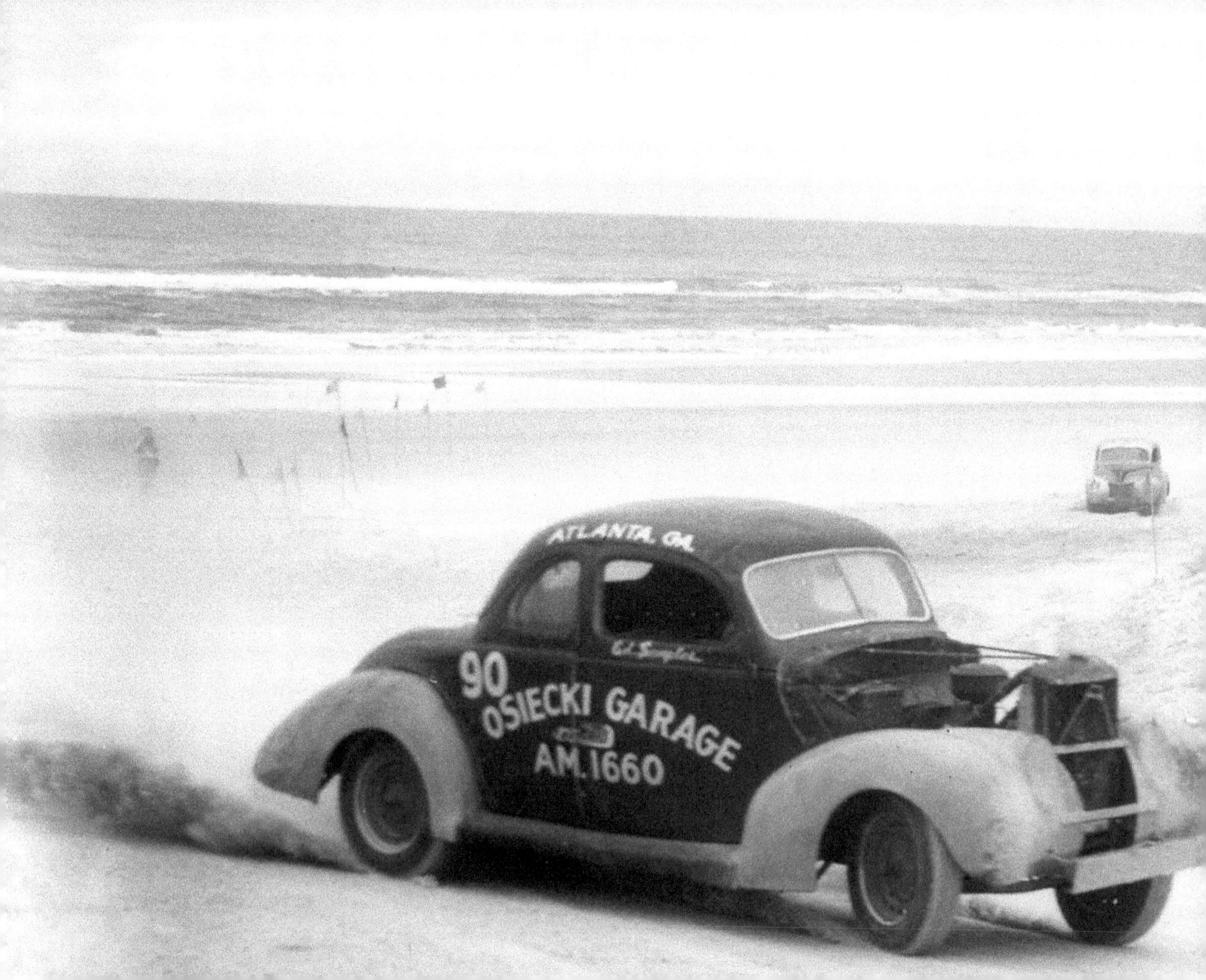

HISTORIC PHOTOS OF
DAYTONA
BEACH

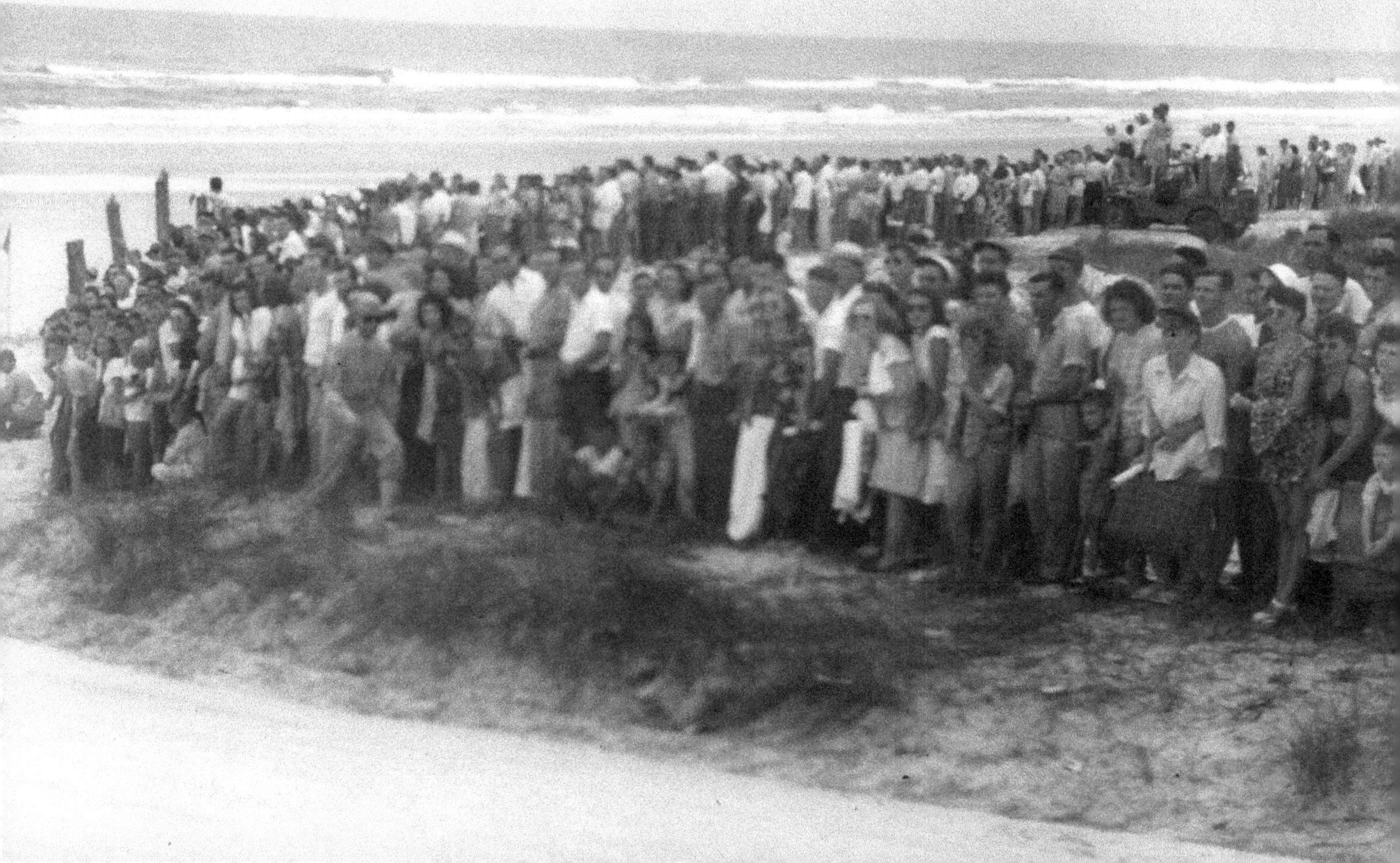

Turner Publishing Company
www.turnerpublishing.com

Library of Congress Control Number: 2006937034

ISBN: 1-59652-326-3

Printed in the United States of America

ISBN 978-1-68336-941-7 (hc)

Contents

The Firecracker 400, Fourth of July, 1963. The race was started with the pace car in front and the qualified drivers following behind. Notice the officials giving their signals to the drivers. Today NASCAR has improved the track with new grandstands for the fans, facilities for the race cars, and new safety measures for the drivers.

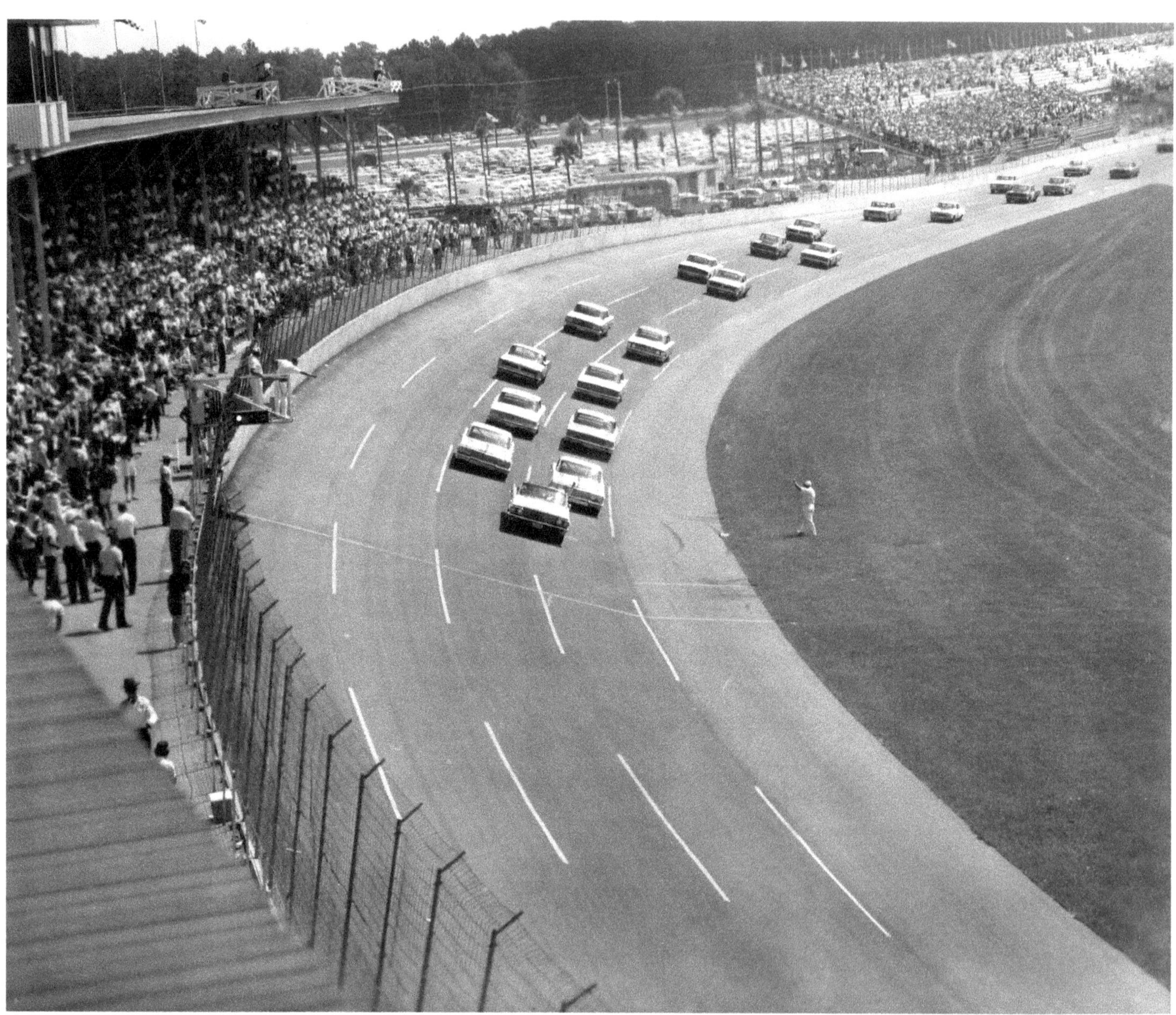

Acknowledgments

This volume, *Historic Photos of Daytona Beach,* is the result of the cooperation and efforts of many individuals, organizations, and corporations. It is with great thanks that we acknowledge in particular the generous assistance of the State Archives of Florida.

We would also like to thank the following individuals for valuable contributions and assistance in making this work possible:

Harold D. Cardwell, Sr., our writer

N. Adam Watson, Photographic Archivist, State Archives of Florida

Preface

Daytona Beach has thousands of historic photographs that reside in archives, both locally and nationally. This book began with the observation that, while those photographs are of great interest to many, they are not easily accessible. During a time when Daytona Beach is looking ahead and evaluating its future course, many people are asking, How do we treat the past? These decisions affect every aspect of the city—architecture, public spaces, commerce, infrastructure—and these, in turn, affect the way that people live their lives. This book seeks to provide easy access to a valuable, objective look into the history of Daytona Beach.

The power of photographs is that they are less subjective than words in their treatment of history. Although the photographer can make decisions regarding subject matter and how to capture and present it, photographs do not provide the breadth of interpretation that text does. For this reason, they offer an original, untainted perspective that allows the viewer to interpret and observe.

This project represents countless hours of review and research. The researchers and writer have reviewed thousands of photographs in numerous archives. We greatly appreciate the generous assistance of the individuals and organizations listed in the acknowledgments of this work, without whom this project could not have been completed.

The goal in publishing this work is to provide broader access to this set of extraordinary photographs that seek to inspire, provide perspective, and evoke insight that might assist people who are responsible for determining the future of Daytona Beach. In addition, the book seeks to preserve the past with adequate respect and reverence.

With the exception of touching up imperfections caused by the damage of time and cropping where necessary, no other changes have been made. The focus and clarity of many images is limited to the technology and the ability of the photographer at the time they were taken.

The work is divided into eras. Beginning with some of the earliest known photographs of Daytona Beach, the first section records photographs through the beginning of the twentieth century. The second section covers the early twentieth century through World War I. Section Three spans a period of time from the close of the First World War to the close of the Second. The last section moves from the postwar era to recent times.

In each of these sections we have made an effort to capture various aspects of life through our selection of photographs. People, commerce, transportation, infrastructure, religious institutions, and educational institutions have been included to provide a broad perspective.

We encourage readers to reflect as they go walking in Daytona Beach, strolling through the city, its parks, and its neighborhoods. It is the publisher's hope that in utilizing this work, longtime residents will learn something new and that new residents will gain a perspective on where Daytona Beach has been, so that each can contribute to its future.

Todd Bottorff, Publisher

This primitive log structure was one of the earliest landmarks along the Halifax riverfront that later became Daytona. It stood about where 154 South Beach Street is today. The logs were hand-hewn and boards were hand split. Later rough-sawn lumber was available to build houses when a sawmill was built in the settlement.

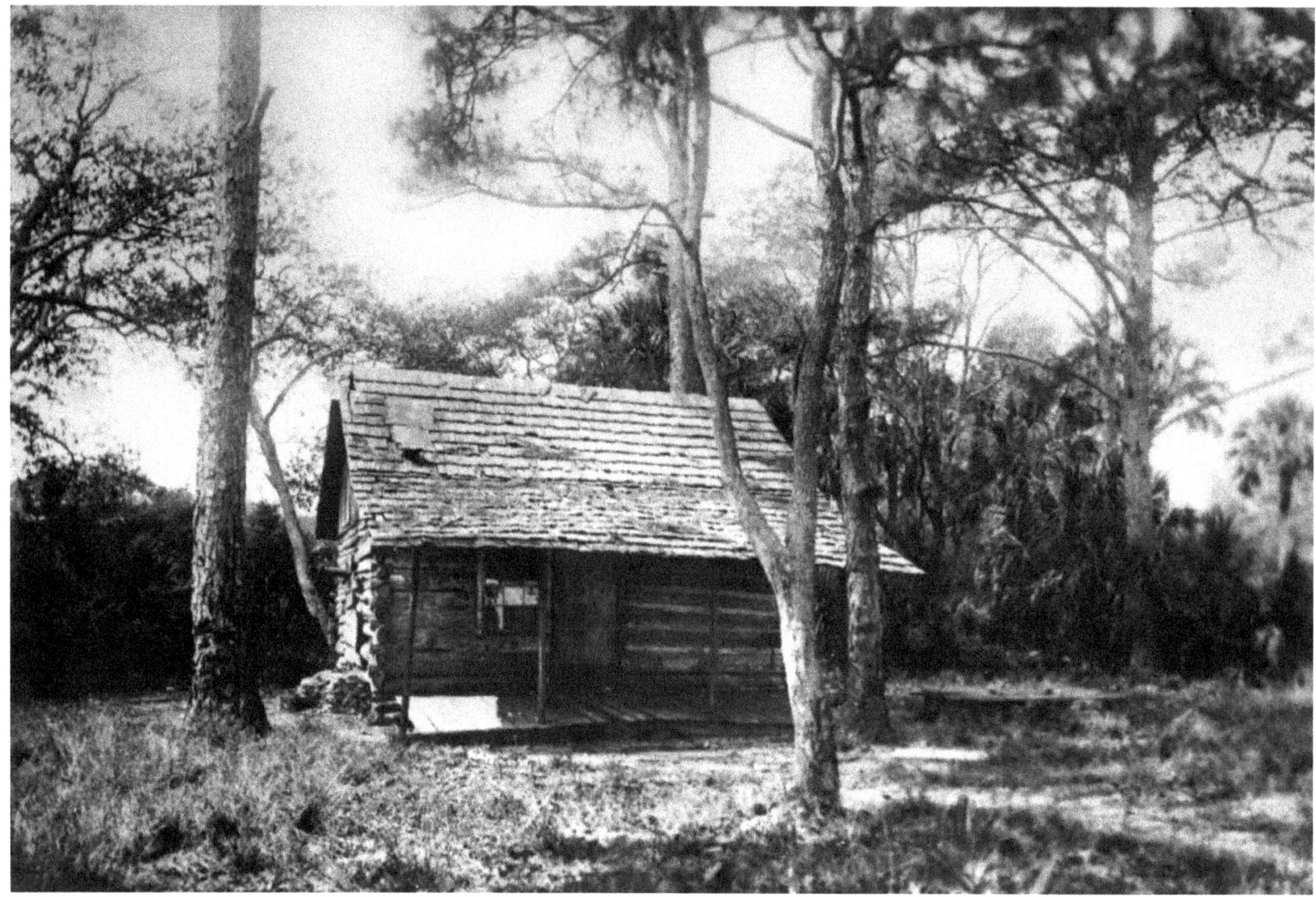

From the Wilderness to a Town

(1875–1906)

The first settlement was carved out of an old, overgrown plantation by Matthias Day. He brought fourteen workers from Ohio to build houses and a hotel where the men could stay. Log cabins were the first shelters to be built out of hewn timbers and split boards.

On July 26, 1876, twenty-five settlers convened at Jackson's store to organize a town. They appointed a council and they named the settlement Daytona to honor Matthias Day.

A second sawmill that started up to produce rough-sawn boards and timbers was Manley's Sawmill. It was located on Orange Isle on the Halifax River north of the settlement. This new source of lumber enabled the settlers to build homes, bridges, boats, and stores.

On December 2, 1886, a steam locomotive named *Bulow* arrived in Daytona pulling the first passenger cars on a narrow-gauge track. Henry Flagler purchased this railroad in 1888 and extended his Florida East Coast Railway Company into Daytona. The first depot was near where Orange Avenue and Beach Street are today. Businessmen started arriving and new stores, hotels, and houses were built. Mrs. Wilmans Post arrived later and established the town of Seabreeze. A yacht club was built on the river and the first automobile appeared in the town in 1898. Beach outings and fishing became a draw for tourists.

At the turn of the century, horses and carriages still plied the streets, which were still unpaved. After 1901, electricity became available. Ferryboats handled crossings but new bridges were being built to connect the mainland to the peninsula. As horseless carriages became less of a phenomenon, speed records were being set at nearby Ormond Beach and on Daytona Beach. The Florida East Coast Automobile Association was organized in 1903, and membership included well-known men like Burgoyne, Vanderbilt, Flagler, and others.

Mary McLeod Bethune started her school to teach the children of railroad workers.

The era ended with Daytona having risen quickly from a primitive settlement to a recognized tourist destination.

This steam-powered sawmill stood on the Halifax riverfront. Logs were floated to the riverbank or brought overland by ox cart. The rough-sawn lumber made possible the construction of houses, boarding houses, and bridges.

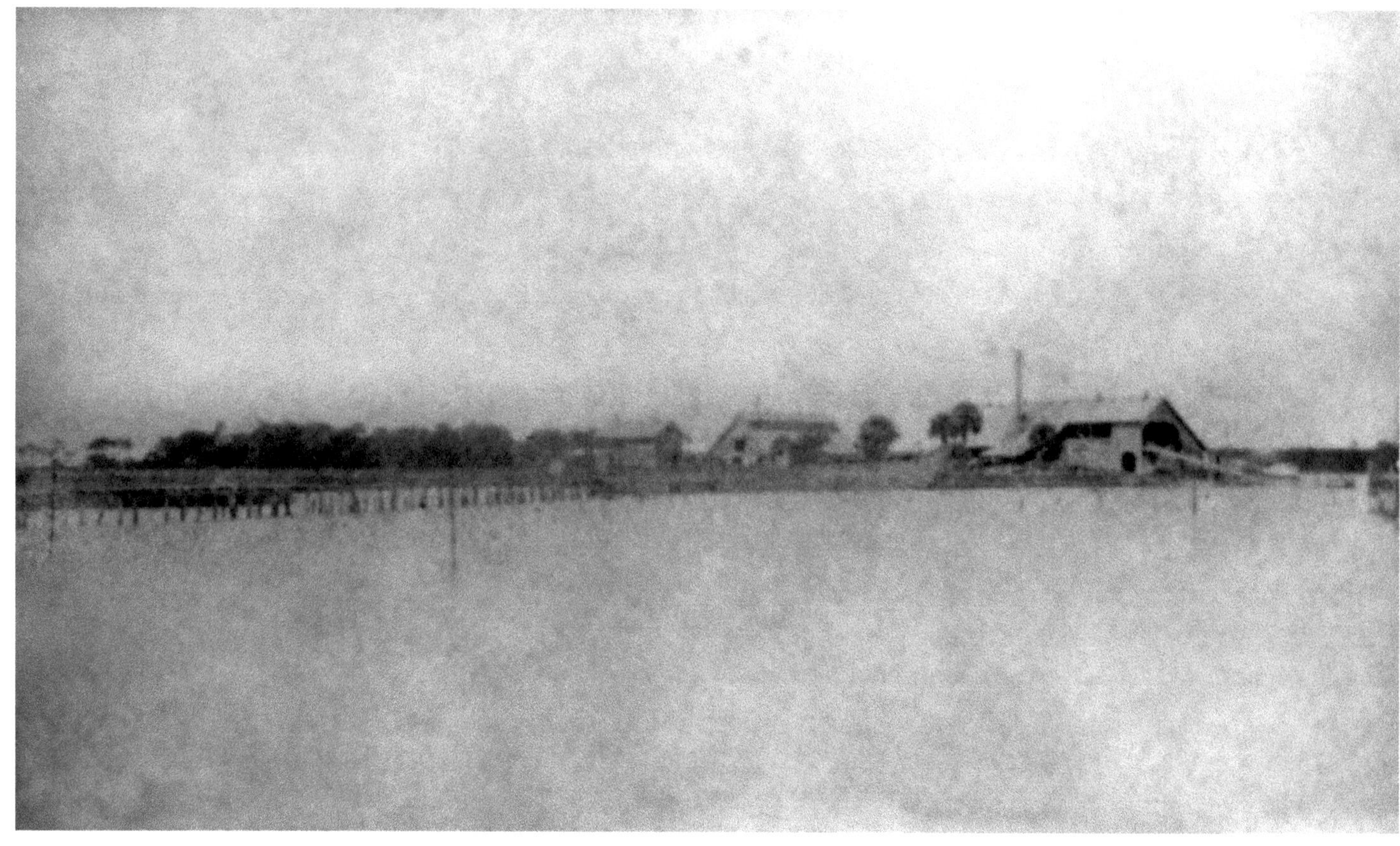

John Botefuhr, pictured, was a boat builder and sea captain. Boat construction was started by laying a long-leaf yellow pine keel. The bow stem and ribs were made from live oak, deck beams and planking were pine, and siding was cypress. All of this was secured with bolts and pins. The size of the boat depended on whether it was to be a sailing or steam-powered vessel.

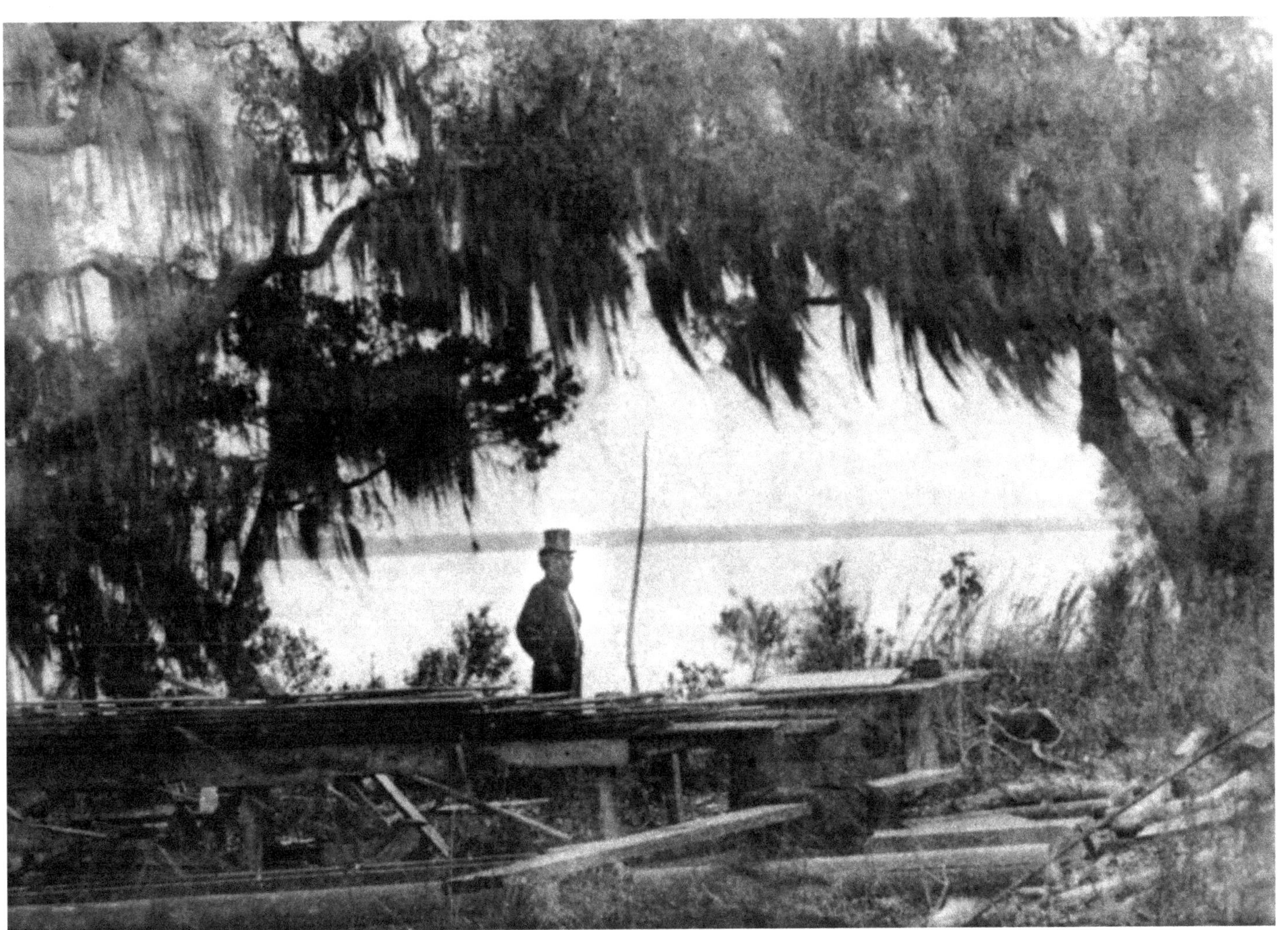

The small town of Daytona was growing. Buildings and houses, boats and docks were being constructed. Daytona was isolated by a lack of overland roads. Boats were the main source of transportation; therefore, the riverfront was most important. Here, Manley's sawmill is present in the distance.

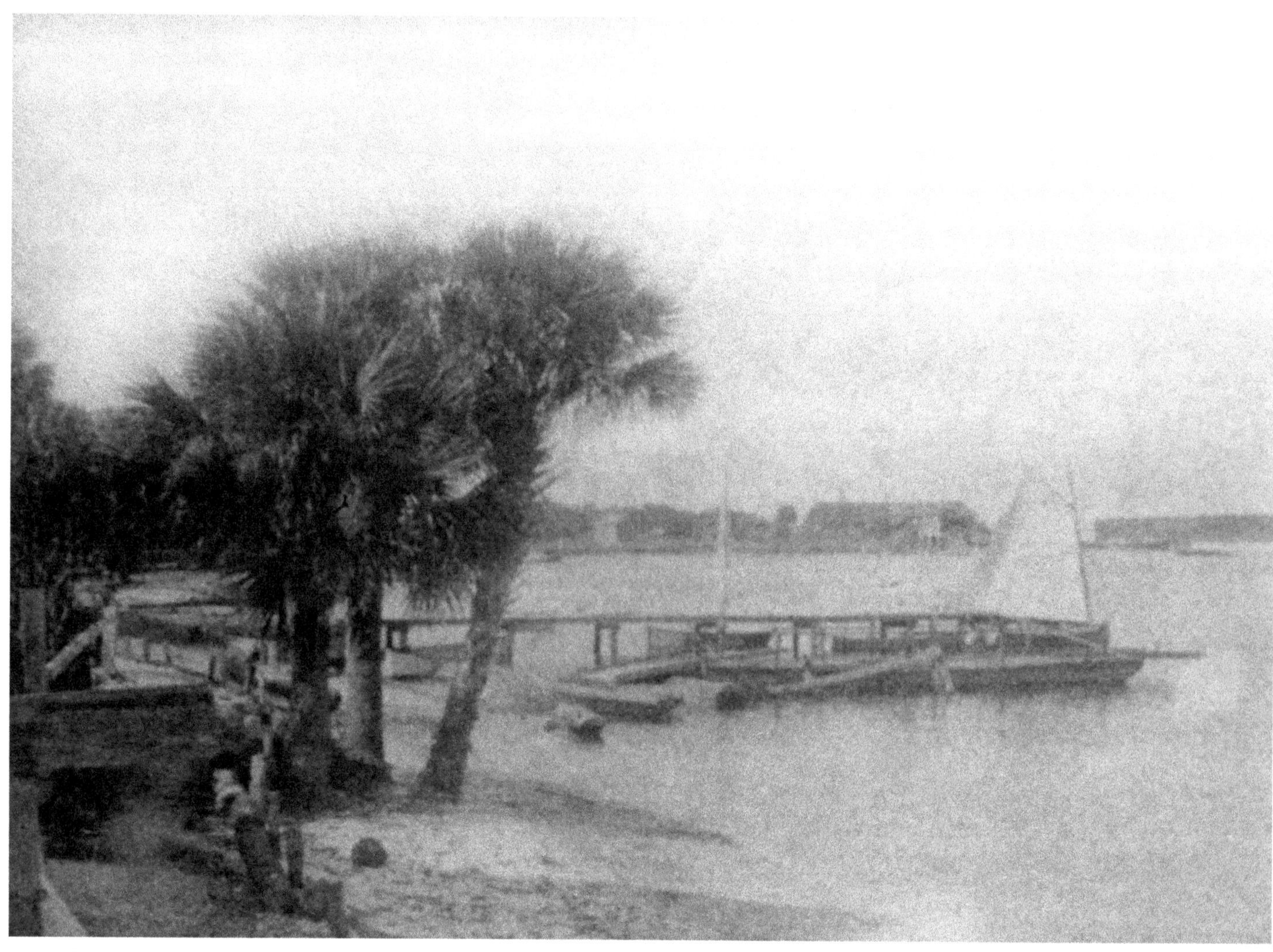

The St. Johns and Halifax River Railway Company brought the narrow-gauge railroad to Daytona, December 2, 1886. The steam-powered locomotive, *Bulow*, was built by the Baldwin Railroad Works. Pulling the first cars with passengers to the terminal at Daytona's riverfront, it introduced a new era of transportation to the settlement.

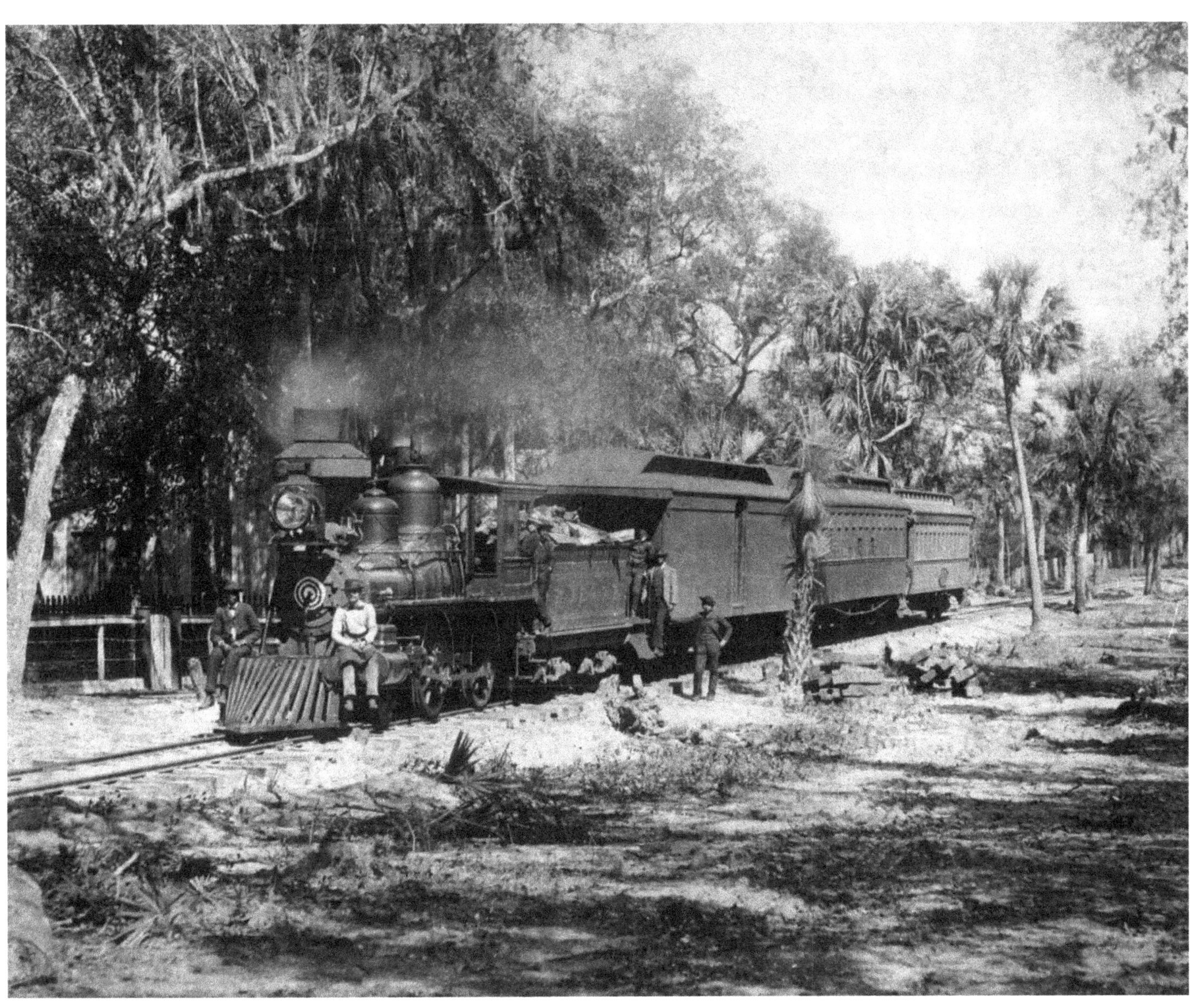

Matthias Day, founder of Daytona, built the Colony House in 1872 for the boarding workers who were building new houses in the settlement. Roofing shingles did not arrive in time for the opening, so palmetto fronds were used—hence the name Palmetto House. Fire destroyed the building in 1922.

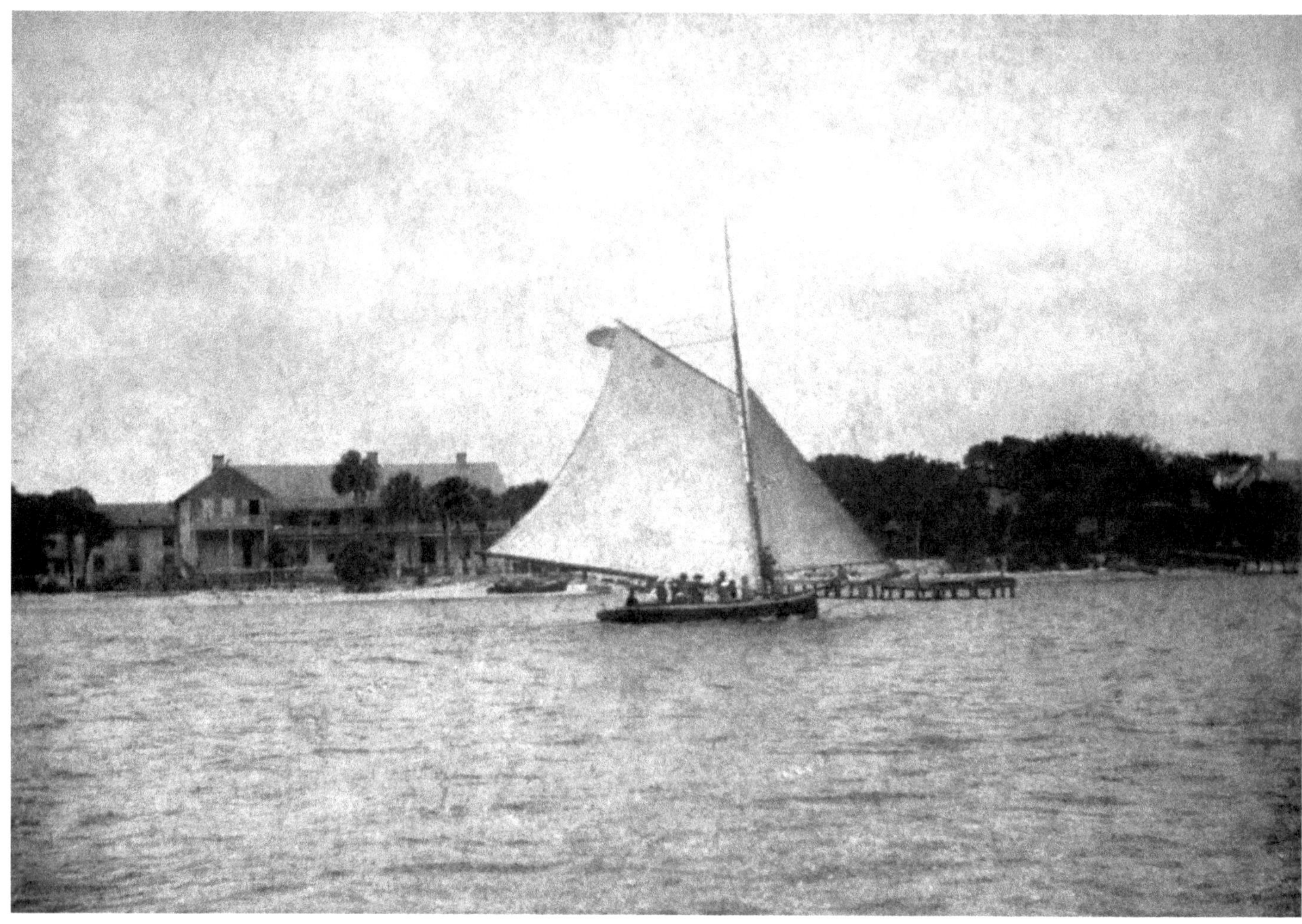

At right is the Thompson Bros. general store and to the left is the Lawrence Thompson residence, built in 1879. The road shown was paved with packed marl and crushed shell and is today South Beach Street near Loomis Avenue.

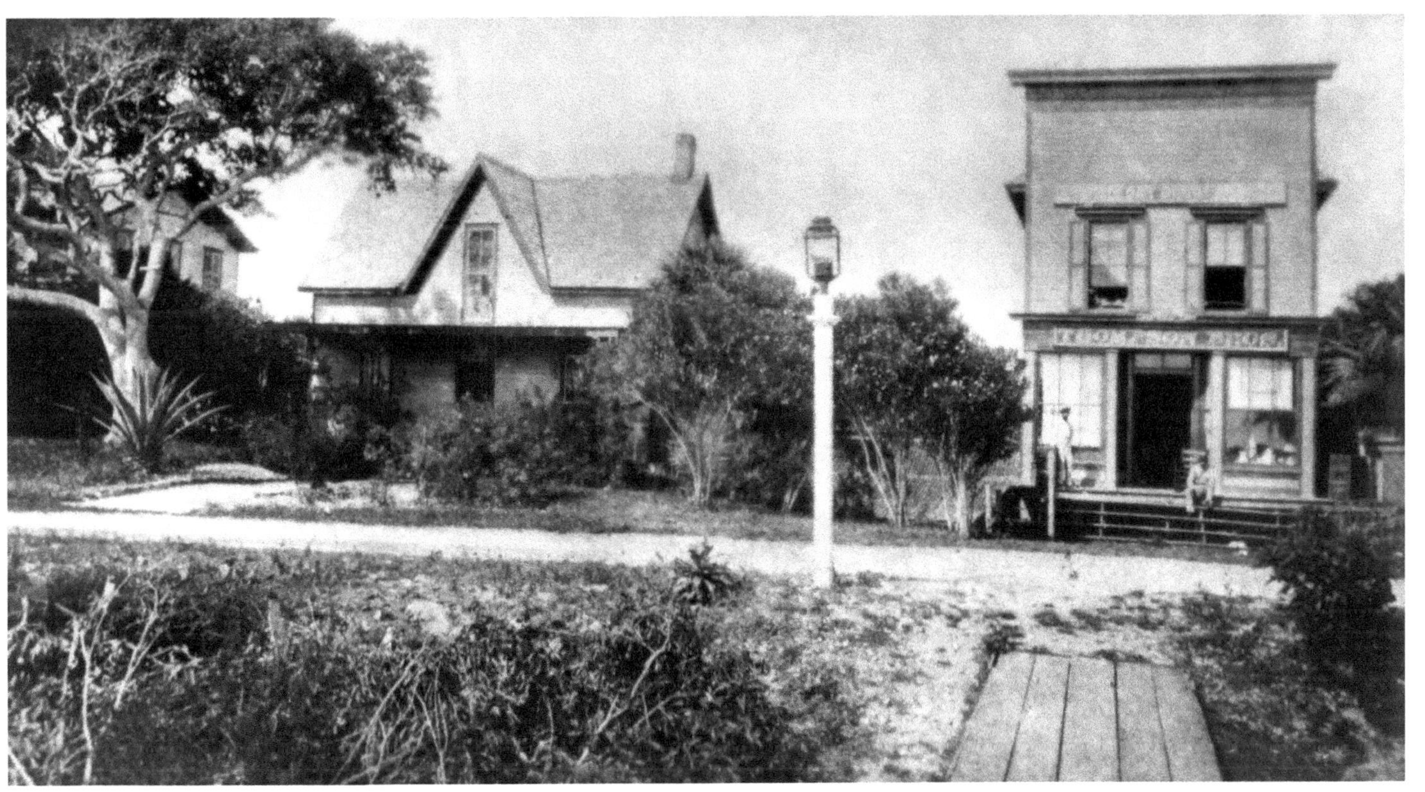

Workers are seen here doing the grading of the right of way for Ocean Boulevard. Mrs. Helen Wilmans Post, riding in her carriage, inspects the construction work. Later the Wilmans Post Opera House and hotel were built on this new boulevard, which became Seabreeze Boulevard.

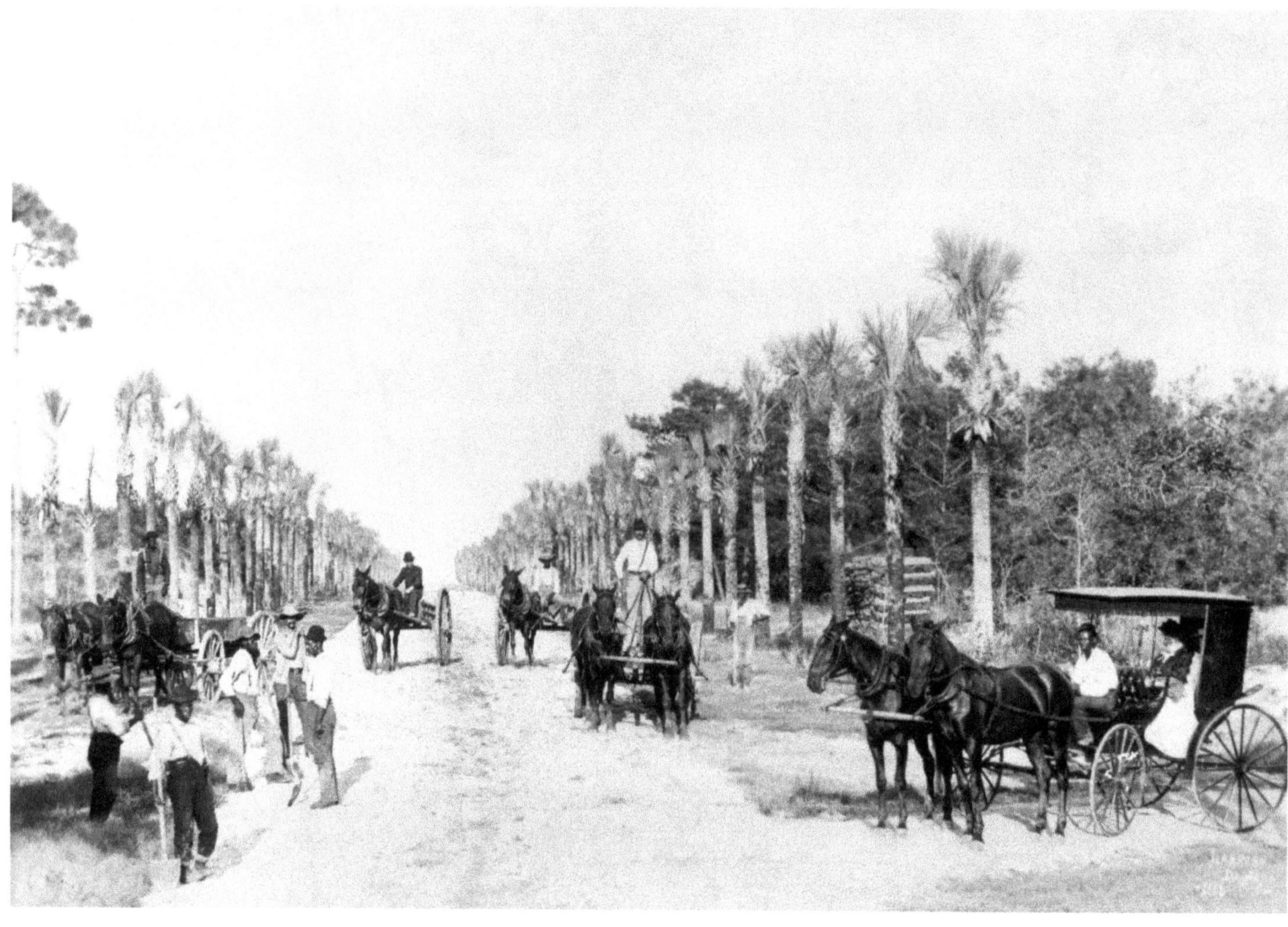

This fashionable vernacular two-story frame home with gable roof stood on Ridgewood Avenue. New houses were being built in this section of town. This photo was recorded by E. G. Harris, well-known author and photographer.

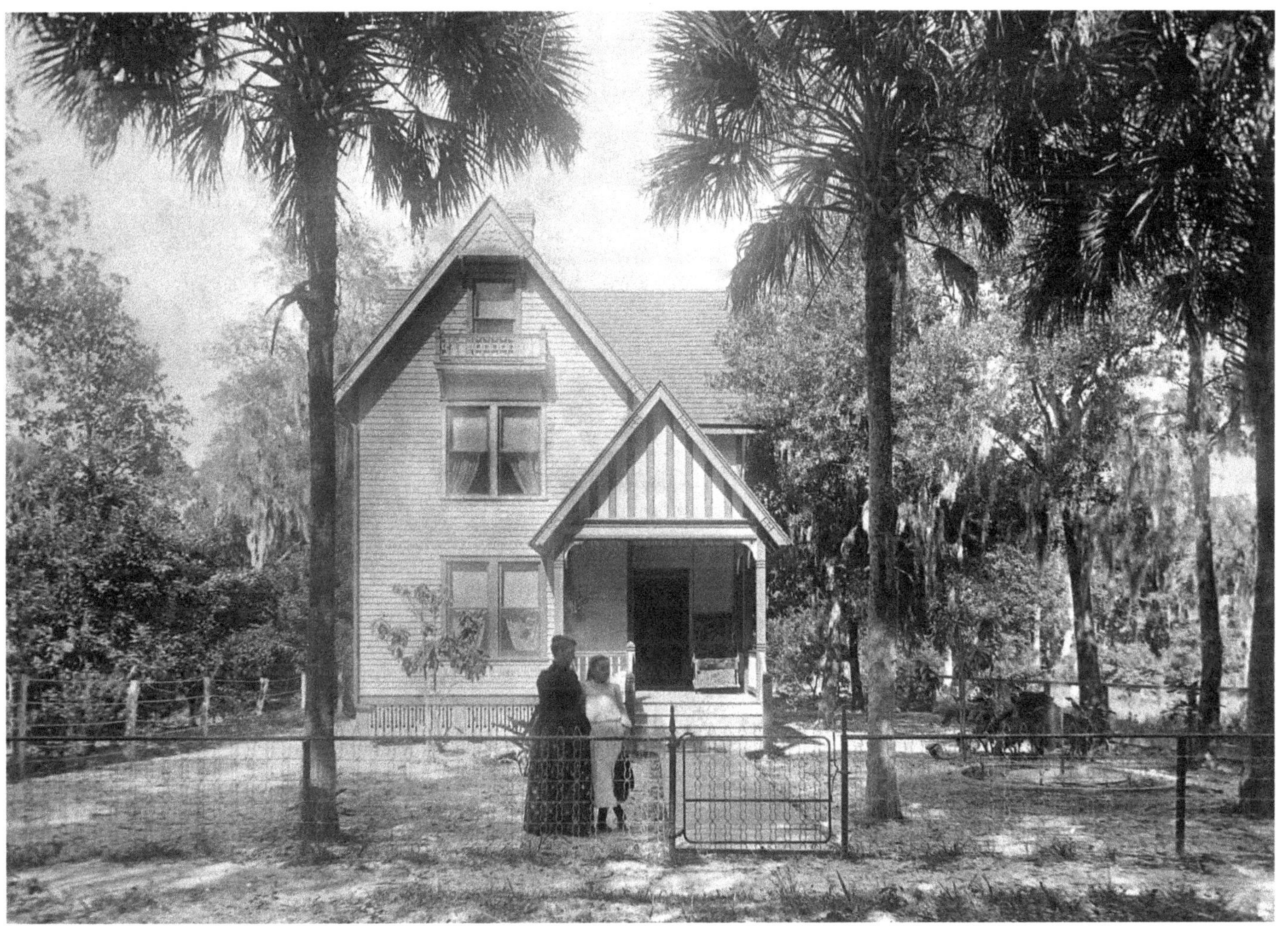

This early photo by E. G. Harris shows bathers on the beach and in the water. In the background are new buildings and hotels, which were beginning to dot the landscape. The beachside was being developed.

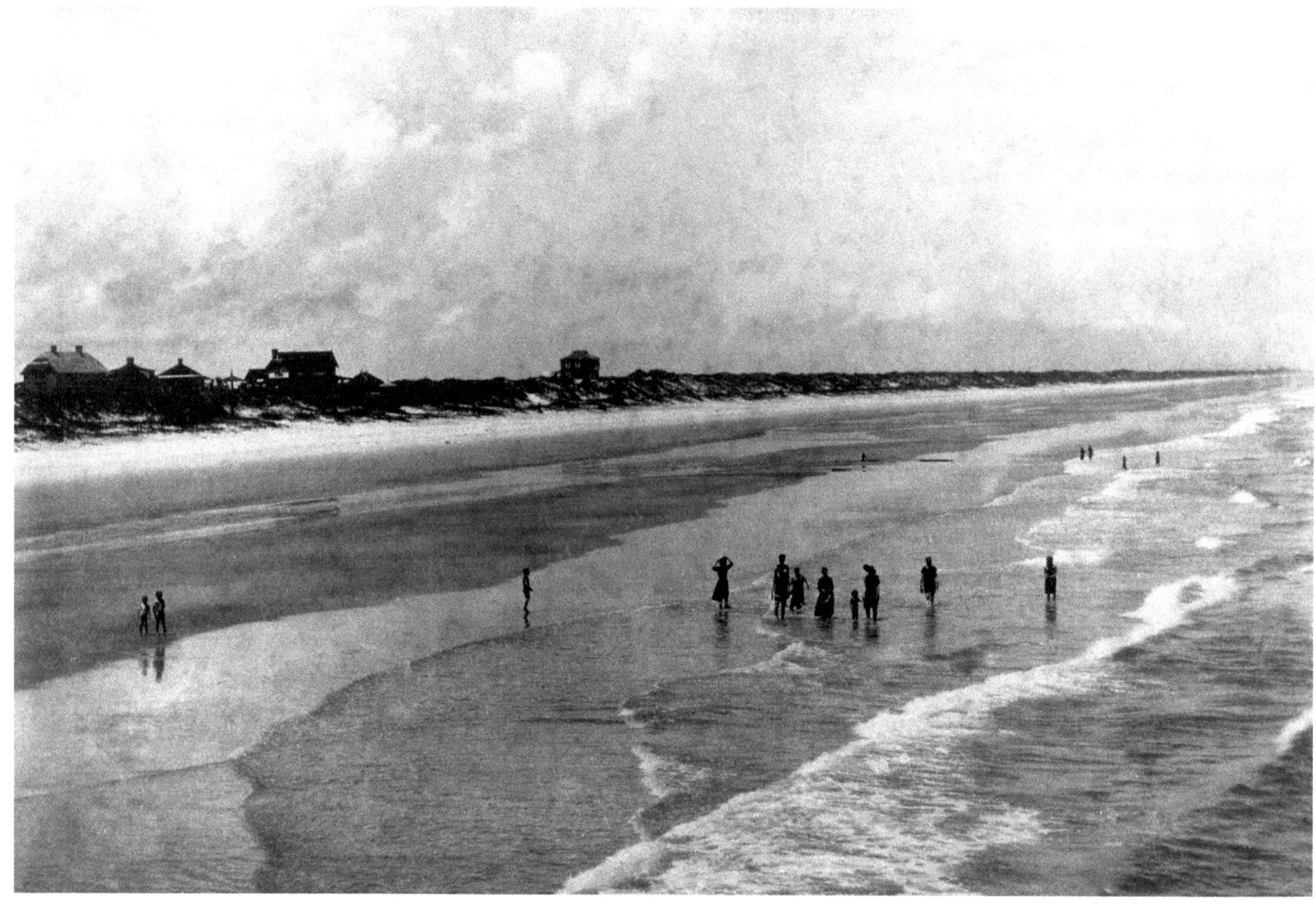

The Yacht Club was chartered in 1896. In this view, log pilings are being driven in preparation for its construction. A new, modern clubhouse was completed in 2006. The old structure was to be dismantled in 2007 because of environmental damage to the waterfront.

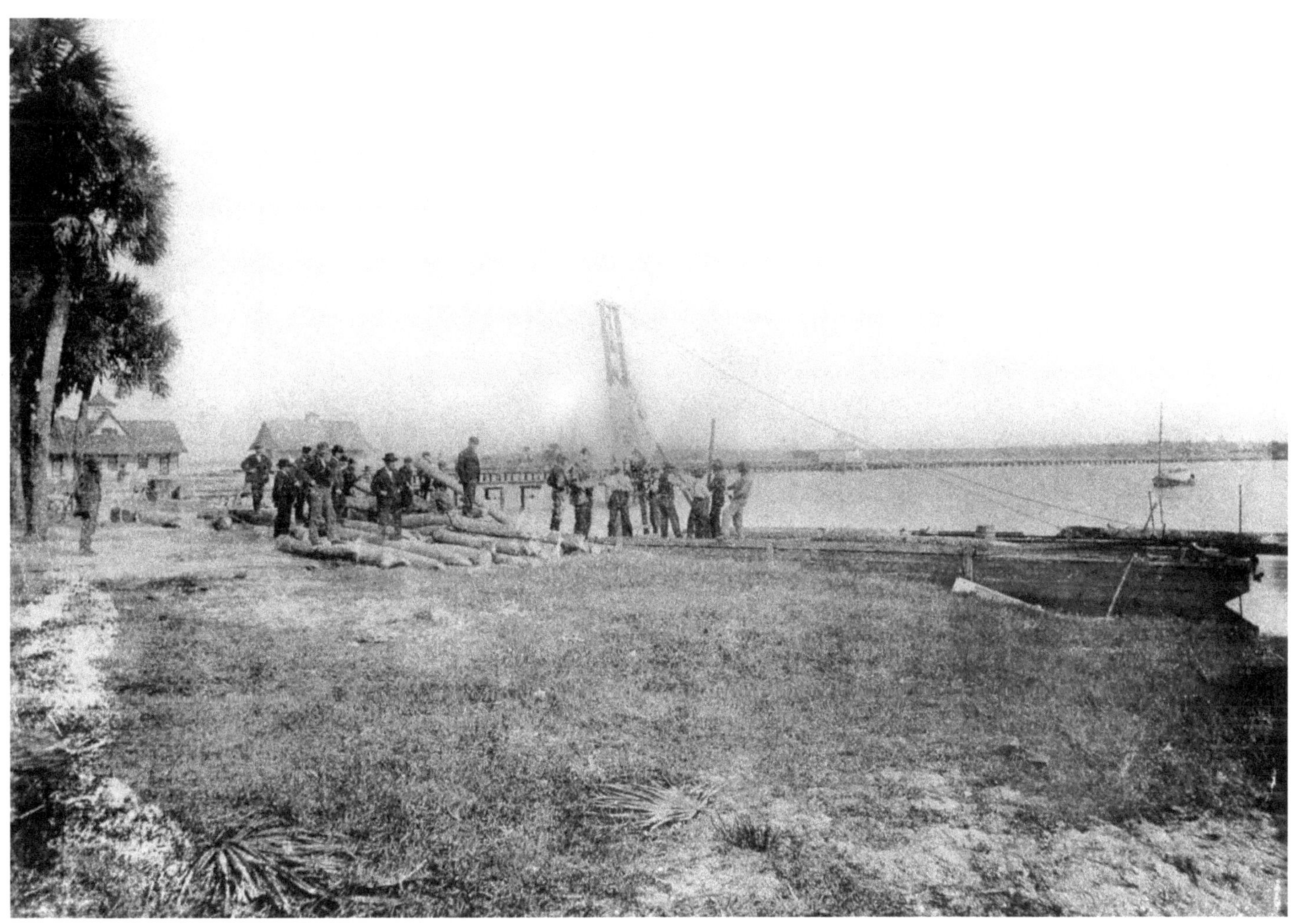

A nineteenth-century version of a day at the beach—horses, carriages, and people in full dress take in the view. The Keating Pier can be seen in the background. It had been destroyed by storms by the turn of the century.

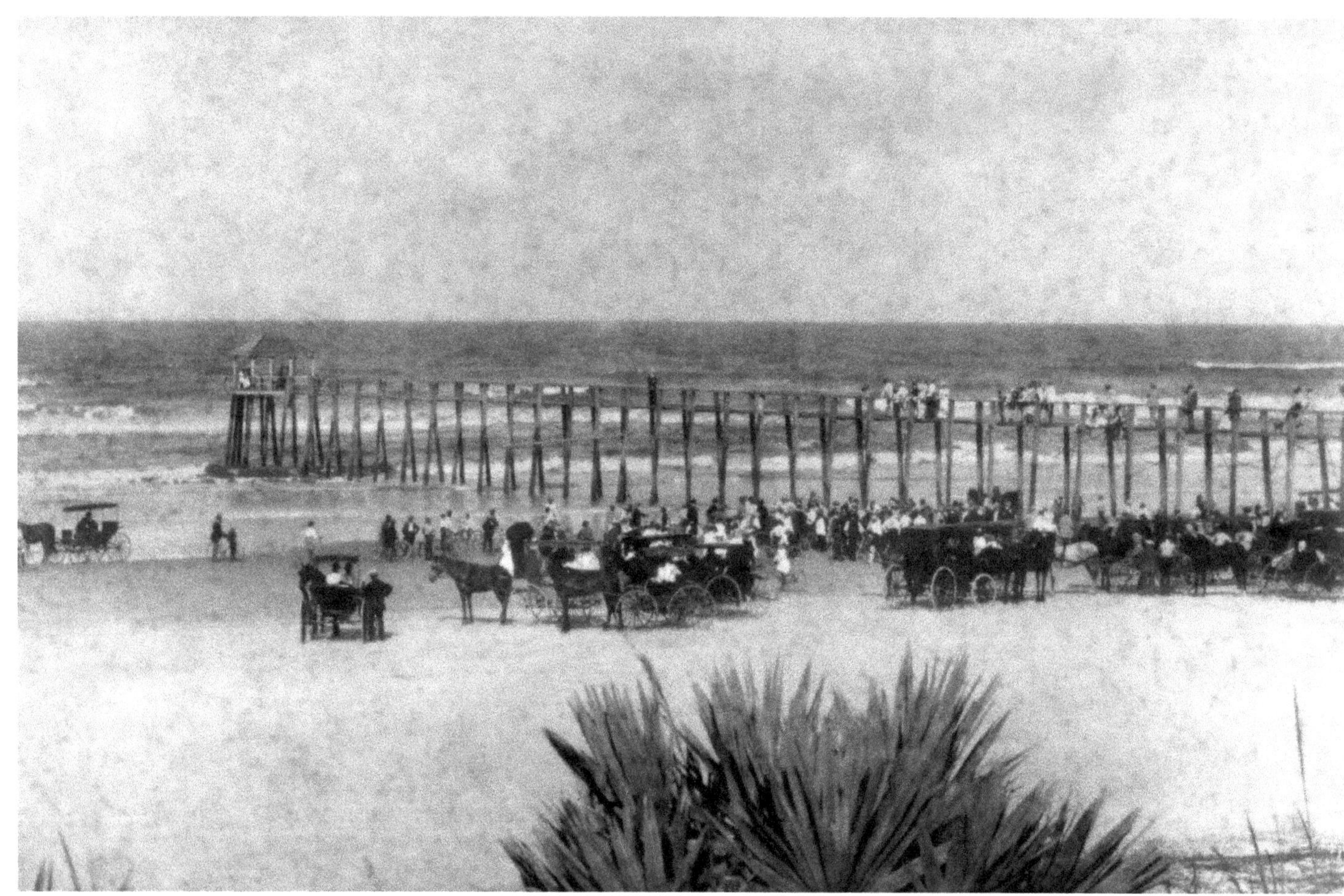

The new, fashionable yacht club is visible to the right. Also pictured is the river pier for unloading and shipping supplies by steamboat. Notice the sabal palms and oak trees with a man on foot in the left foreground.

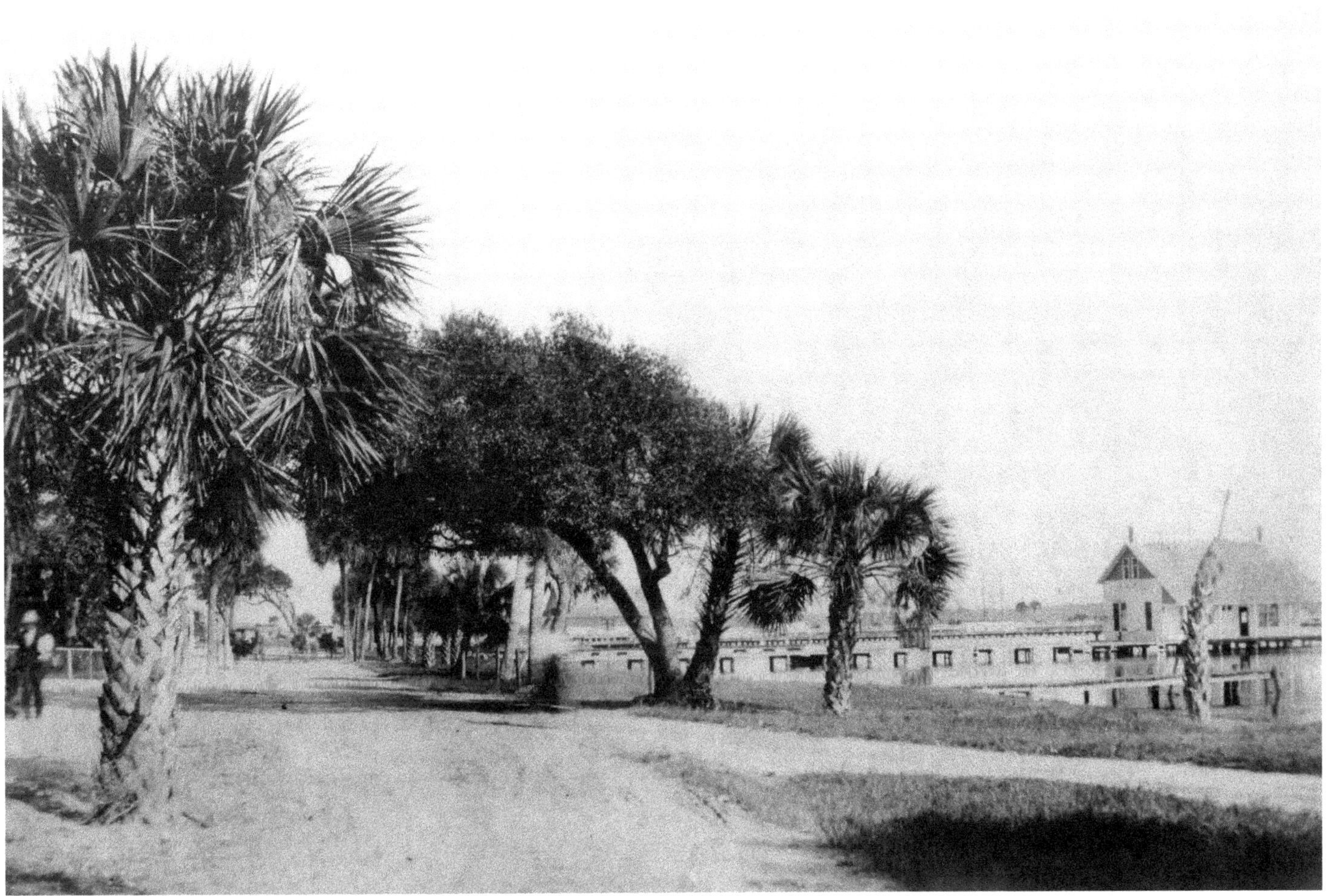

This automobile was owned by H. H. Seelye, who helped form an auto club. In 1903 the Florida East Coast Automobile Association was organized. The club was responsible for promoting races on the beach. This photo was taken after 1898, in front of the Colonnades Hotel, Ocean Boulevard.

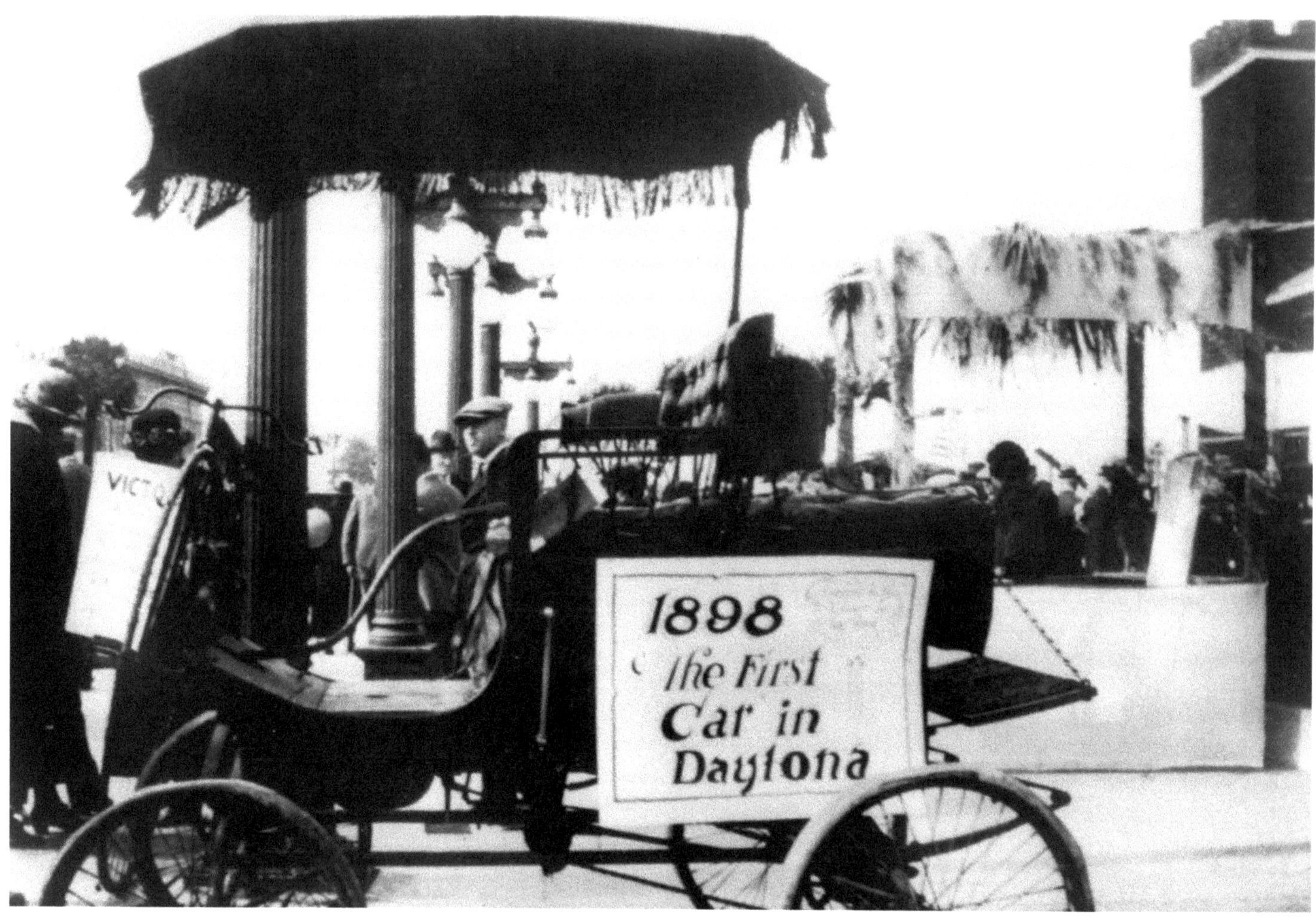

The South Bridge was a great achievement for Daytona. This bridge enabled horse and carriage and later the horseless carriage to cross from the peninsula to the mainland. Note the bridge tender's house at the draw and in the distance the Halifax River Yacht Club and Palmetto House.

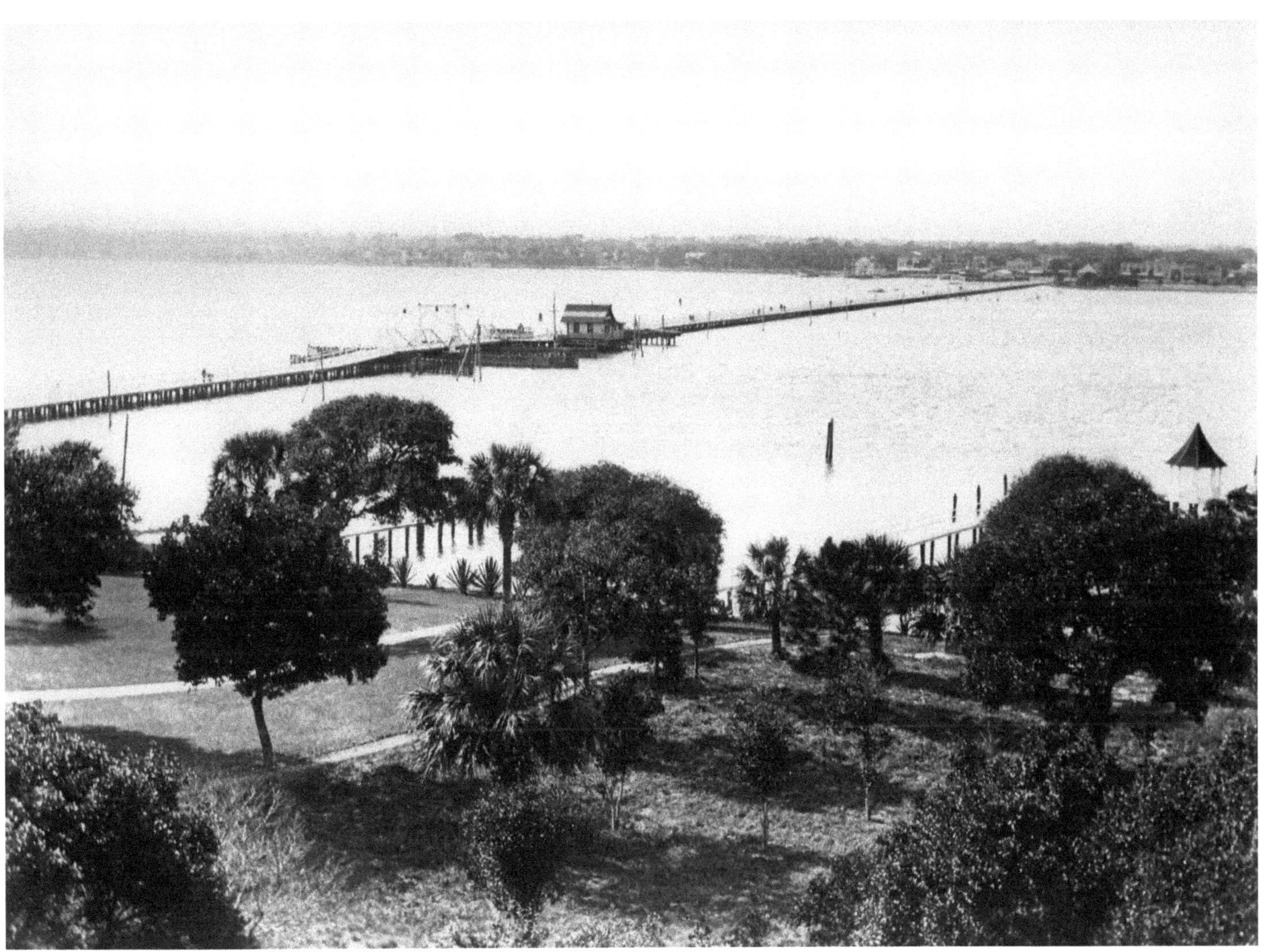

Palmetto House accommodated new settlers and workers who came to live and work in the new town. This hotel was advantageous to fishermen, who could leave in boats nearby for a daily catch, and hunters, who could retreat into the backwoods for a day of hunting deer and turkey. Mary Hoag was manager and proprietor.

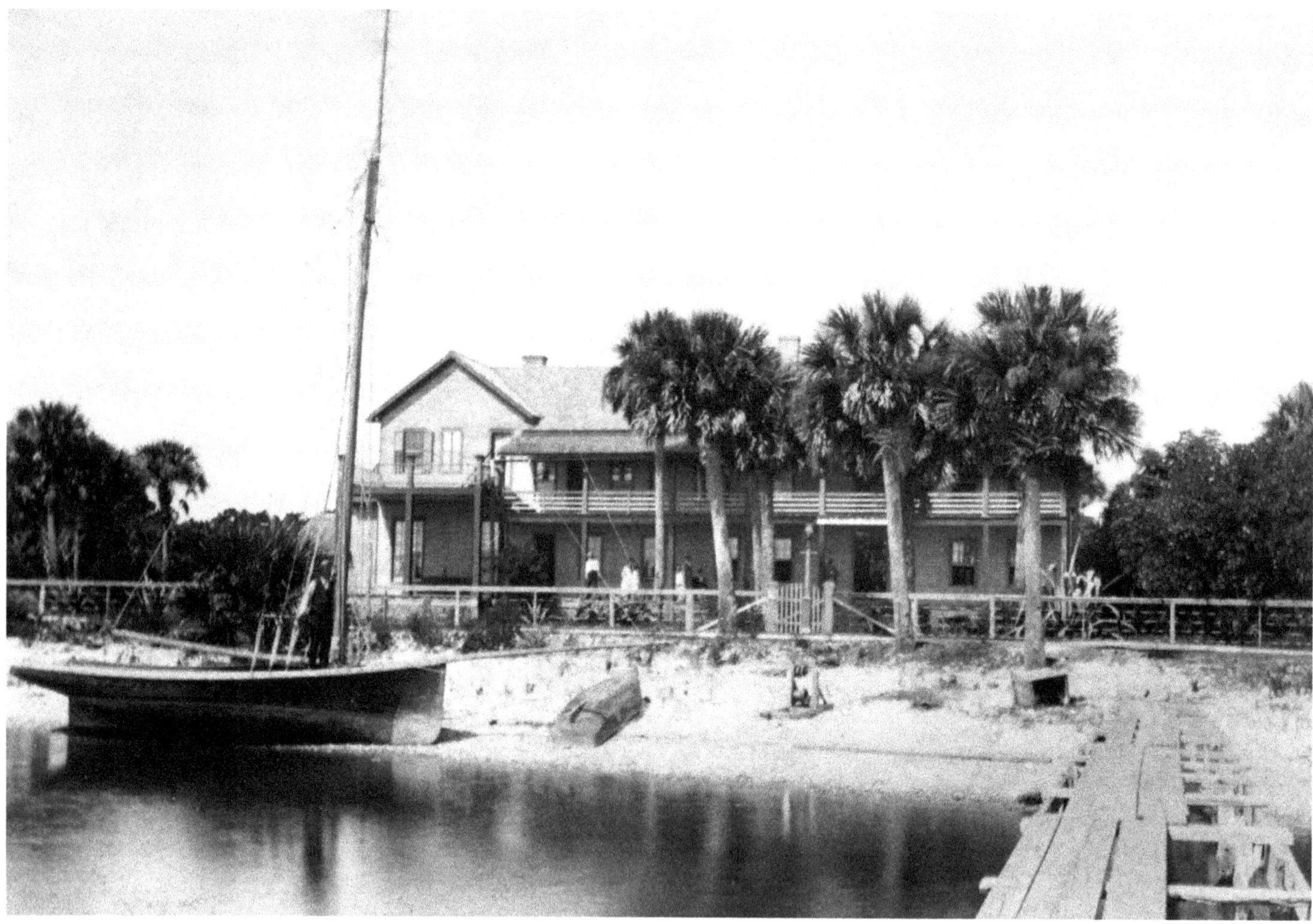

Wind-sailors, bicycles, steam-powered, gas-powered, and human-powered vehicles gather at the beach for E. G. Harris to make this impressive photograph. A lone horse and buggy stands apart in the distance, as though to suggest its passage into history.

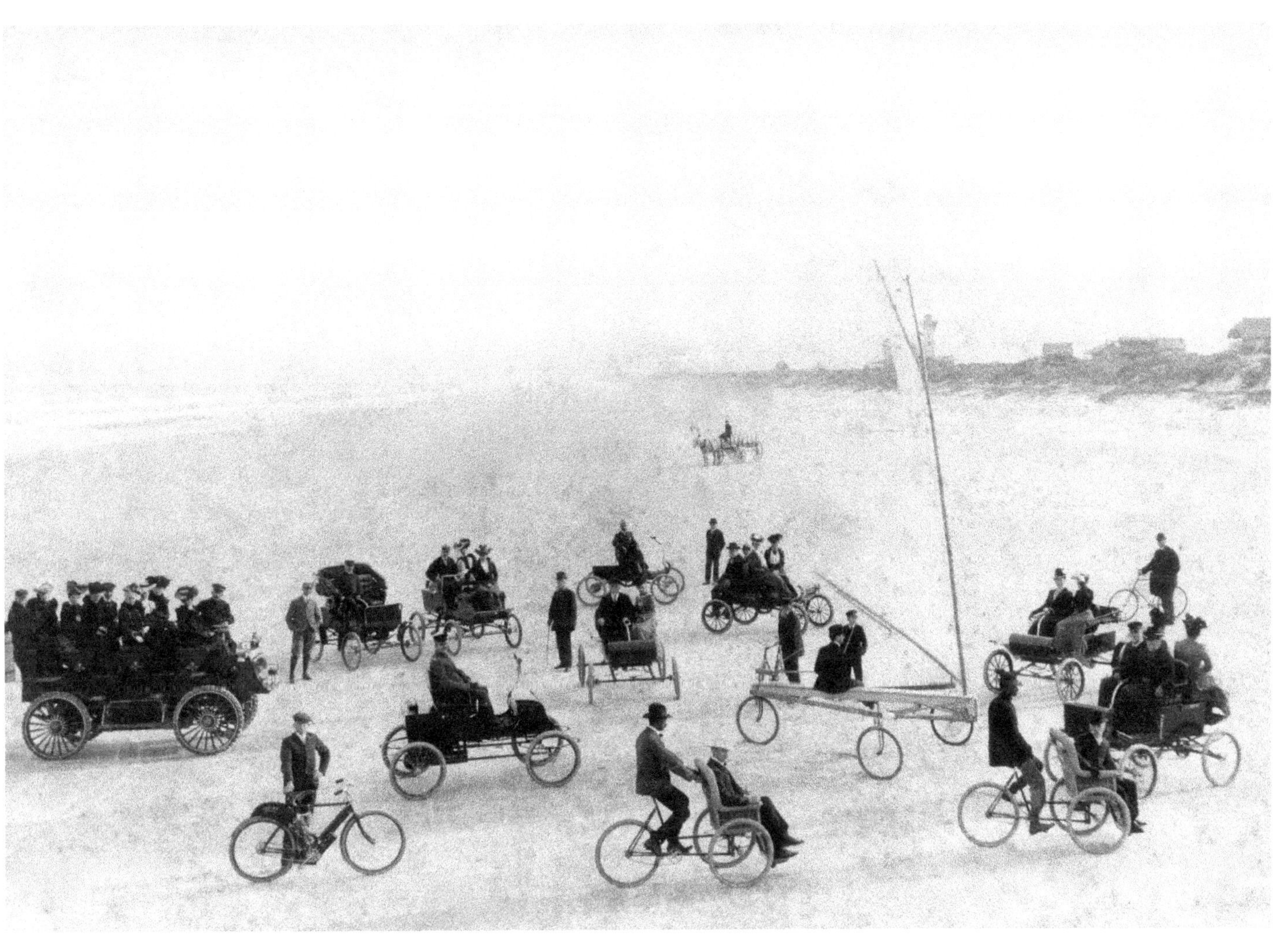

This building was moved from what is now Main Street to Ocean Boulevard with the approval of federal authorities. The move was necessary to accommodate the heavy bulk mail of Helen W. Post's publishing business. As a result of protests regarding the move, south of Main Street (today) became a dividing line for what was called Goodall (town).

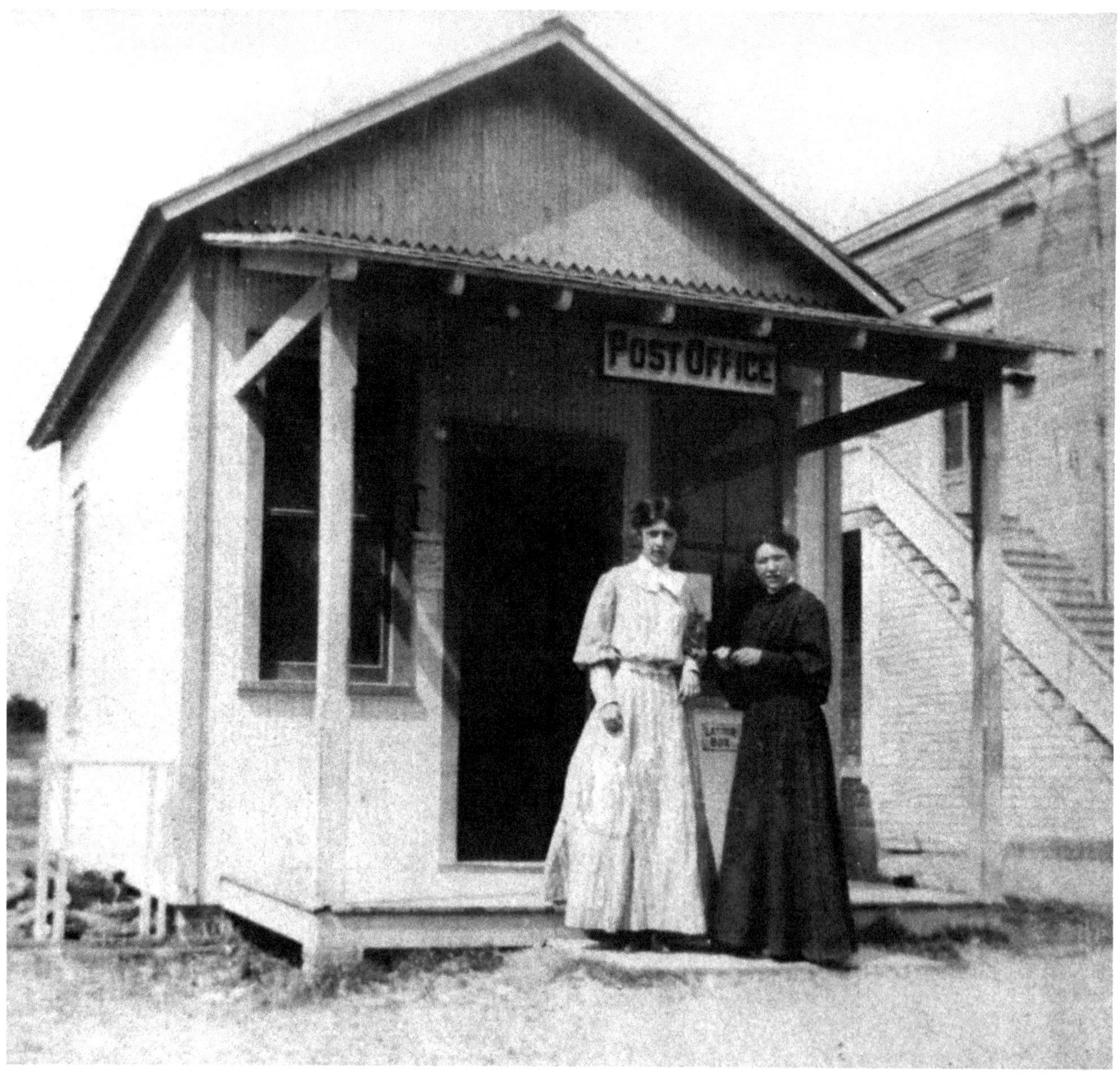

This early, winding river road, later named Beach Street, is seen here with its native palms. These were a source of food and fiber. The fronds were used for early thatched roofs and their trunks were used in the early days for building log cabins.

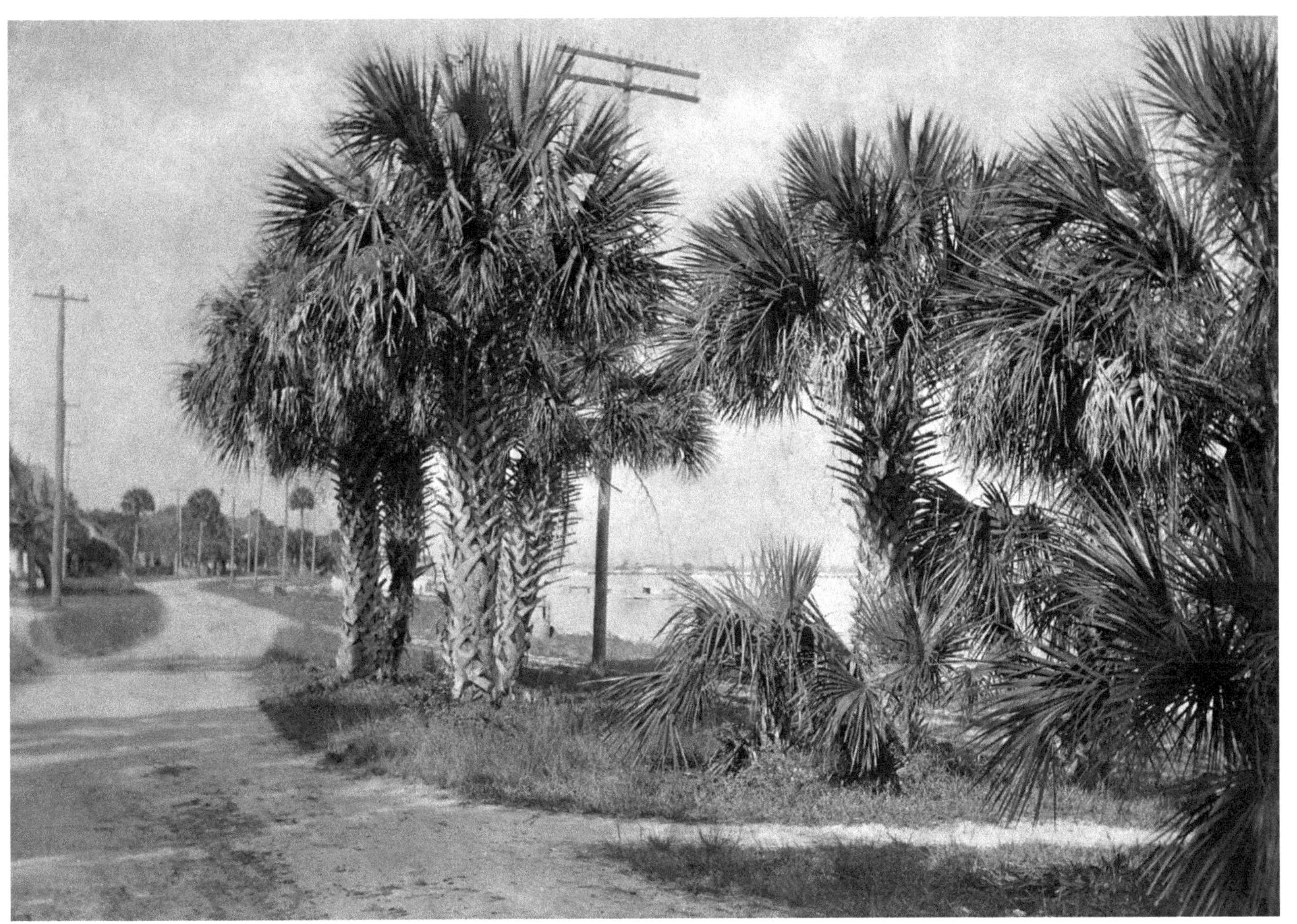

The jitney, pictured here, was a forerunner of the city bus. It brought passengers from the depot to hotels or for sightseeing tours or shopping. Canvas tops were later added to protect riders from inclement weather.

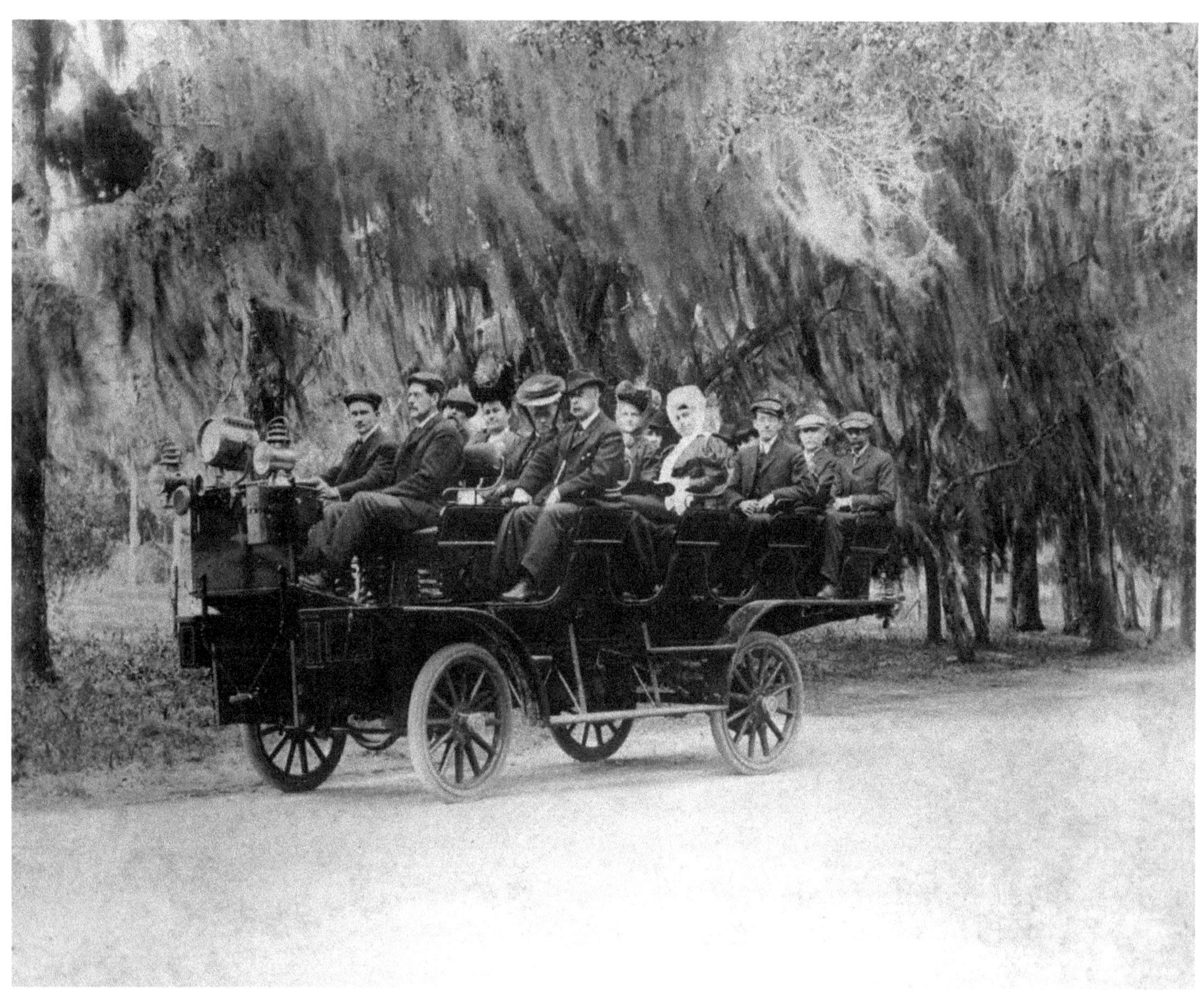

The prominent lady dressed in a blouse and long skirt below was the wife of Henry K. DuBois, a well-known physician of Port Orange.

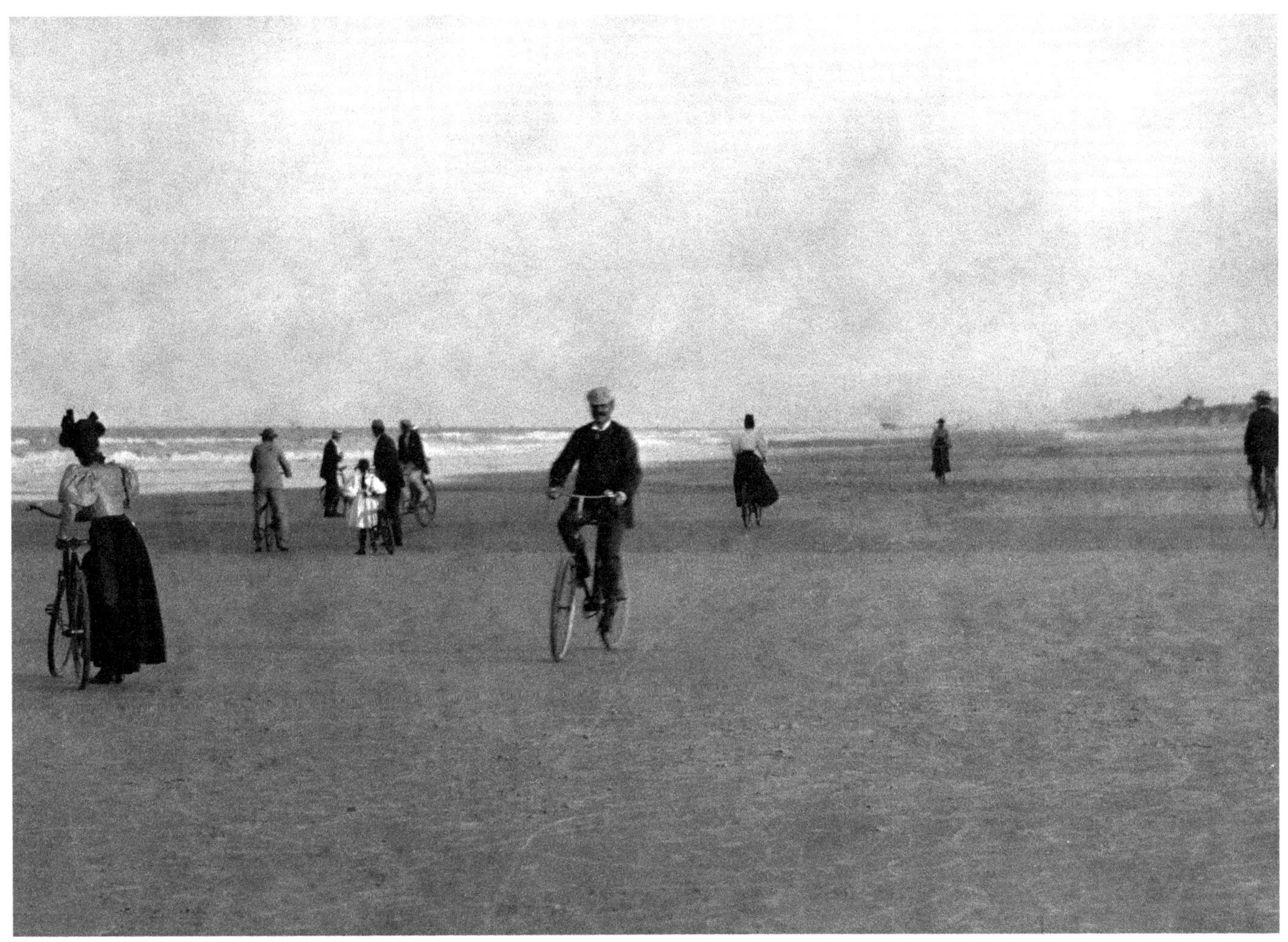

This early photograph shows buildings along an unpaved South Beach Street. In the distance a horse-drawn enclosed wagon delivers supplies. In the foreground is a barber shop and the City Hotel.

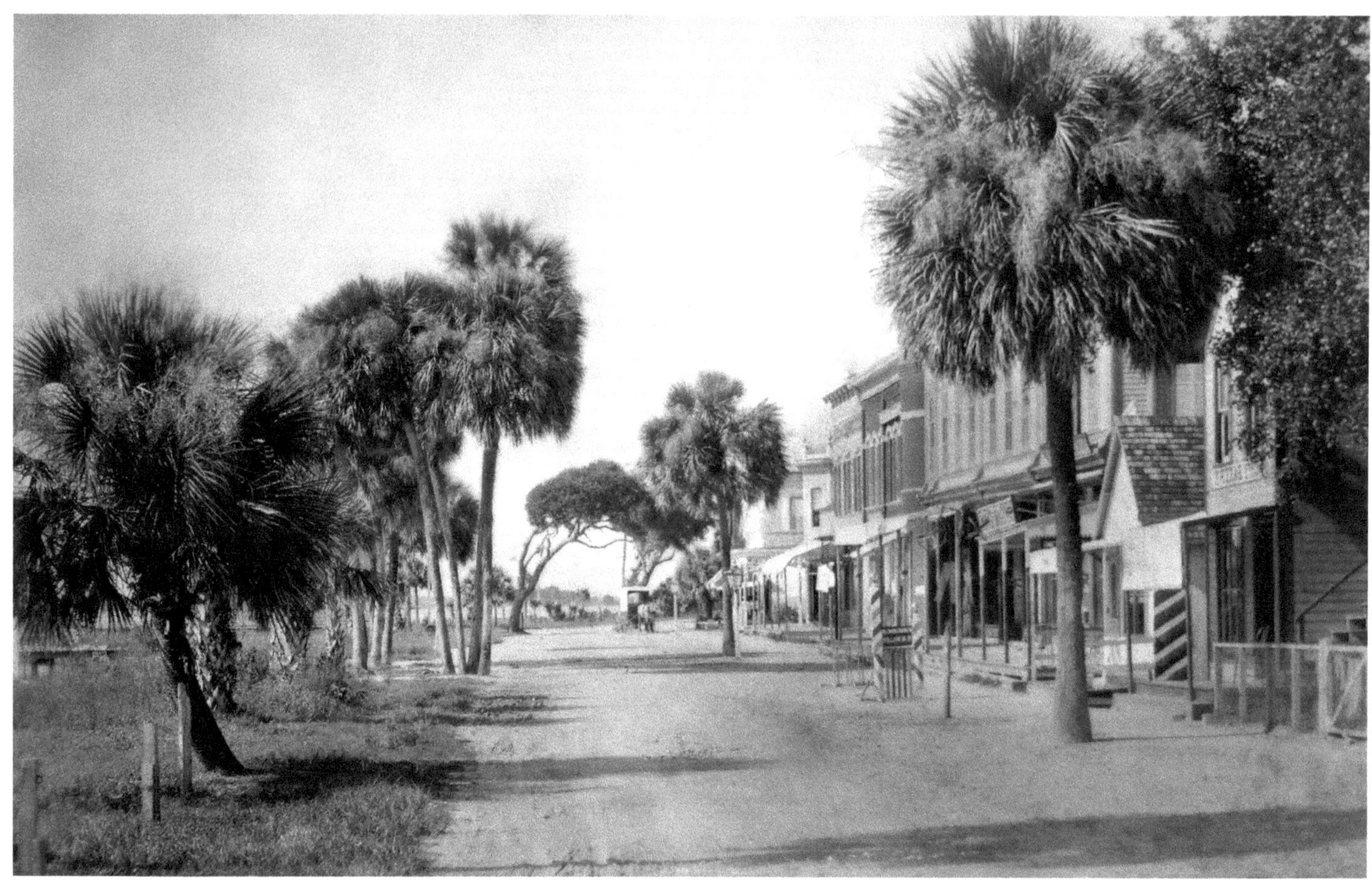

D. D. Rogers, civil engineer, was well known throughout Florida as a land surveyor. It was appropriate that these engineers hold their convention at Daytona. The Florida East Coast Railway offered the best transportation at that time for them to attend.

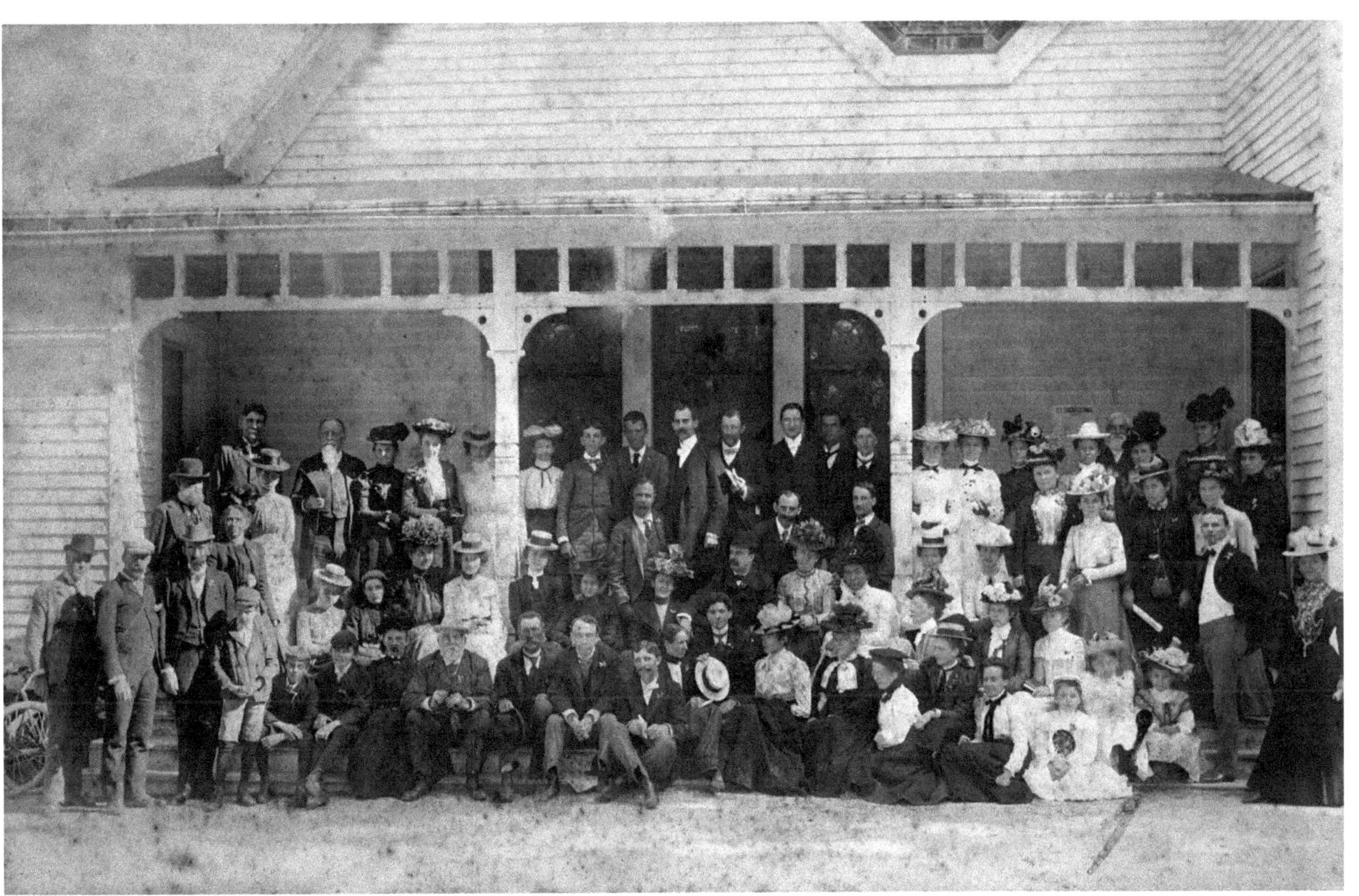

This wooden pier gave fishermen and tourists a chance to catch fish. Occasionally they got a big one to photograph and show friends up north. Sightseers could stroll out on the pier to breathe the salt air and in summer to cool off in the sea breezes.

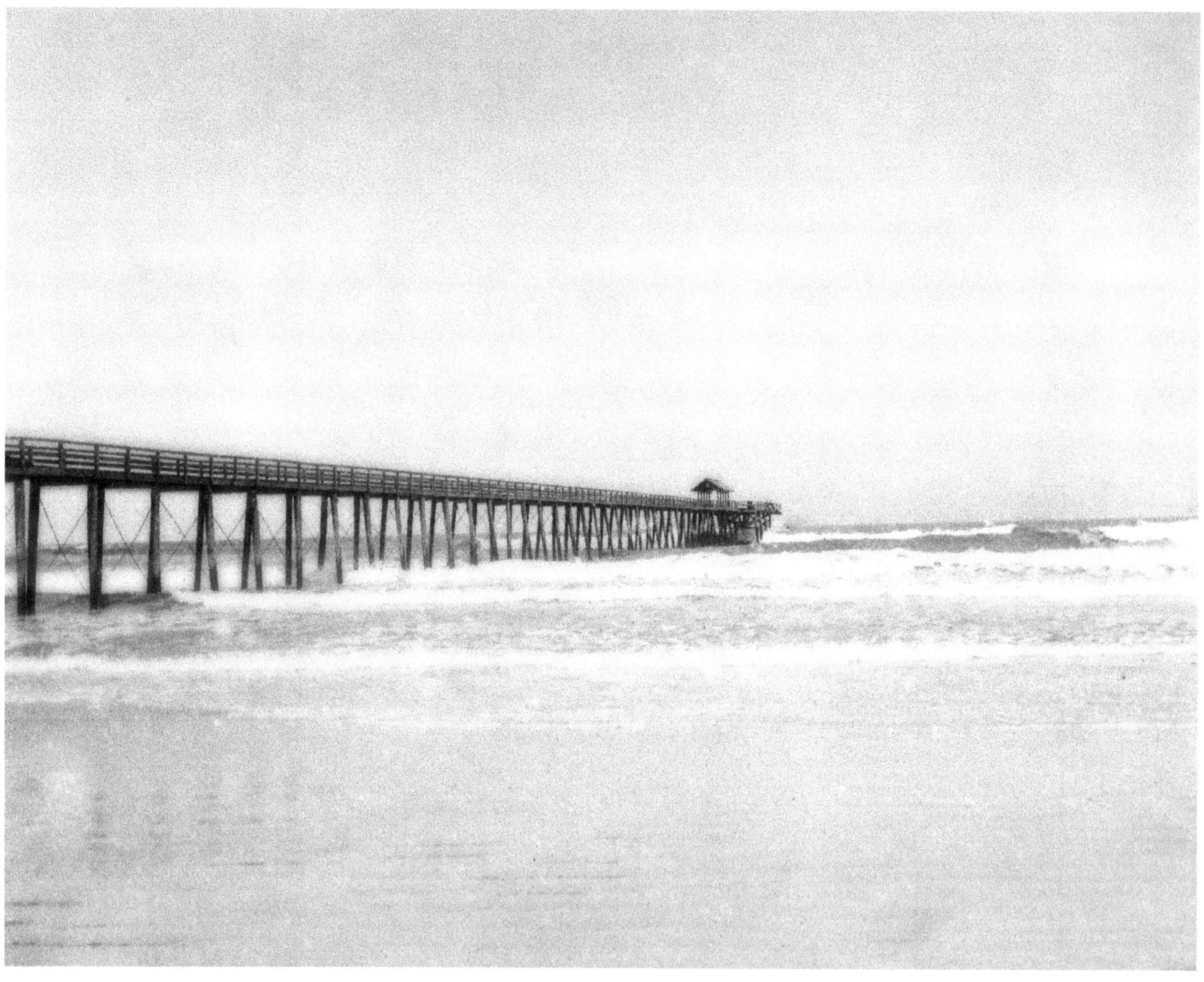

Daytona had a busy railroad station. Tourists coming from the north to stay in sunny Florida brought their bags and trunks to stay at homes and hotels during the winter season. Horse-drawn carriages and wagons could be obtained from a nearby livery stable.

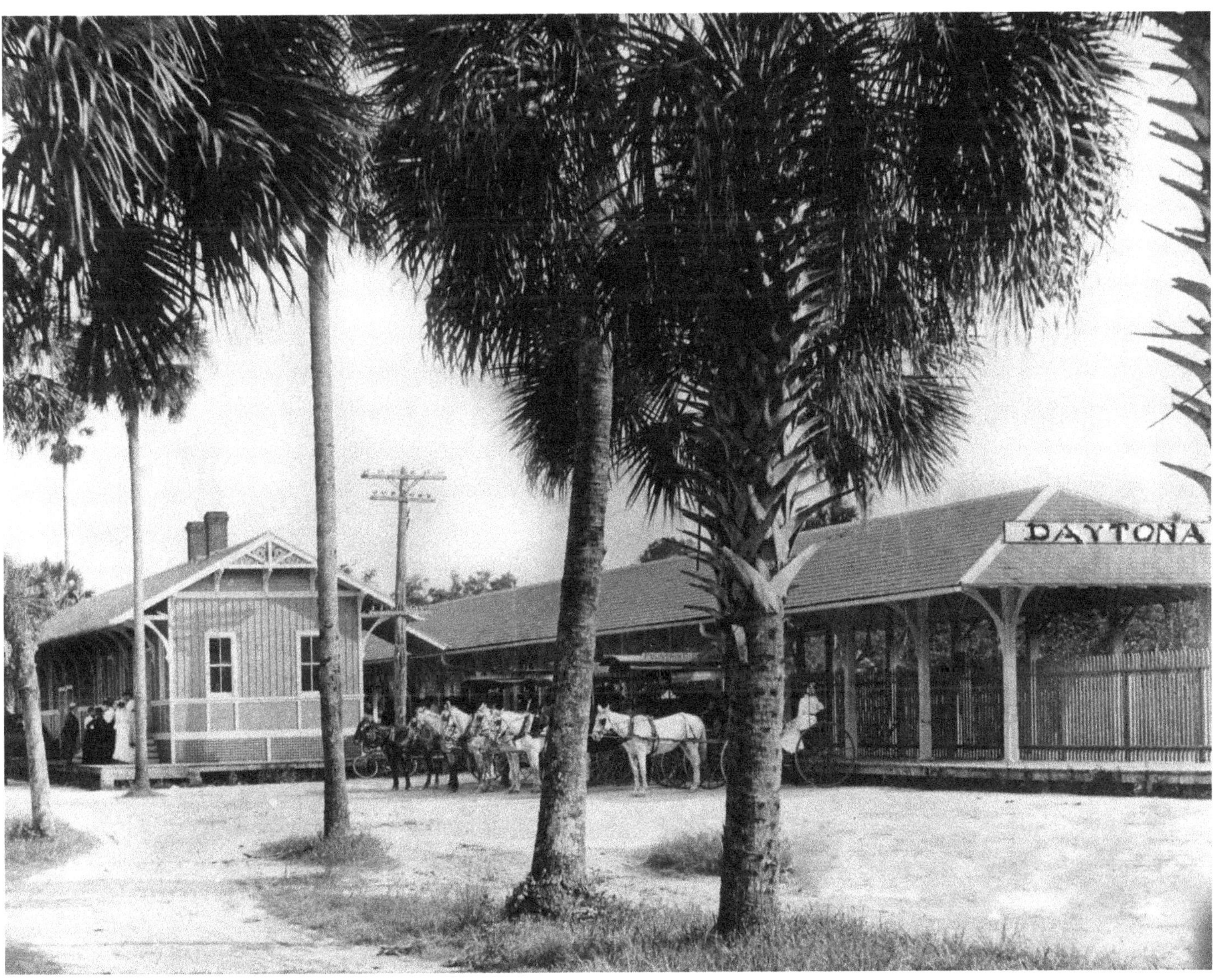

Helen Wilmans Post published her mental science paper *Freedom* on the ground floor of the opera house seen here. Colonel and Mrs. C. C. Post developed Ocean Boulevard with hotels, stores, a post office, and cultural events in the opera house. They platted the town of Seabreeze, which she called the City Beautiful.

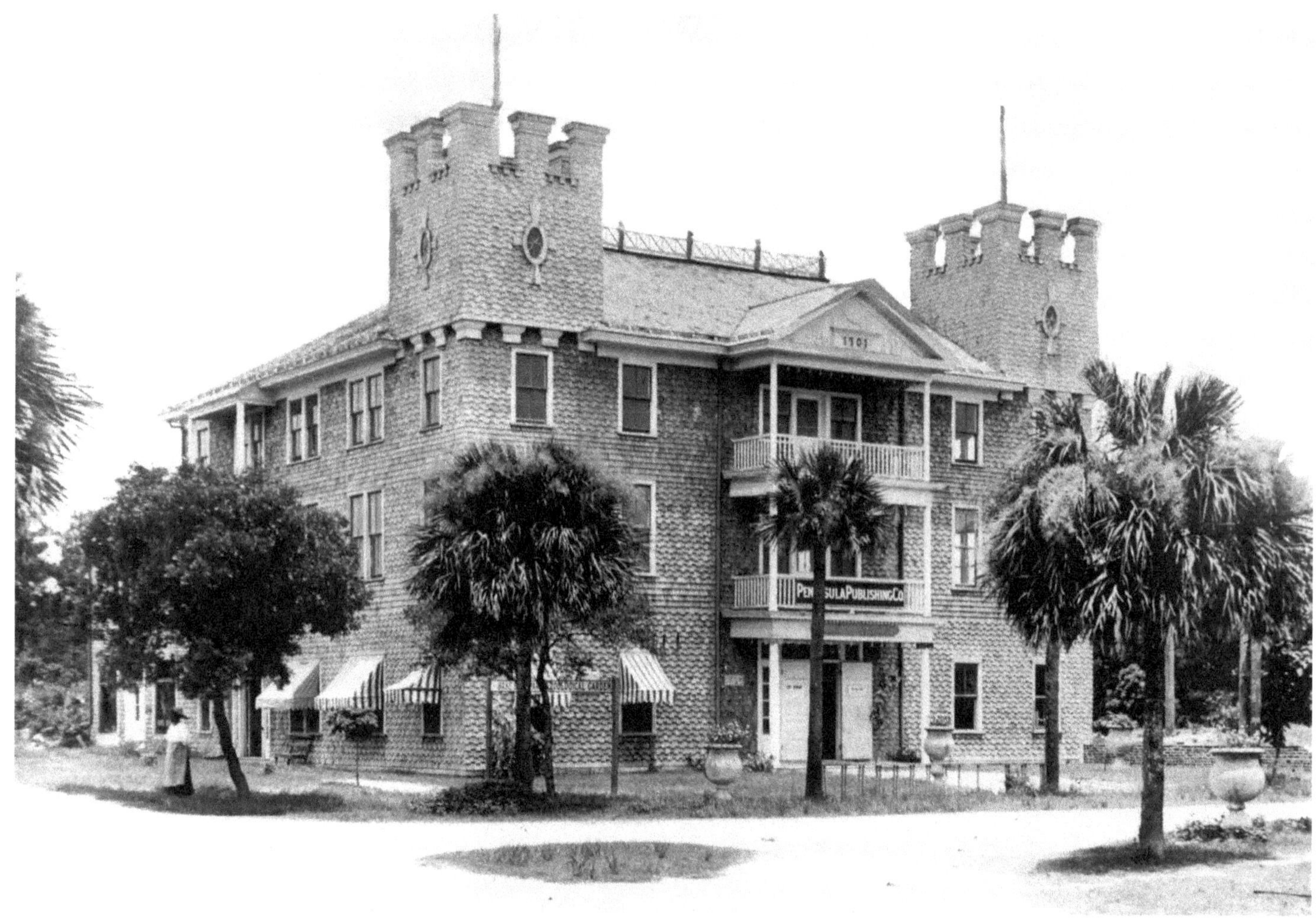

Buildings on Ocean Boulevard in this view looking west are the Clarendon Inn, several homes, the Shell House (later the Geneva Hotel), and the Wilmans Opera House. Near the river stood the Colonnades Hotel.

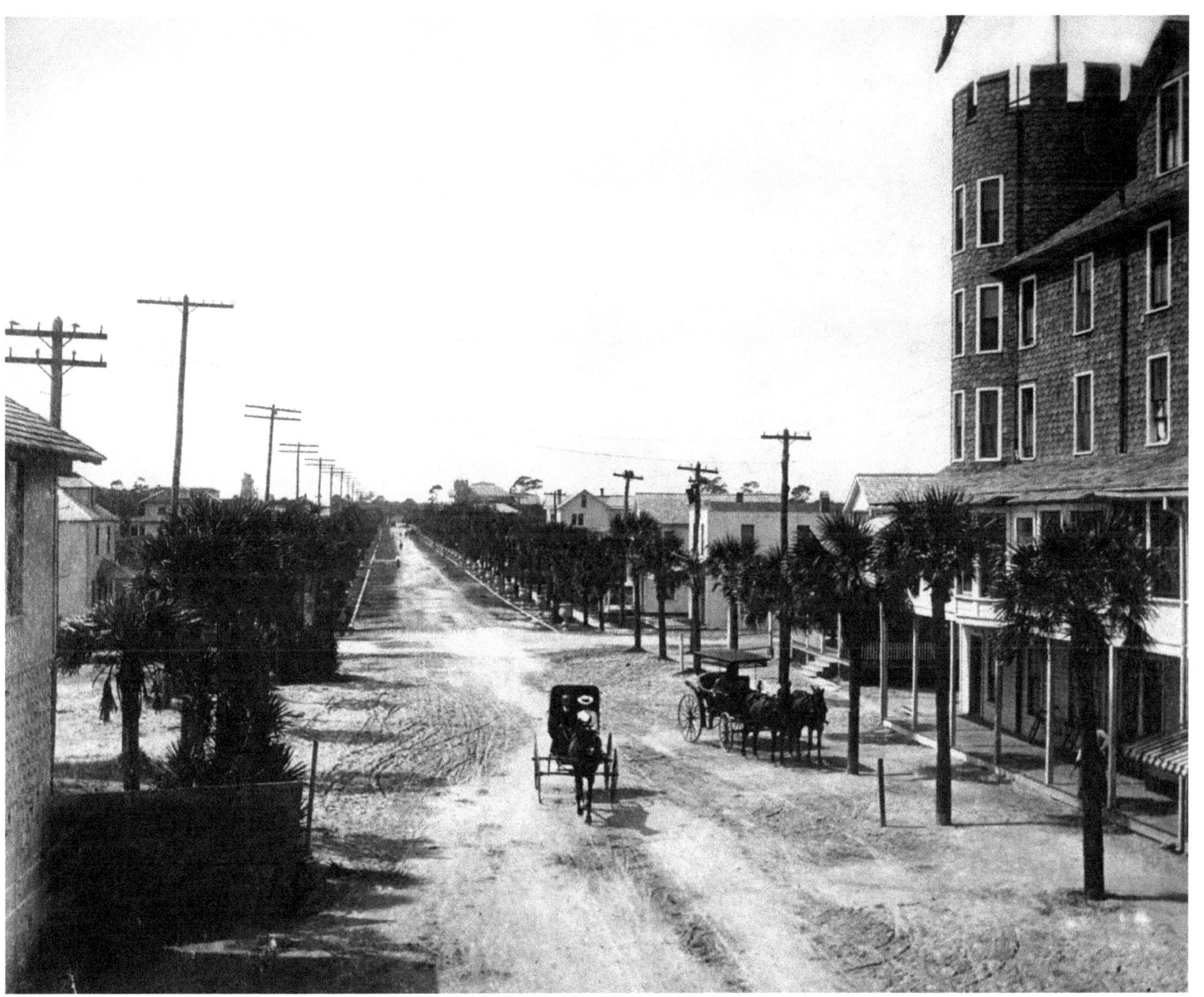

Ormond Beach to the north was known as the birthplace of speed, but speed trials were often run farther south on Daytona's beach to take advantage of its smoothness and length. Mr. Ross ran this speed trial in his twin-throttled Ross Steamer on January 29, 1903, at low tide with a record speed of 1 mile in 38.05 seconds.

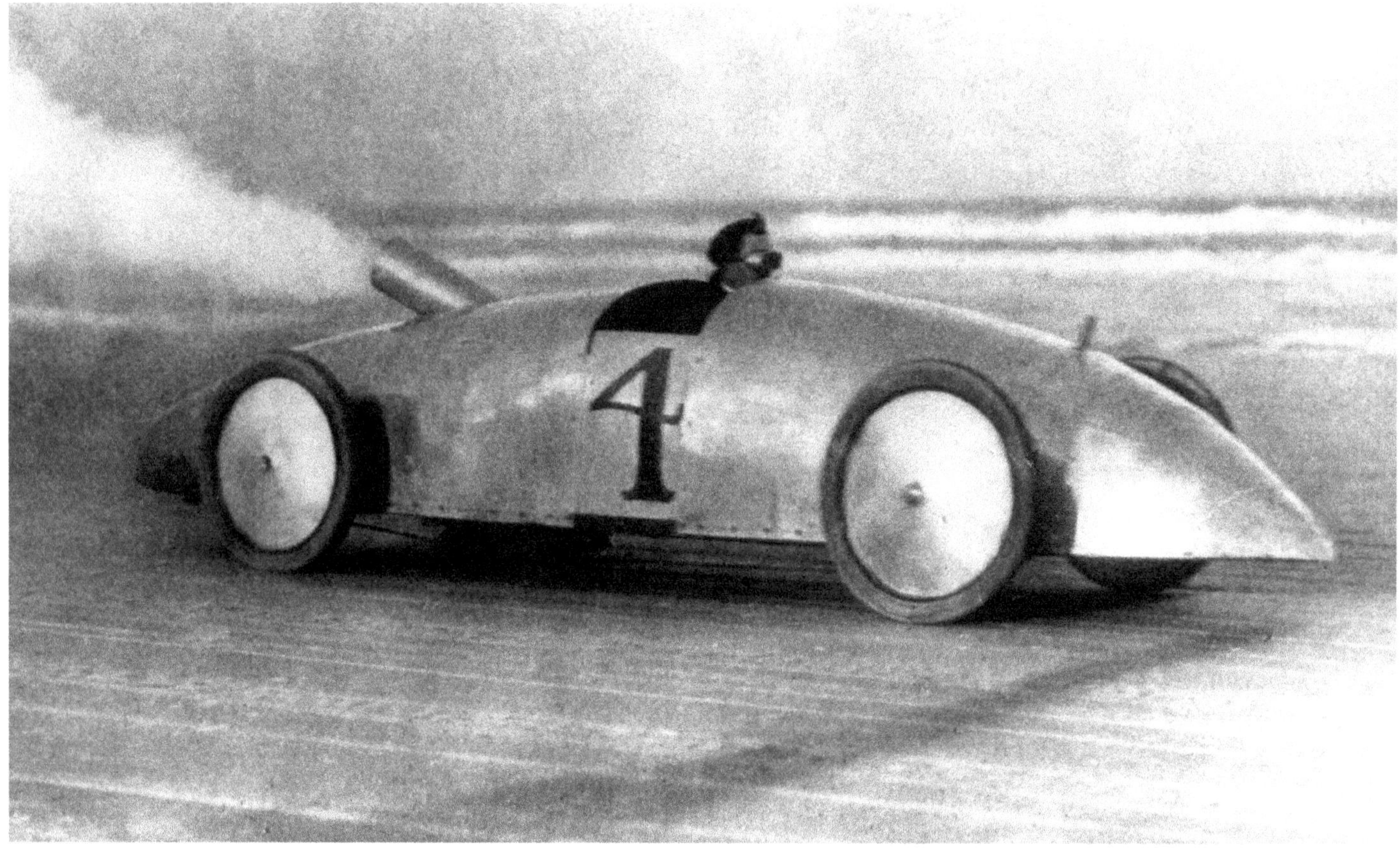

Visible at lower left on this tree-lined avenue, a stone step serves as a horse carriage stop, enabling passengers to step into a carriage or wagon. A homeowner poses with his bicycle.

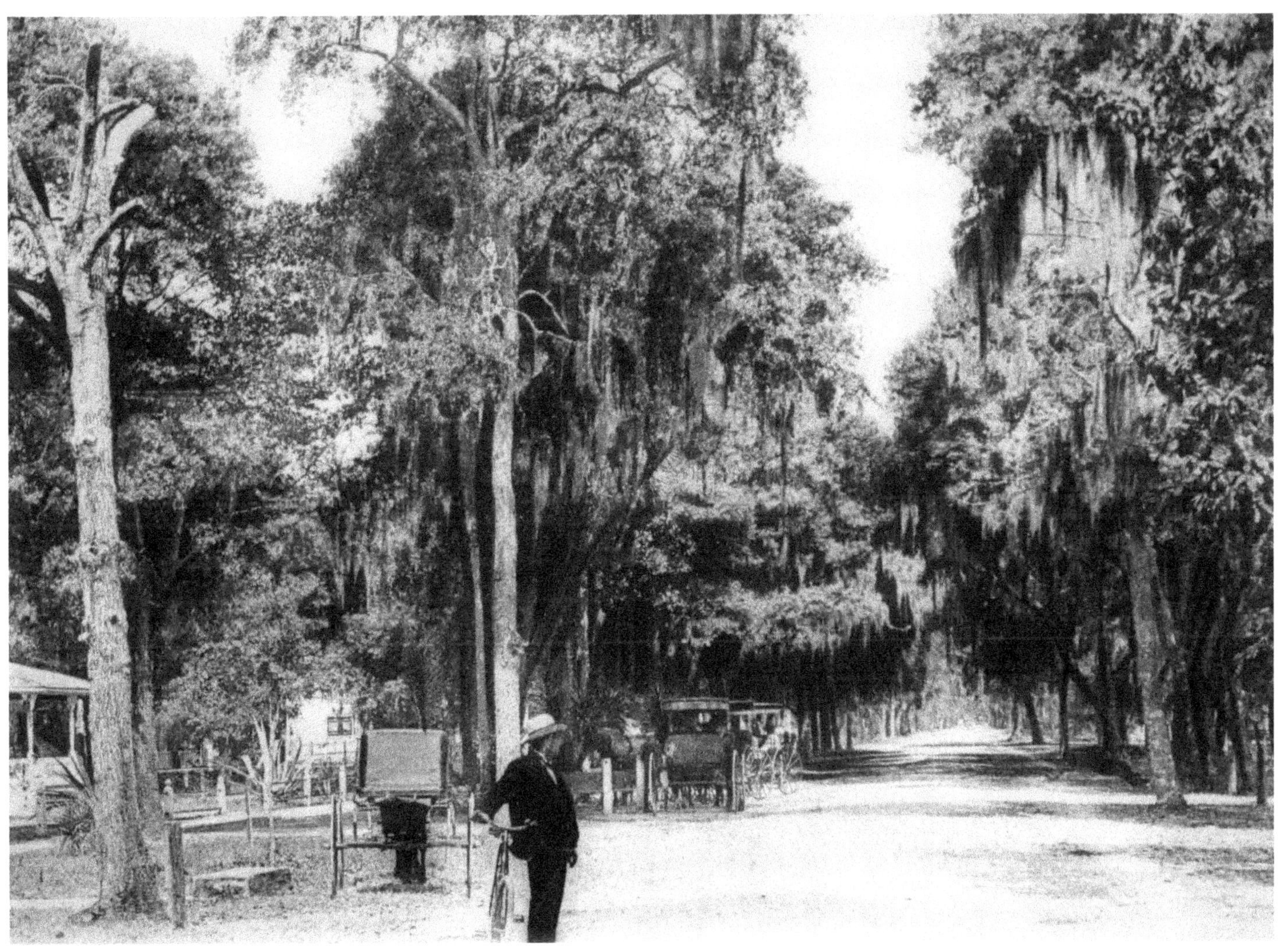

This launch moored at a dock on north Beach Street ferried passengers across the river to a landing near today's Main Street. Captain L. E. Ellenwood operated the *Dixie* for several years from the mainland to the peninsula. He was owner from 1903 to 1913. Tokens were used for fare and could be purchased in advance of boarding.

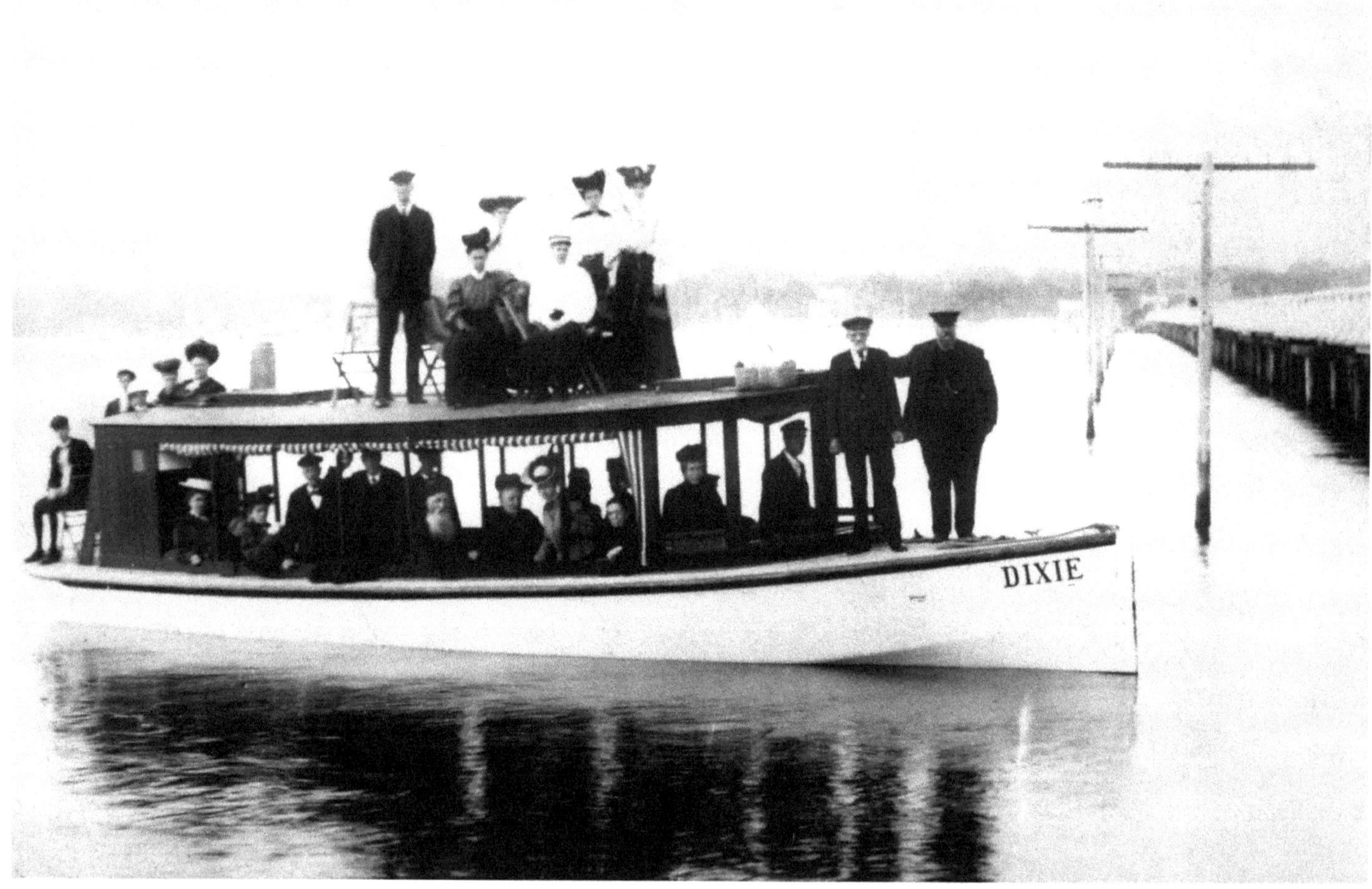

The first building at left was Burdine's Pharmacy. Hitching posts for horses are visible on the unpaved street. In a few years, masonry buildings would replace wooden and old Beach Street would take on a new look.

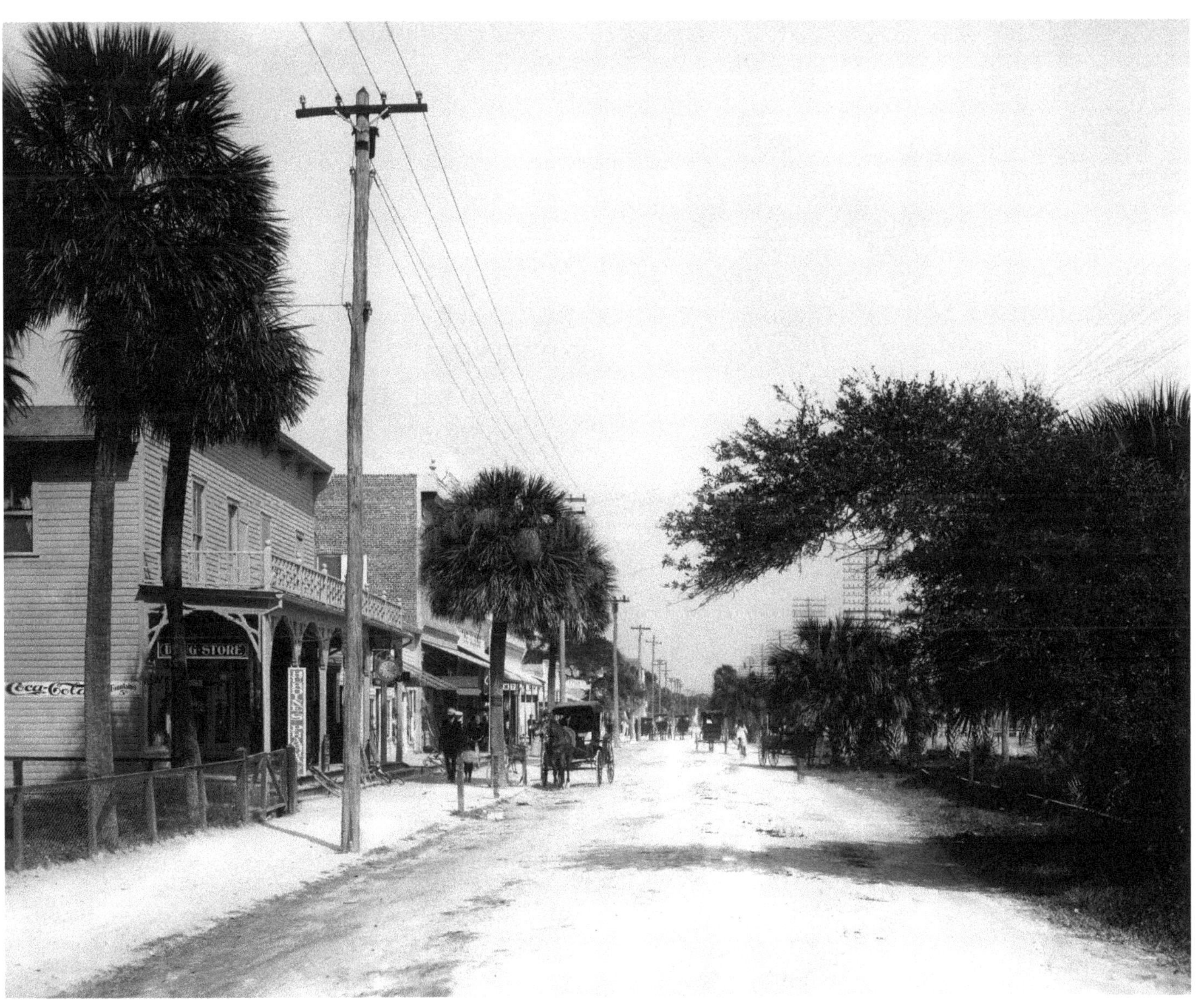

Ormond Beach was known as the birthplace of speed and the measured area was known as the flying mile. Racing cars however often needed more distance to obtain their high speed, so Daytona's beach came to be used for speed trials. The Florida East Coast Automobile Association honored Mr. Vanderbilt for the speed record set here: 1 mile in 39 seconds.

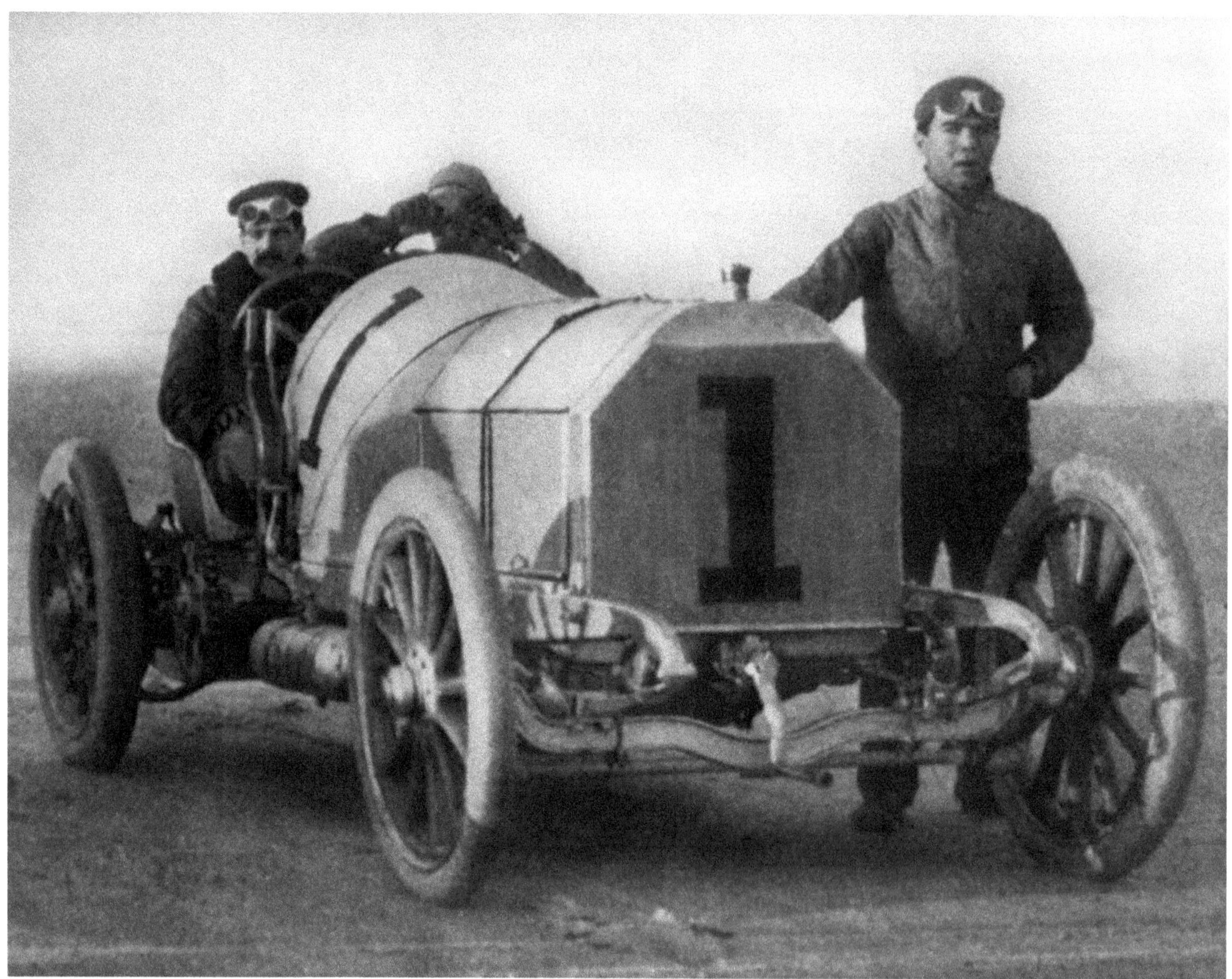

The *Cherokee* launch prepares to leave its dock. This boat took passengers and freight as far north as the Tomoka River and south to New Smyrna. The first city hall and fire station are visible in the background.

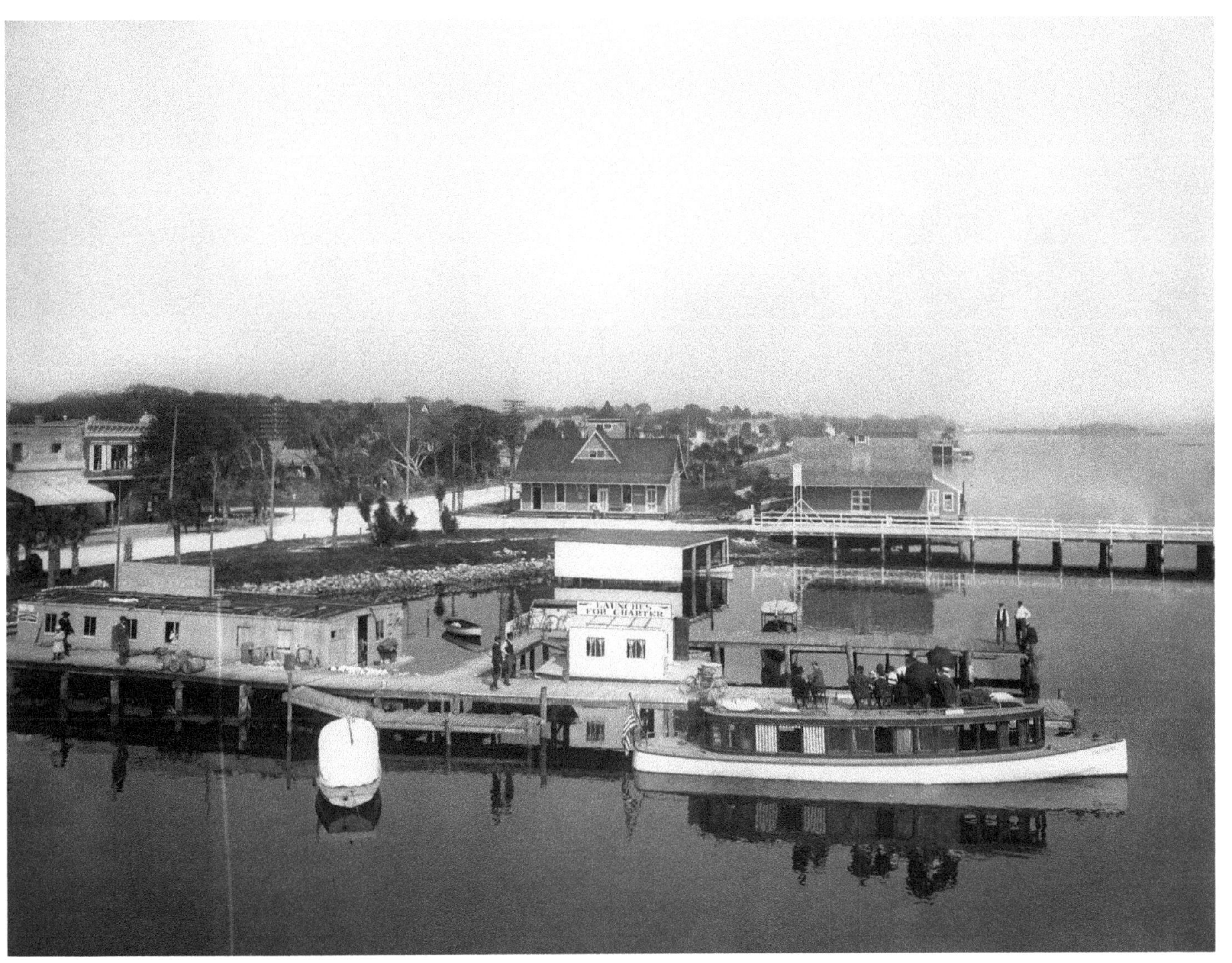

The *Uncle Sam* made daily trips to Tomoka and three times per week to New Smyrna. This boat carried passengers and light freight. It also conducted scenic tours for tourists on the Halifax and Tomoka rivers.

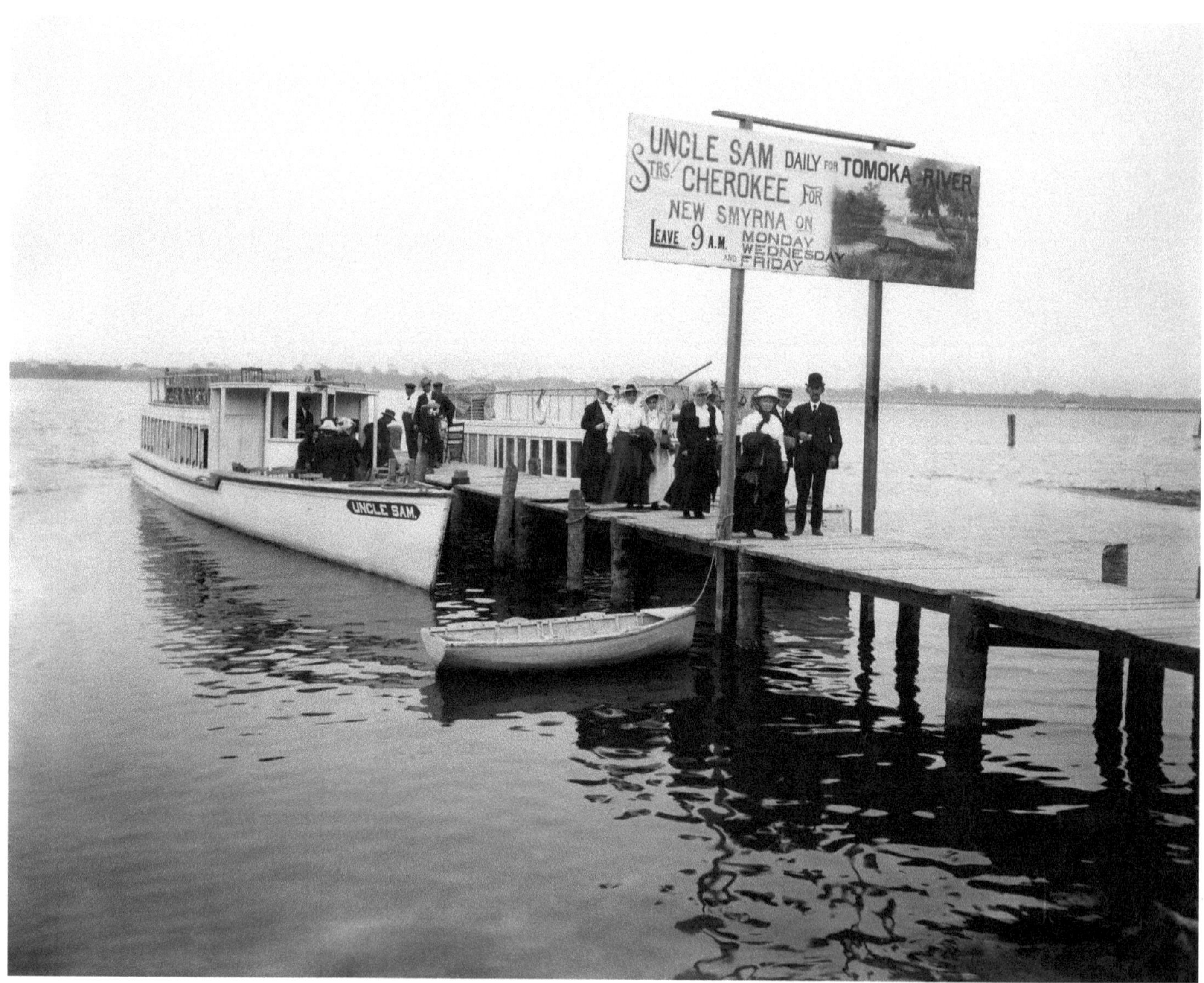

Mary McLeod Bethune established a school for the children of Florida East Coast railroad workers. She started her school under primitive conditions with a class of five girls. The school grew into the Daytona Normal and Industrial Institute, later merging with a Methodist Church school to become Bethune-Cookman College. Bethune died in 1955, widely known and much esteemed.

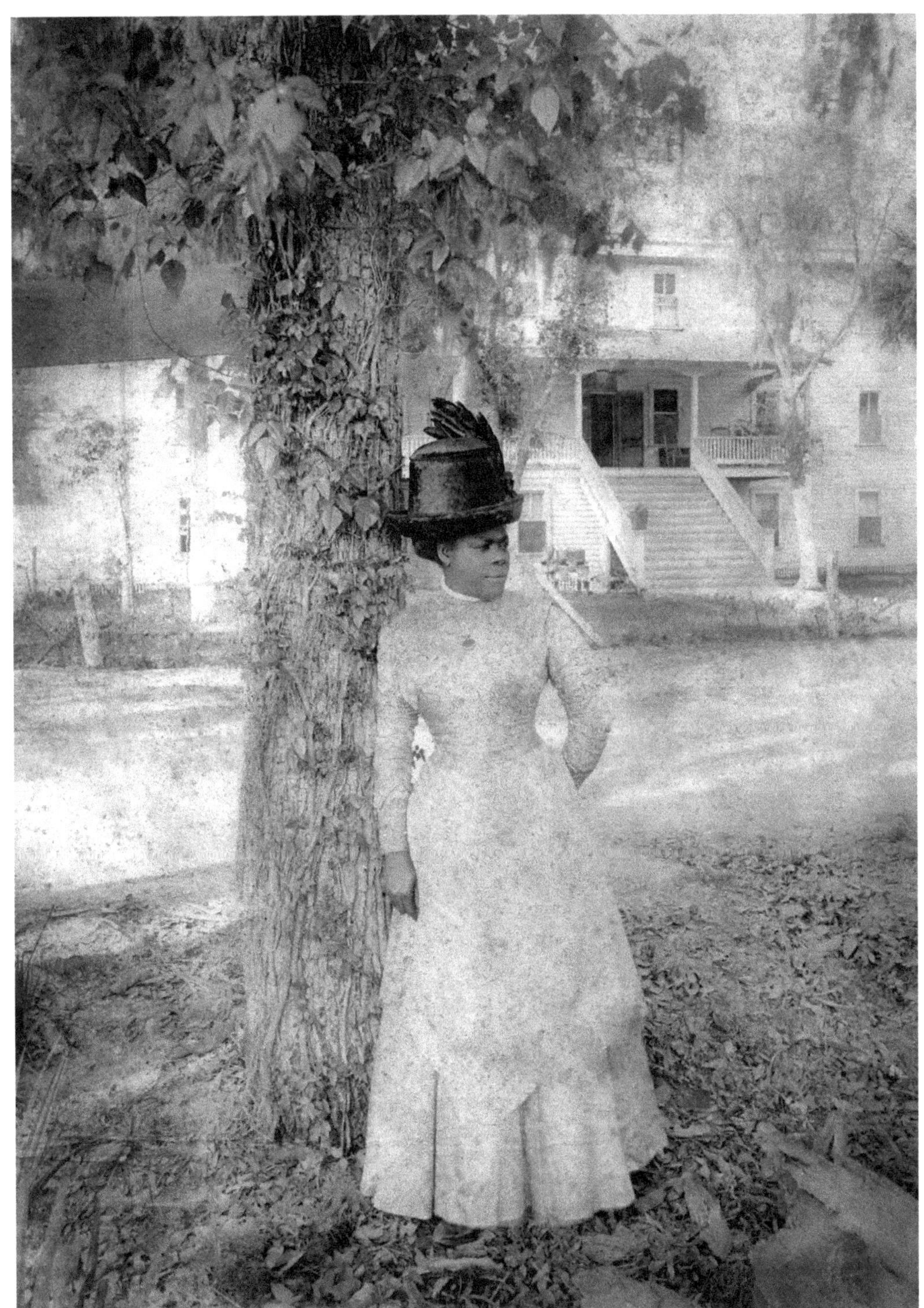

To the left is Daytona's lumberyard, which later became City Island. On the right midway across is the city jail. Across the bridge to the left, just visible, is the Lawrence Thompson home and to the right James N. Gamble's home. This route led east to the Atlantic Ocean and today is known as Silver Beach Avenue.

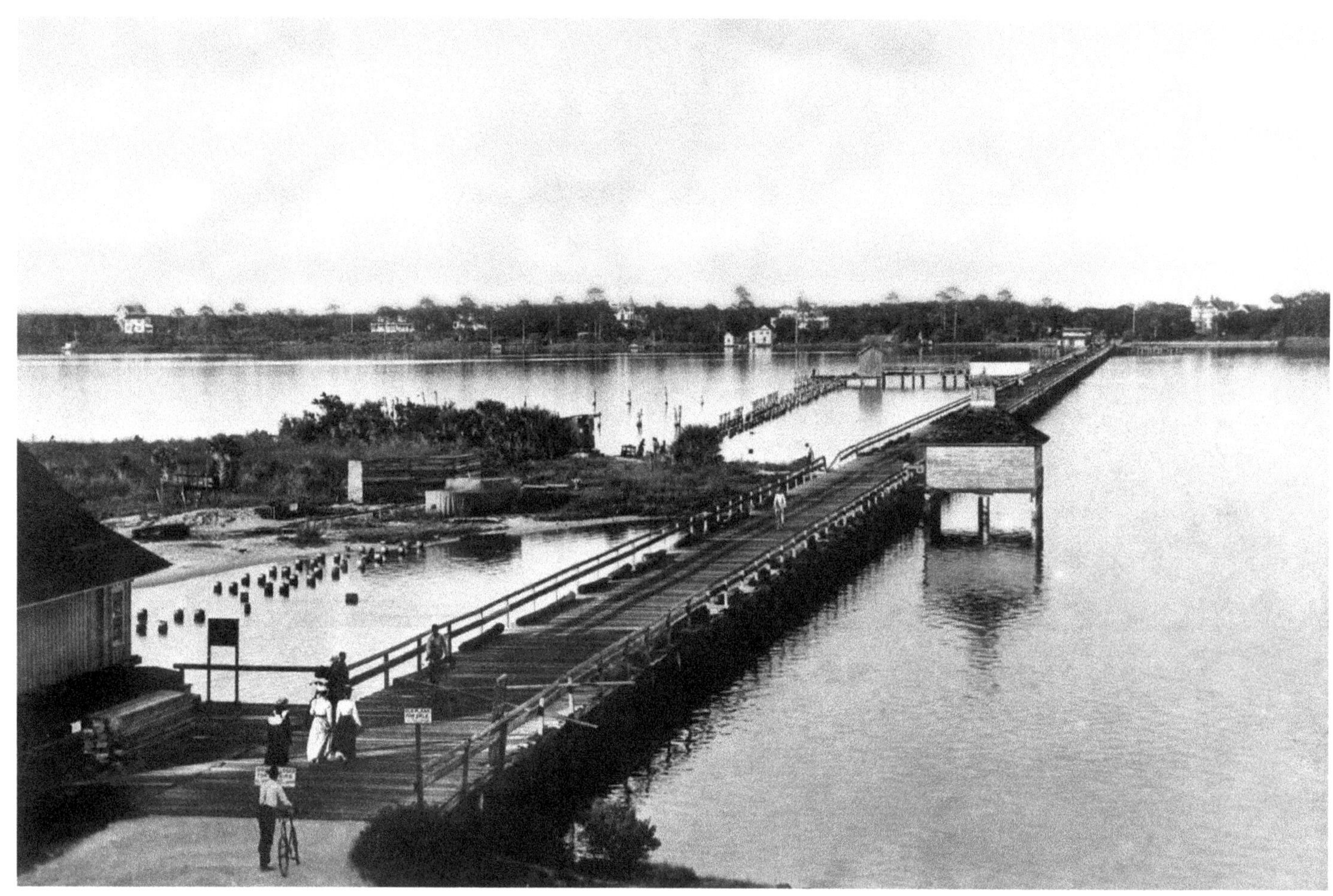

Tourists and visitors at the beach enjoy themselves on a pleasant day. Here a single horseless carriage sputters along, wending its way through the milling crowd.

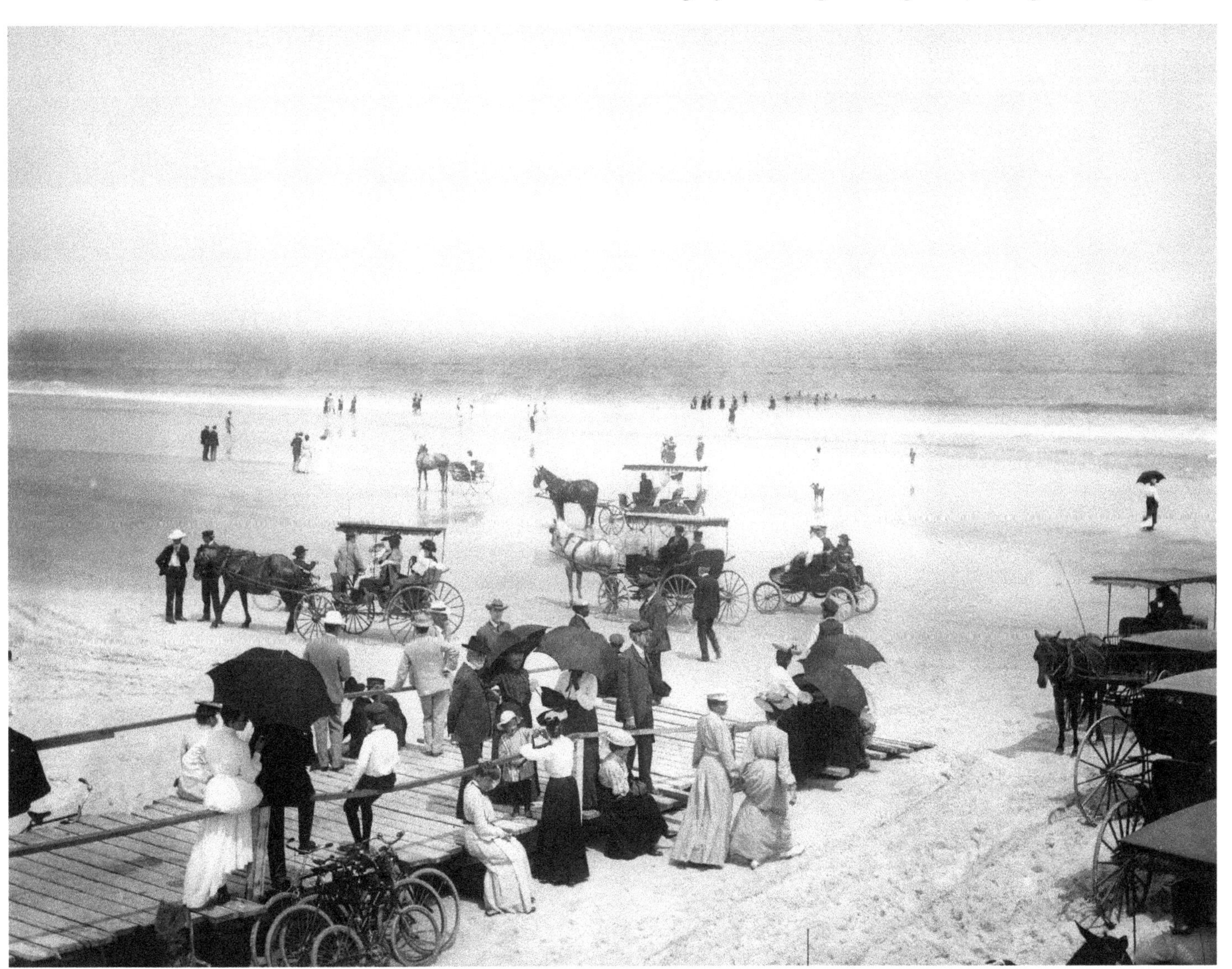

In this image tourists and townspeople have come out to watch two sport racers, just visible in the distance.

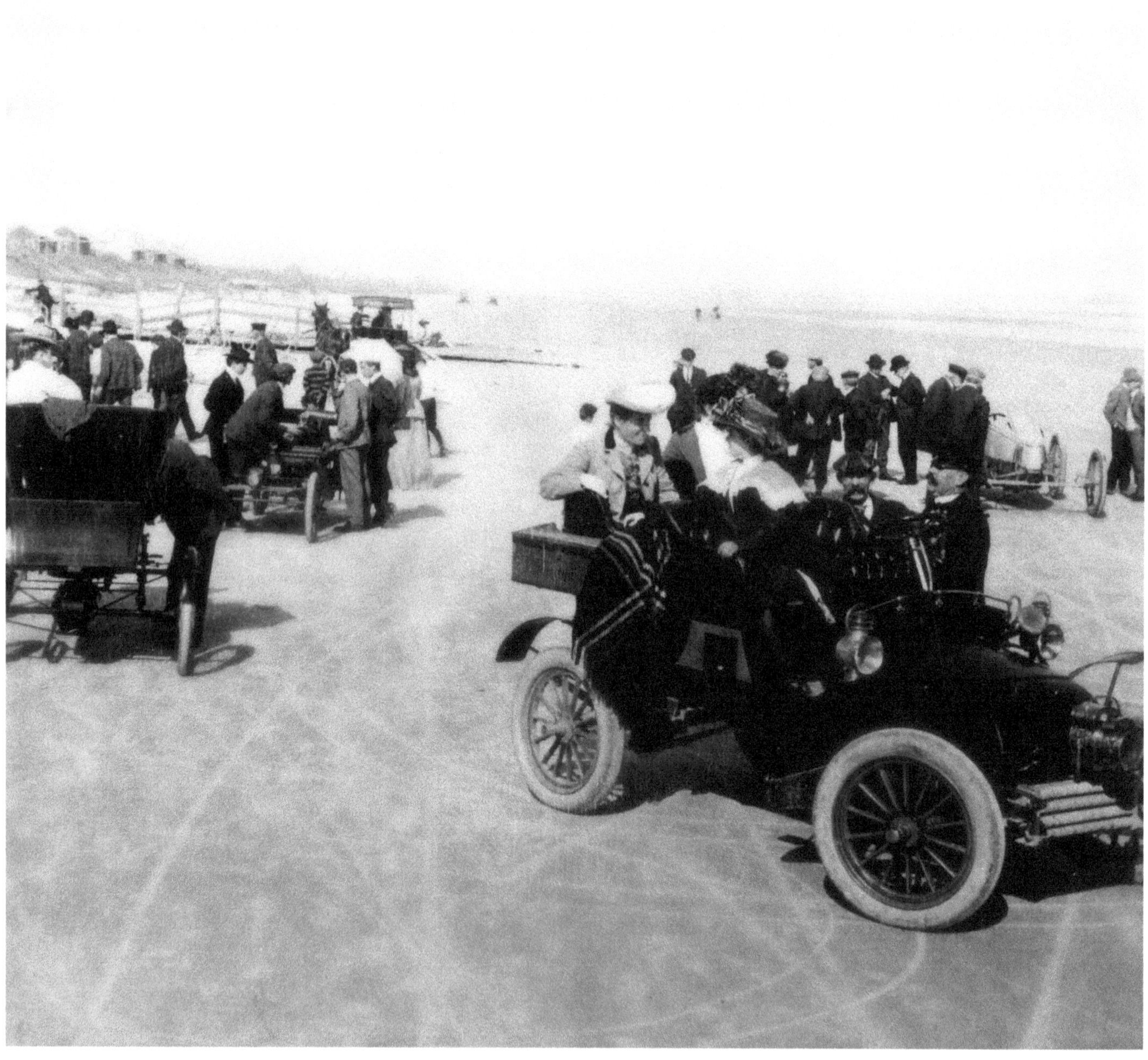

This estate covered most of the block surrounded by Beach Street, Bay Street, and Palmetto Avenue. The Queen Anne mansion, enclosed by a stout rock wall, was home to Mr. Burgoyne, a retired printer from New York City. He died in 1916 and the mansion was demolished in 1941 to make way for a new shopping area along Beach Street.

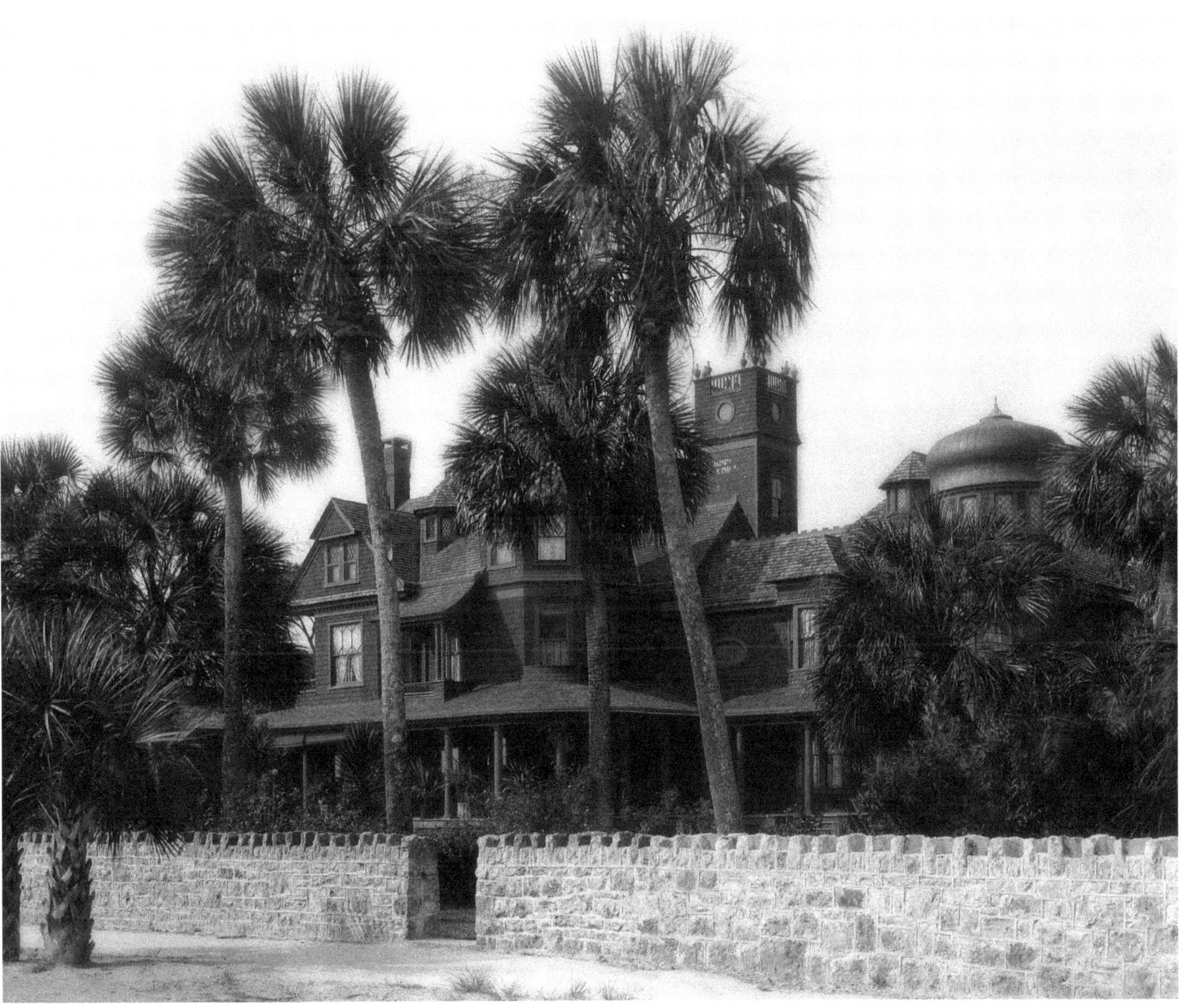

This boat is moored at a dock north of City Island. The Public Library and City Jail are visible to the right. To handle well, the sailboat required skill, especially during races, and was a common sight on the river.

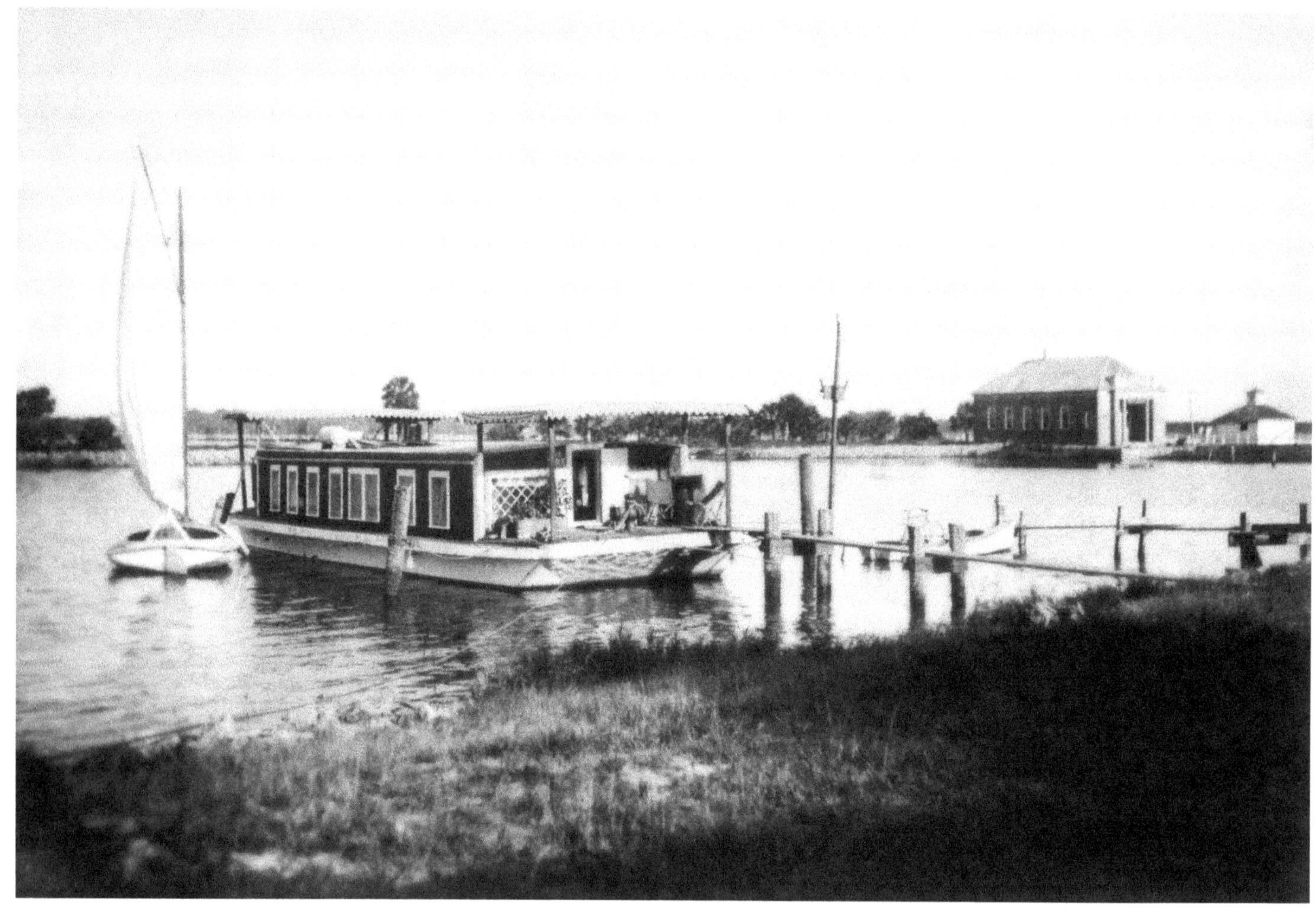

Logging employed teamsters to snake logs up a ramp and onto high wheels, for pulling by oxen overland to a sawmill. The teamster had to be well trained in handling the oxen and the load of logs. Heavy loads frequently made ruts in the road.

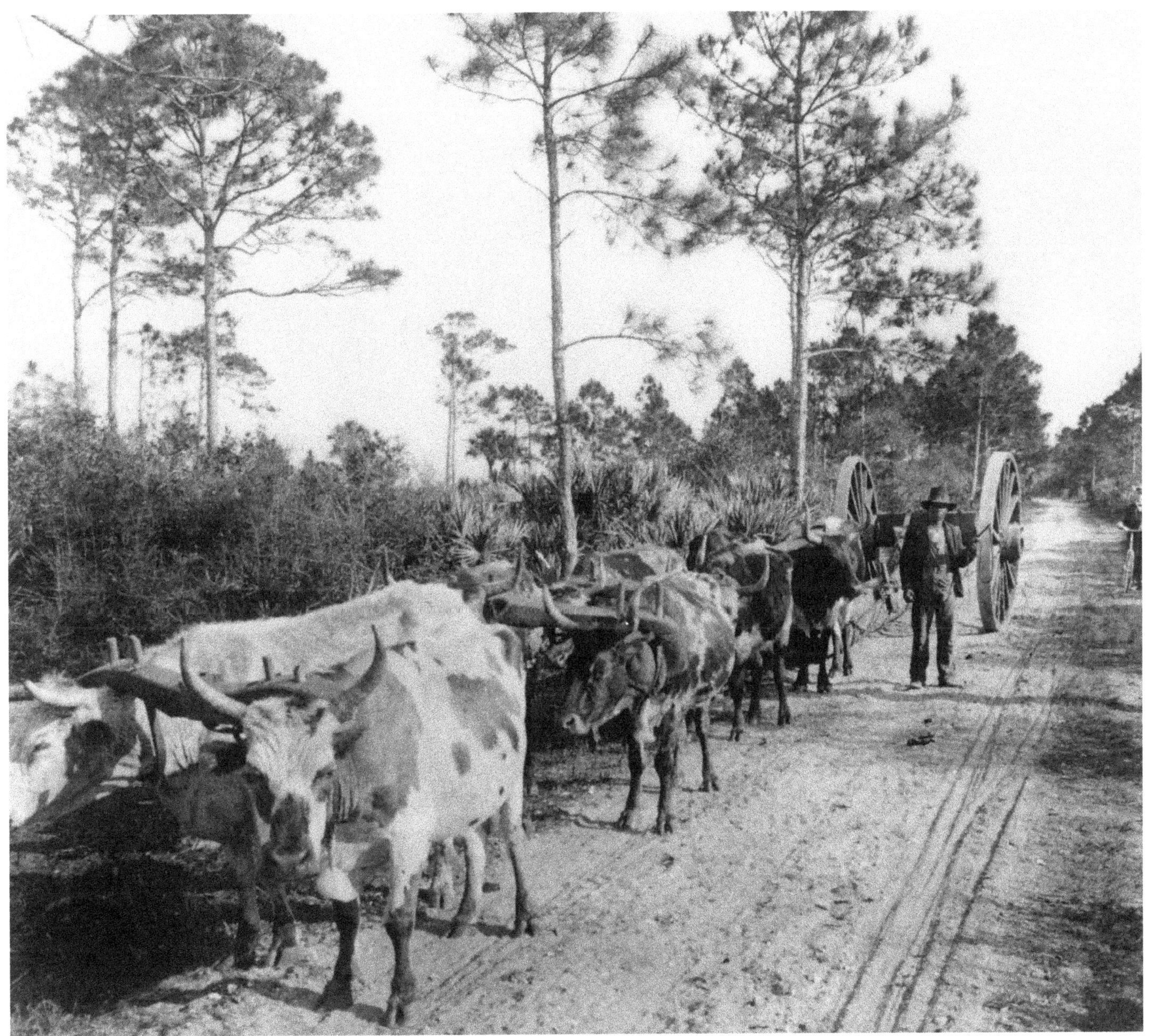

This odd assortment of early automobiles forms a line on the beach January 14, 1905, near Ormond Beach and the Flying Mile. Speed seconds were calculated for the measured mile.

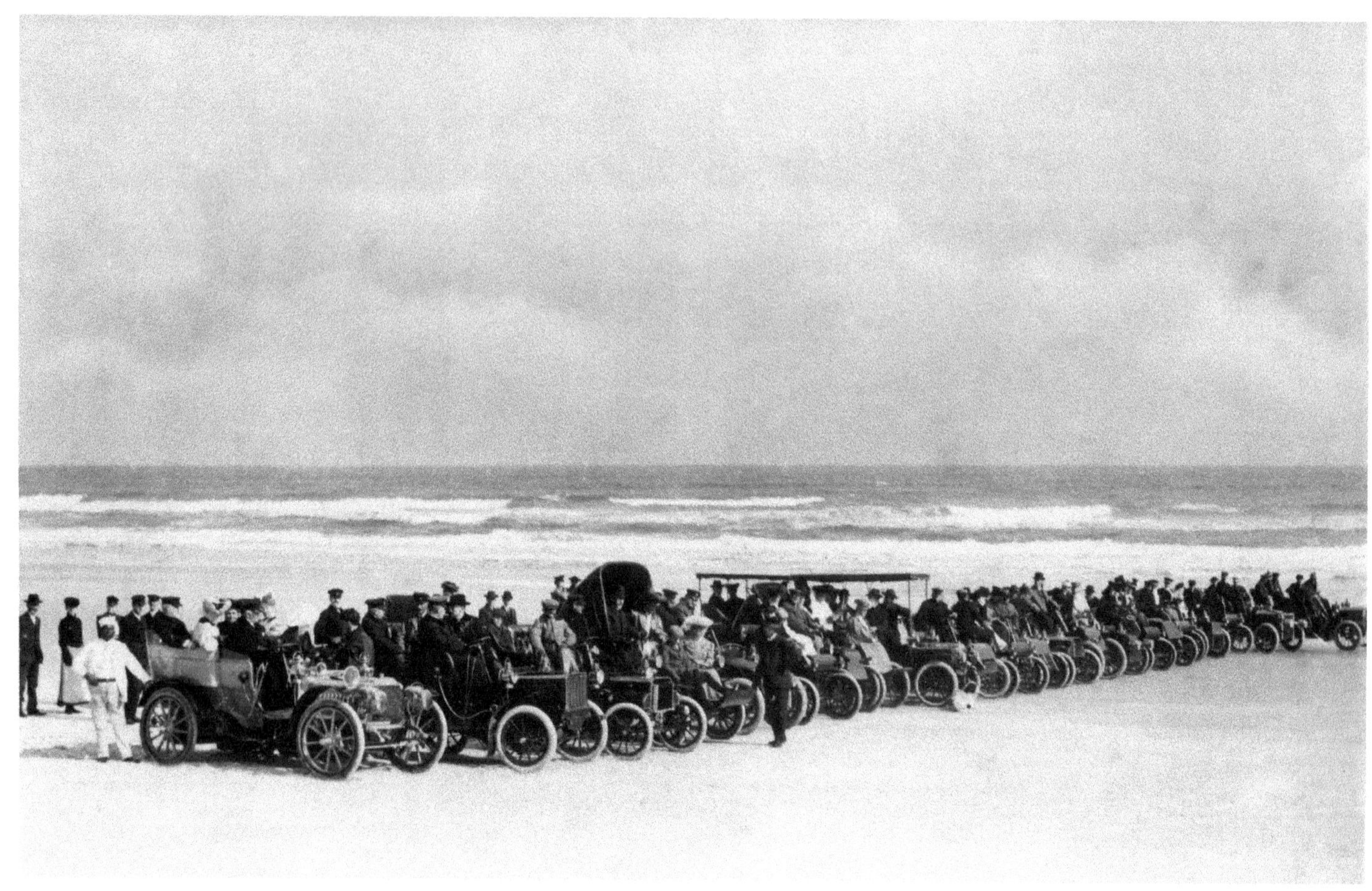

Each winter large numbers of speed trial events were held. During a practice run, Frank Croker, to avoid a bicyclist in his path, ran into the ocean overturning the race car. He and his mechanic Alexander Raoul did not survive the wreck.

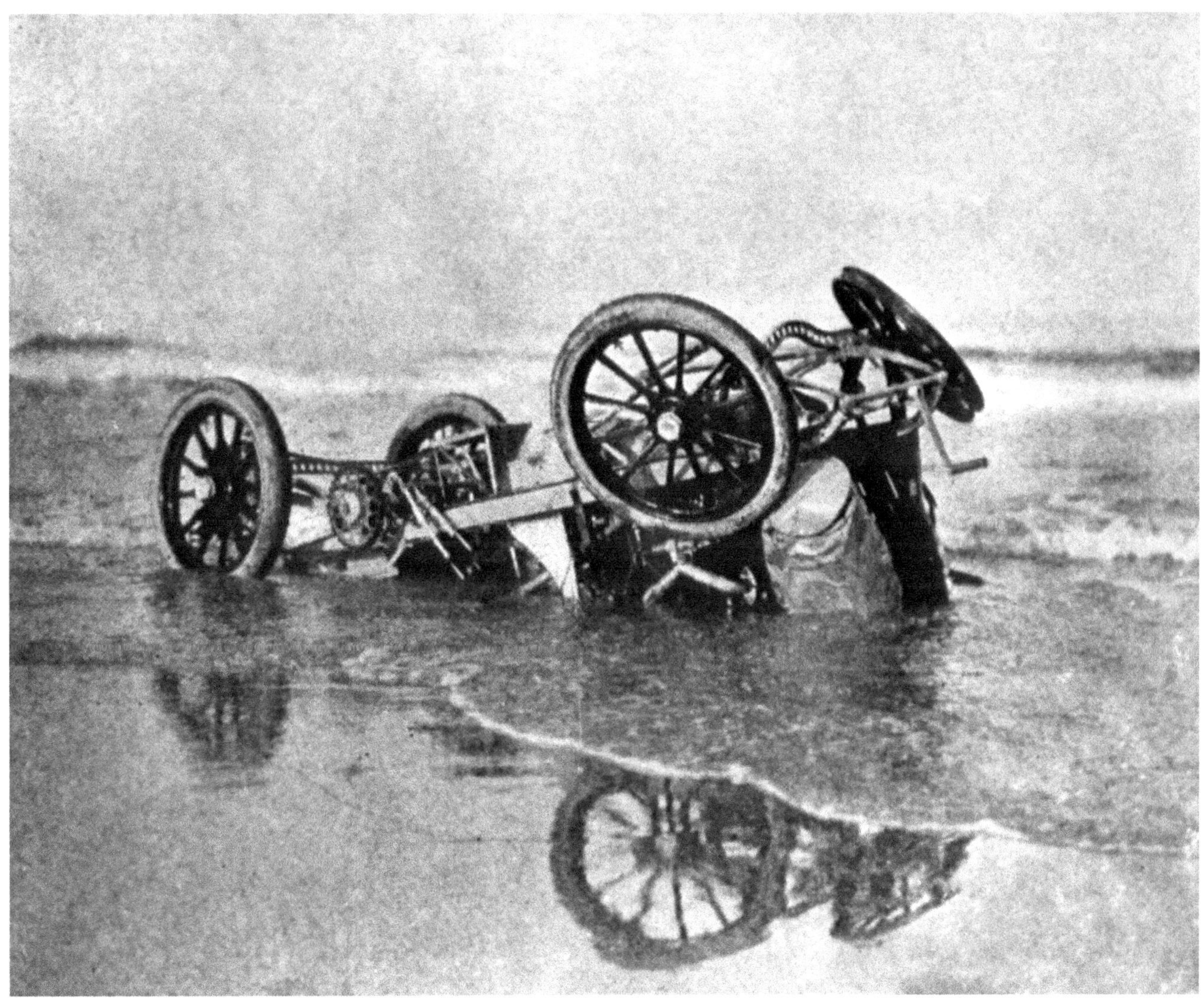

Mary McLeod Bethune started her school teaching five girls. She taught them to work with their hands and improve their social skills. She was able to persuade the industrialists who lived in Daytona in the winter and local businessmen to assist her with funds and supplies, the result of which was a flourishing school. Those contributing included James N. Gamble, Thomas White, H. D. Rhodes, and Lawrence Thompson, as well as other local citizens.

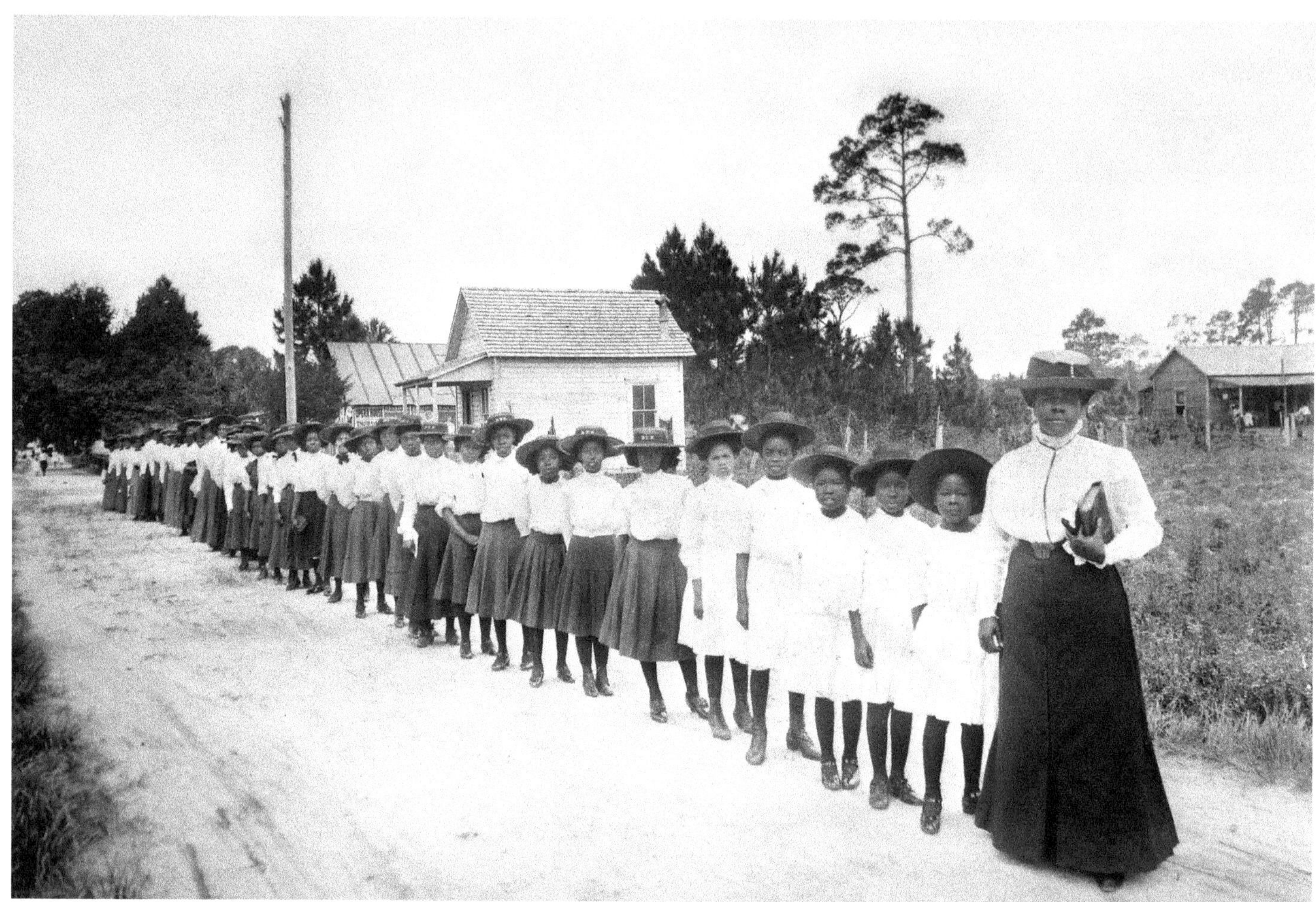

Beach Street as seen from atop adjoining boat house. Ellenwood's dock and landing are visible in the foreground. Captain L. E. Ellenwood was owner of the ferry from 1903 to 1913. Facing an unpaved Beach Street are various businesses. On the riverfront are clusters of sabal palms. In the distance is the former Florida East Coast Railway Depot, which became the city hall. Nearby is the city jail.

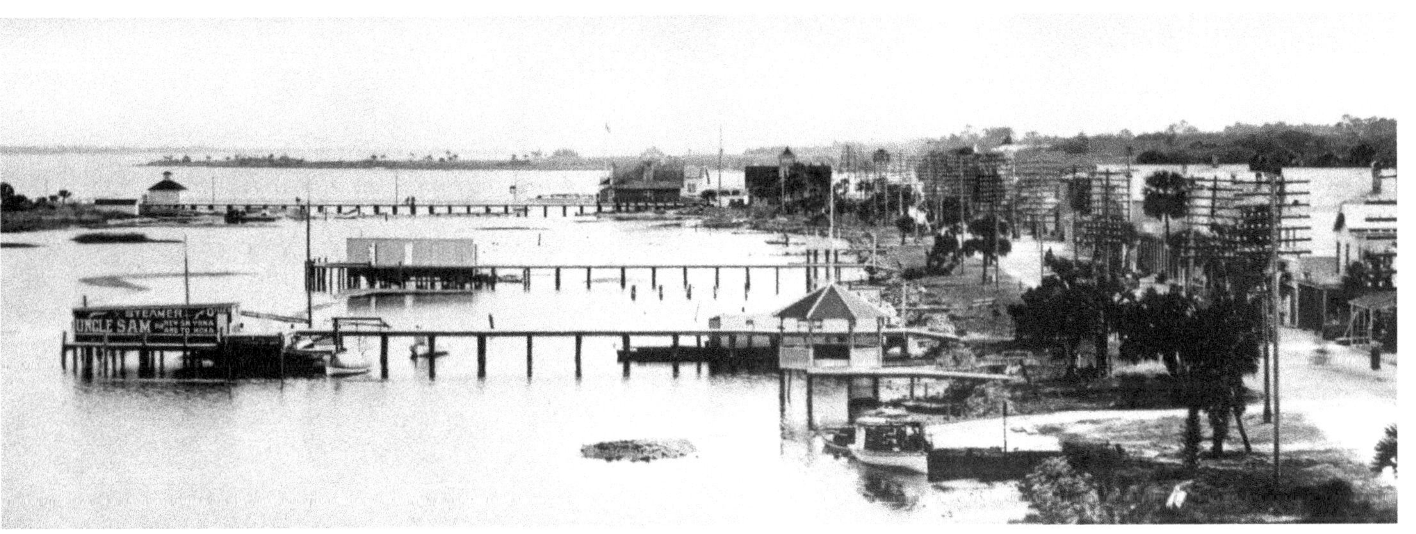

Daytona has always been associated with auto racing, but early time trials were held in Ormond through the flying mile area of the beach. As cars became faster they had to use the full length of the beach at Ormond, extending runs through Daytona's beach. Arthur MacDonald, pictured here, has an English-built, six-cylinder, ninety-horsepower Napier. His record speed was 104.651 m.p.h.

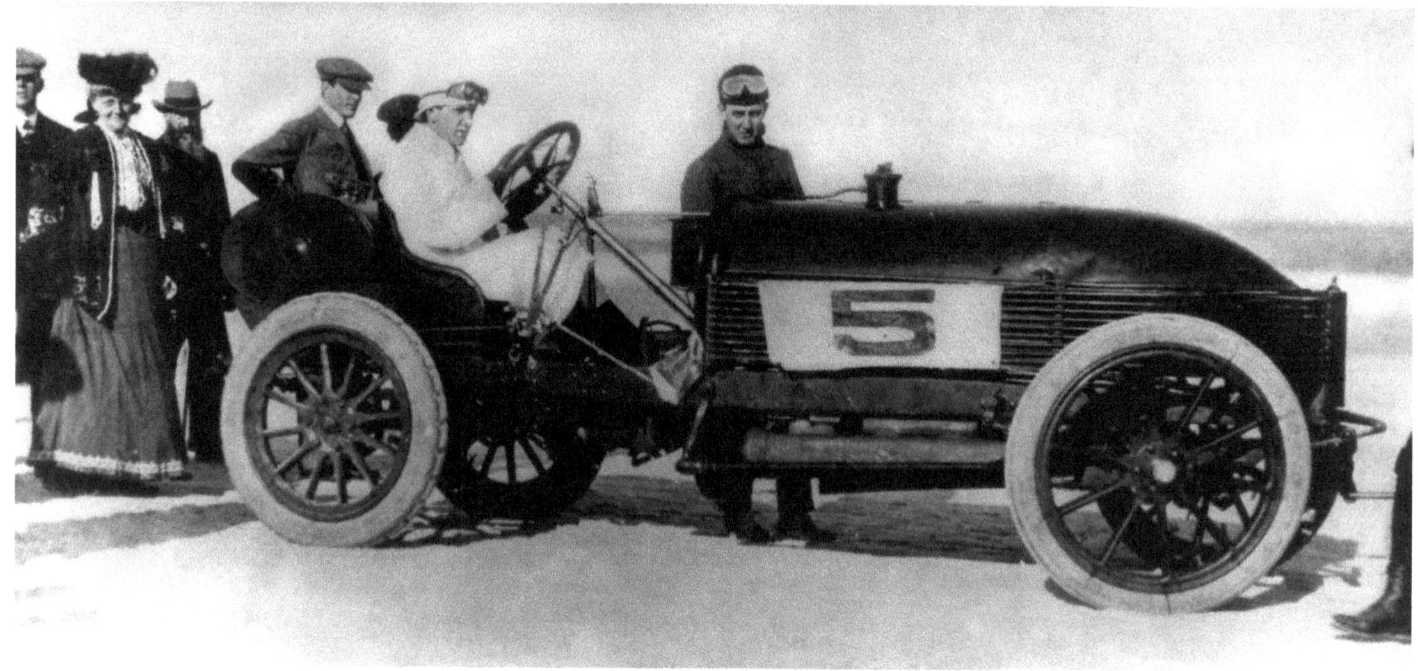

In this view north, on the left is Burdine's Pharmacy, and in the distance the Hotel Despland is visible.

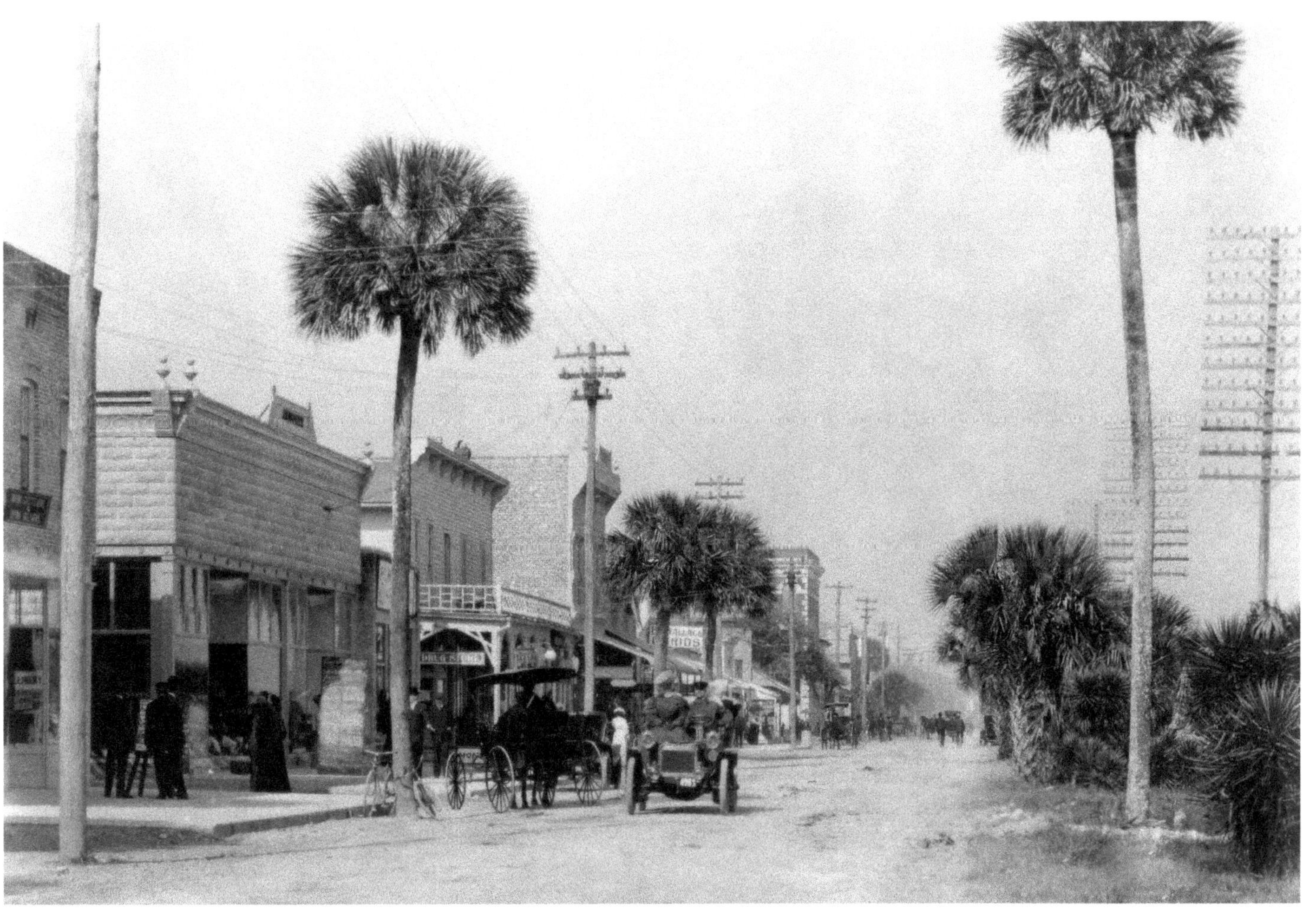

Turpentine was one of the most important products of the pine forest near Daytona. Mr. Paxton shipped turpentine and rosin to Savannah, Georgia. He was manager of the entire operation including the commissary, barrel making, and the living quarters for the workers. Paxton worked for many years at the naval stores operation.

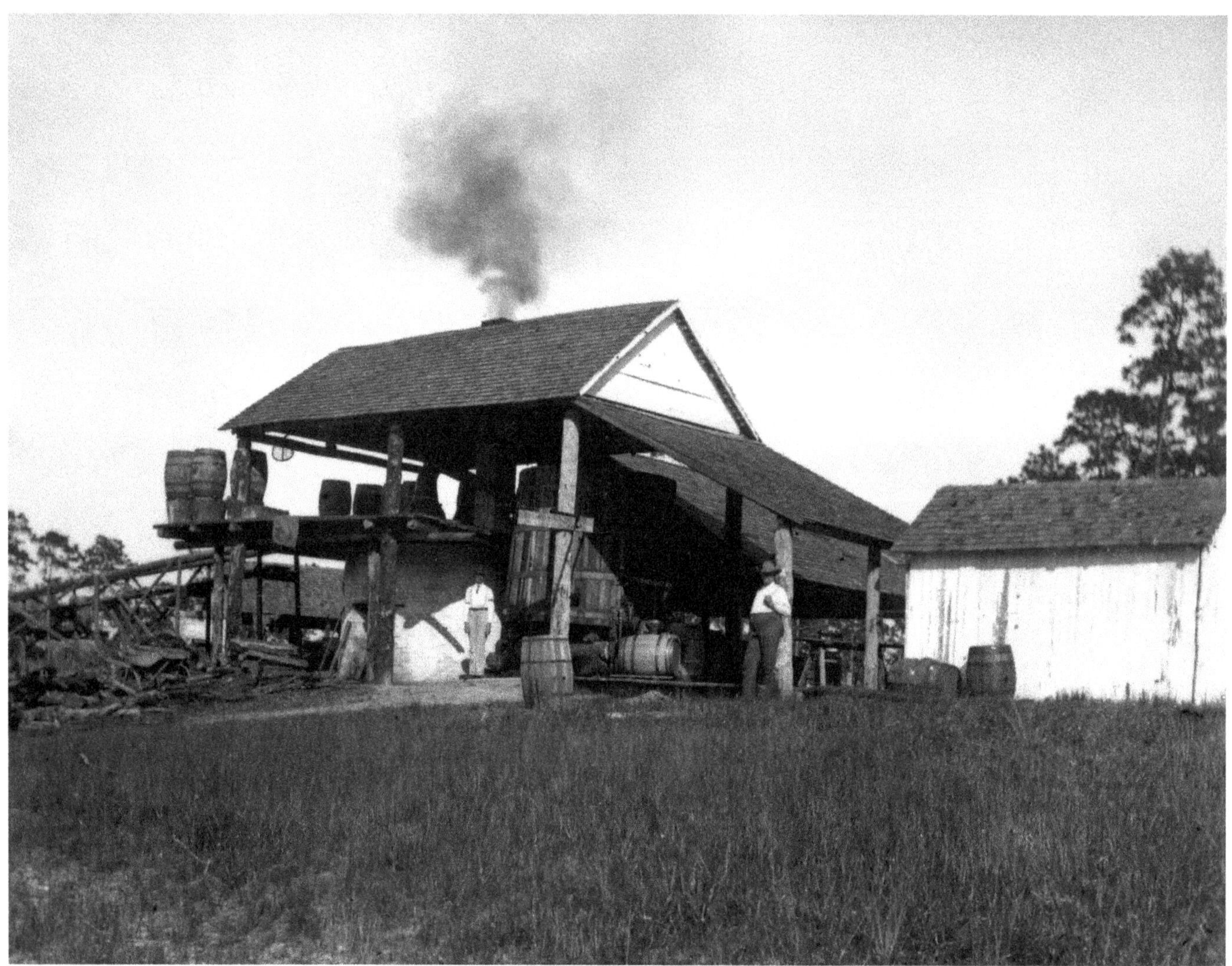

Transportation, Industry, and World War I (1907–1918)

As the Florida East Coast Railroad connected Daytona to places like Jacksonville, St. Augustine, West Palm Beach, and Miami, the town was growing. Increasing traffic on the railroad provided more finished lumber, and finer glass windows and interiors were being installed in homes, boarding houses, and hotels. The growth of industry included lumber and fiber production, the naval stores operation, and citrus and produce. The tourist industry, however, was by far the largest, drawing visitors from colder realms north to the beach, the river, and Florida seafood.

The Keating Pier was drawing more visitors who liked to fish. The beach always had crowds on weekends. The winter tourist particularly liked the boarding houses, but many others preferred the hotels. Visitors would gather in the lobbies during the day just to see and be seen and to find out where other guests were from. The Burgoyne Casino was operating with band concerts and other programs during the winter.

Streets were still unimproved. Animal-drawn vehicles were less numerous and the automobile was here to stay. A new concrete bridge was built during this time and trolley service was available from Beach Street to Seabreeze. The improved transportation by rail enabled local citizens to travel throughout the United States; businessmen, families, and vacationers could enjoy traveling in unaccustomed luxury.

The black population was growing, but the town was segregated. The railroad was an arbitrary boundary separating the white population to the east of the tracks from the black sections of Midway, New Town, and Waycross.

In nearby Ormond, new automobile ground speed records were being set. A lot of attention was given to steam-operated automobiles. The favorite, by far, was Barney Oldfield, who challenged the Stanley Steamer. Fred Marriott in his steamer had been one of Oldfield's competitors; however, a wreck on the beach diminished the competition from the steam-powered automobile. Gasoline-powered vehicles would set future ground speed records.

After the Wright brothers made their first flight at the Kitty Hawk sands of North Carolina, it did not take long for the first flying machine to find the hard-packed sands of Daytona Beach. The first machine to arrive was a biplane piloted by Carl Bates from Chicago. Unfortunately he could not substantiate his time or distance for the beach flight and was not nationally credited. Many old timers would argue that the actual event was proof enough and did not require documentation.

As aviation advanced, the U.S. Army Signal Corps first saw the advantage of the airplane as a modern surveillance machine much improved over the balloon. Just before World War I, the U.S. Army Service Aviation Section was established. Pilots were trained to fly biplanes—at the time, the latest innovation for national defense. The beach at Daytona was a natural landing runway and could be reached by U.S. Army pilots from nearby training fields in Florida.

During World War I many men left from Daytona to join the Army and then came home from Europe with innovative ideas about improving houses and hotels. The flu epidemic of 1918 ravaged citizen and soldier alike, but did not affect the economy of Daytona to the extent it did in the north.

Fred Marriott, trying to break the speed record near Ormond, hit an uneven spot on the beach, losing control. The racer broke apart, stopping near the surf. Marriott was injured but did recover.

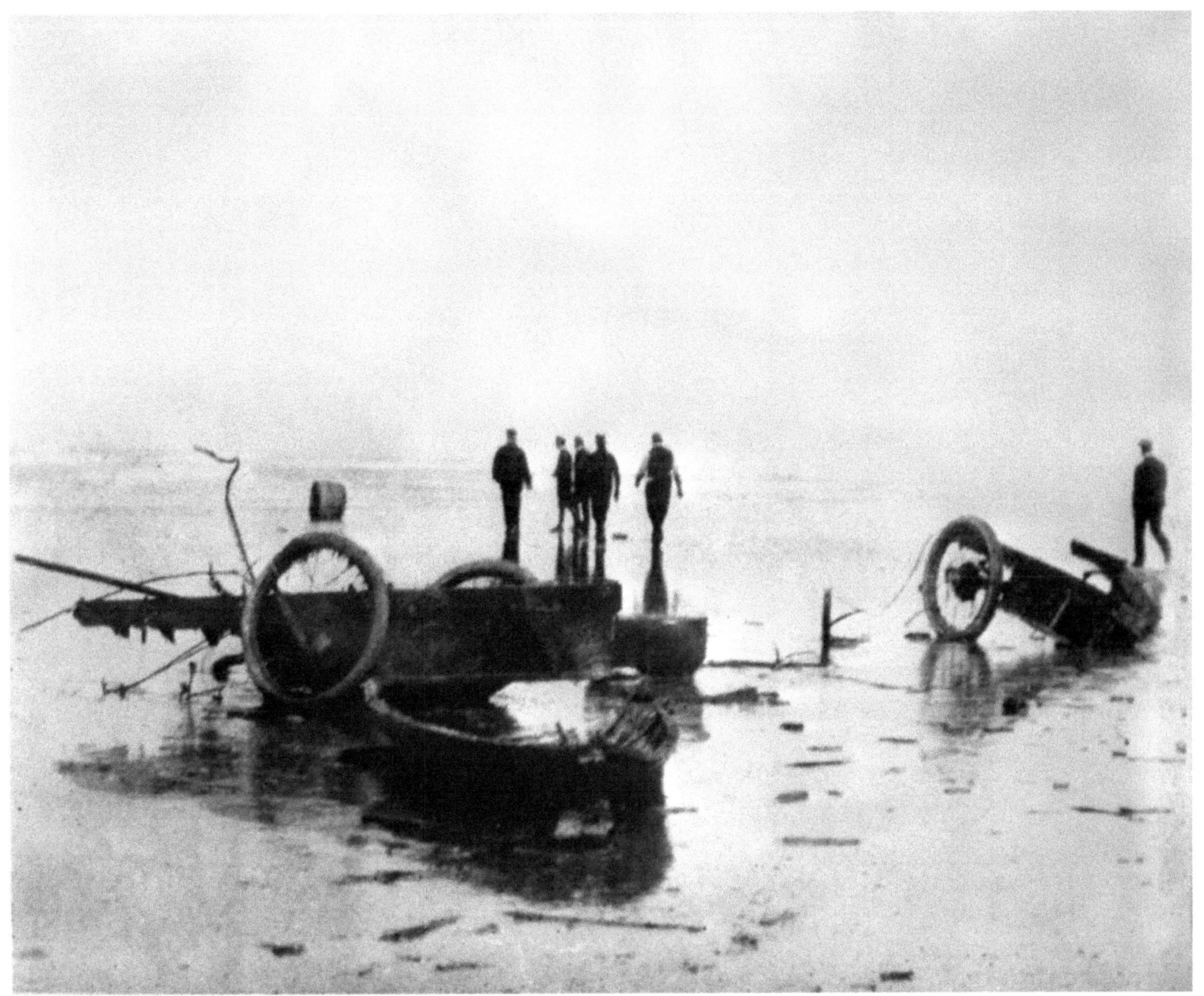

Today this bridge is called the Main Street Bridge—the main entrance to the ocean beach. Women in long skirts, cyclists, and pedestrians all stop to pose for the photographer, but a little dog has more important business on the agenda.

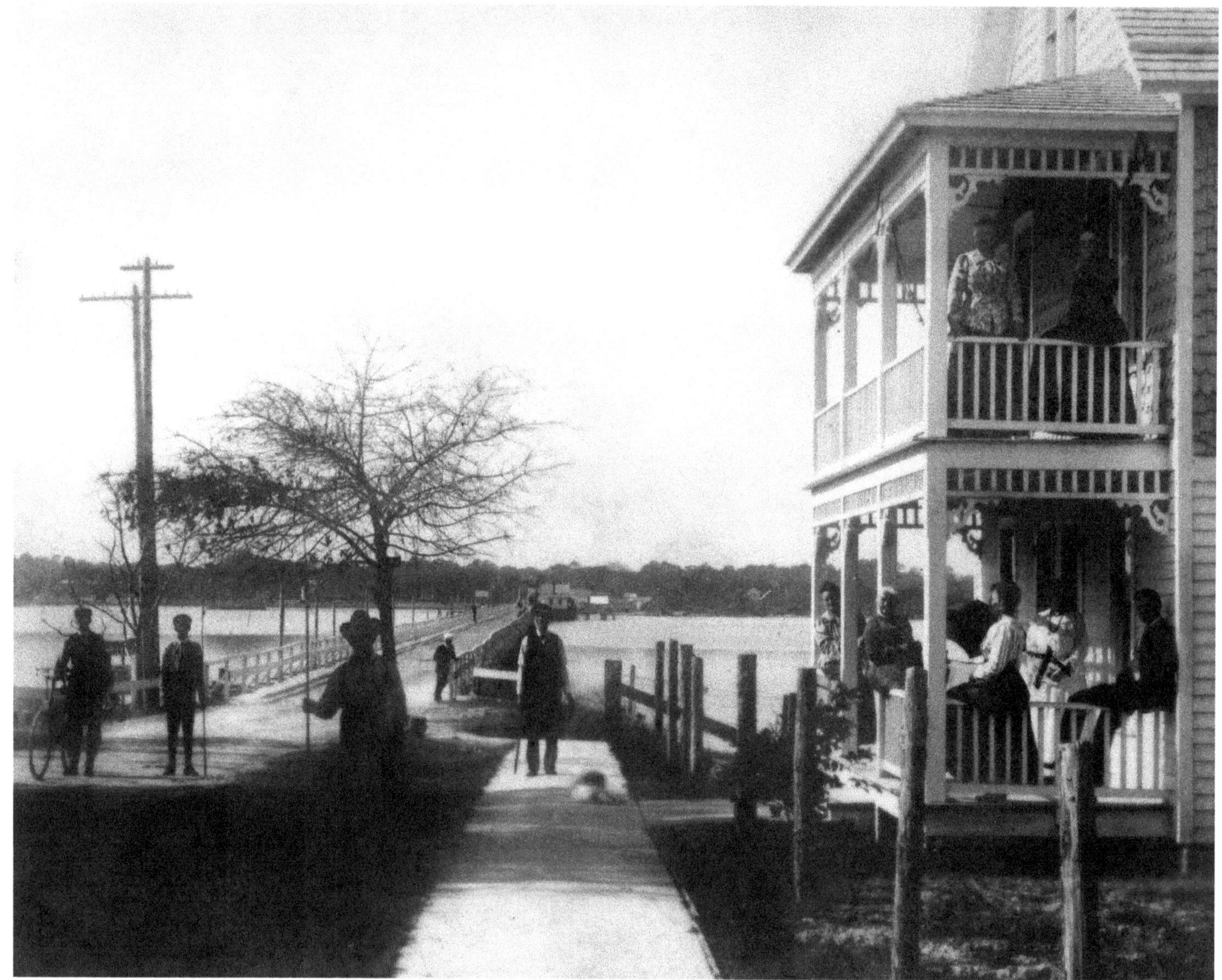

This fashionable home was a masonry vernacular styled building. Features were bay windows, dormers seen at the roof line, and a back extension of the home including a chimney.

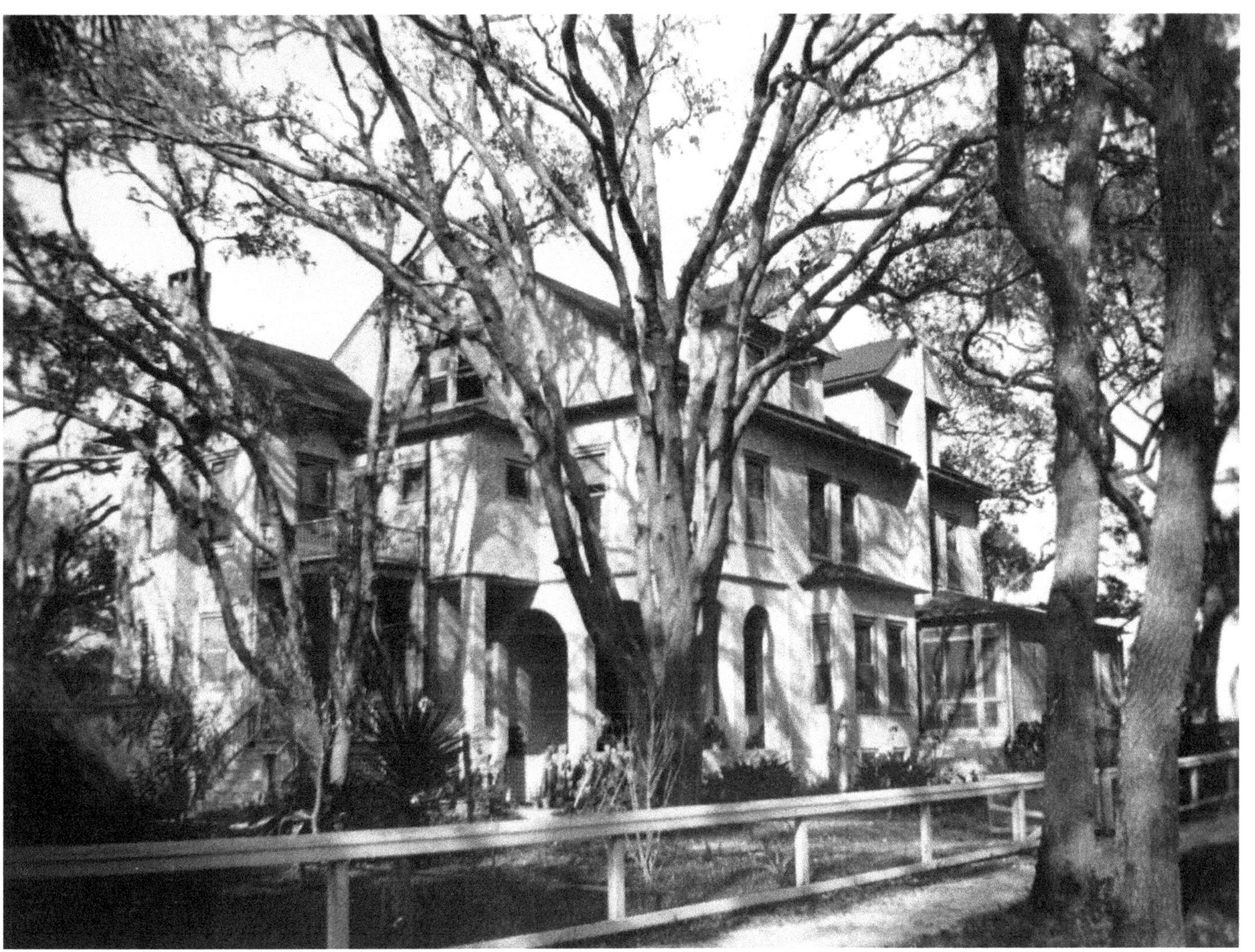

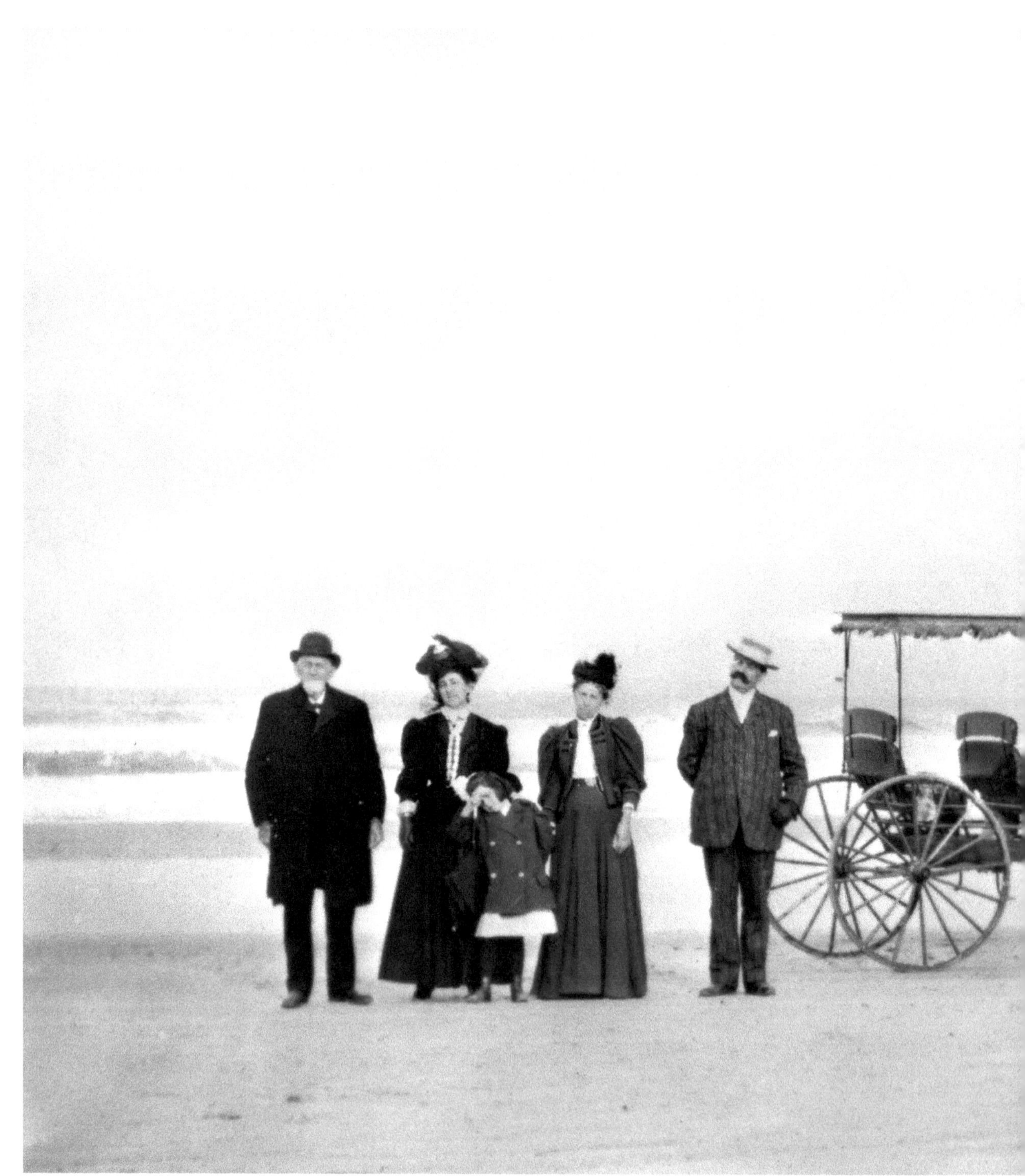

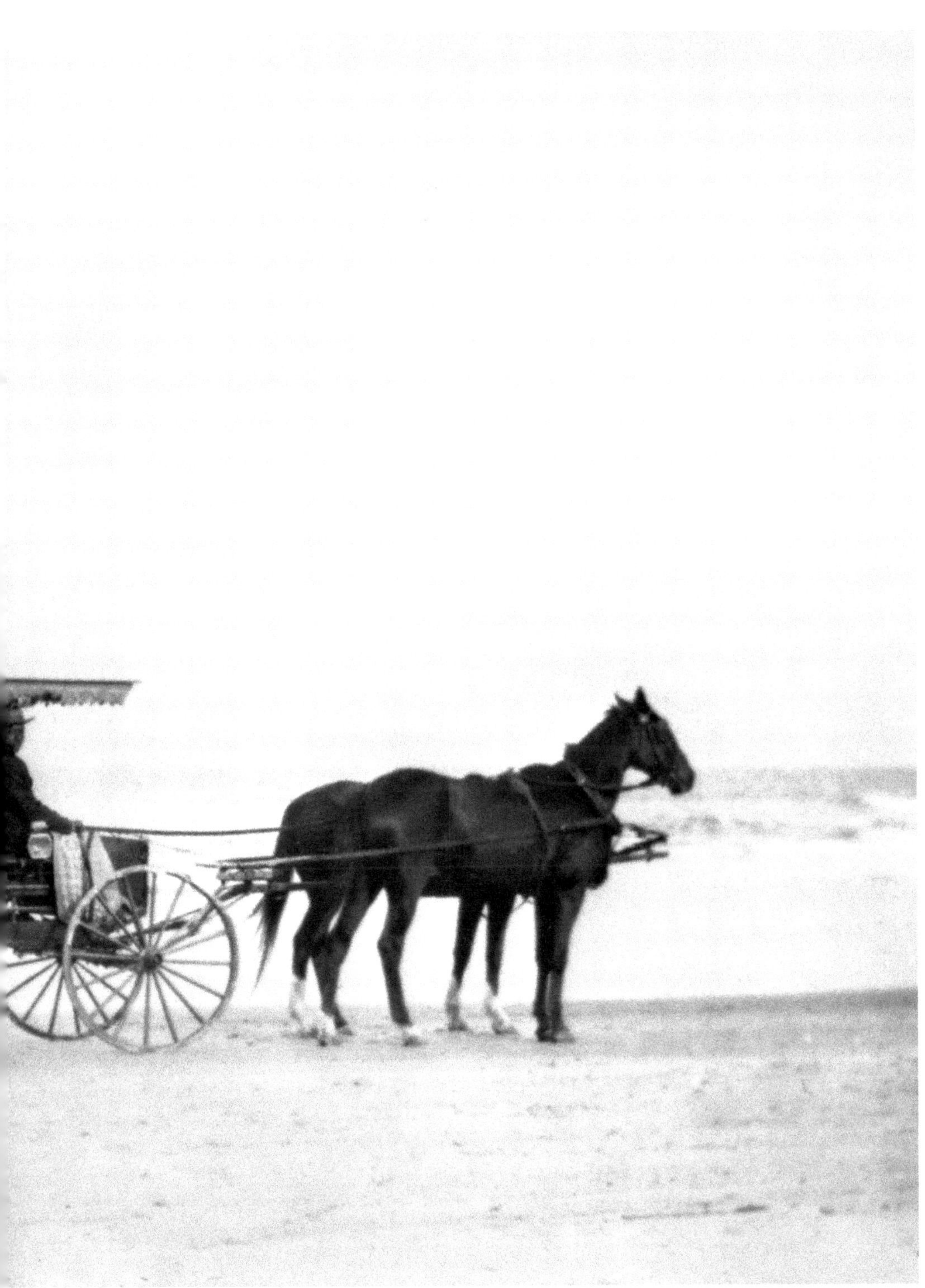

Dressed in attire appropriate for autumn, three generations of one family gather on the beach to pose for the photographer while team and driver wait nearby.

Later named Main Street, this was the main approach to the ocean. At left is the Pinewood Cemetery and its wall. At right in the distance a church's steeple (First Methodist Church beachside) is visible. An early canvas-topped auto sits parked in front of a store.

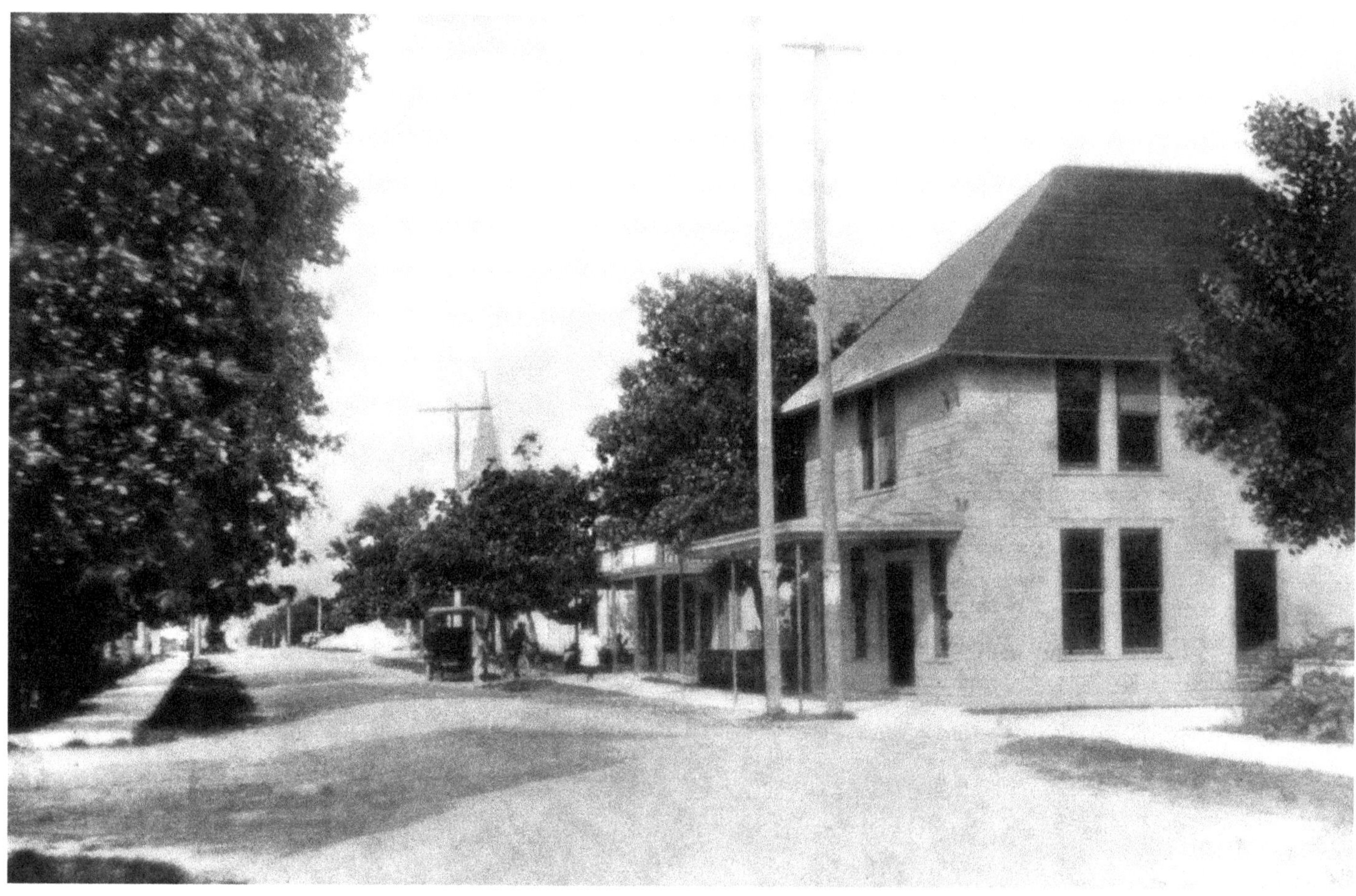

This was a typical street scene in Daytona when pedestrians gathered at a store or a boarding home. The organ grinder depended on gratuities for his living. The monkey often held a cup for loose coins. The two women are being entertained by the well-kept monkey.

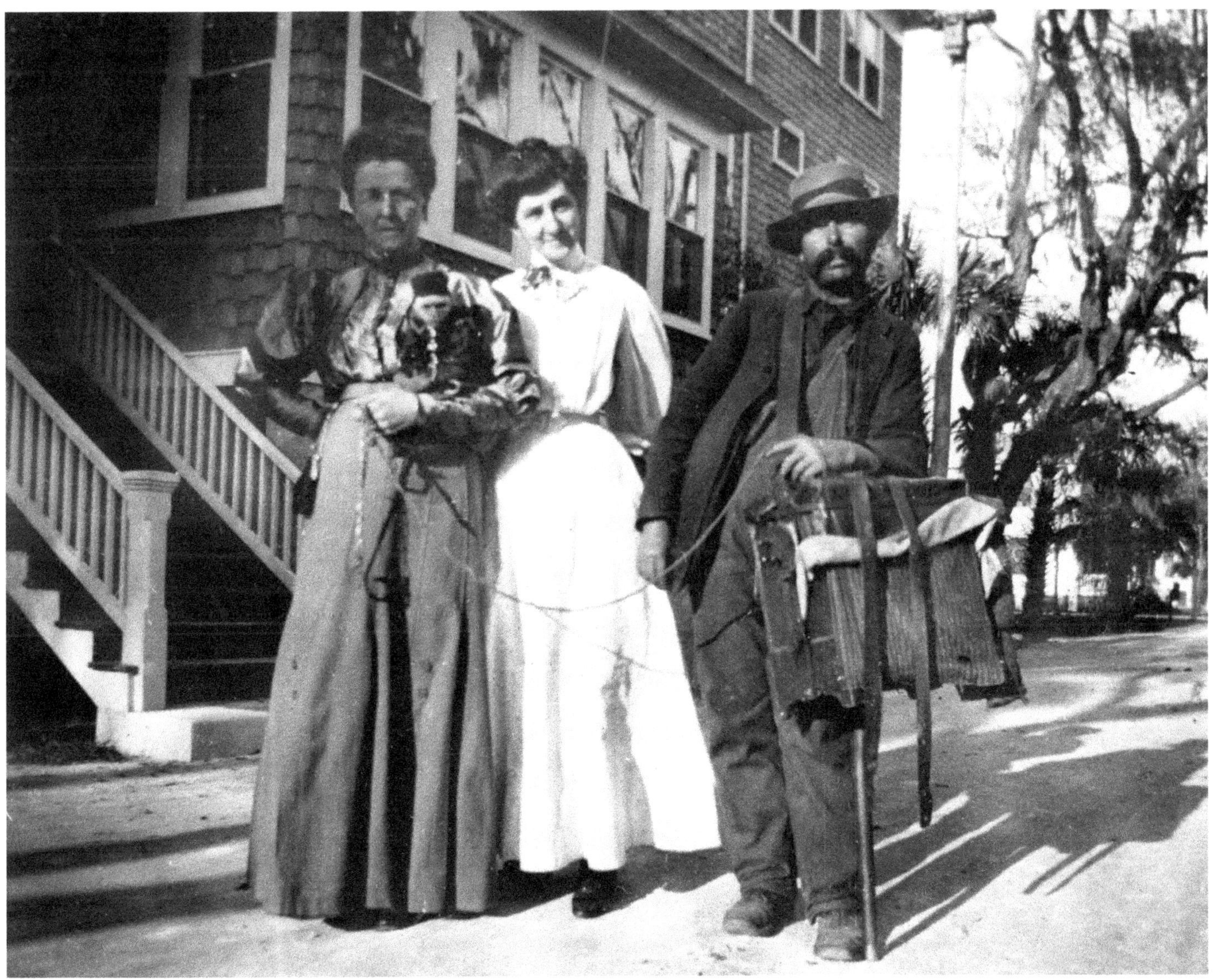

The original Putnam House in Palatka was built in 1885. Later it was razed, one wing being dismantled for the yellow pine lumber. The joists, framing, and siding were taken to Daytona and incorporated into the Hotel Neptune. Often heart pine lumber was salvaged and reused in new construction.

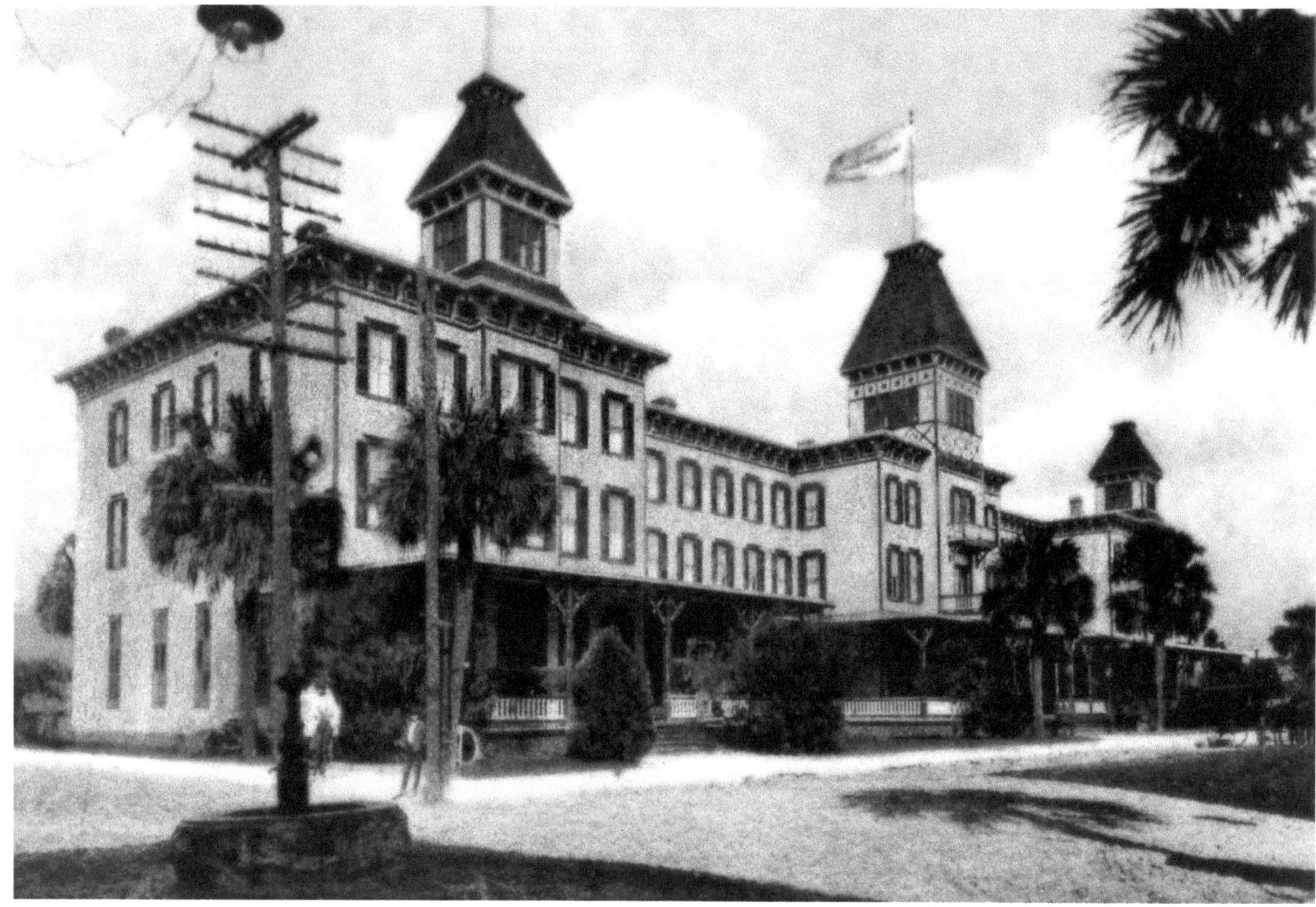

Left to right are Ed Lindberg, oiler; George Young, engineer; and Chief Messmore, superintendent, standing in front of a new generator installed to make possible electric lighting. In the beginning electricity was available only for an allotted number of hours. Many facilities had to close late at night.

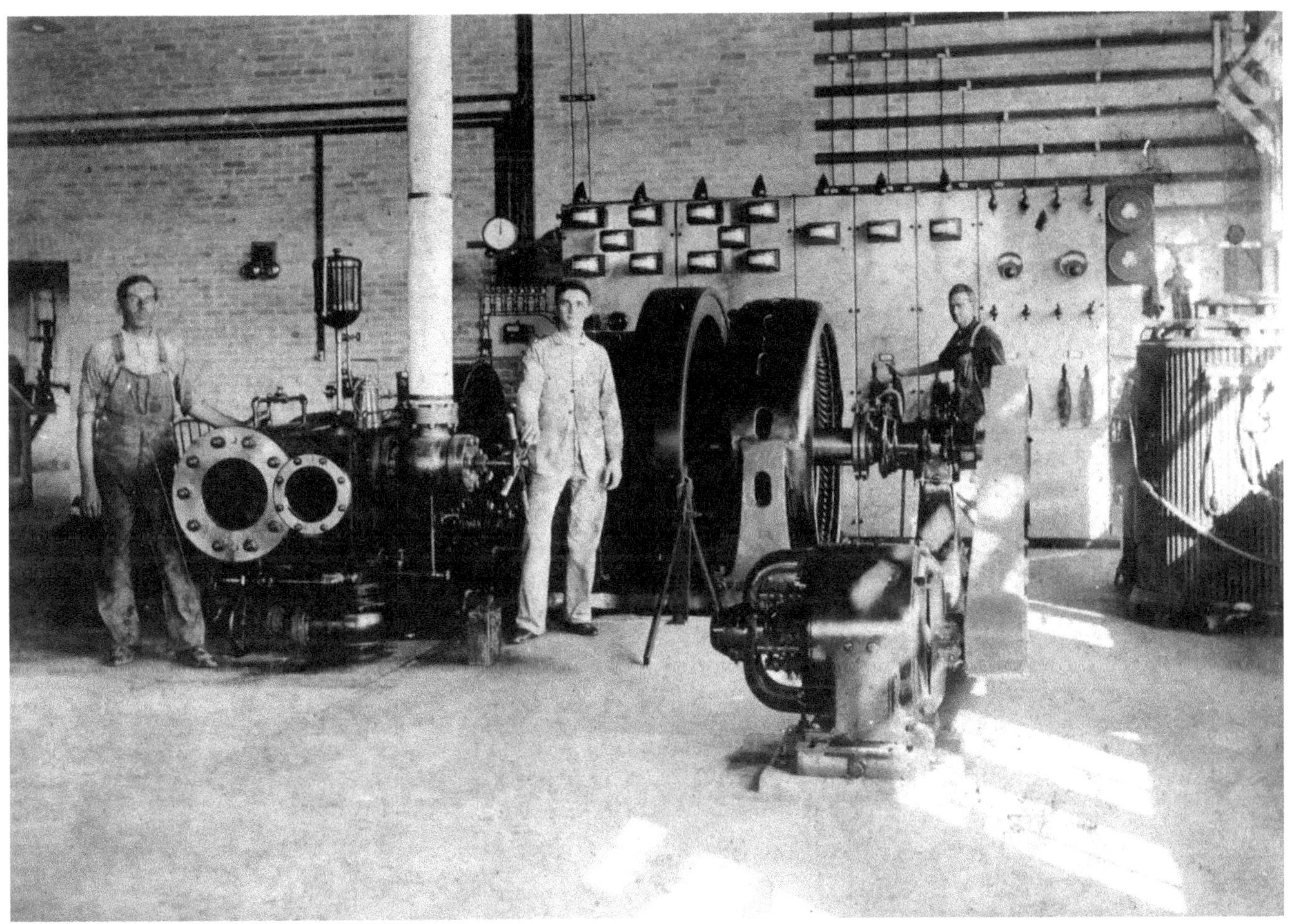

These whales, 35 to 40 feet long, washed ashore along the beach south of Daytona. Frank Sams, Albert Moeller, Elmer Oliver, Jerome Maley, John Pettigrew, and Captain S. Bennett partnered to chop up these sea creatures and make whale oil. They used the giant kettles from the Dunlawton Sugar Mill. Their method failed.

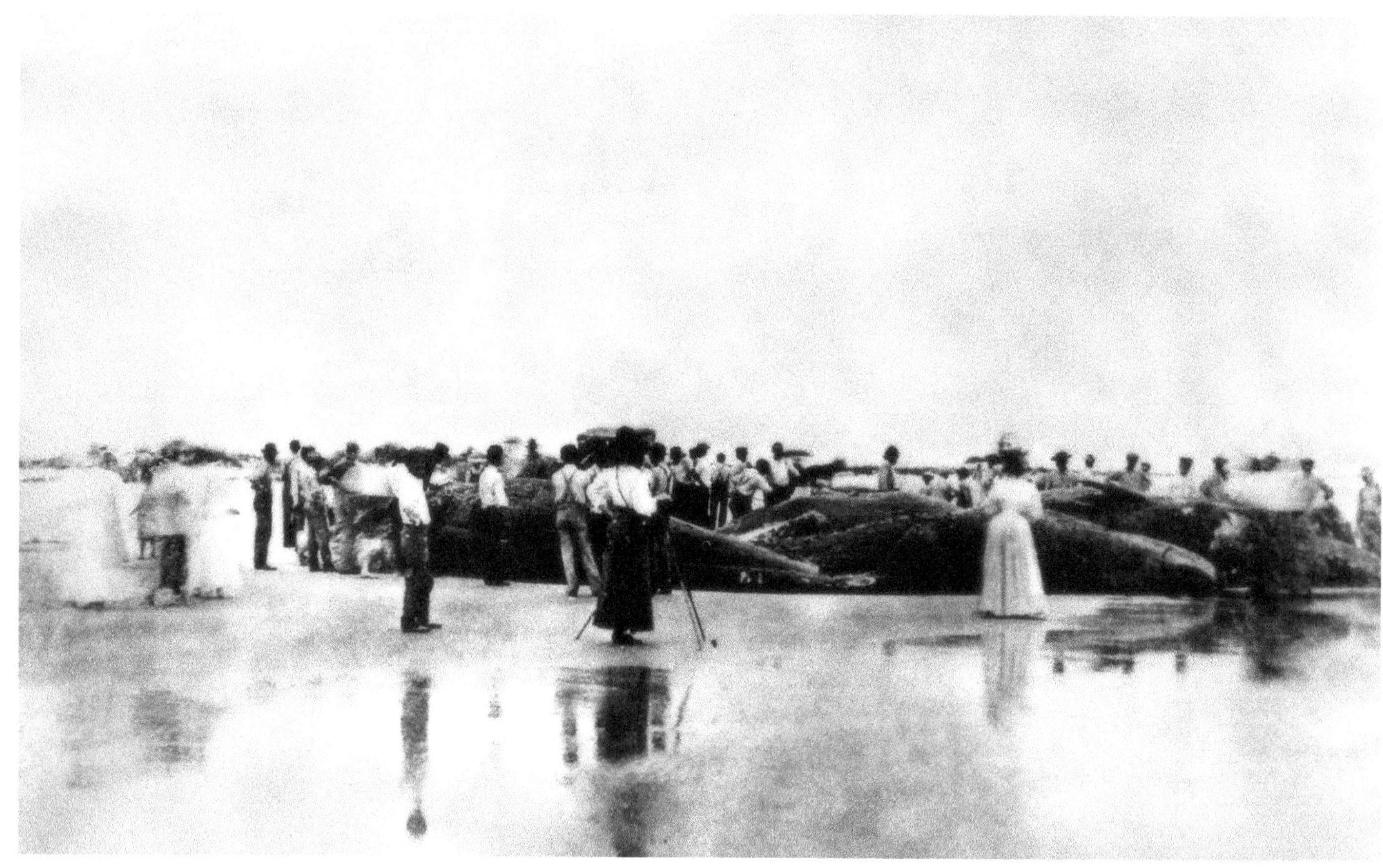

This large, well-known inn was home to many winter visitors. Some guests came back to the same room each year. Standing at the northeast corner of Palmetto and Ivy Lane for many years, the inn was eventually demolished to widen Palmetto Avenue.

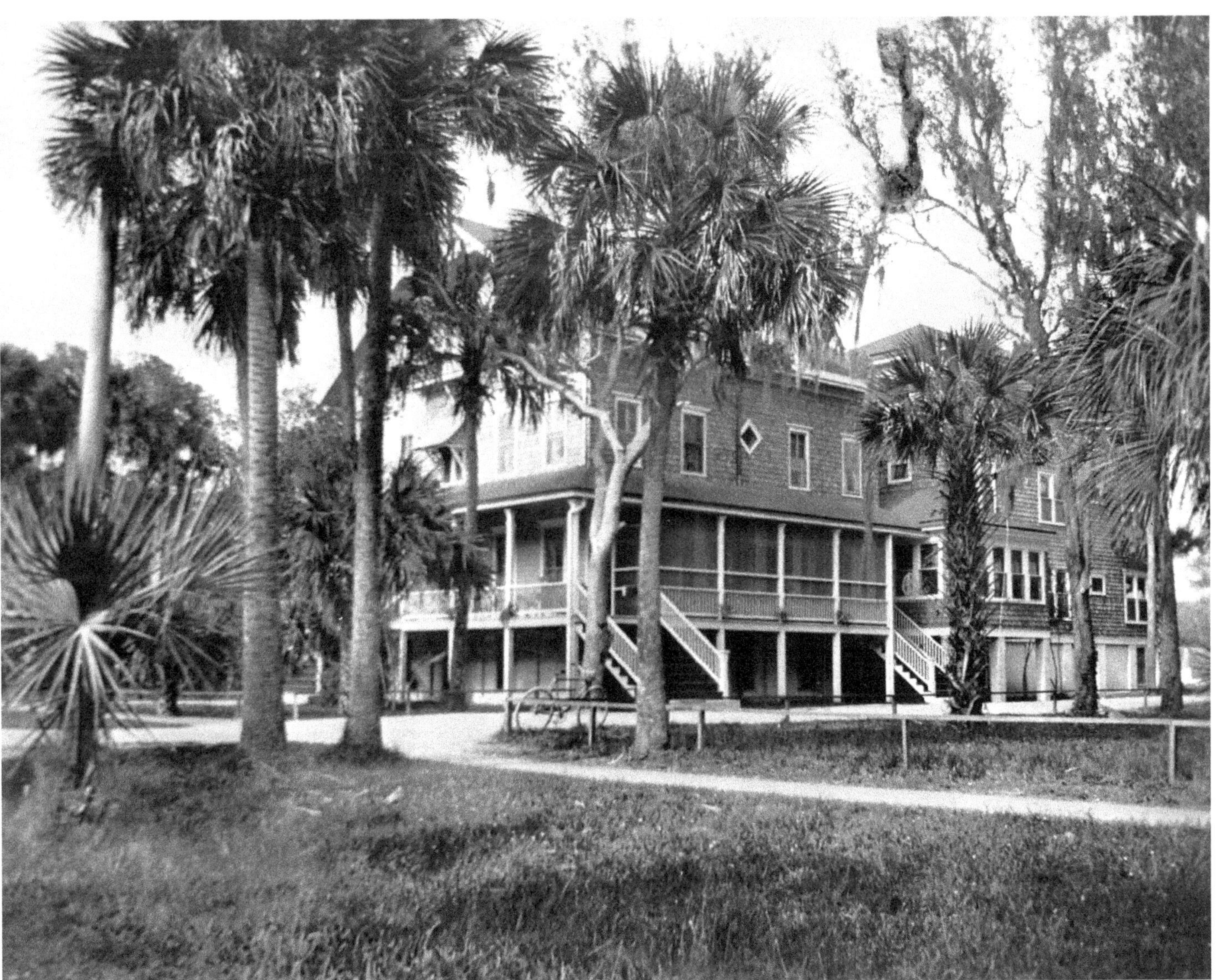

This bridge was constructed of yellow pine timbers. Planking was rough sawn to accommodate the new autos crossing the bridge. The library building to the left was a masonry brick structure and the jail to the right was a wooden structure with enclosed iron cell.

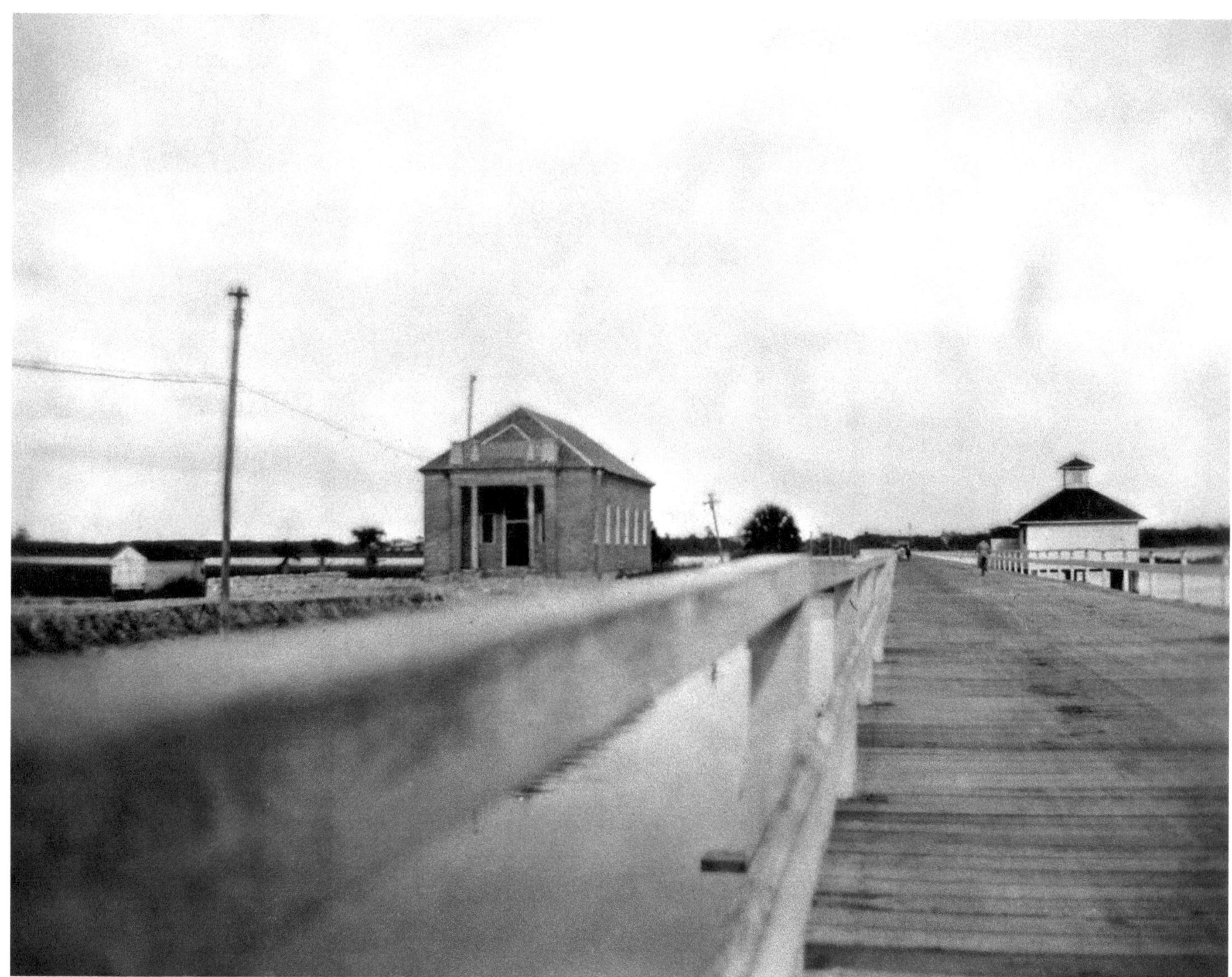

Daytona's Midway was west of the railroad. Most blacks lived segregated away from whites, in Midway and other sections. Stores, schools, and churches served their area of town.

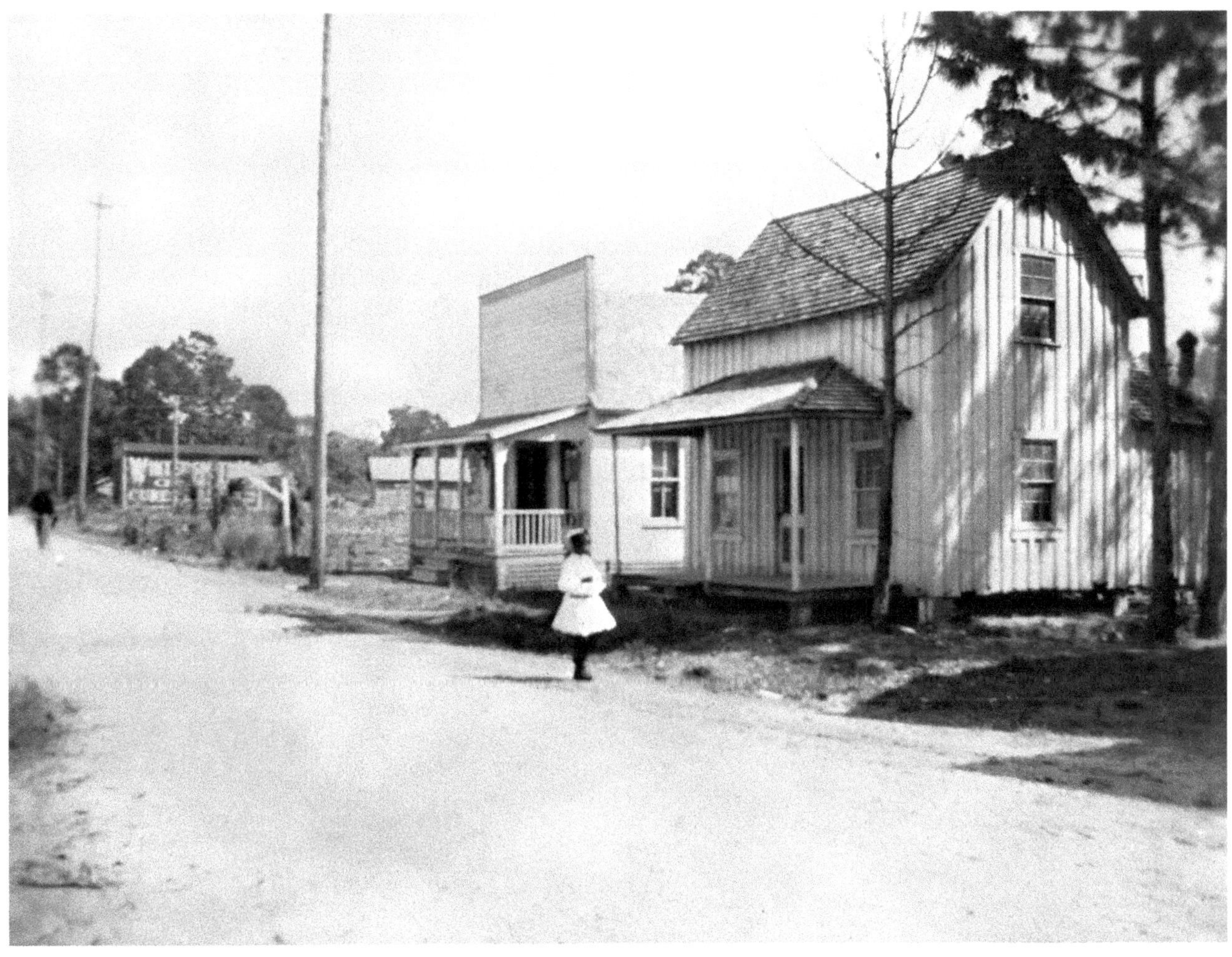

This boat once plied the waters of the Halifax River. A steam-powered craft with two decks and a pilot house in front on top, it featured an open area for entertaining guests.

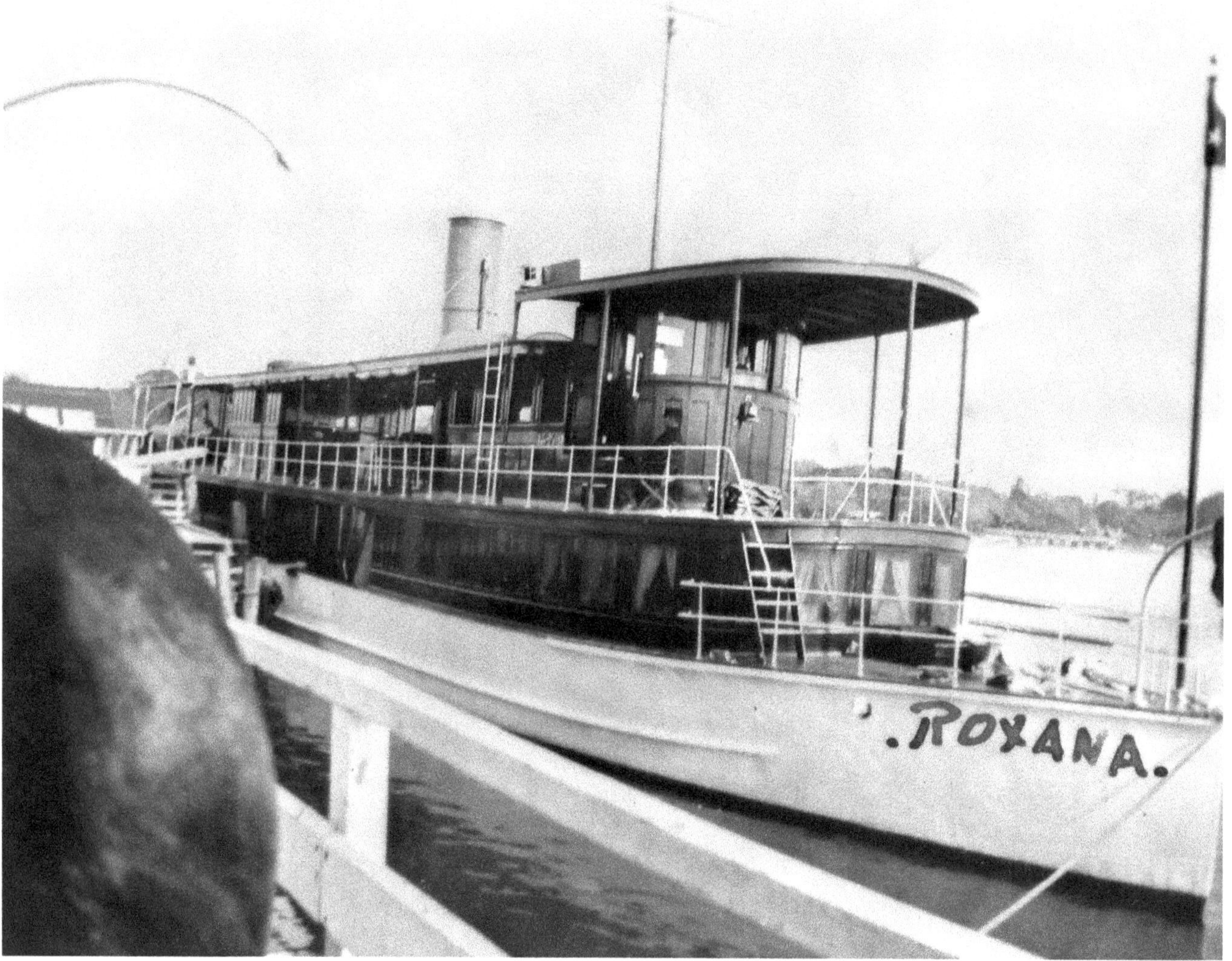

This outstanding home was on Ridgewood Avenue and encompassed several architectural styles, mostly classical revival. Masonry walls are hand-formed block made in molds. Artistic porch railings and columns adorn the front and side elevations. A sun room with chimney is at the side.

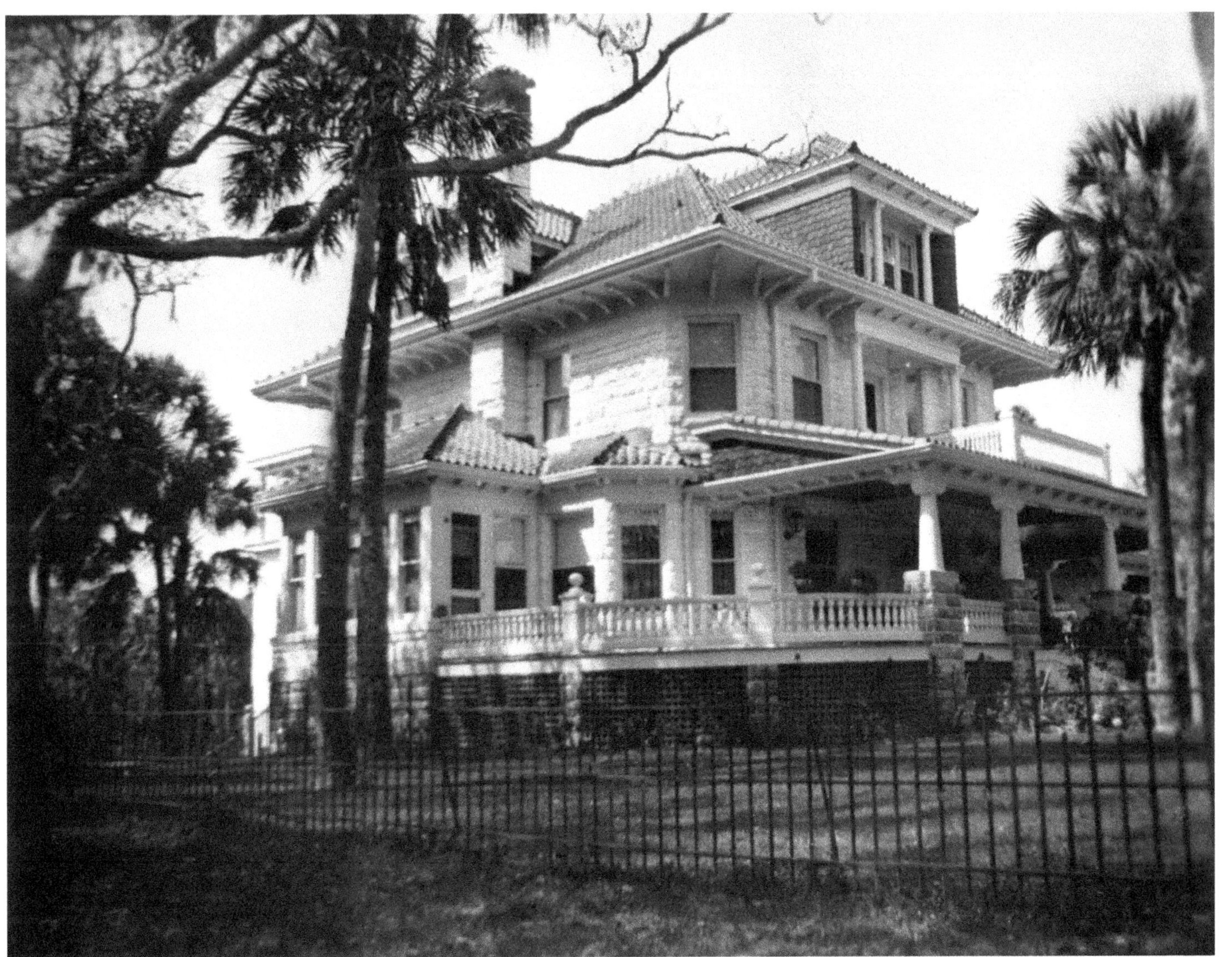

The Keating pier was the forerunner of the Main Street Pier today. The hexagon-towered house with porch was reported to be Charles Burgoyne's beach house. To the north in front of the old Claradon Inn was the Port Pier, which was destroyed many years ago by a northeaster storm. Often these storms did as much damage as a hurricane along the oceanfront.

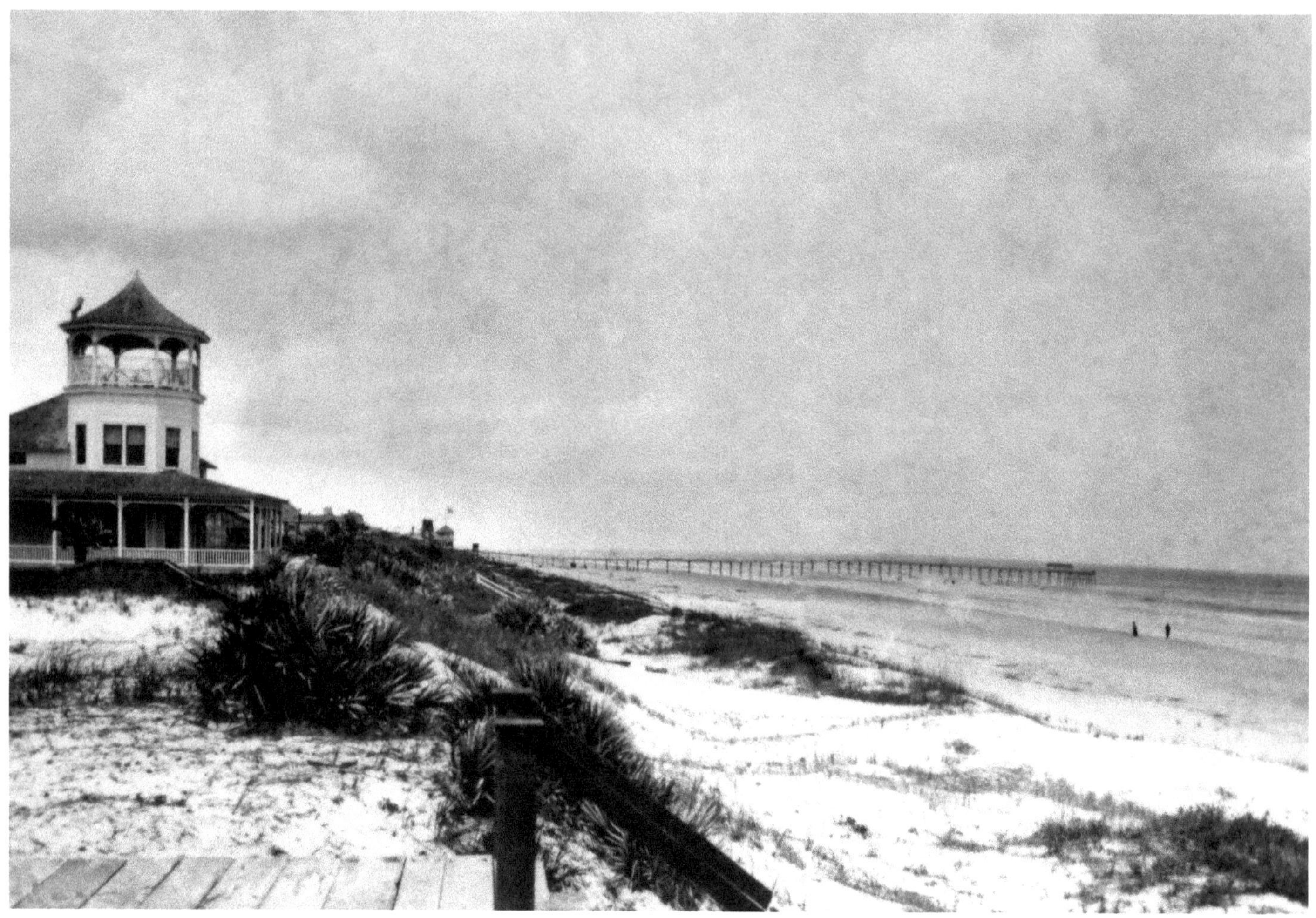

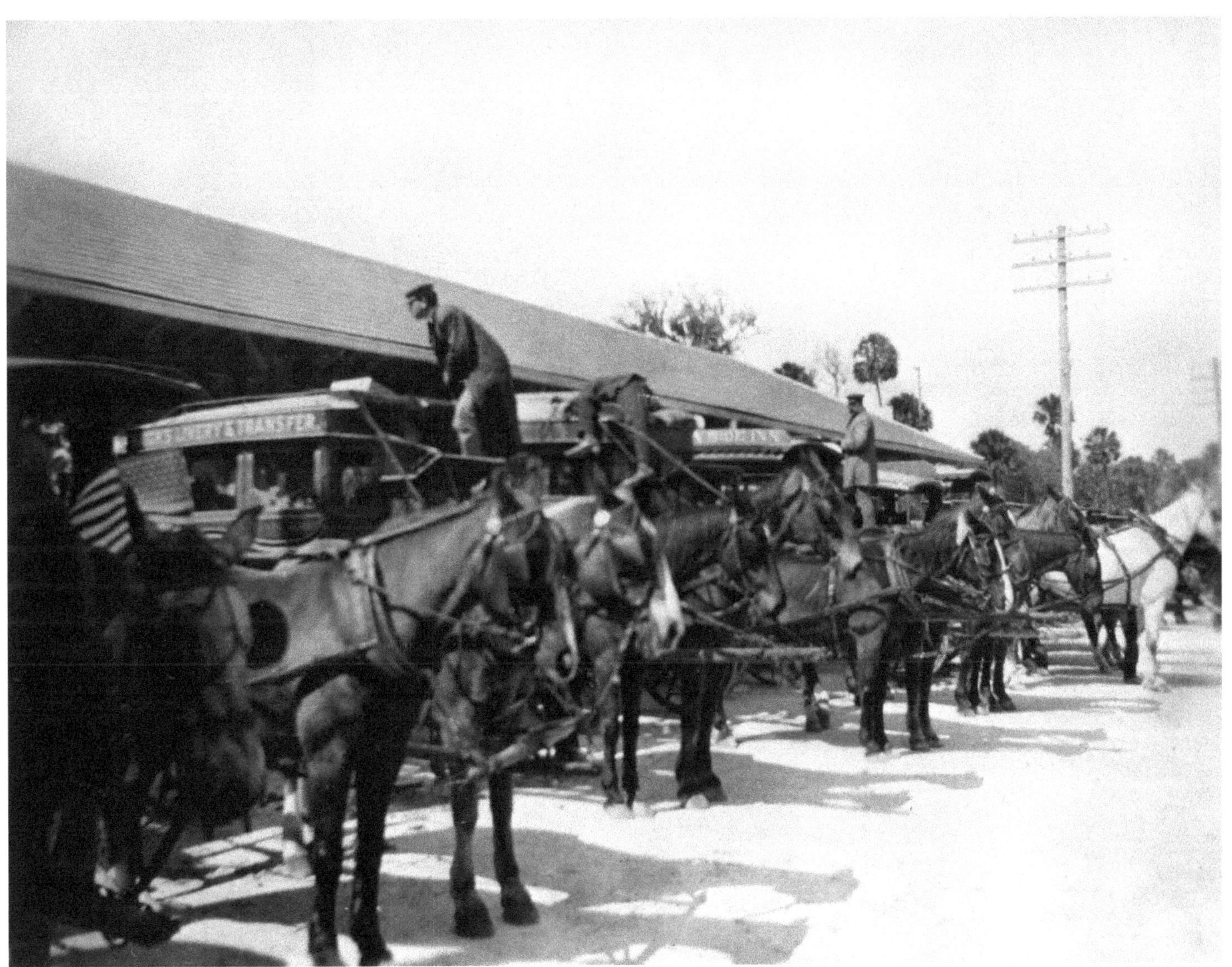

This crowded depot loading area was awaiting the unloading of luggage and steamer trunks. Tourists brought all of their clothing and accessories for the winter when they arrived in town.

A haberdashery and other stores line this Daytona street.

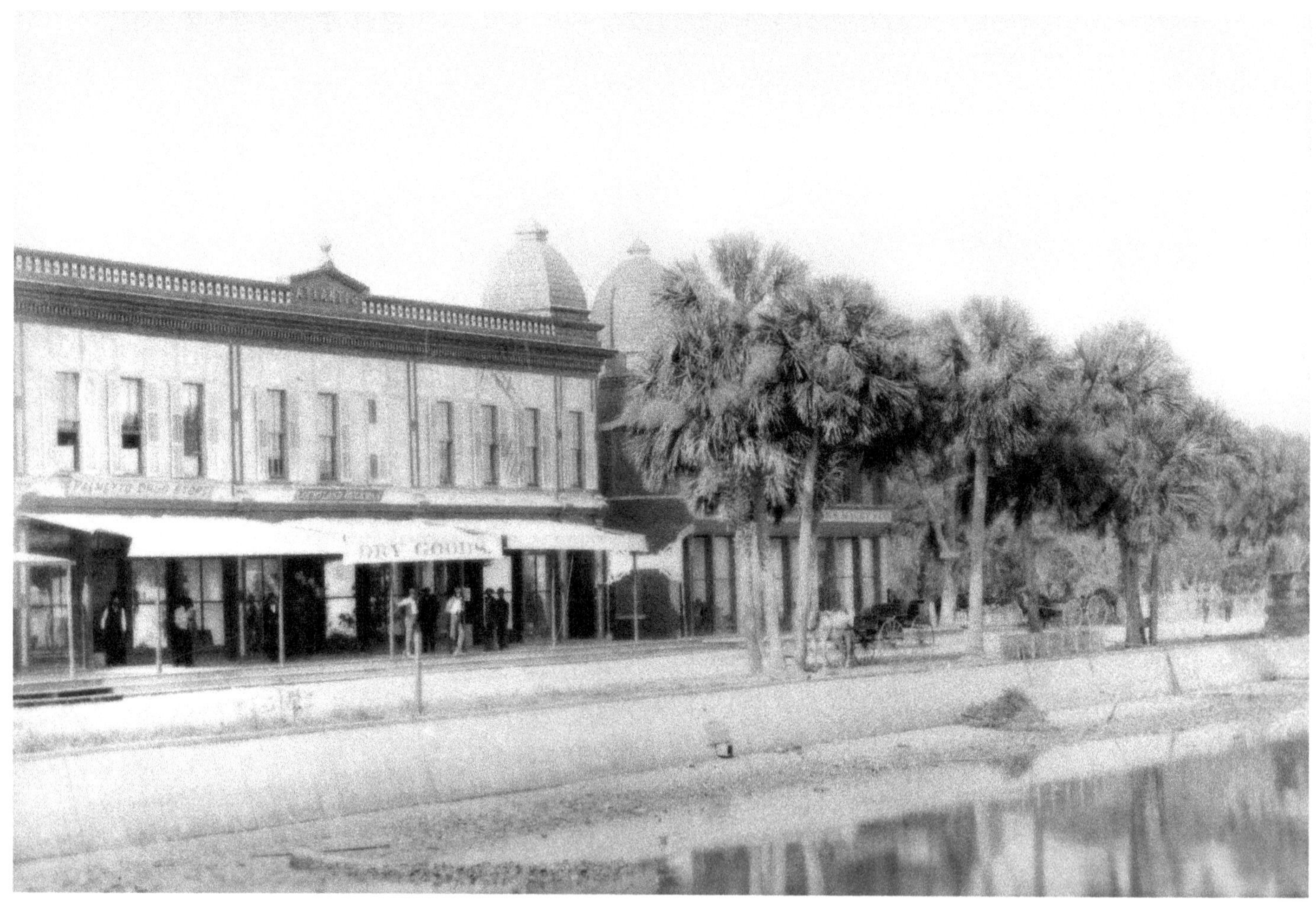

Harry B. Shefts in his Hotchkiss racer participates in a day at the races, March 5, 1908. Time trials and individual races used the full length of the beach from Ormond to Daytona.

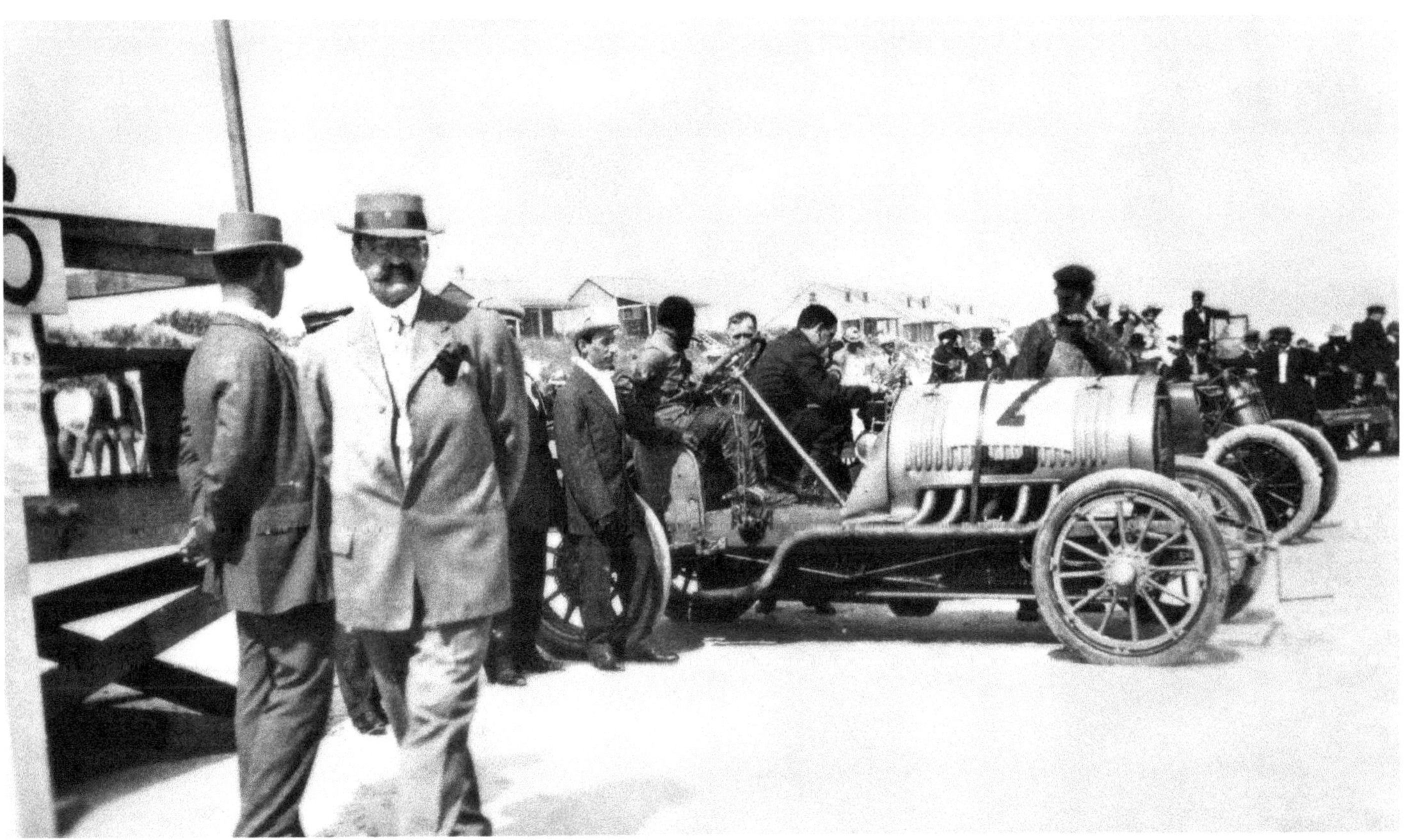

A disastrous fire leaves enough time for guests and hotel workers to remove personal belongings. Furnishings were stored at nearby homes. The belongings of some guests were taken to the beach for safety.

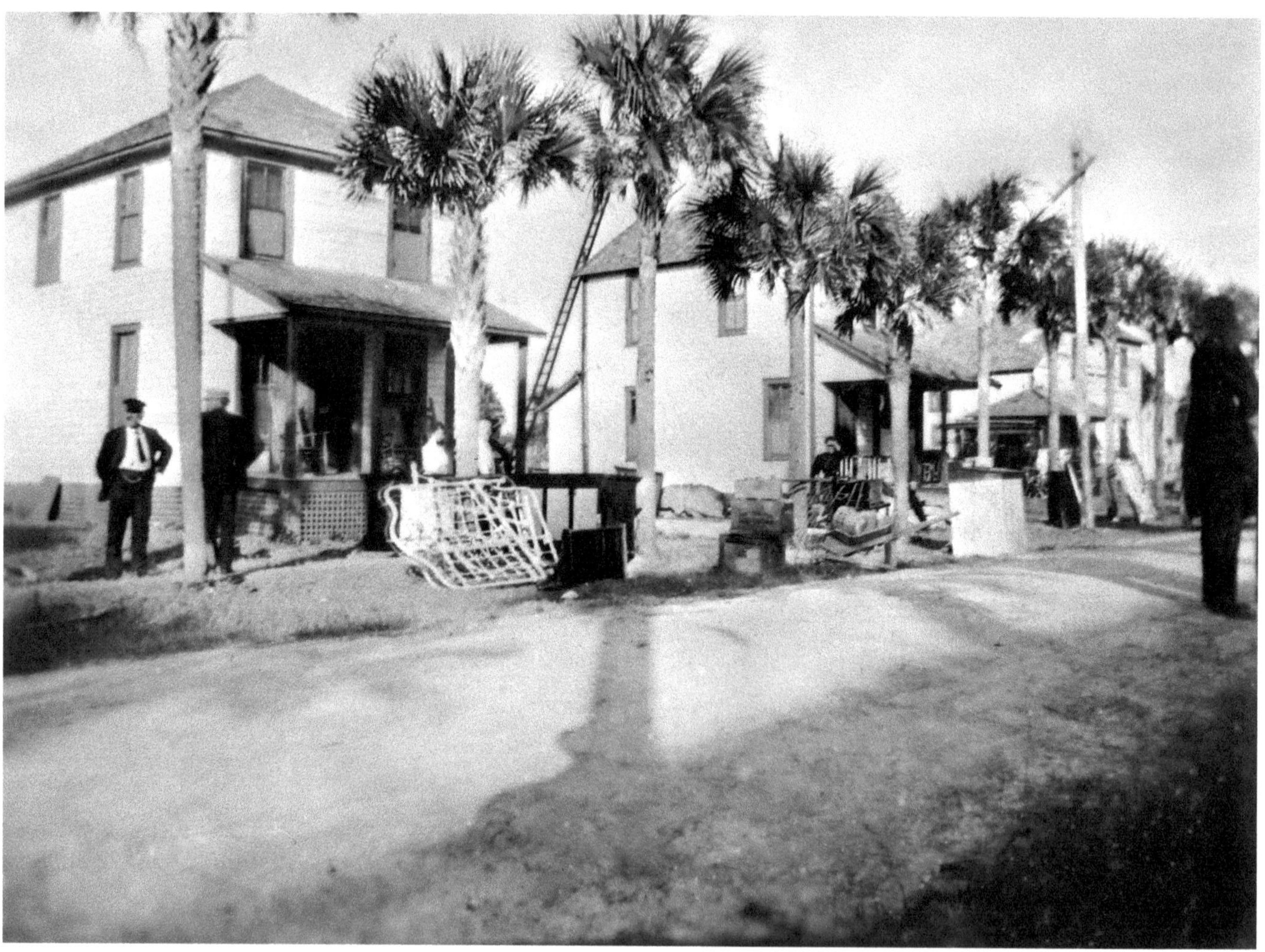

These bathers appear to be enjoying the surf in their store-bought wool bathing suits. The lady at right sports a nautical collar, wool skirt, and leg covers. Both women are wearing shoes.

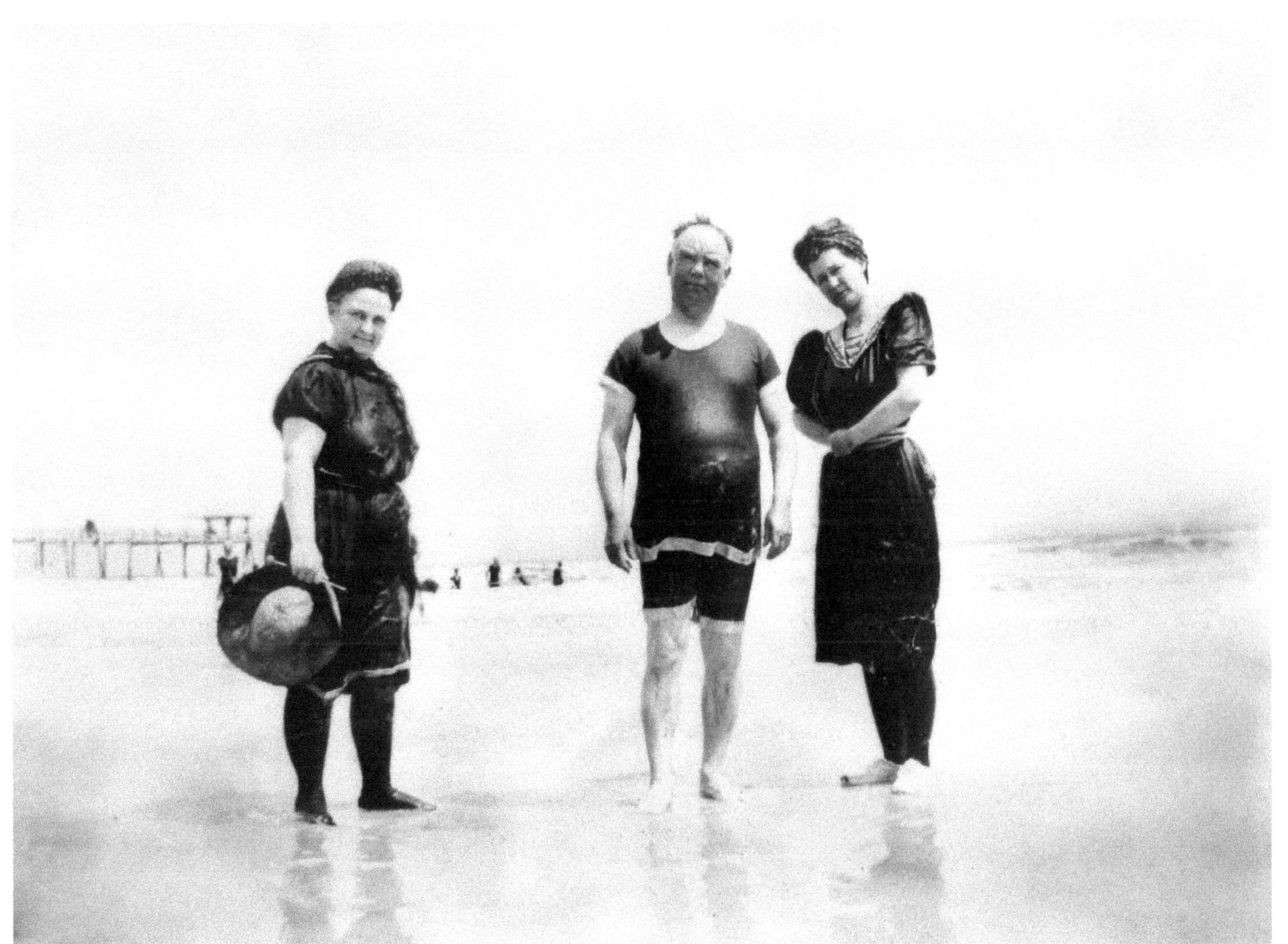

Carl Bates and two other men from Chicago built this biplane. He successfully flew over the beach for a short distance, rising 10 to 20 feet off the hard-packed sand. A broken fly wheel led to engine vibration and he landed abruptly. He was not able to substantiate the time or distance so was not credited with the first flight in Florida.

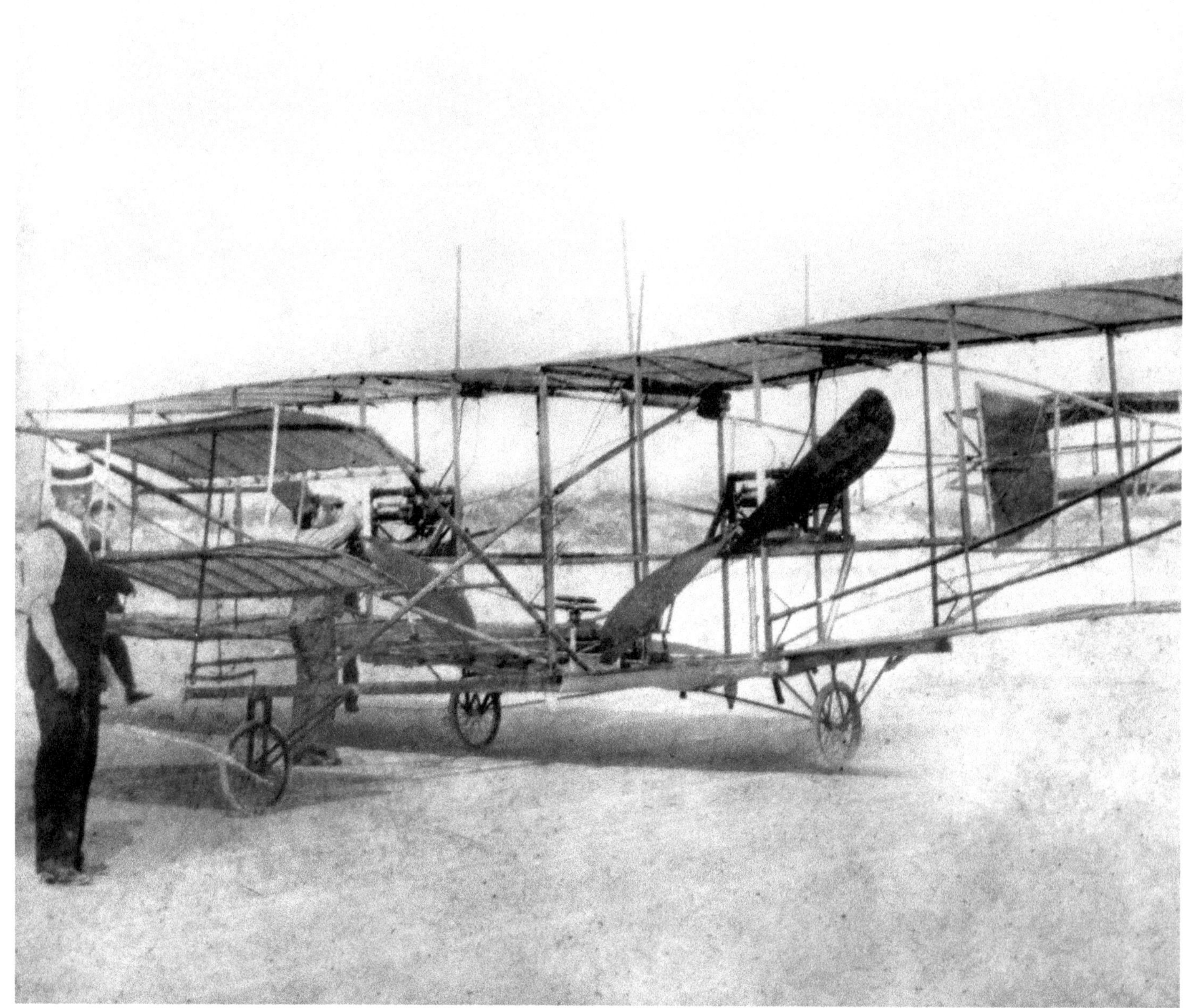

Leon Despland was a hotel magnate. He first had a hotel on the northeast corner of Beach Street and Magnolia, which he sold. He built a new hotel, pictured, at the southeast corner of Palmetto and Magnolia streets. He sold this hotel and it was renamed the Williams Hotel, which stood until after World War II.

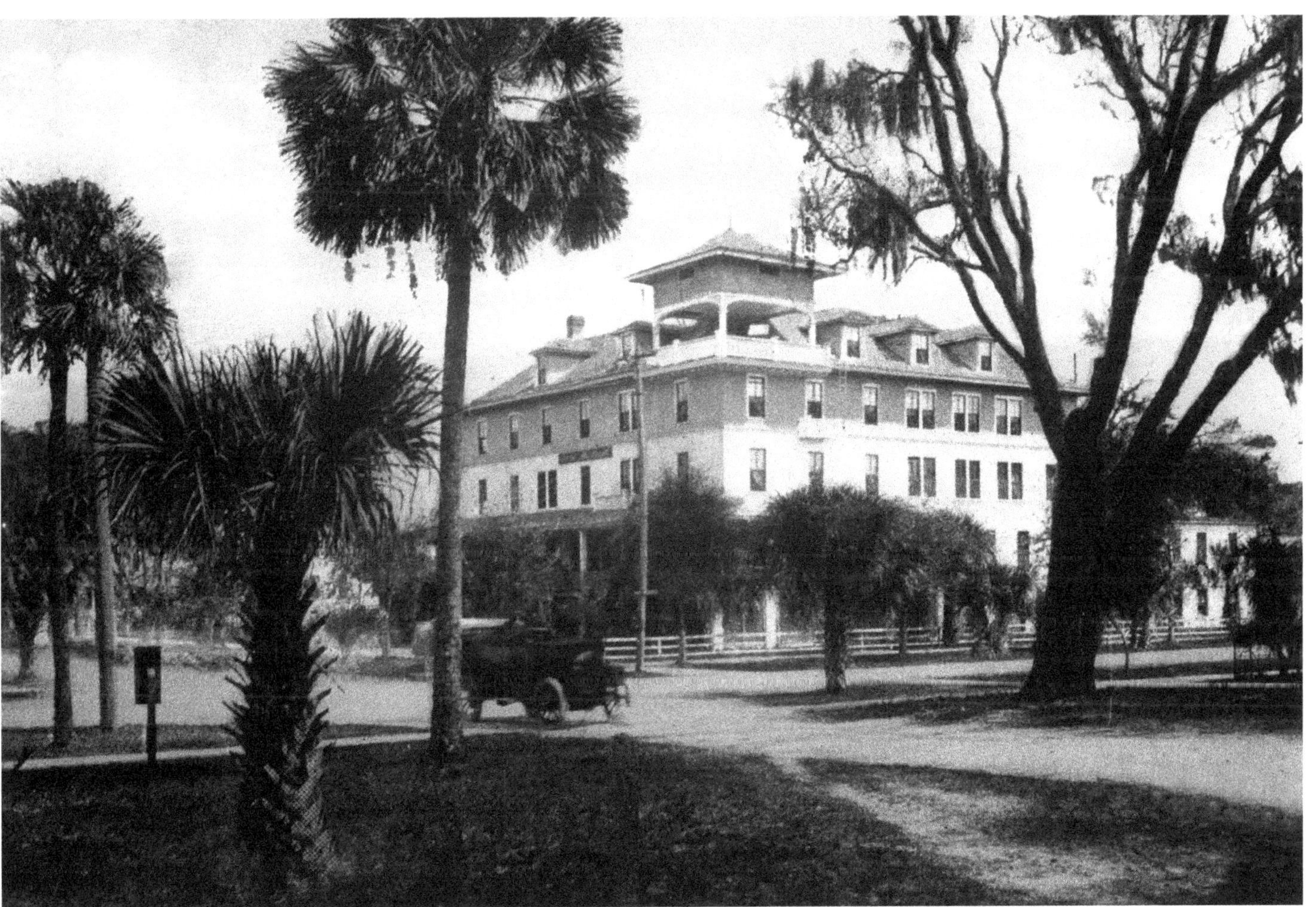

When young ladies came to the beach and stayed in hotels, they always had a chaperone. Parasols offered protection against the sun. This photograph was taken near the beach pier on a sand dune.

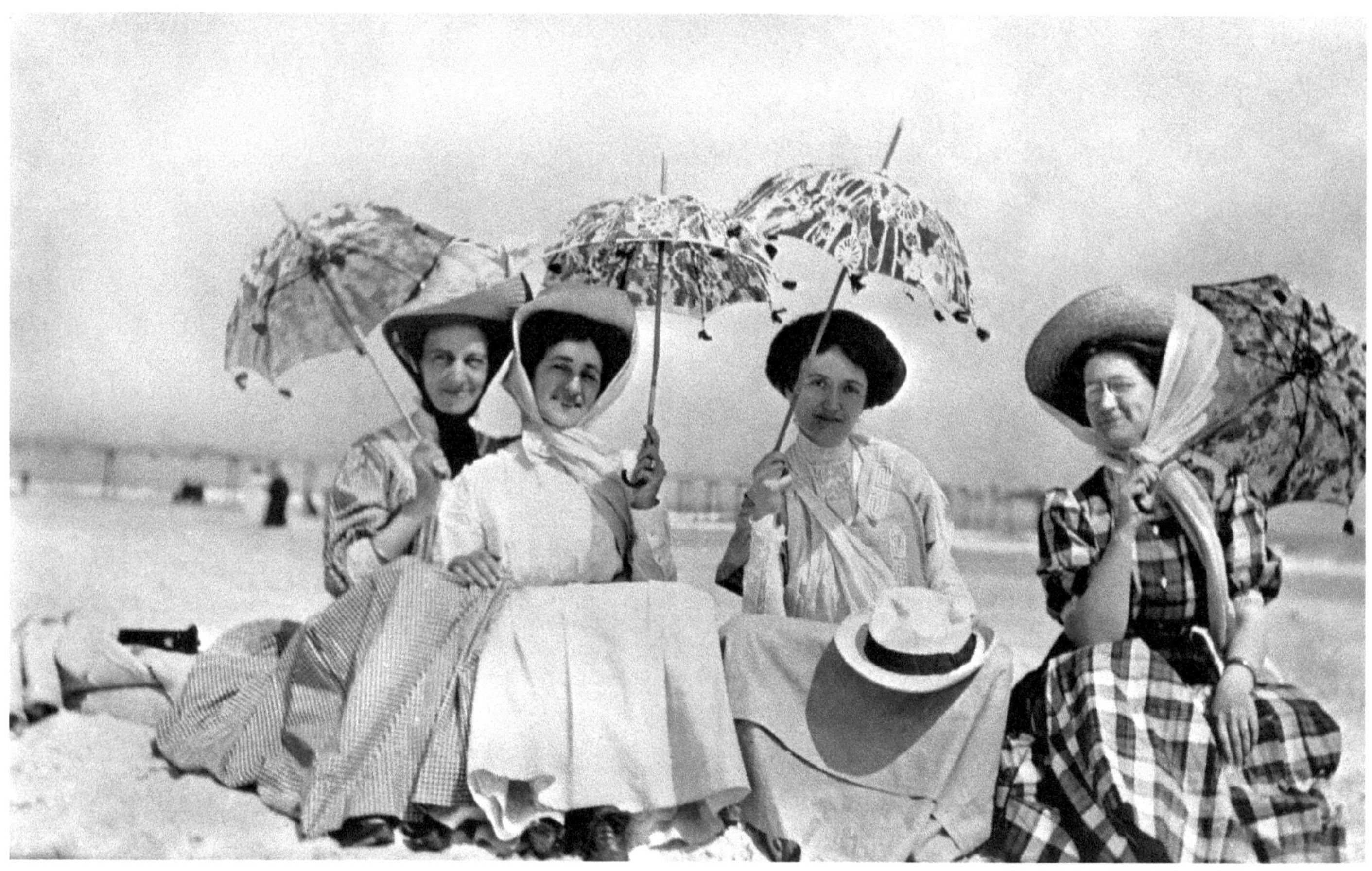

Visitors to the city founded by Matthias Day take an afternoon stroll on an unpaved Loomis Avenue named for Matthias's son, Loomis Day.

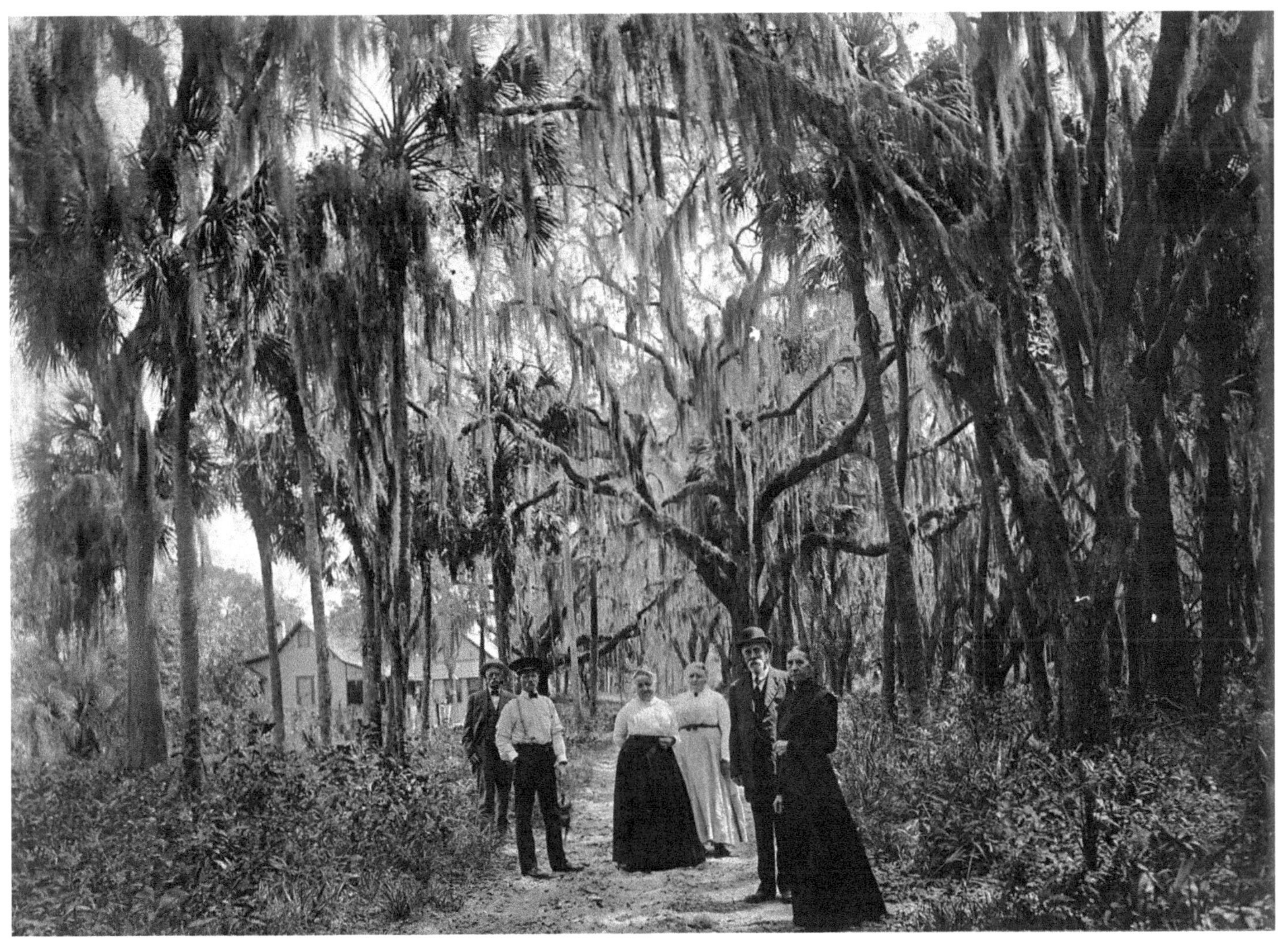

The Halifax Yacht Club was a place to see and to be seen. If you were the commodore, you were the most prestigious person in town. Membership comprised city officials and businessmen who frequently met for lunch to promote Daytona. Here various types of boats are moored at the club's dock.

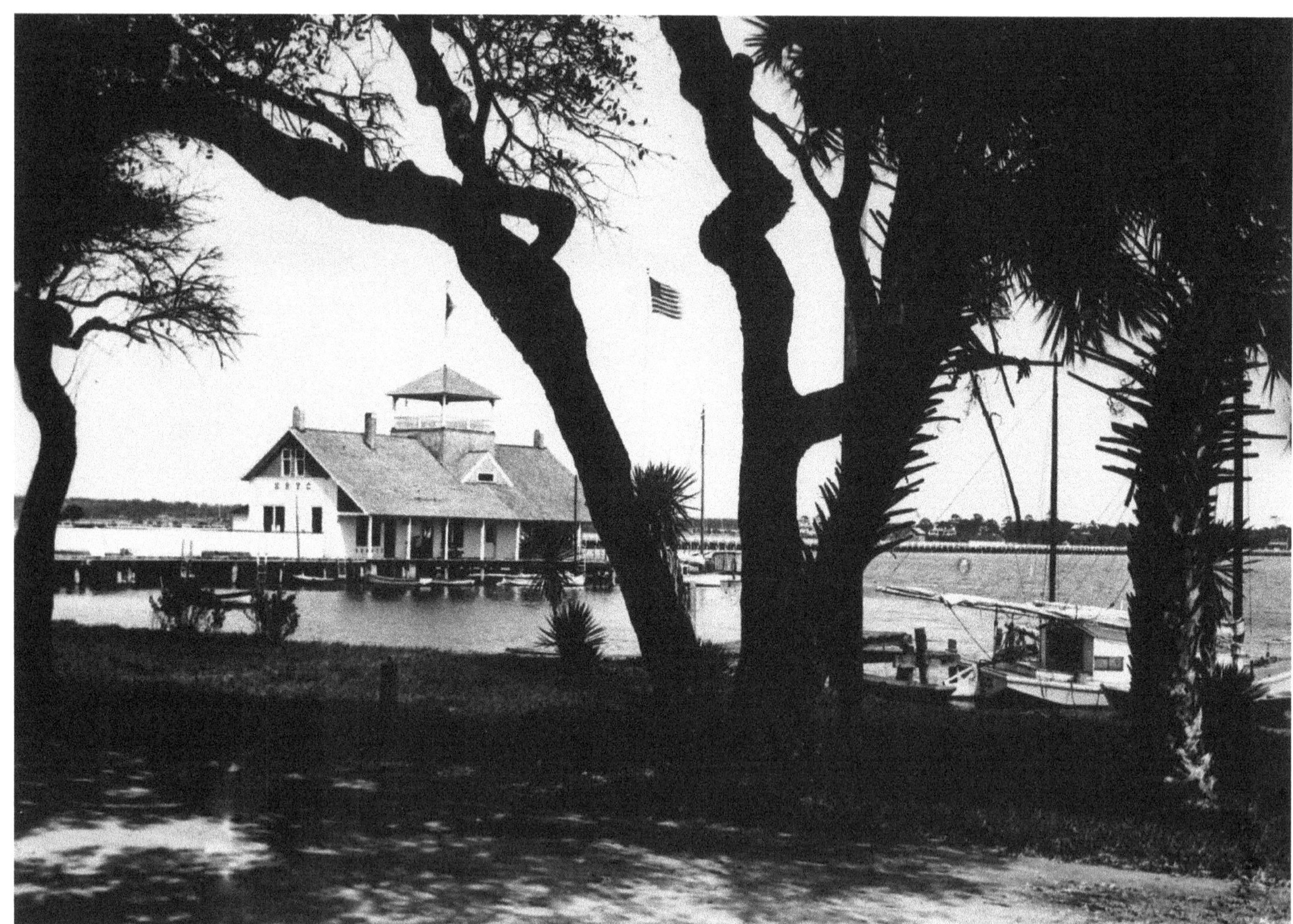

Each winter Charles Burgoyne paid for a band to play concerts in the special gazebo built for entertainment. People came from near and far just to hear this band. A variety of music was played, including martial music, today known as parade music.

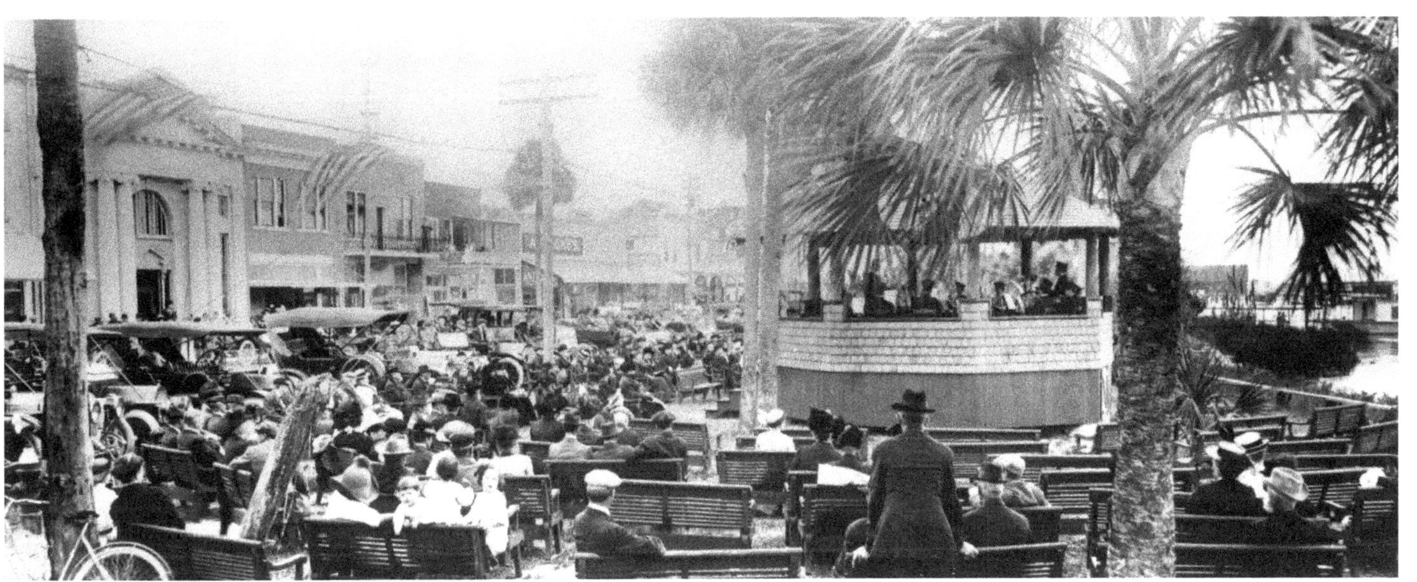

Famed aviator Glenn Curtiss came to Ormond and Daytona many times. Businessmen paid Curtiss $3,500 for his pilot, John A. D. McCurdy, to make three flights off the sands of Daytona Beach. Curtiss's early craft, pictured here, features a rather bulky-looking water-cooled engine.

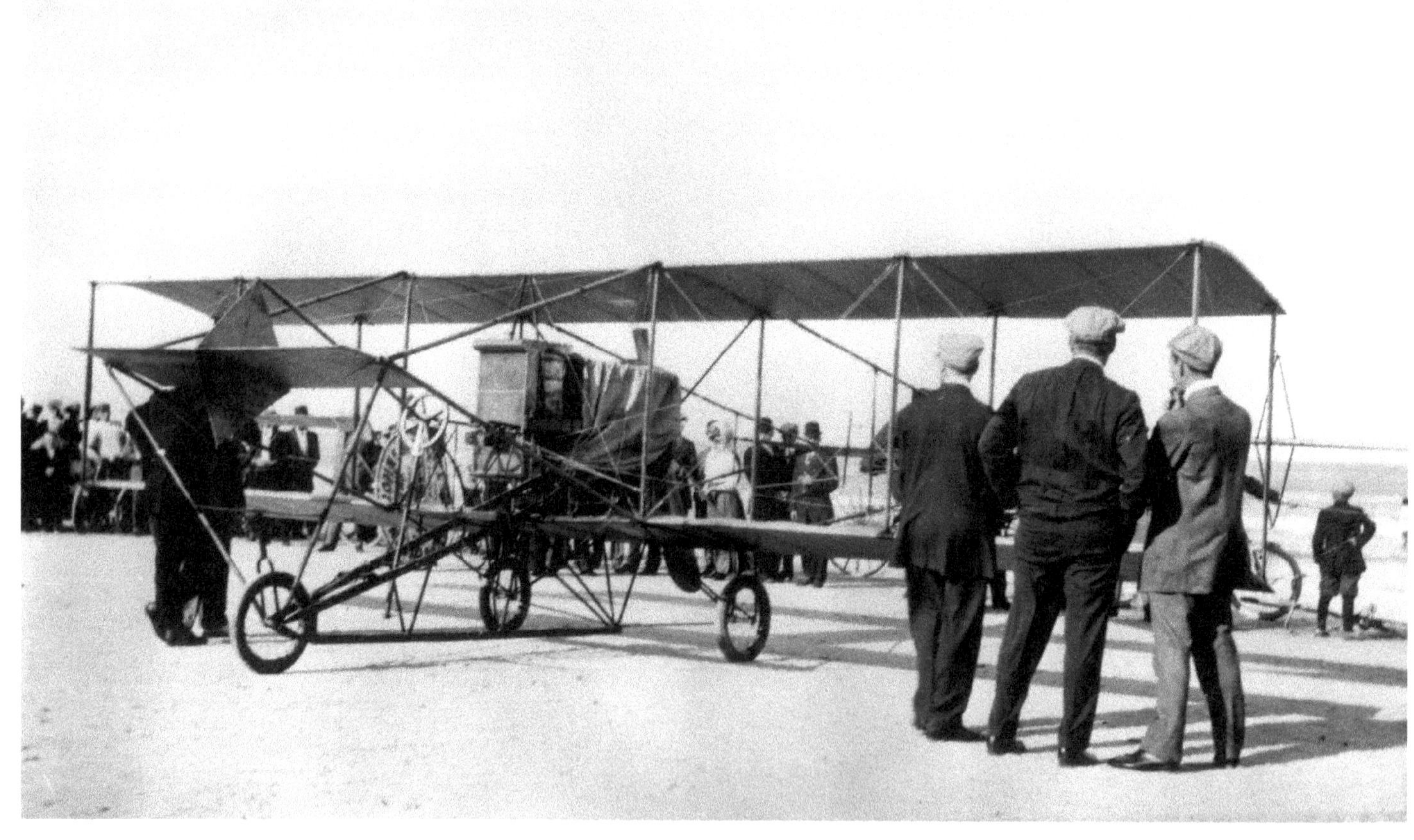

This school was established to train girls. They were taught to work with their hands, etiquette, and social skills. The school was becoming well known under the tutelage of Mary McLeod Bethune.

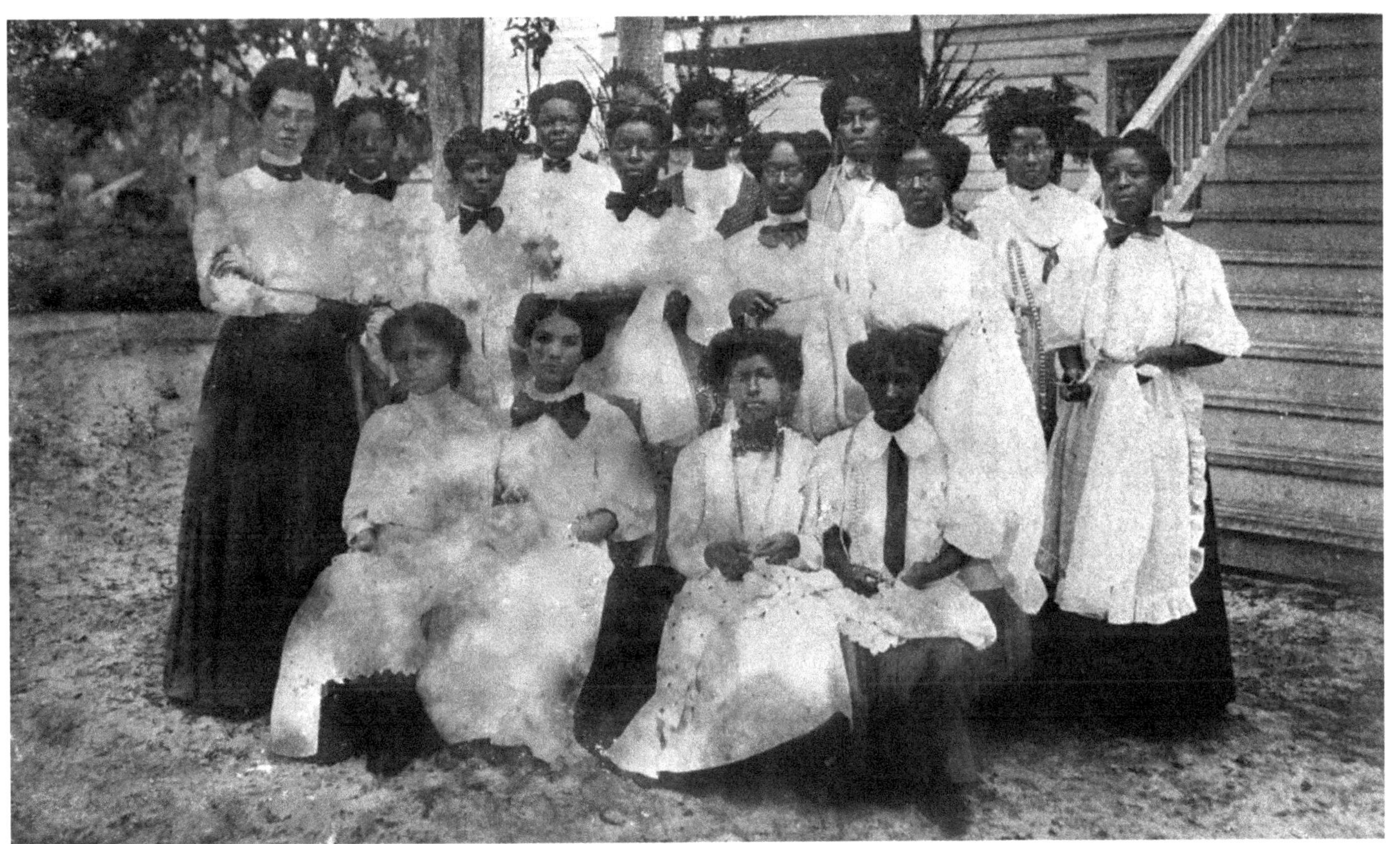

Barney Oldfield, on the beach at Ormond and Daytona, sped through the measured mile at 131.72 m.p.h. He was one of the most colorful drivers to break a speed record. The machine pictured here, dubbed "Blitzen" (German for lightning), was built to challenge the Stanley Steamer, March 16, 1910.

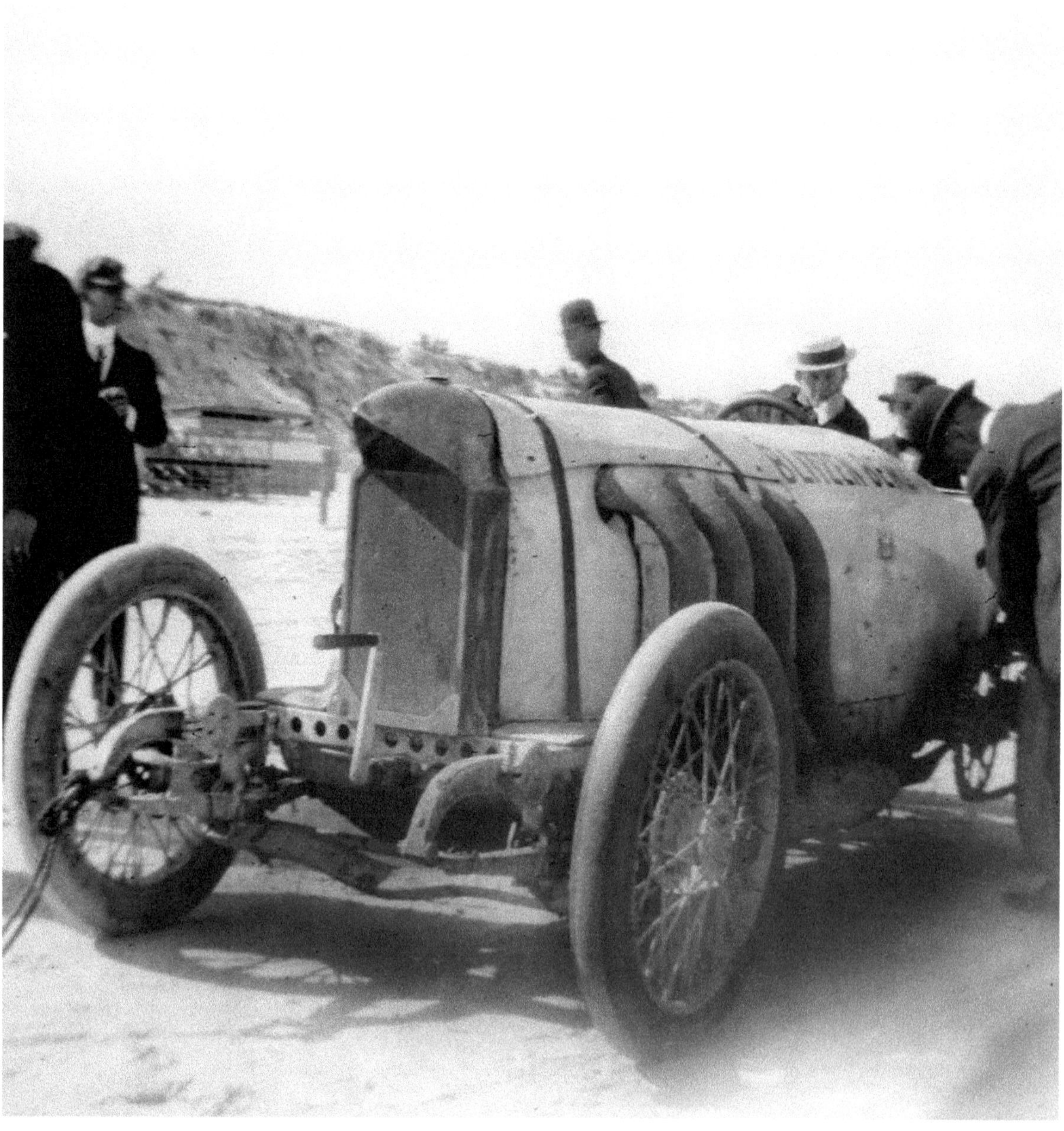

Passengers await the ferry at the landing to cross the Halifax River to beachside. Captain Ellenwood was always on schedule and reputedly very polite to his passengers. Roundtrip tokens were available in advance for the return to the west side in downtown Daytona.

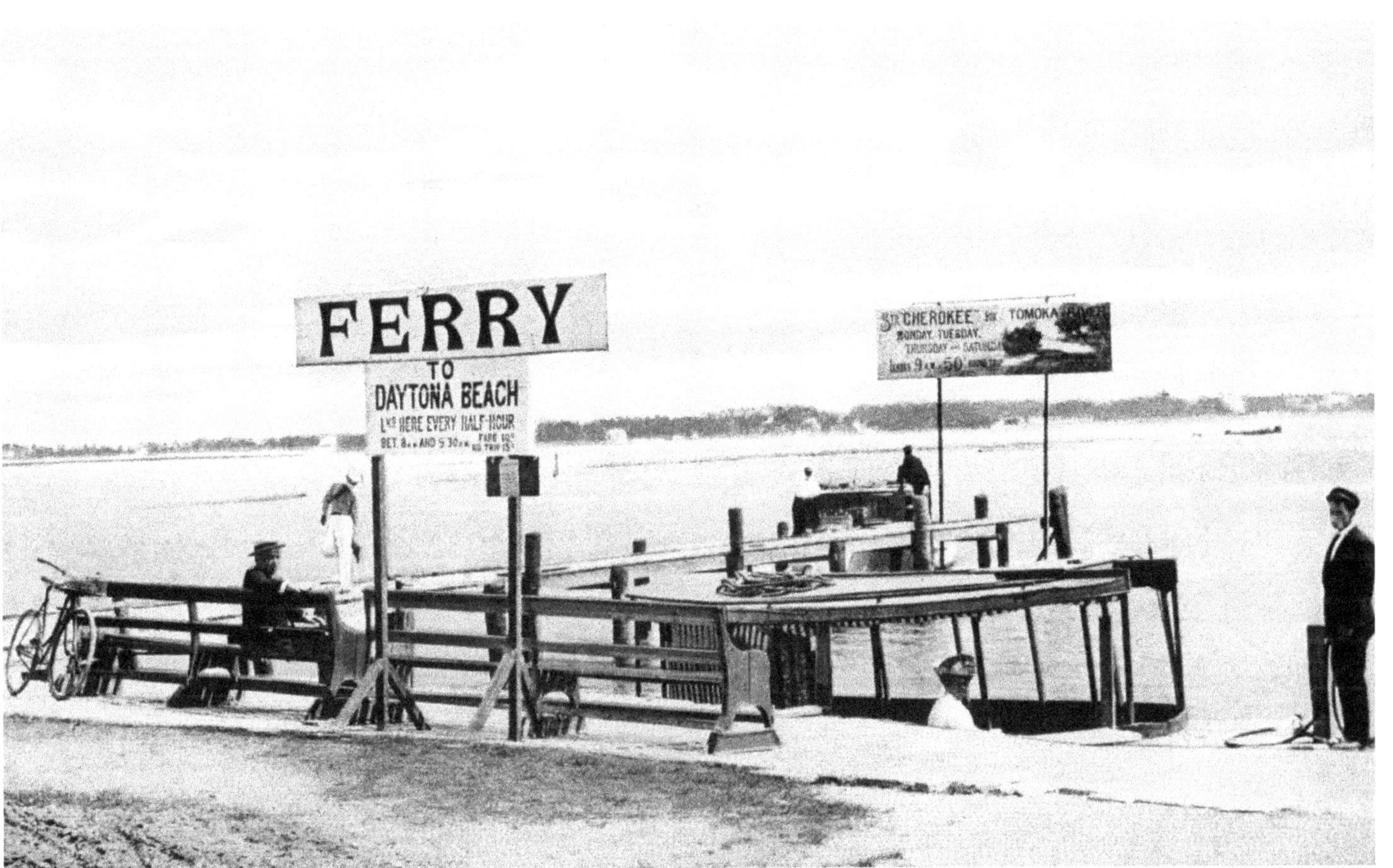

Blowing palm trees attest conspicuously to a northeaster that did a large amount of damage along the entire beachfront. Today Main Street runs where the northeast winds cut the sand dunes away and left an embankment.

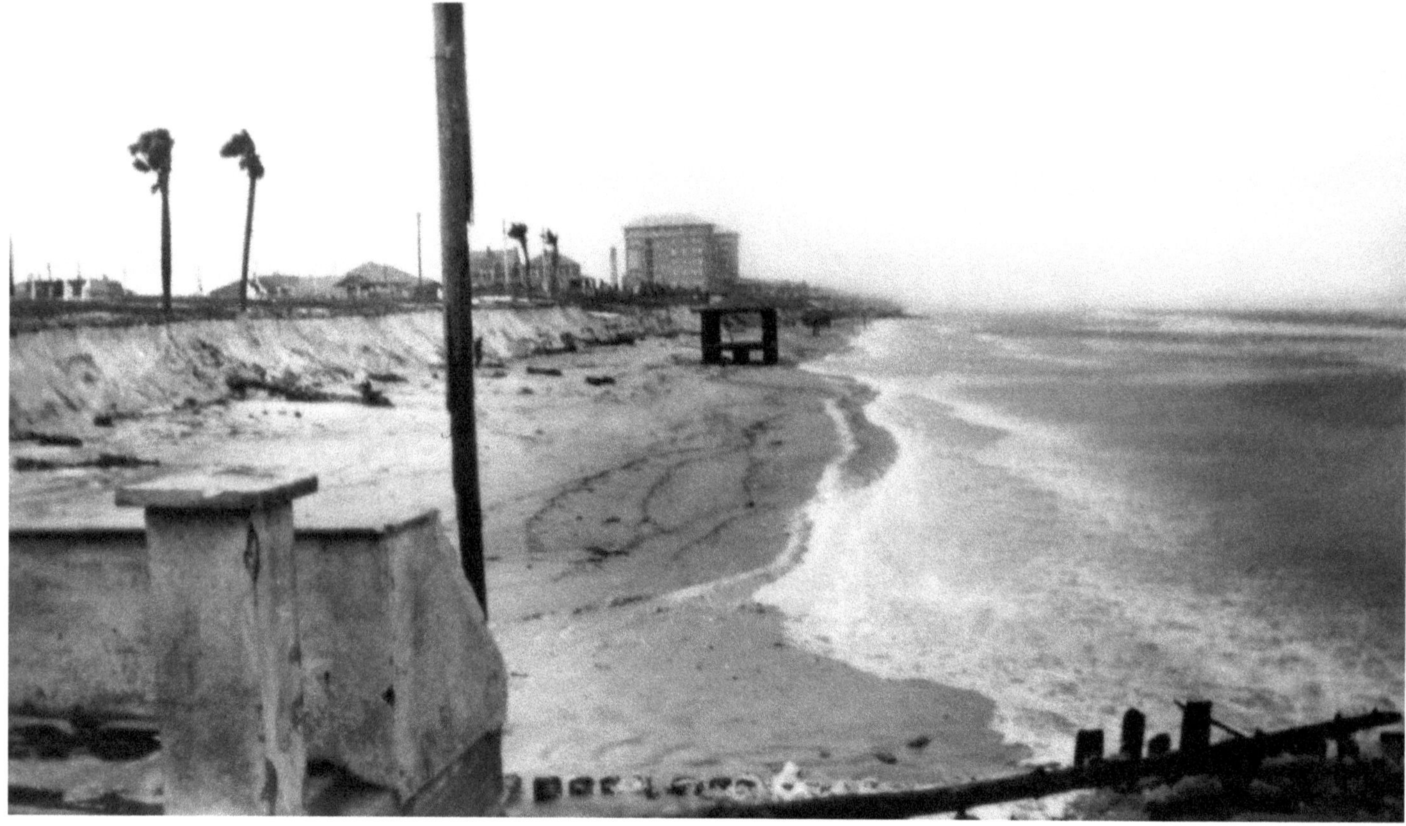

The well-known Hotel Austin was a gathering place for winter tourists in Daytona. The accommodations were superb, and many of the patrons returned each year with friends. This frame vernacular building was built out of yellow pine and cypress and stood on brick piers.

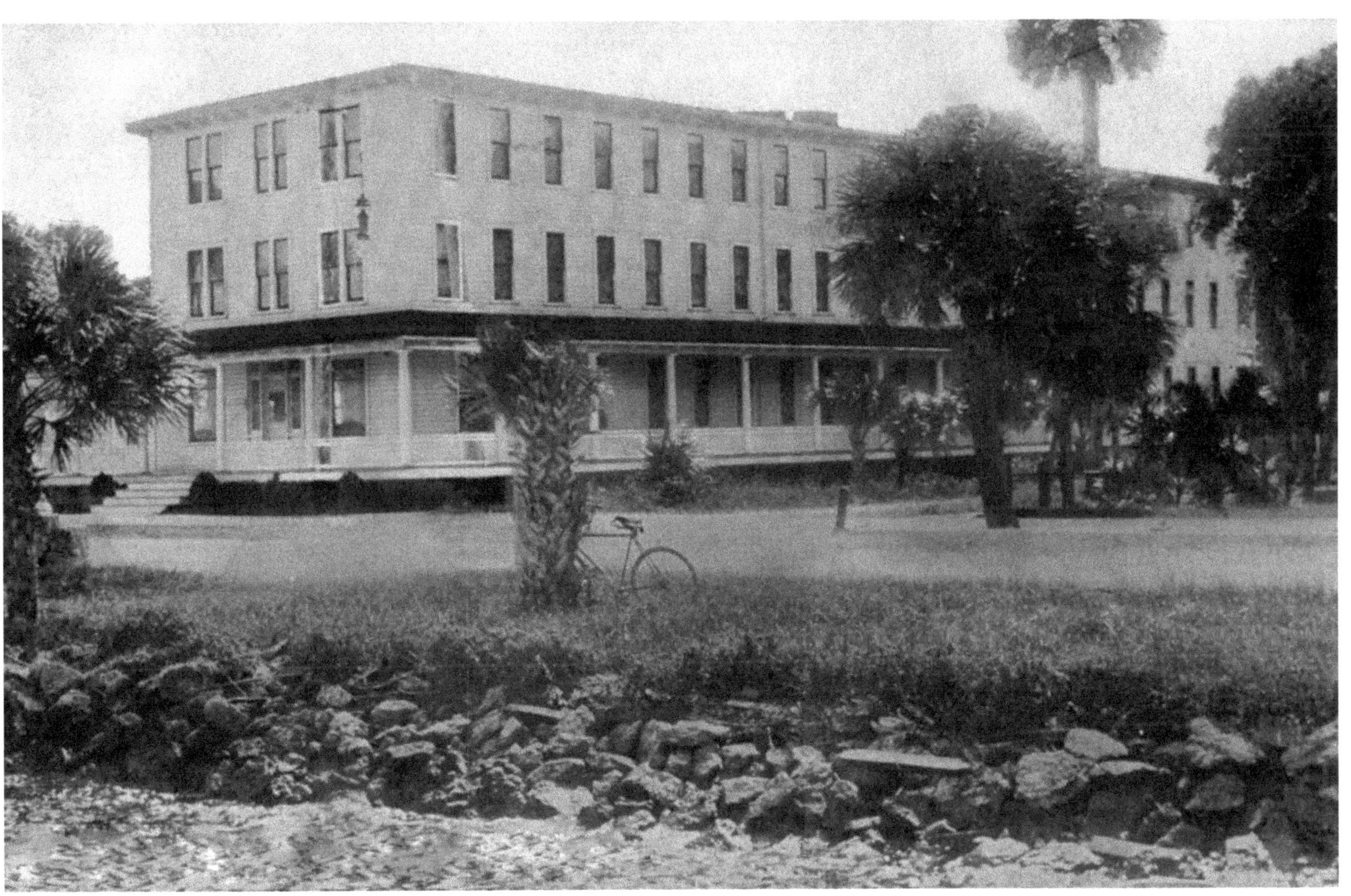

Two young girls enjoy an outing at Daytona Beach. Young people always wanted to be photographed in front of the new automobiles. Replaced by the horseless carriage, the horse and carriage was disappearing fast.

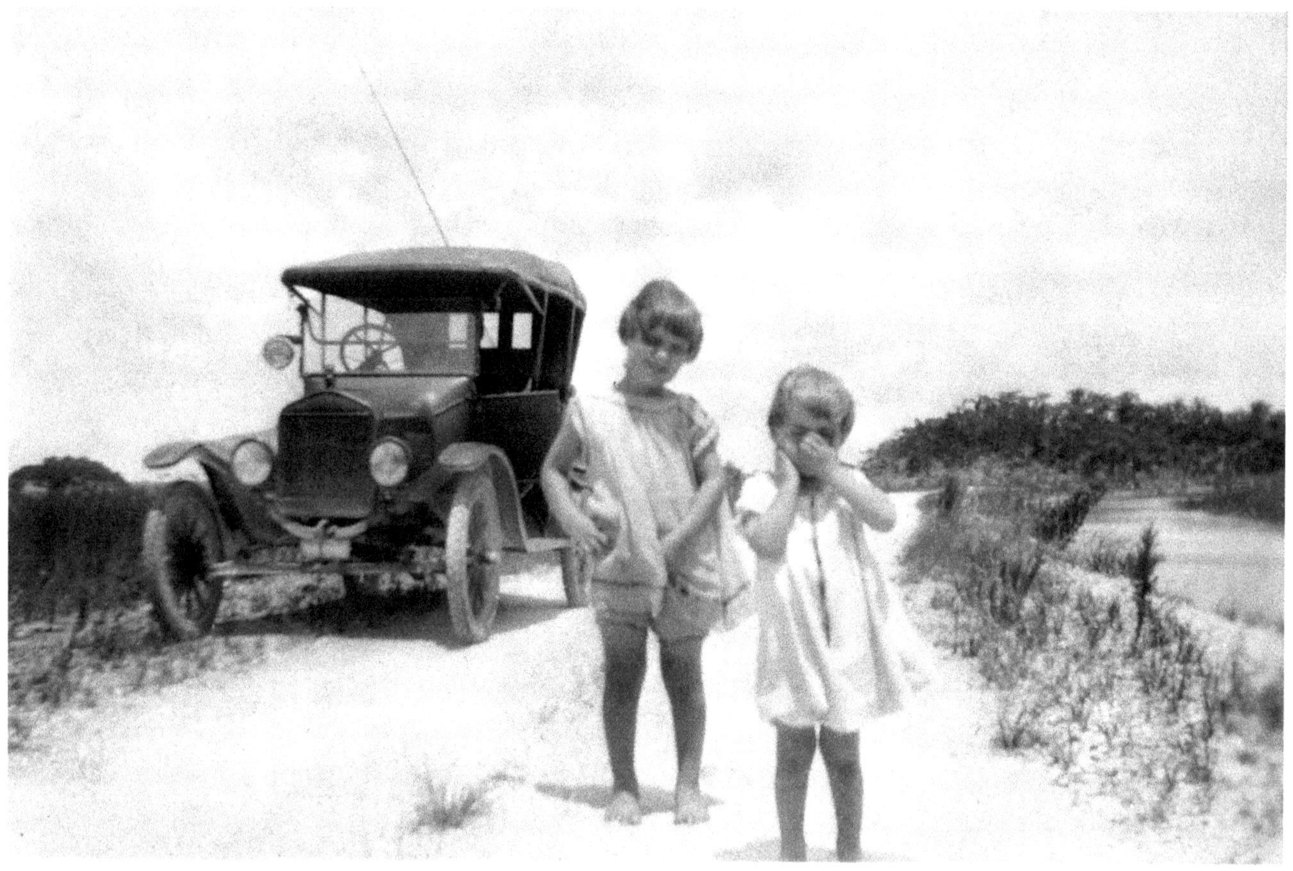

The first bridge to cross the Halifax was great news for people building homes on the beachside. Lumber and other materials no longer needed ferrying. Here townspeople ride and stroll, taking advantage of the river breezes.

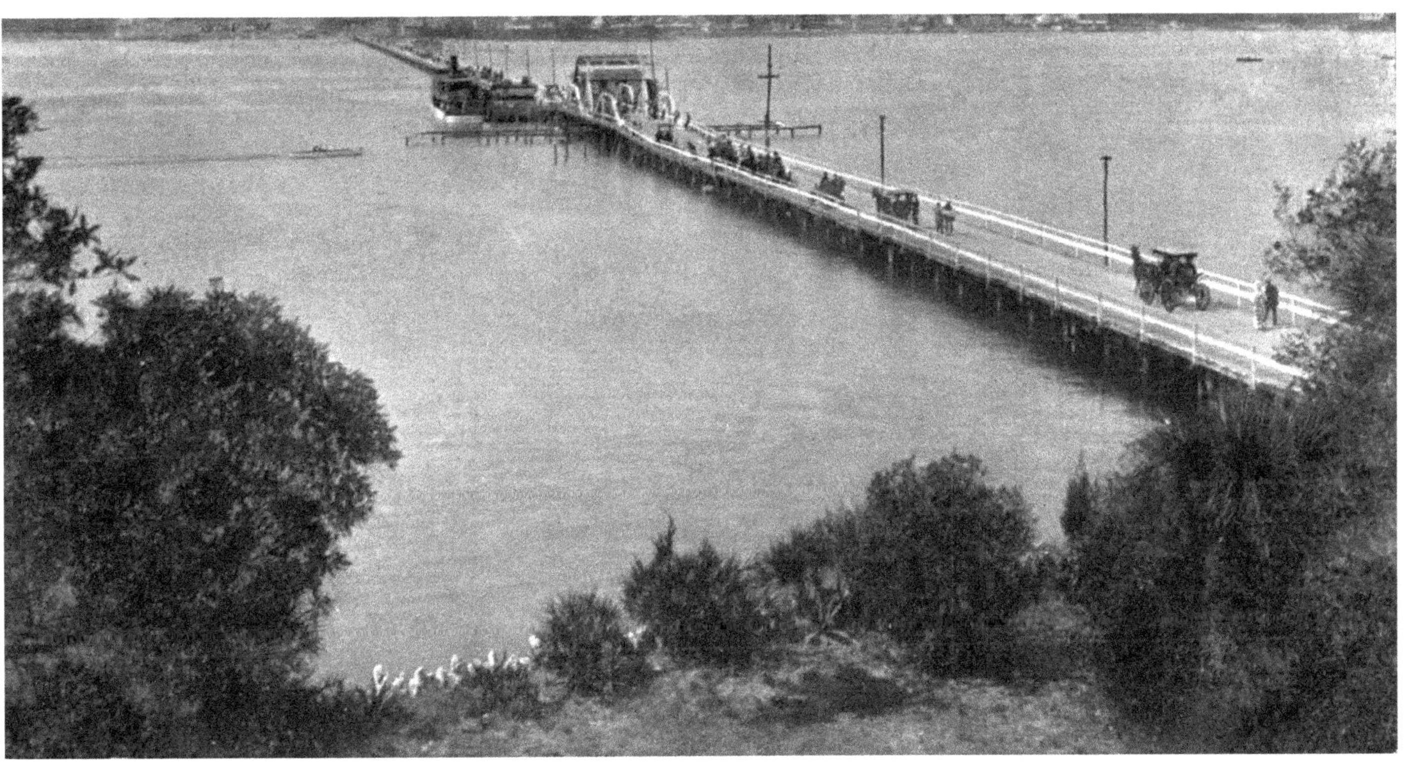

This clubhouse was constructed for the Elks at the northwest corner of Volusia and Palmetto. Featuring brick masonry construction and columns on the front, this building stood for many years at this location.

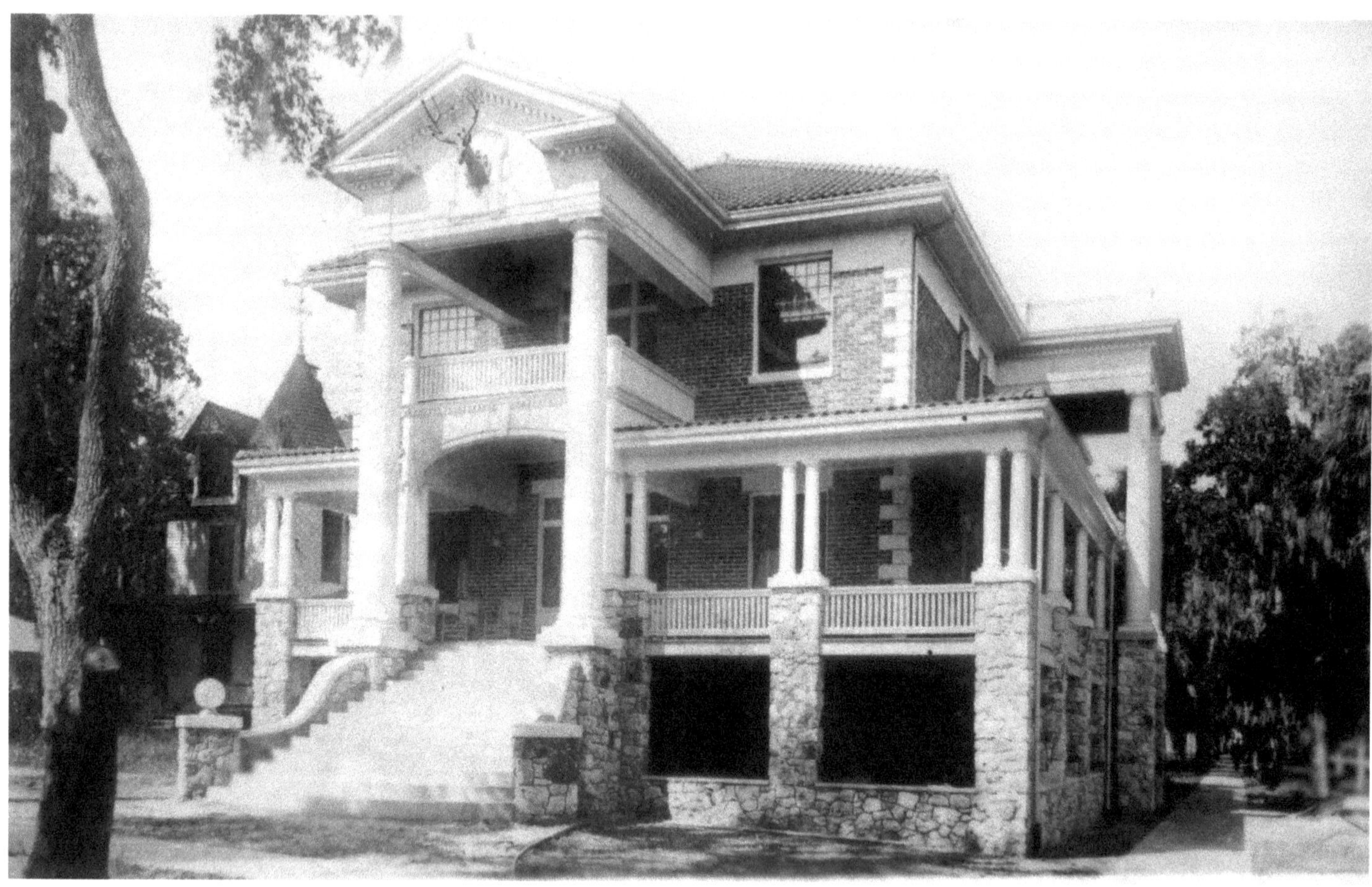

In a neat and tidy kitchen, Mary Bethune, the lady dressed in black, instructs her students in how to prepare food. This is the earliest image of the interior of Faith Hall (ca. 1912).

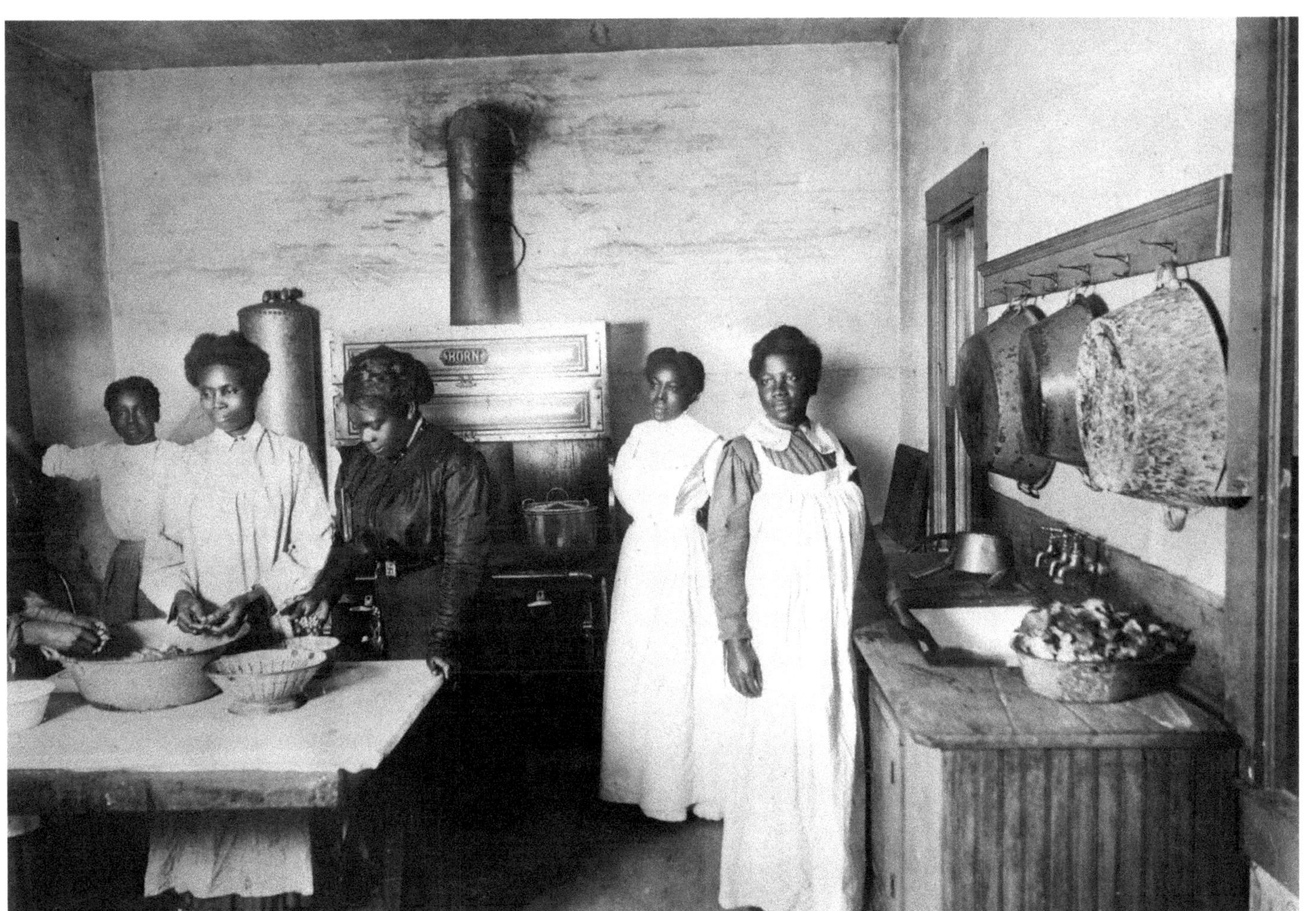

Designed by architect Sumner Hale Gove, this three-story school was built in 1909 of masonry construction. In front on Bay Street, footbridges crossed the north canal to the entrance. The school was steam-heated and had an auditorium and a manual training department.

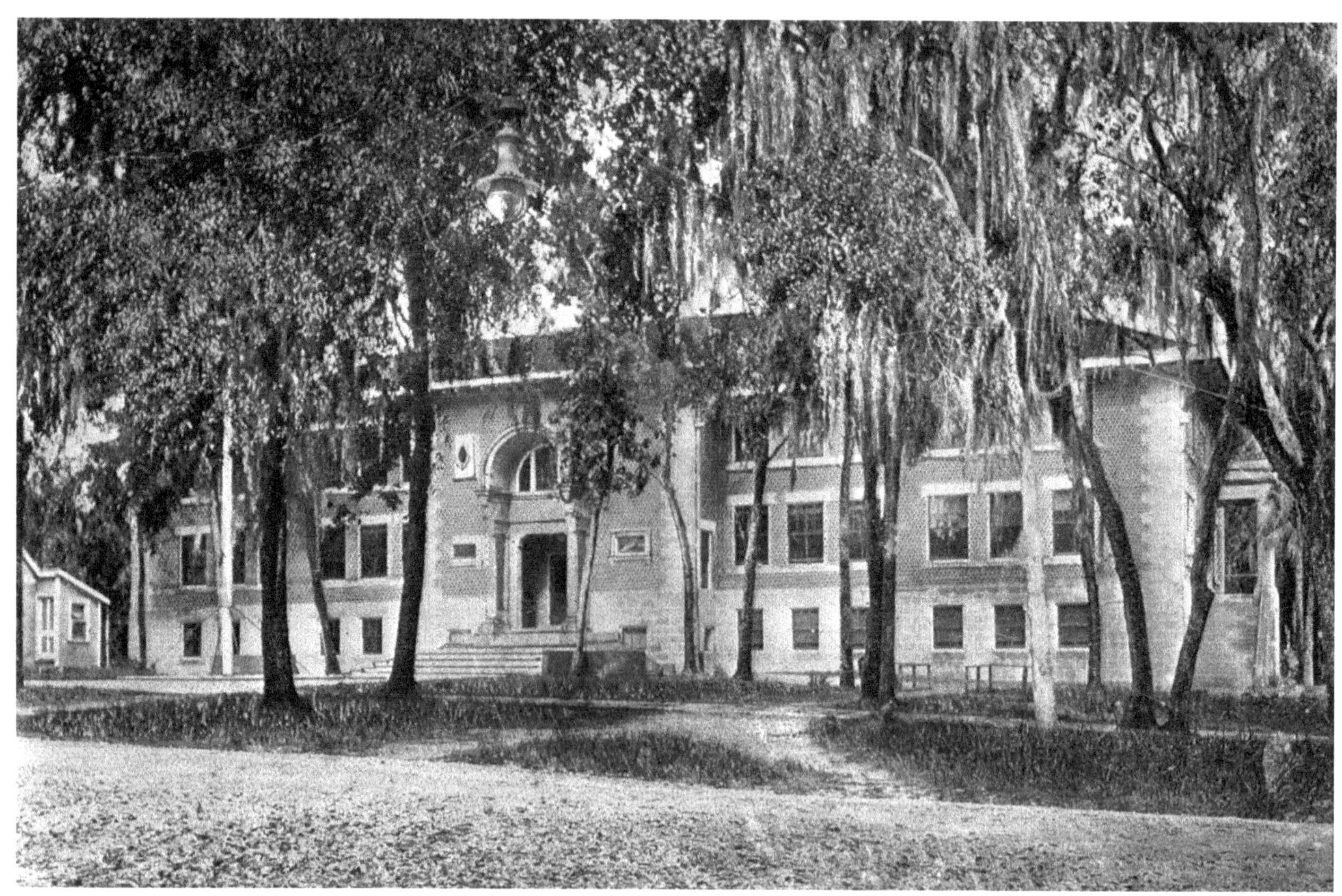

At one time, an electric trolley crossed Daytona's concrete bridge and went all the way over to the peninsula to what today would be within a block of Seabreeze Boulevard. The trolley, very popular at the time, was a transitional mode of transportation between the horse and carriage and the automobile then appearing on the street.

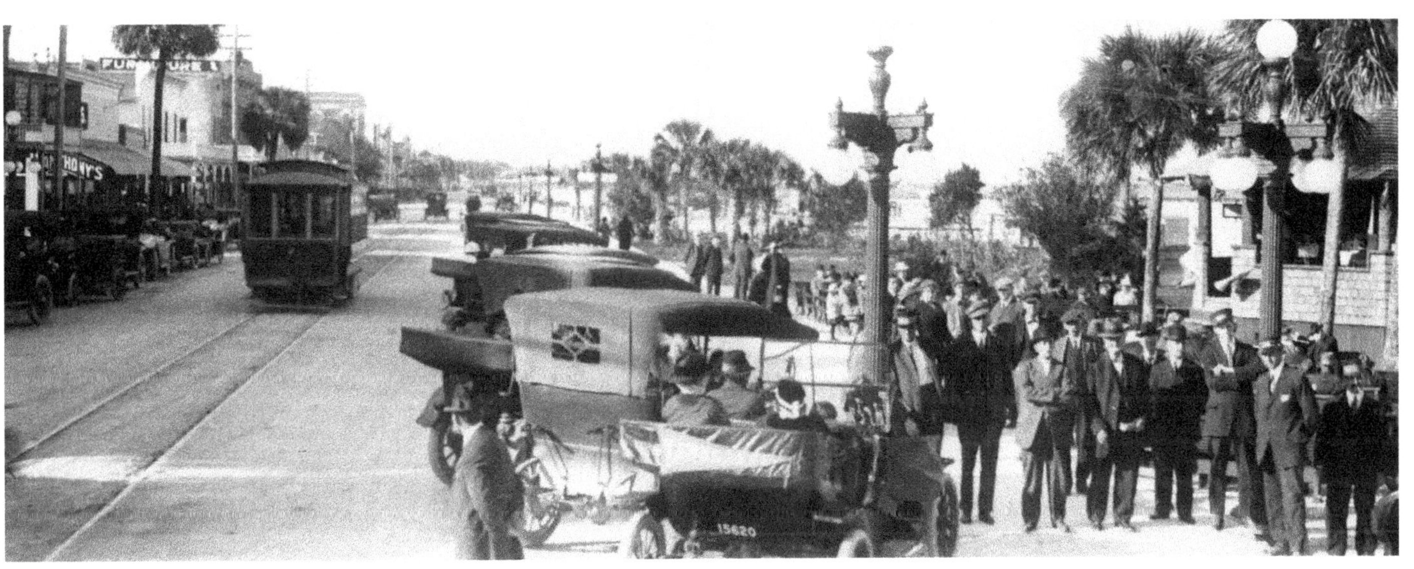

This clubhouse was built in 1905. It honored many of the race car enthusiasts who were trying to break speed records in Ormond Beach and Daytona Beach. The number 39 was placed on the top railing to honor Vanderbilt, who did a mile in 39 seconds, and it stayed there as long as the clubhouse was there.

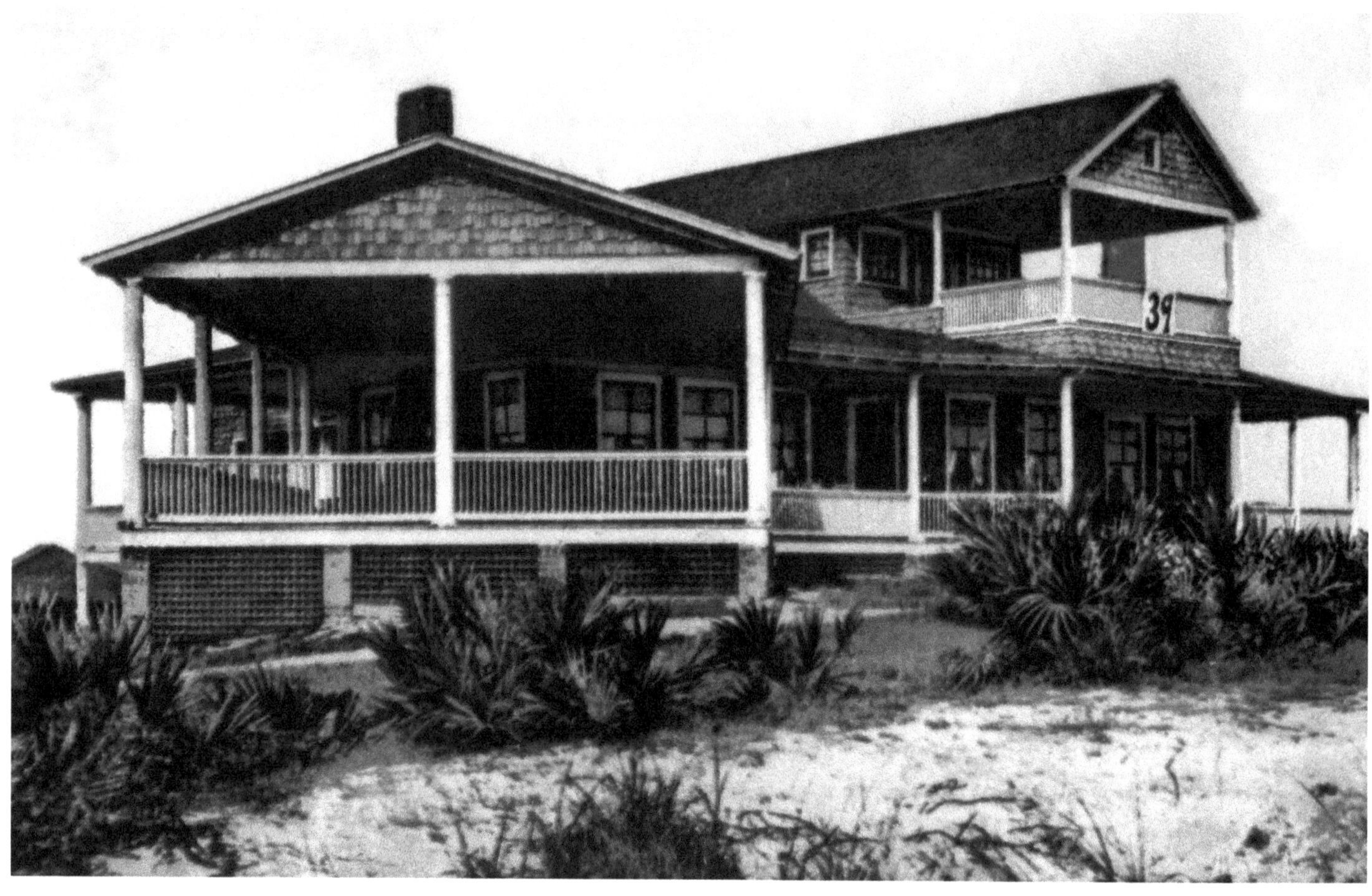

Ruth Law, aviatrix, and Mrs. Robert Goelet, her companion, flew this biplane off the beach and landed it on the beach, Daytona Beach's first landing strip or airport.

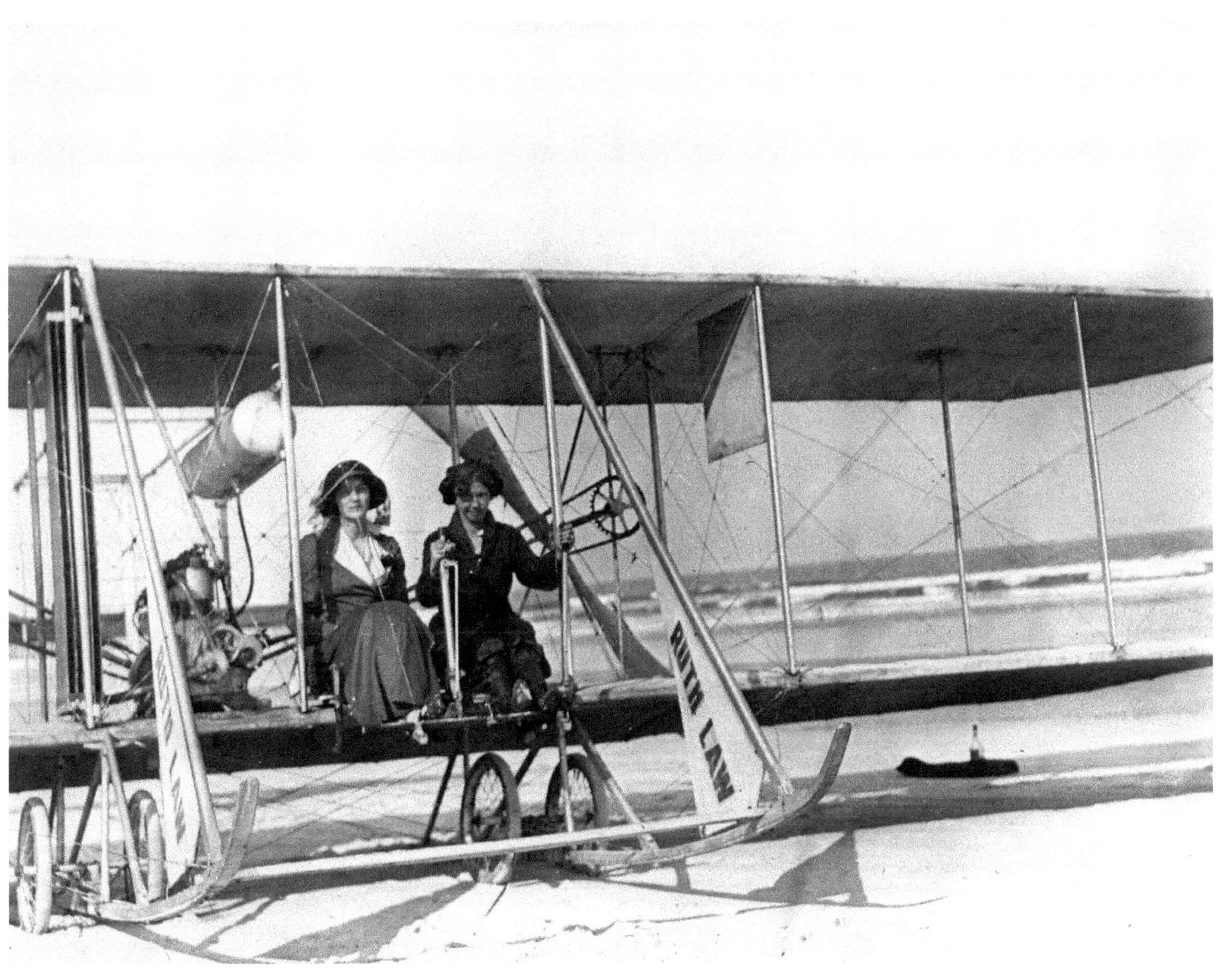

The U.S. Army Aviation Section trained pilots at Carlstrom and Dorr fields near Arcadia. Later they had training flights in Daytona Beach, making beach landings. Several pilots were lost in training. This Jenny plane in the tree illustrates the kinds of crashes that befell pilots.

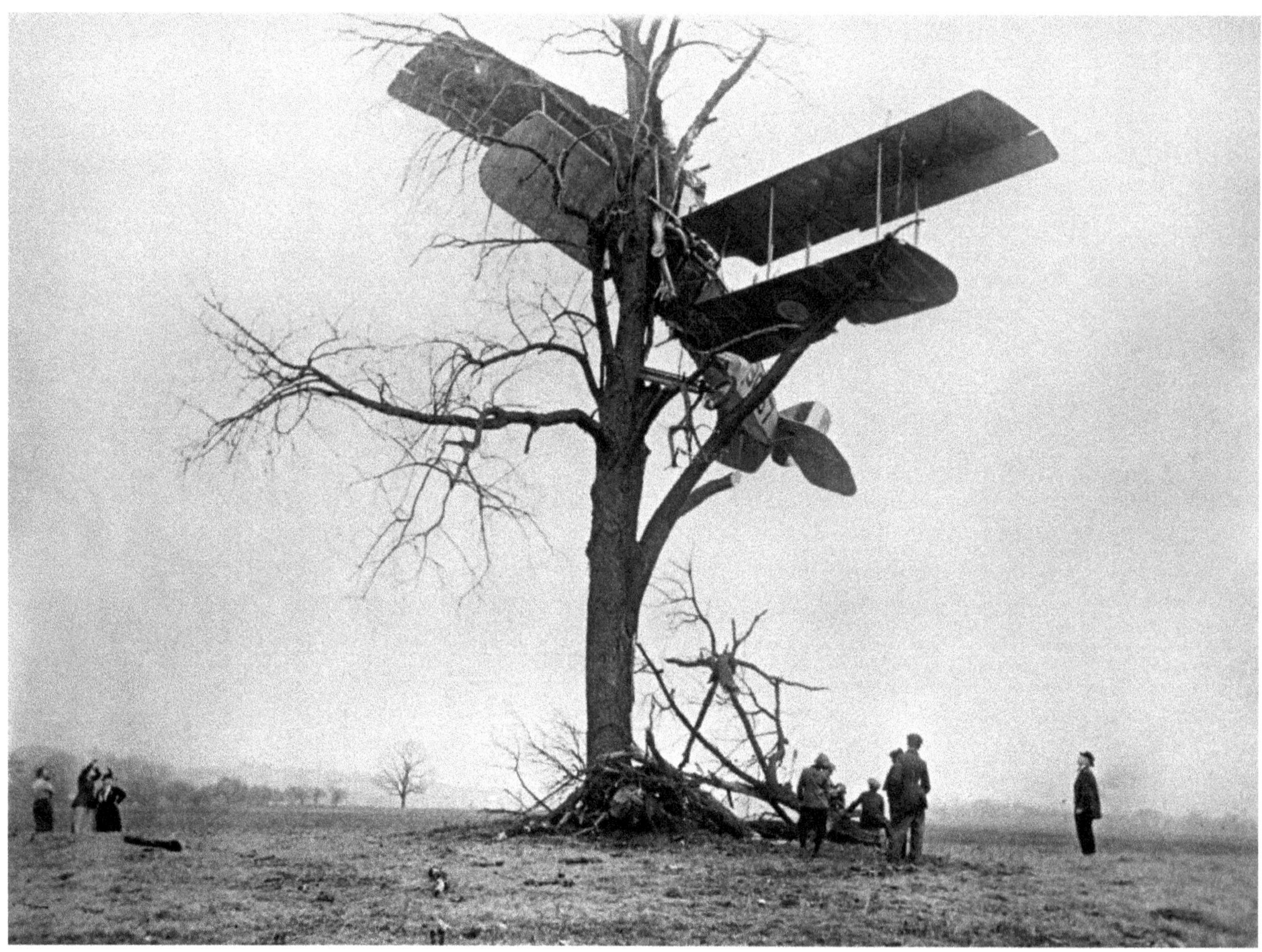

The fashionable Gables Hotel was on old Volusia Avenue. A fire eventually consumed part of the building. When rebuilt, it was called the New Gables Hotel. As buses began transporting passengers, a bus station with a restaurant was built under the east end of the new hotel.

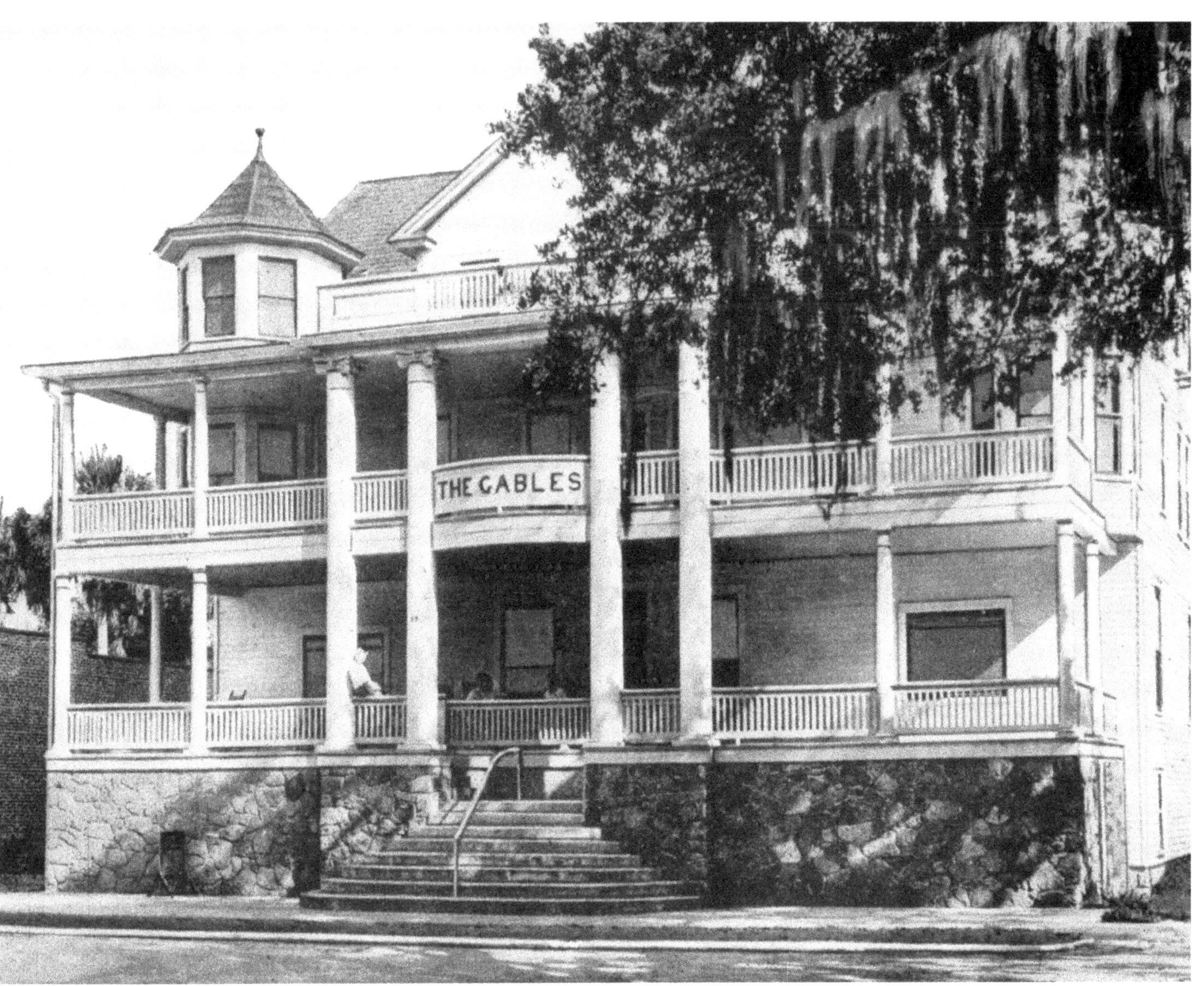

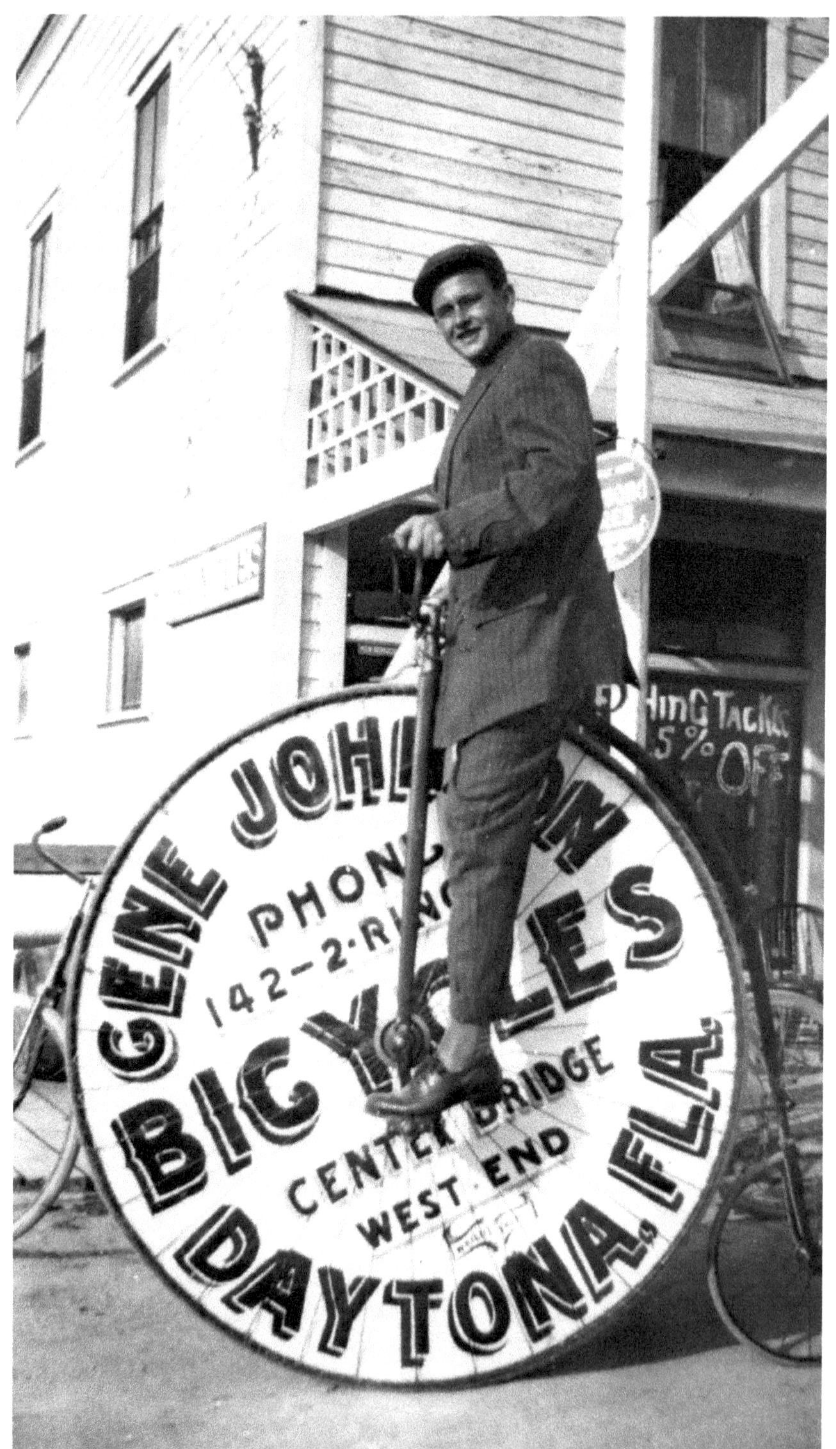

Gene Johnson's fishing and tackle store was on North Beach Street at Fairview. He sold all types of sportsmen's supplies including bicycles. In this image, Koert DuBois demonstrates the advertising bicycle for Johnson.

Beachgoers of the day frequently wore white, the idea being that white shed the most heat. Automobiles were now the vehicle of choice for those of means, who drove and parked on the beach to see and be seen, as persons of prominence in the community. Beach houses are visible in the distance.

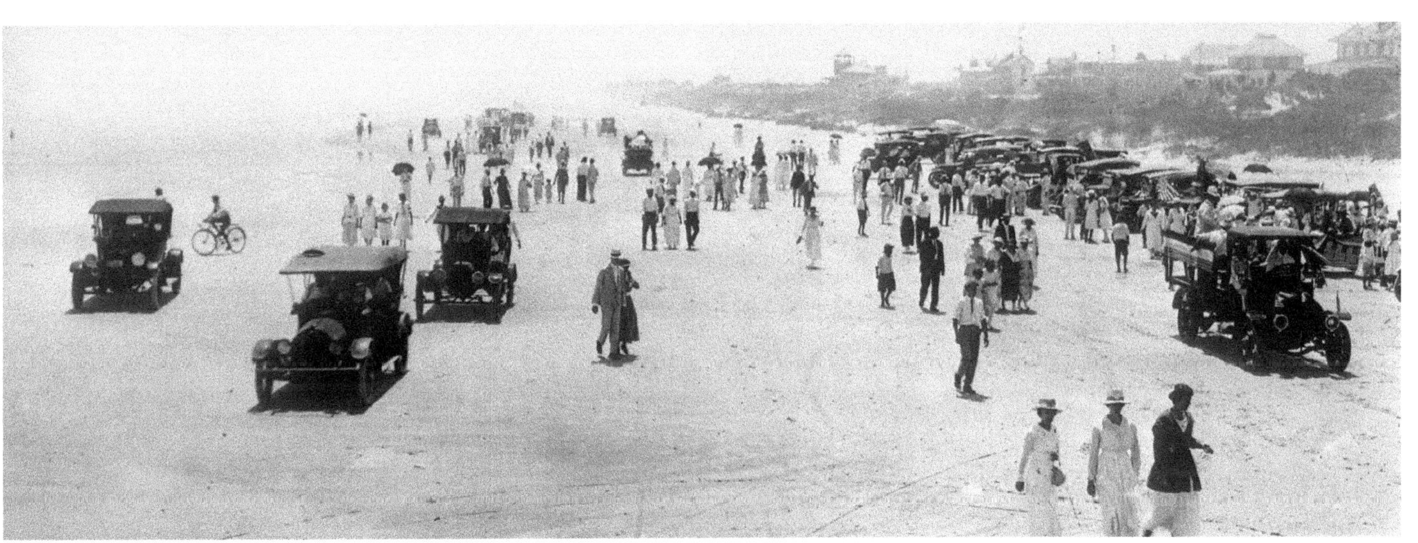

This party of DeLand revelers spends a holiday at the beach. The two cars are parked peculiarly and these heavily clothed fun seekers appear to be looking for a coin in the sand. Perhaps they had heard of buried treasure.

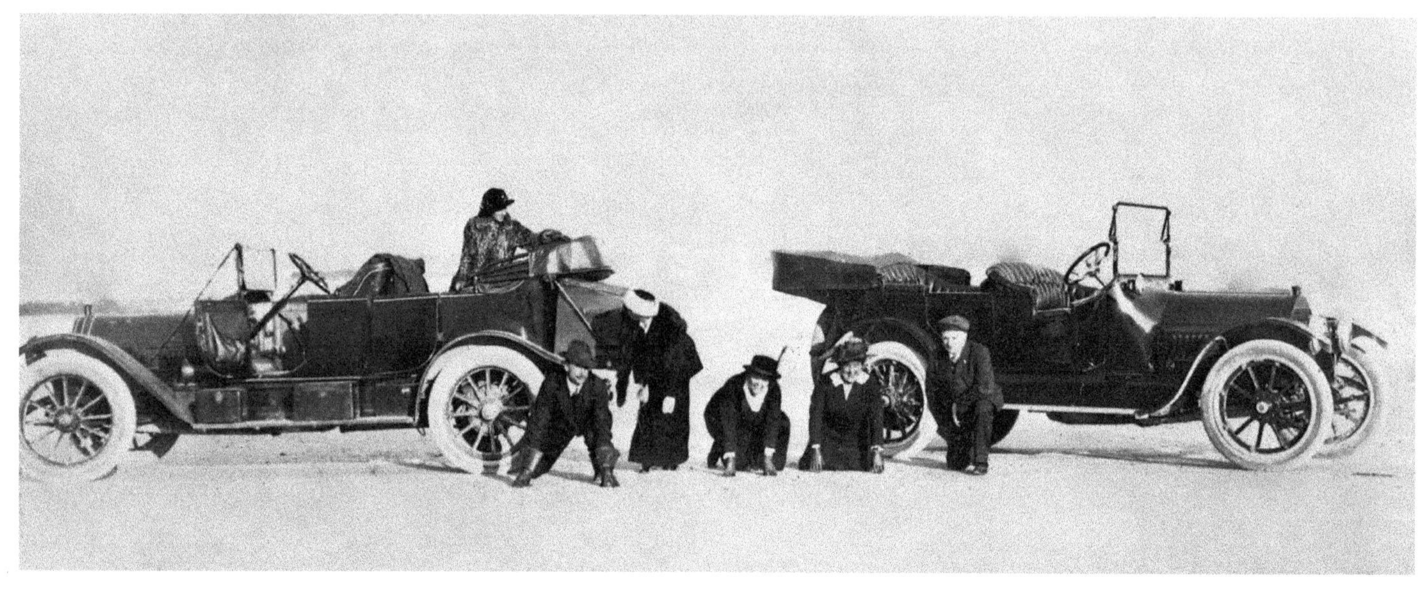

Mr. Norwood used his horse, Bob, for transportation. He preferred riding Bob or taking a bicycle even to go long distances, refusing to use a horseless carriage.

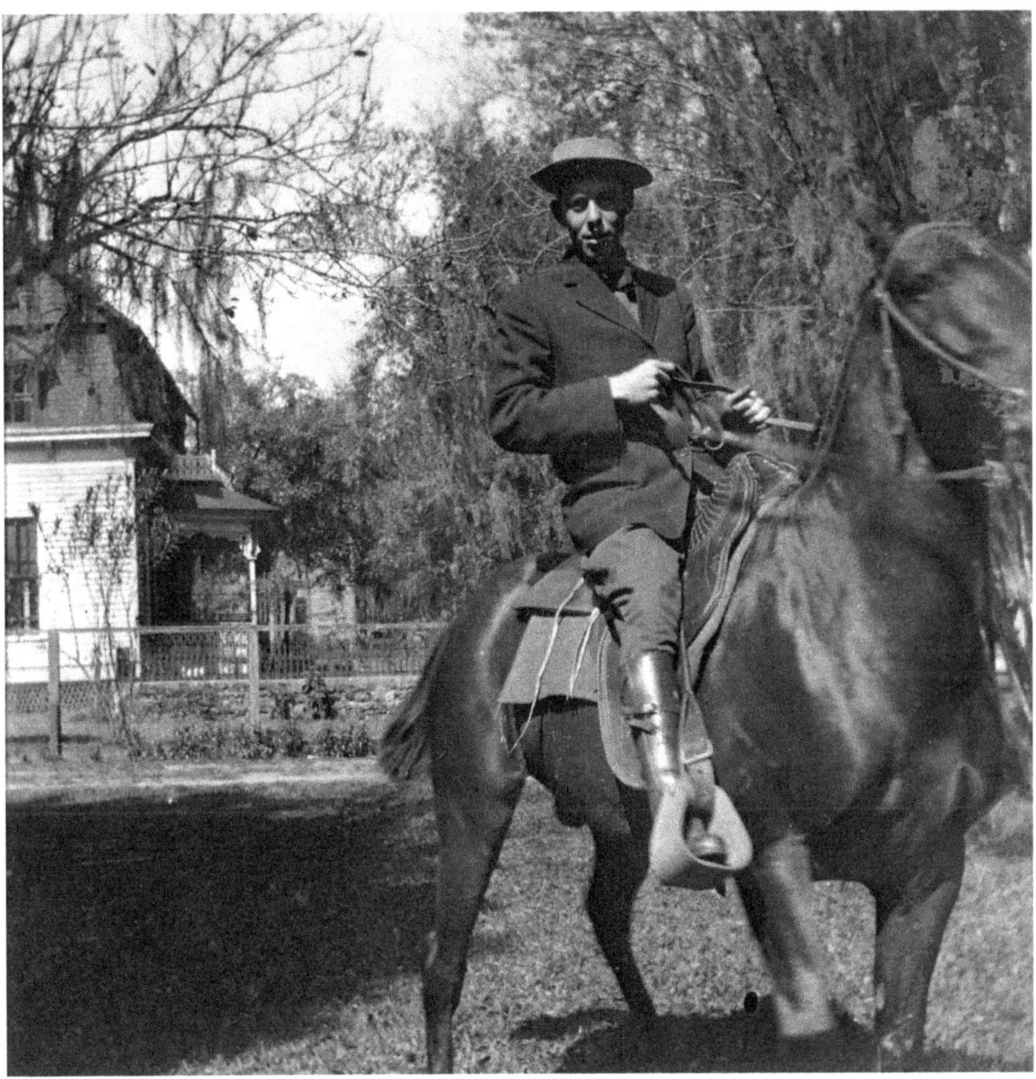

William Usher Norwood was well known throughout Volusia County. He is pictured here in his Coast Line office reading railroad schedules for the railroad traffic north and south. Of note is the pigeonhole old-fashioned desk that most workers used before World War I.

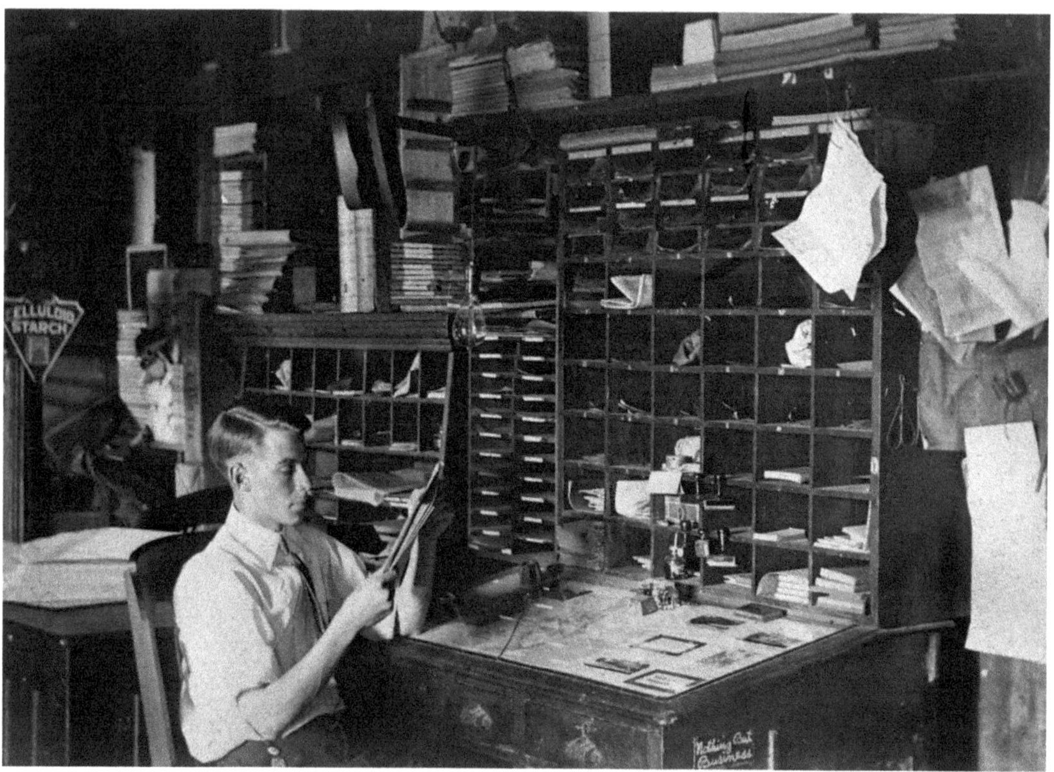

Charles G. Burgoyne had the promenade constructed leading all the way from the casino on the corner of Beach and Orange streets to his home at Beach and Bay streets. The seawall, sidewalk, and street lights along Beach Street were all provided by Burgoyne and his wife.

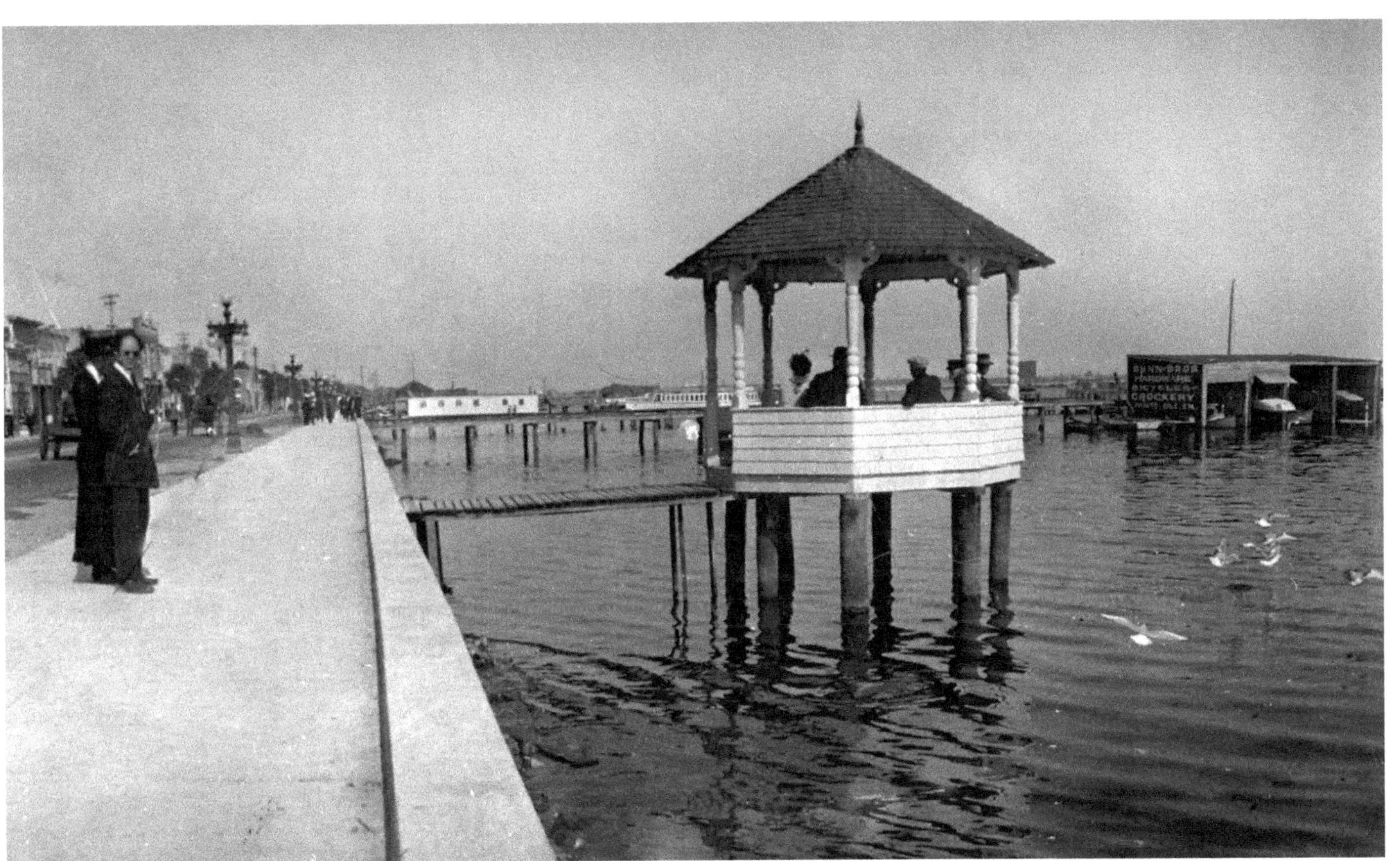

Built on piers of yellow pine and cypress lumber, this two-storied gable roof home was a landmark in Daytona Beach.

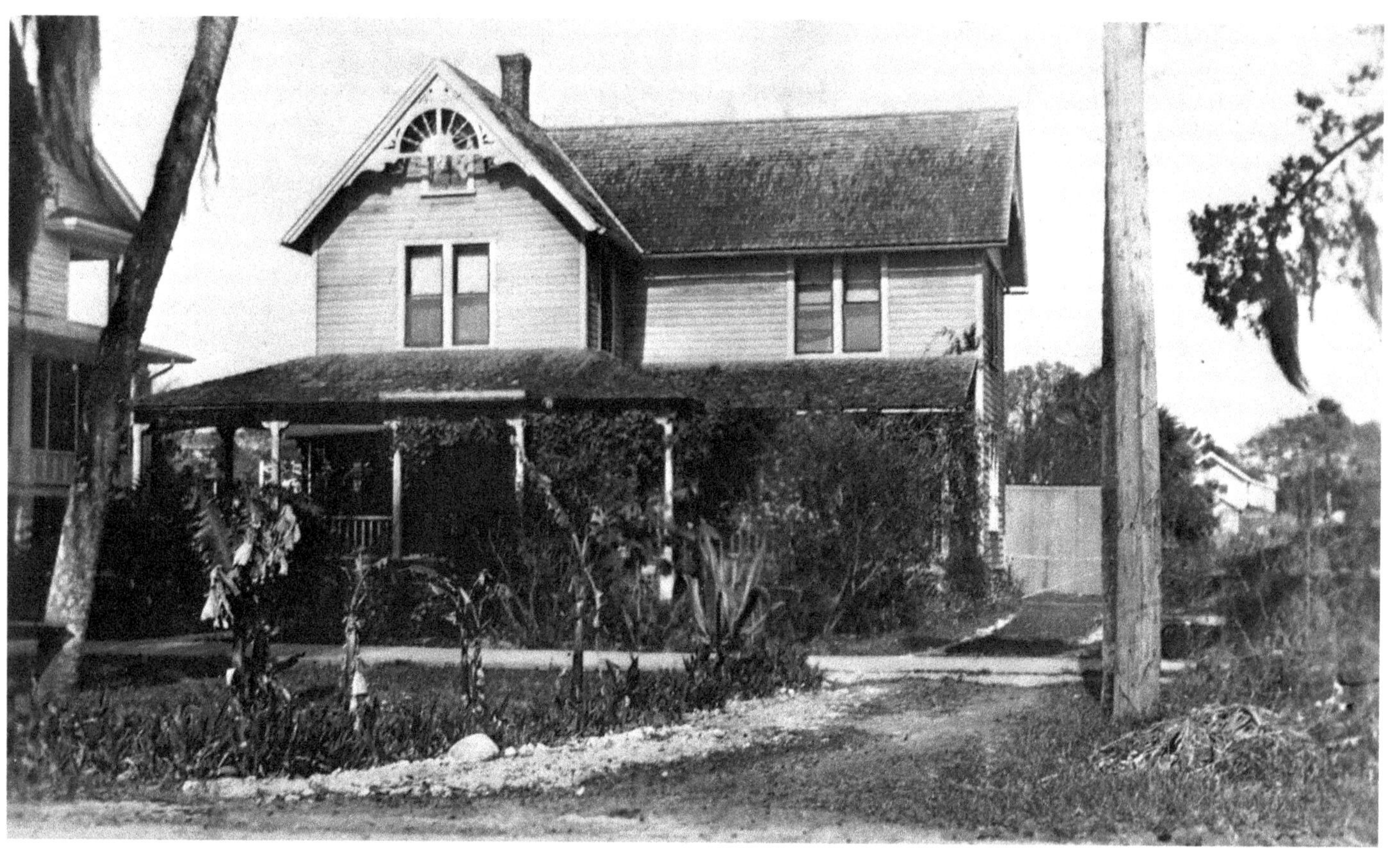

The Pepper family was well known and was active in the Jewish synagogue. Mr. Pepper sold new and used plumbing supplies and also store fixtures. Leonard, sitting at left on the car's running board, attended the University of Florida and became a lawyer and Assistant Attorney General. He owned a large shopping center and other properties in Tallahassee.

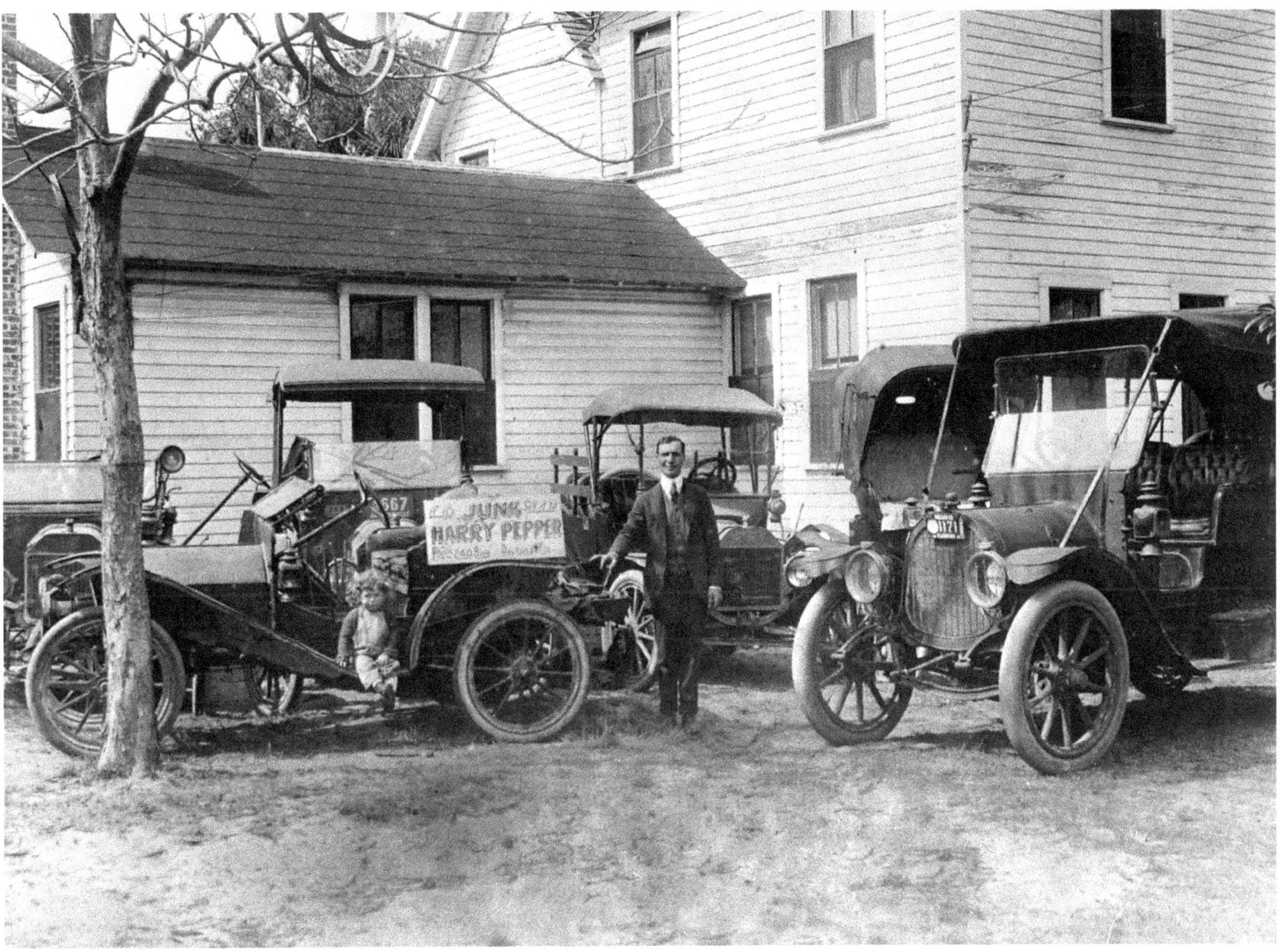

Two men and five women stand in the surf with the waves lapping at their knees. It would appear they are afraid to go into deeper water. Bathing suits at this time were mostly made from wool fabric, but light canvas was added to give more of a decorative look. Sometimes men used their undershirts above their swimming trunks. The ladies wore rubber bathing caps to keep their hair dry.

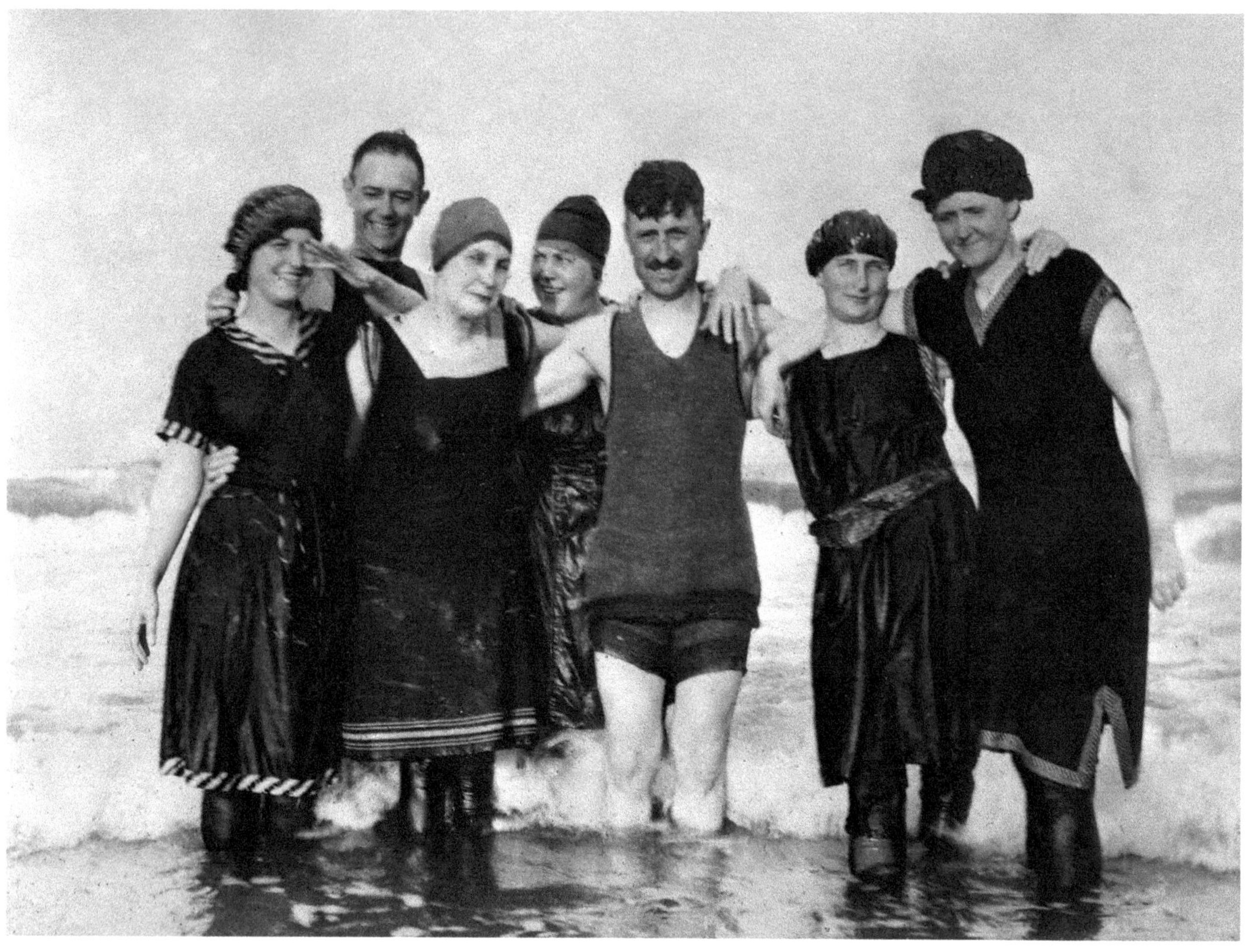

The river width north of Daytona Beach was excellent for landing and taxiing seaplanes to the shore. In later years it became Raymond's Seaplane Base and is known today as Holly Hill. Charles Burgoyne's boathouse was moved to Holly Hill after his death, part of which is seen here down the river. In this image, observers have watched Captain Charles H. Hermann, just arrived from Palm Beach, land his seaplane.

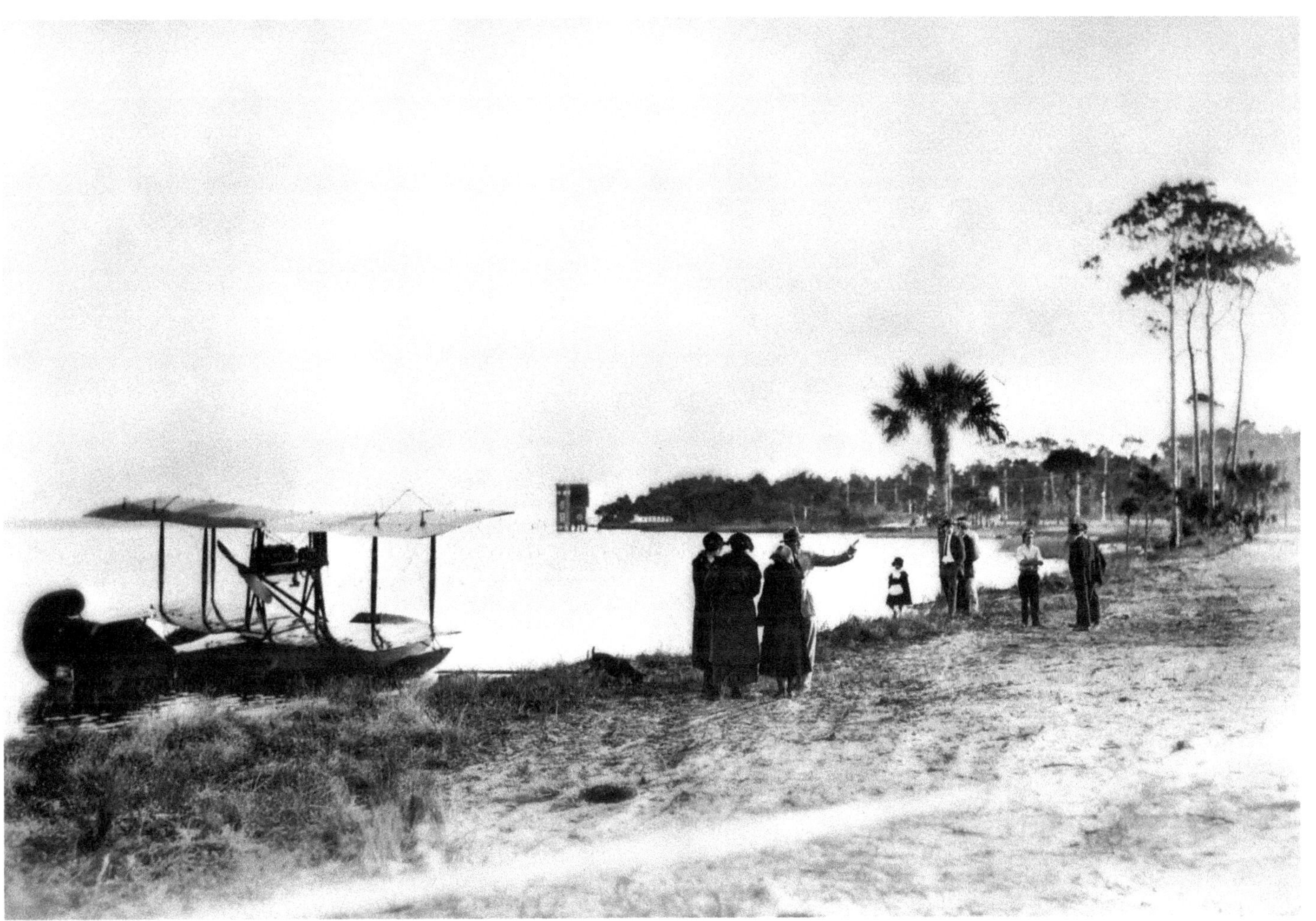

Indian motorcycles were very popular for speeding down the beach, which at low tide was an excellent area for driving vehicles at top speed. The outgoing tide packed the sand, creating a hard surface that prevented wheels from slipping. A typical way to get noticed was for the passenger to stand on the running board of a car.

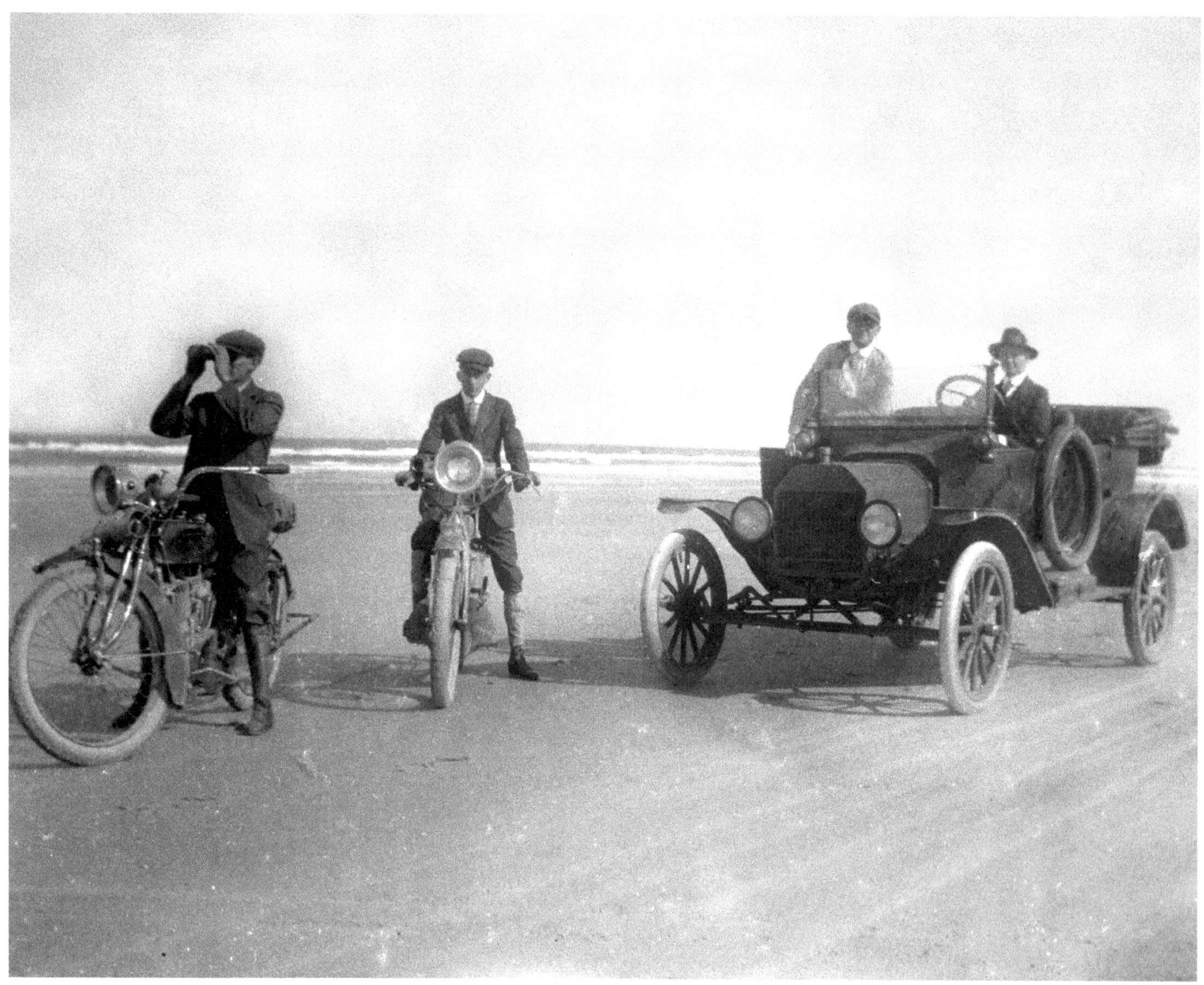

Members of the Daytona Flying Club stand in front of the Curtiss trainer biplane. Among those present are William Lindley, pilot-mechanic, Frank Stanton, chief instructor, and Eugene Count DeBoliac, pilot-chief mechanic. Students came from all over the United States and Canada.

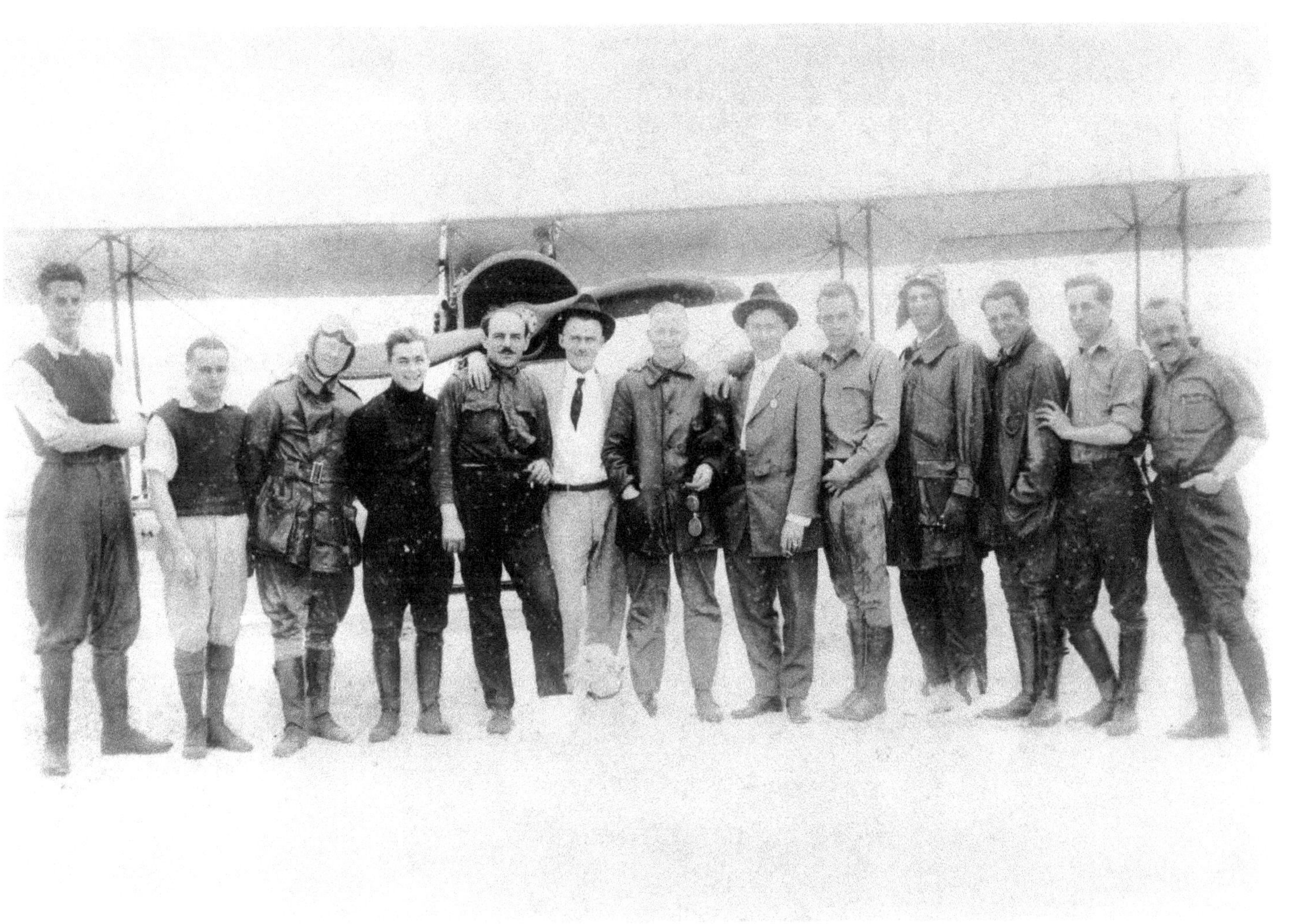

Ralph DePalma and his car with admirers. His car featured a Packard V-12 engine based on the World War I Liberty aircraft engine, both of which were developed by the Packard engineer Col. Jesse G. Vincent. DePalma raced through the measured mile at 149.875 m.p.h., which set a new world record February 12, 1919.

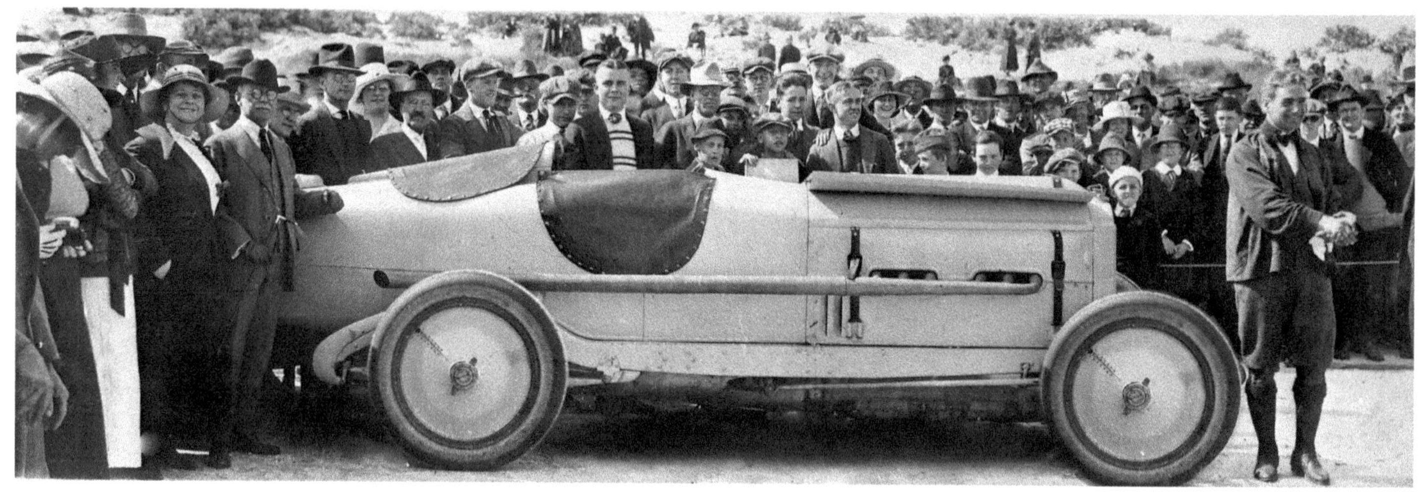

Real Estate Boom, Depression, and World War II

(1919–1945)

World War I was over and Daytona was enjoying unbelievable growth. Land values were rising and a real estate boom was in full swing. Lots were being surveyed and speculators were buying land. In the mid twenties, the Highlands Subdivision and its builders were the most progressive group in Daytona Beach. They specialized in Mediterranean Revival–style houses.

Incorporation of Daytona Beach took place January 1, 1926. The town of Daytona, the town of Seabreeze, and the town of Daytona Beach (Goodall) joined together to become one progressive city. Many banks were flourishing and it looked like the growth would never end.

New ground speed records were being established on the beach. On February 12, 1919, Ralph DePalma was the first to race through the measured mile at 149.875 m.p.h. Sig Haugdahl, a famed driver, was also an early racer to seek ground speed records in Daytona, eventually making his home in the area. He was also credited with planning the first 3.5-mile road-beach course in 1936 for stock cars at Daytona Beach. Other challengers were Campbell, Segrave, Lockhart, Keech, Bible, and Don.

Air flights were becoming more frequent with planes using the beach as their runway and landing strip. In the late twenties, a landing field was constructed at Bethune Point.

The real estate business suffered a reversal when banks started closing and, on Black Friday, October 29, 1929, the stock market crashed. The Great Depression did great harm to the local economy during the thirties. Campbell's speed trials through 1935 continued as a winter draw for tourists, and the PWA and the WPA programs built the boardwalk, bandshell, and other public buildings, giving workers a job and helping to bring groceries to the family table.

War clouds were looming over Europe, and the U.S. started producing war materials. The Daytona Beach Boat Works was established during World War II to build sub-chasers and liberty boats. The Navy Base, the WACs, and the Welsh Convalescence Hospital gave employment to local citizens during the war.

Pilots landed their planes on the packed sands at Daytona Beach. These planes flew in from Carlstrom Field, near Arcadia. They parked south of the pier where tourists and local folks could take a look at new models, such as the new U.S. Army Air Service planes.

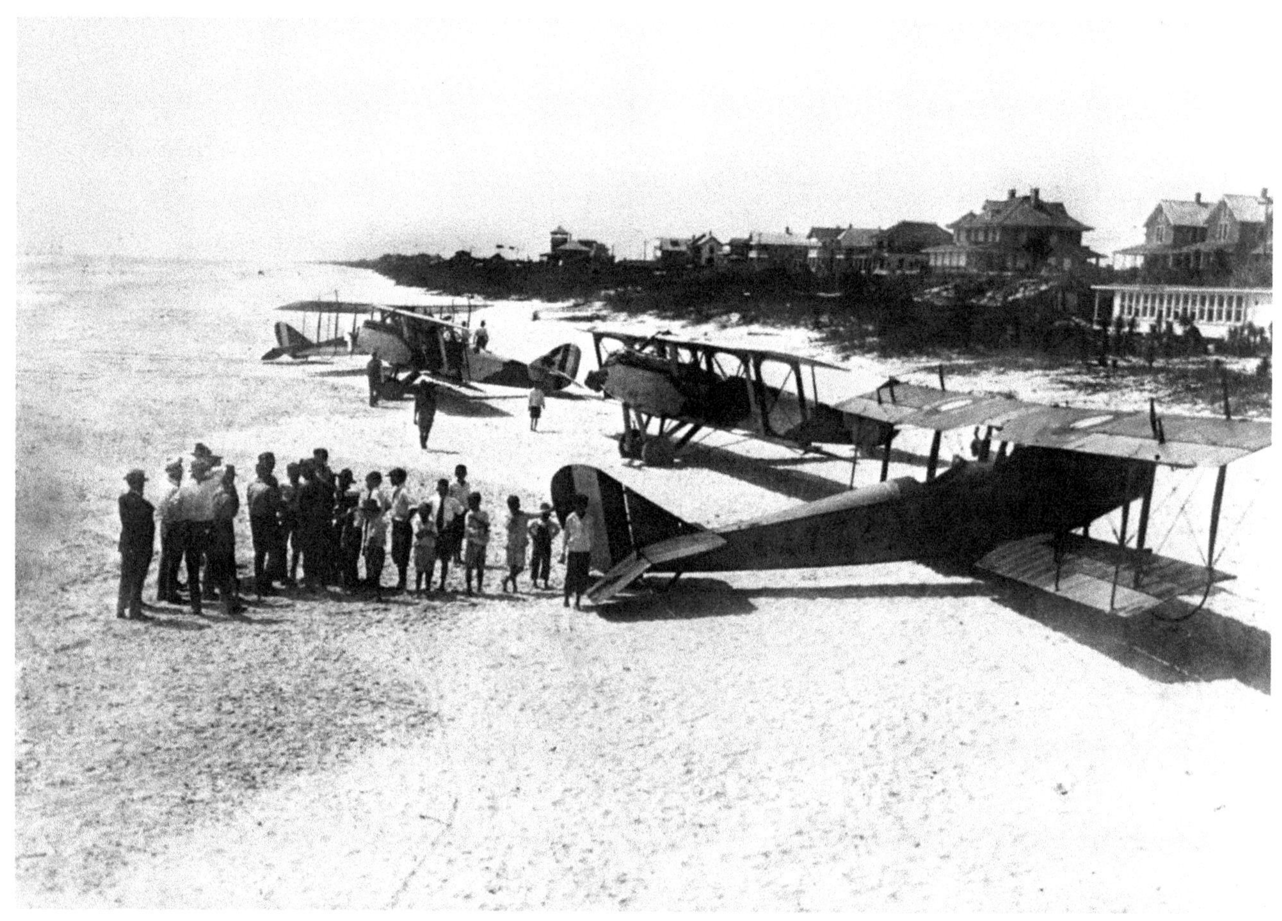

A famous World War I pilot, U.S. Ace Major David McKelvey Peterson, was killed in a crash on the beach March 16, 1919. The U.S. Army Air Service pilots used the beach for landings and take-offs. The major's plane reached a height of 75 feet before the engine cut off and the plane nosed down and crashed.

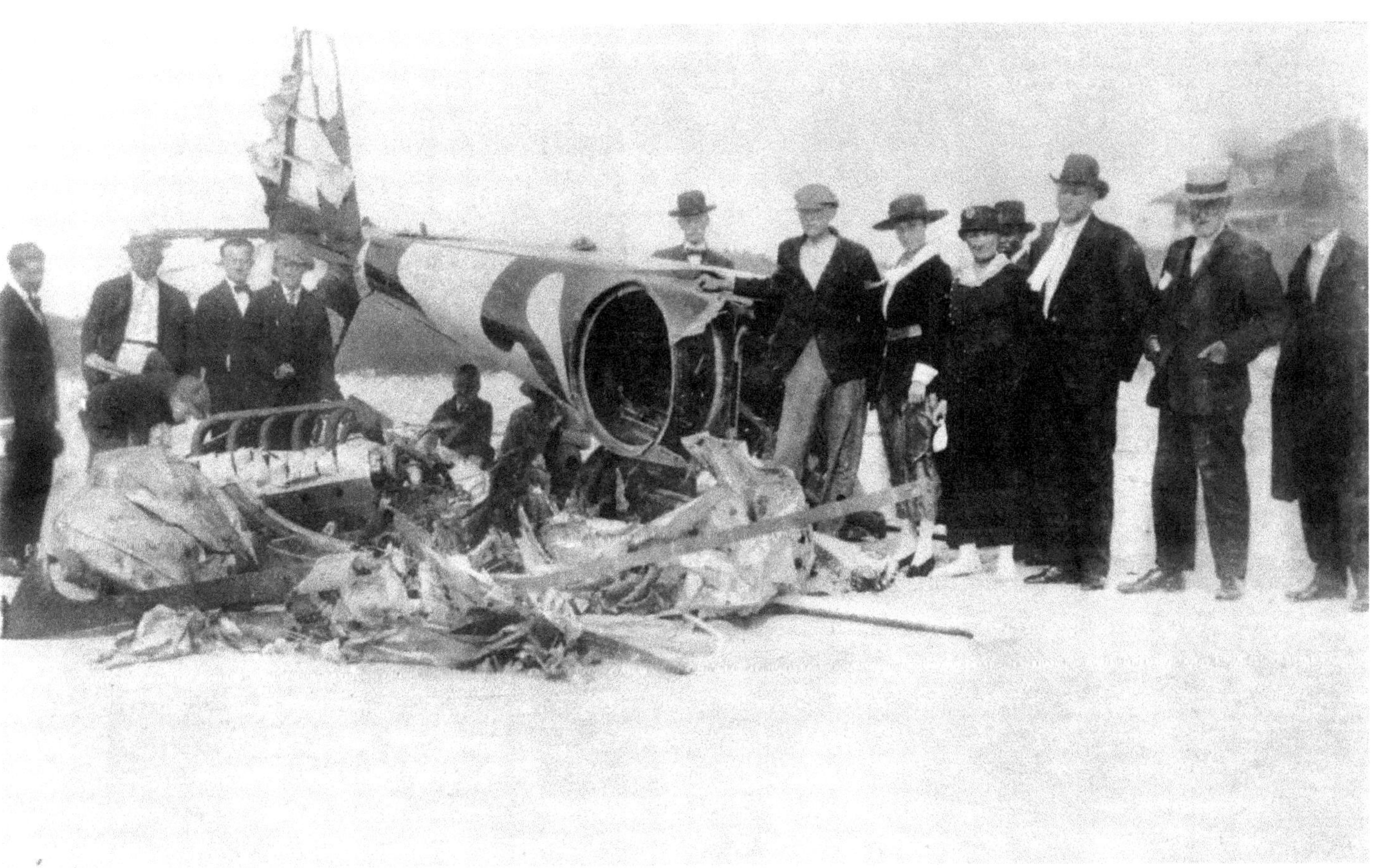

During Prohibition Daytona Beach had its speakeasies and taverns. Gambling ran rampant in the local nightclubs. Law officers were turning their heads until citizens demanded enforcement of the law; overnight the clubs were raided and slot machines confiscated.

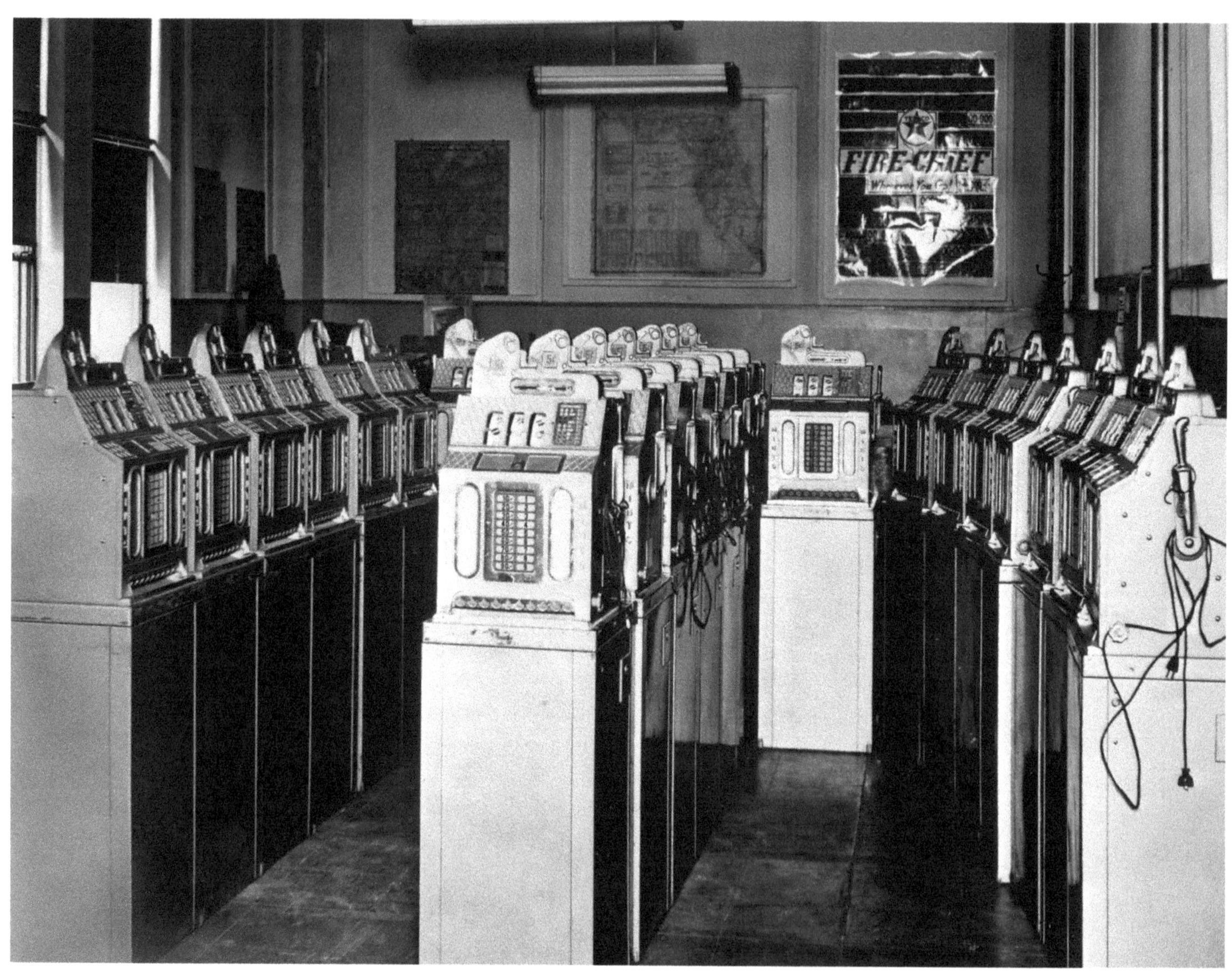

Ervin Ballough (standing), pilot, and Alfred Borden, New York banker and passenger, made this trip to Daytona, the first land-based flight. The plane was a Canuck-Curtiss Jenny, built in Canada.

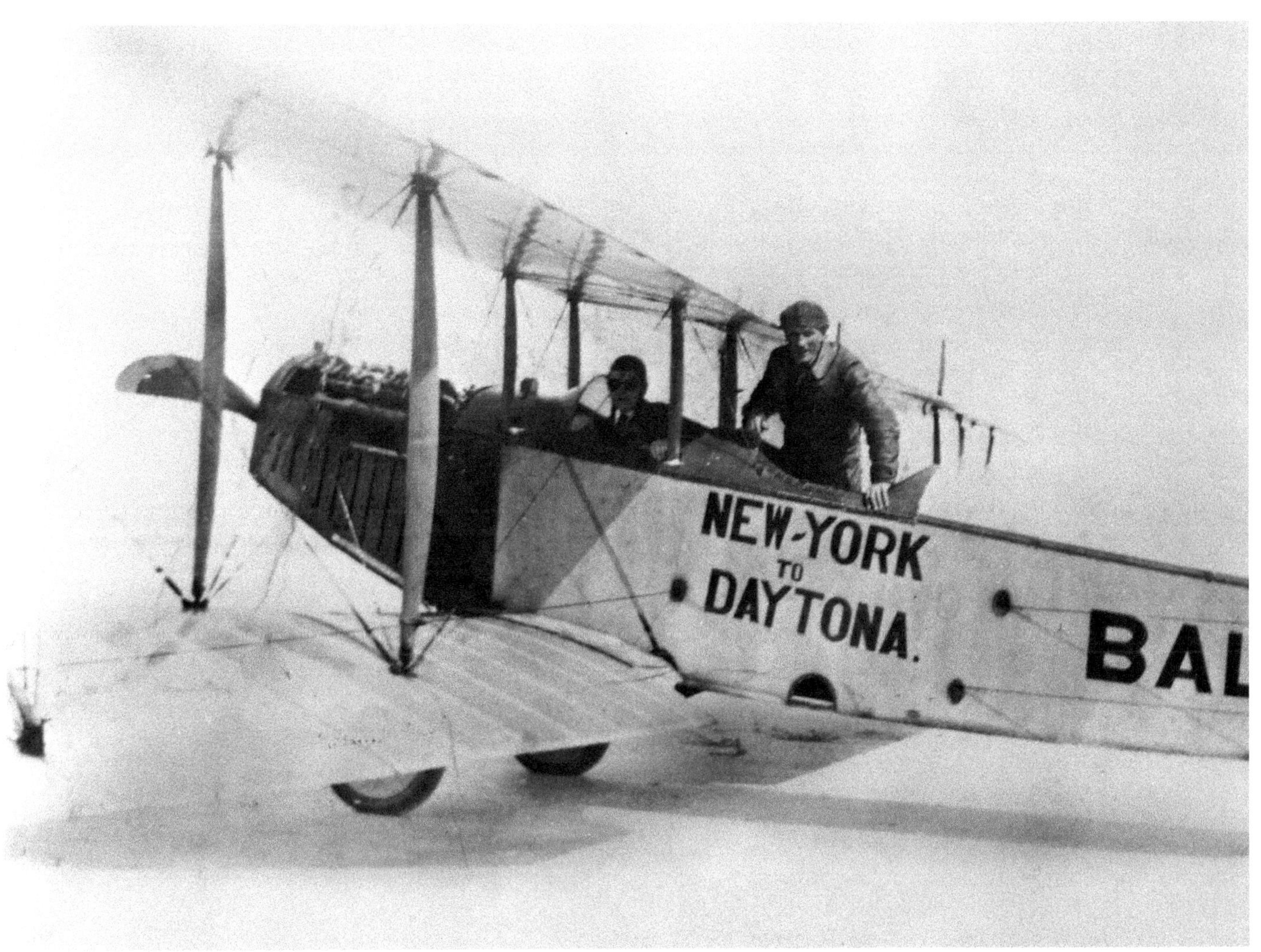

At center in this aerial view are the Halifax River Yacht Club and city docks. To the right is City Island Ball Field and the city library. Other buildings are the Burgoyne Casino and the business block from Orange Avenue to Volusia Avenue including the concrete bridge.

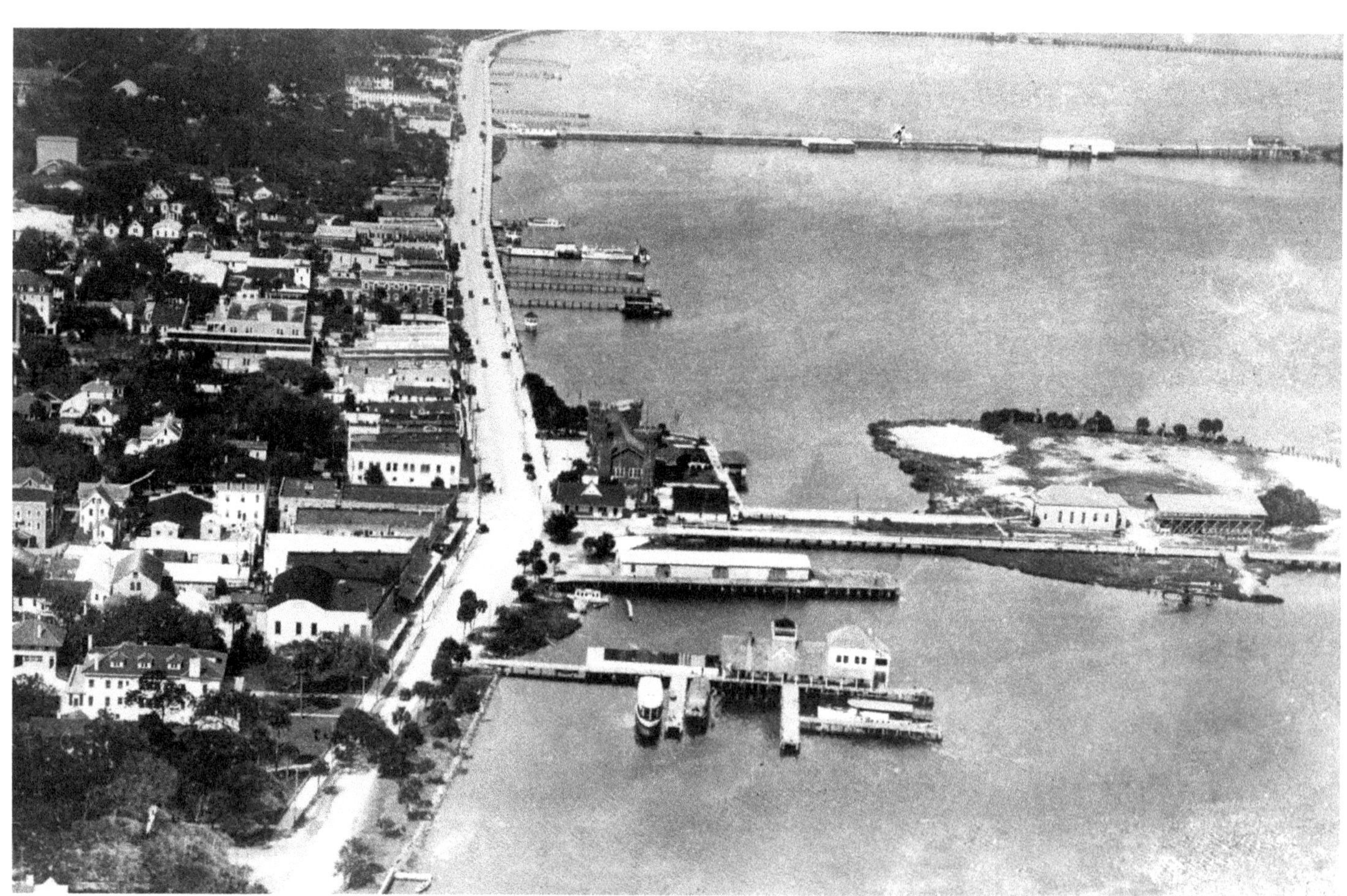

A typical scene on the beach and near the surf, from early days to the present. The pier provided shade from the sun when desired. For the more ardent, fishing and enjoying the beach could be pursued in the same day. The ocean pier pictured was later rebuilt.

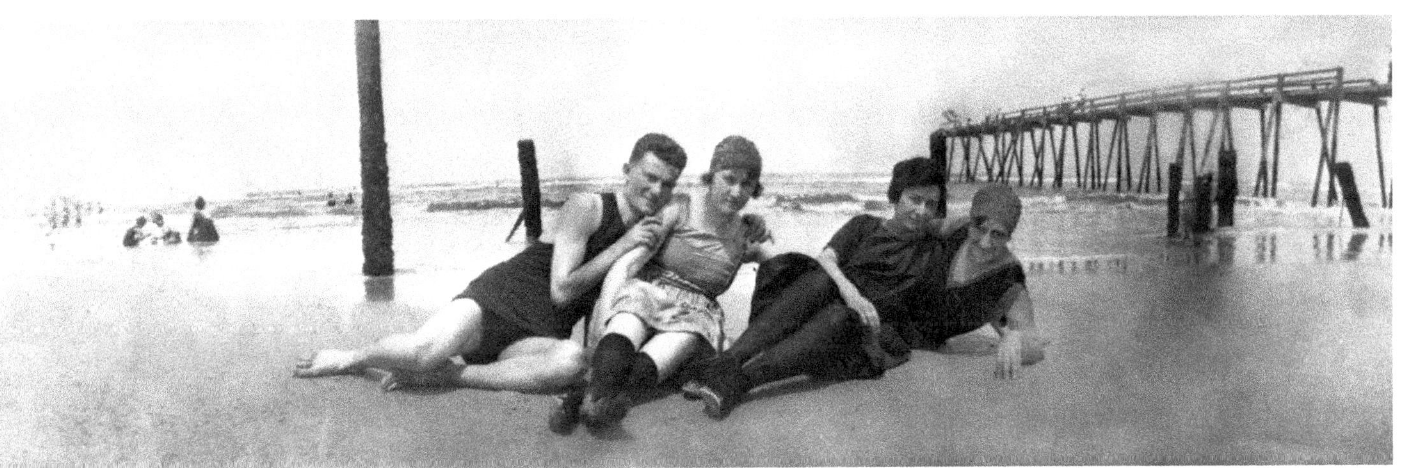

In the days pictured here, Daytona had no mainland airport. The beach served as the landing strip. In view here are various modes of transportation: auto, airplane, and bicycle. The Clarendon Hotel is visible in the distance.

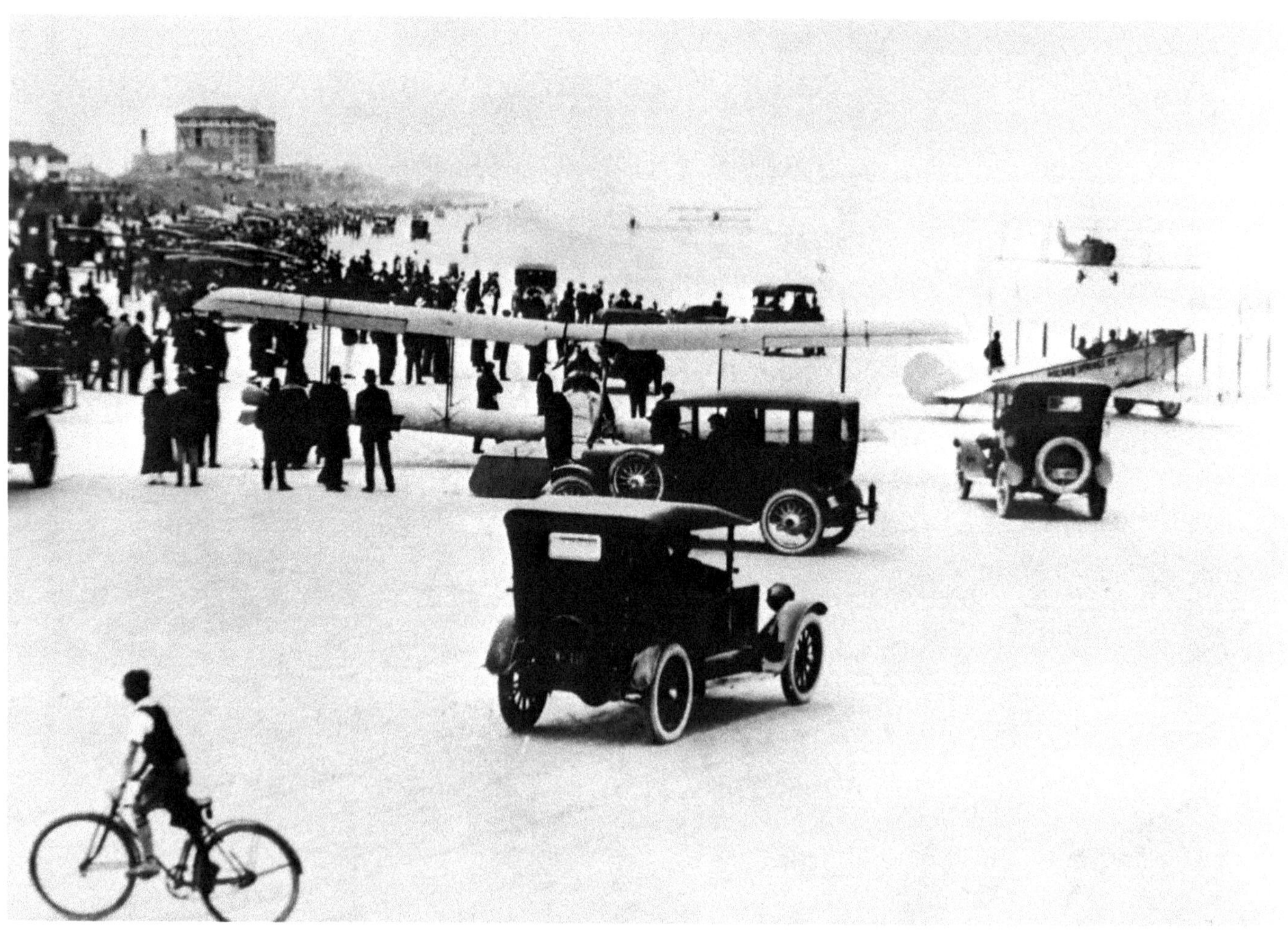

St. Mary's Episcopal Church included beautiful stained-glass windows. The church was to have been named St. Mark's, but in 1883 the cornerstone arrived with "St. Mary's" engraved on it, a mistake the congregation excused.

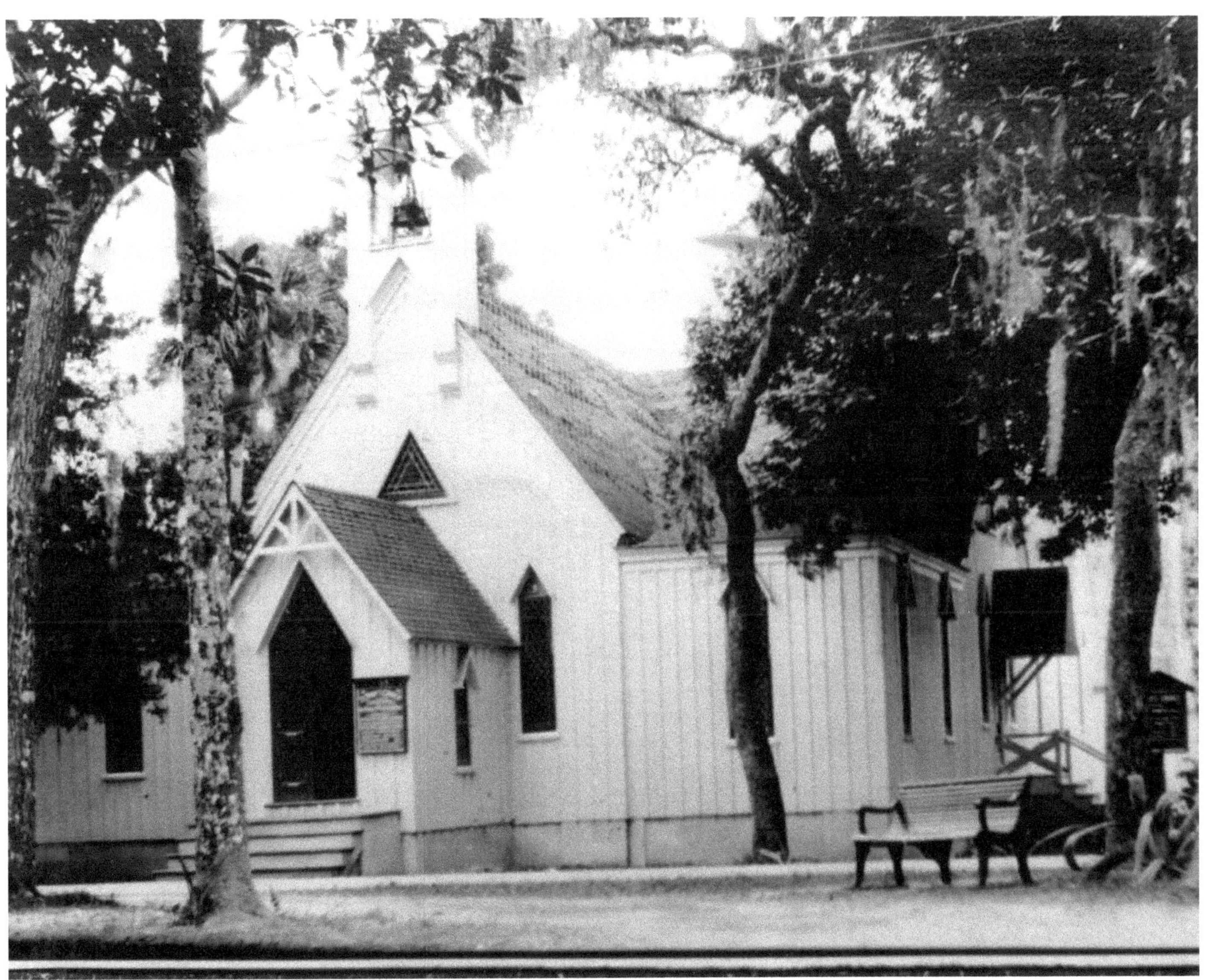

Left to right are Bob Green in his Fronty-Ford; Bob Putnam, Simplex; Pop Daily, Deusenberg; Sig Haugdahl, Miller Special. Sig Haugdahl later made his home in Daytona. In the rear are eager want-to-be racers.

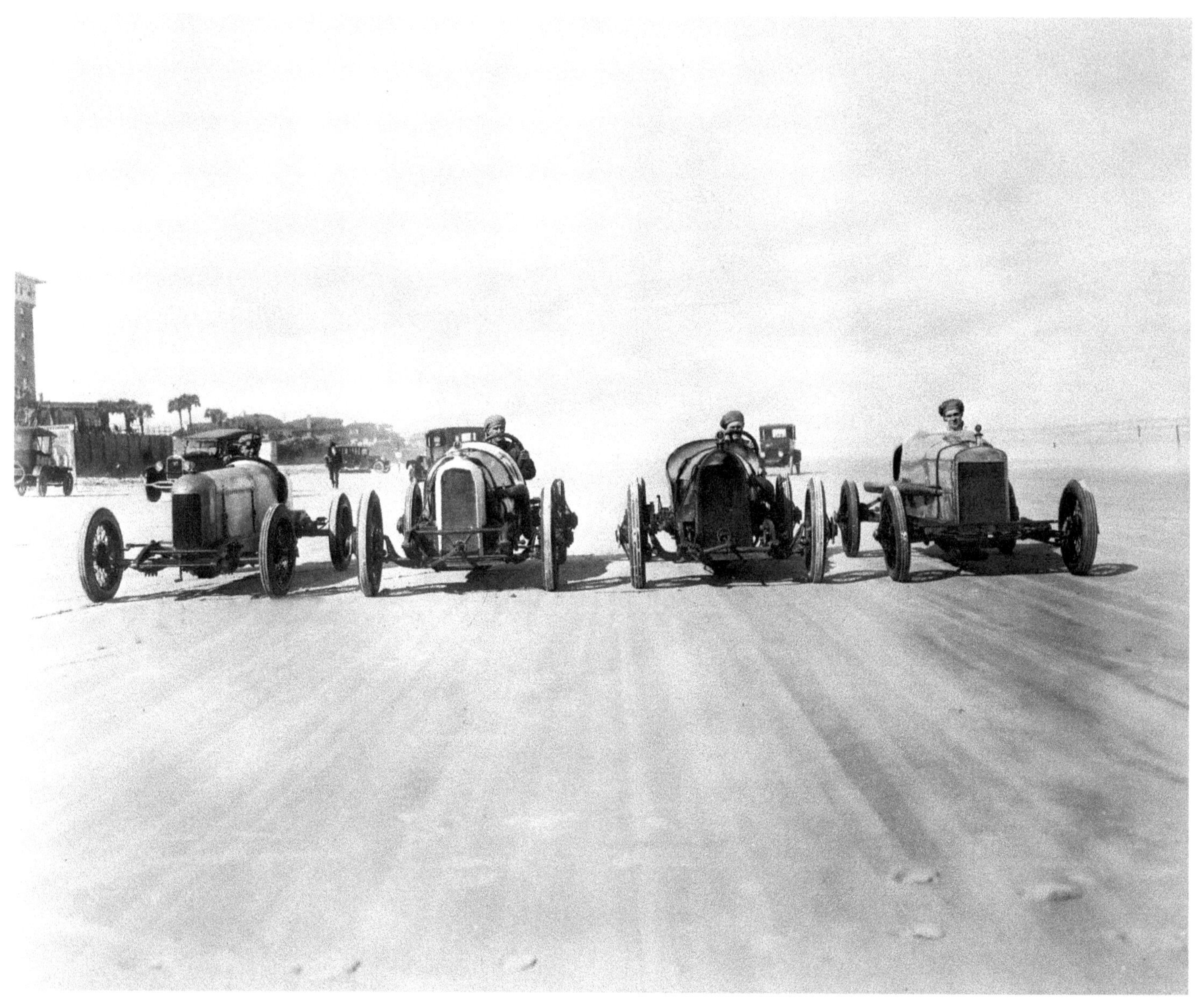

These men volunteered for the honor of service in the home guards, the frontline of defense in Daytona and the home state. Some were Spanish American War veterans and many had served in World War I. The home guard was forerunner of the Florida State Guard and the Florida National Guard.

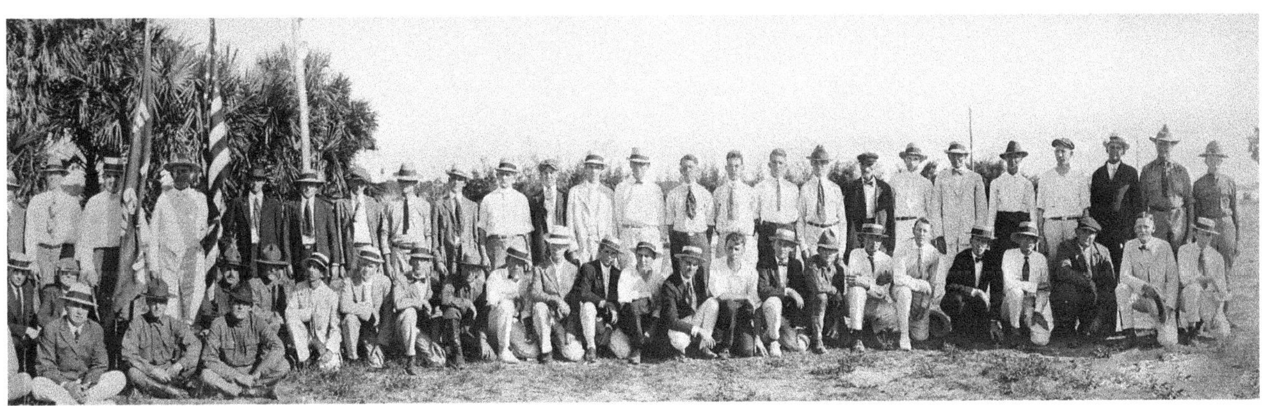

William Usher Norwood and family. This well-known Volusia County resident and his family are being photographed on the beach in their Sunday best, Junior sporting his sailor's suit.

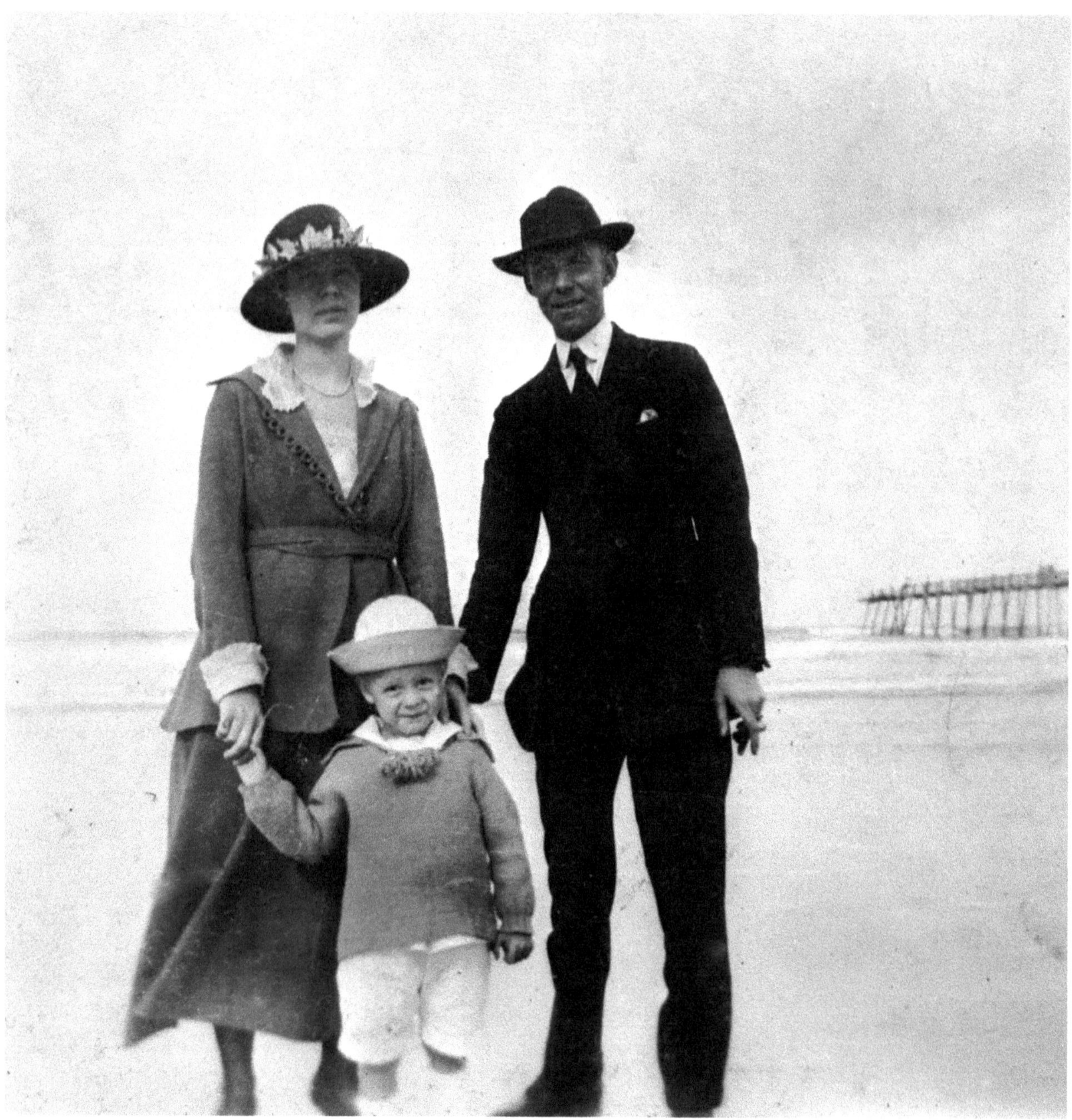

A Flying Circus on the Beach—daredevil shows that often took place on the beach where crowds could gather. Here a pilot flying Mable Cody's Flying Circus plane glides above Sig Haugdahl's Miller Special while daredevil Bugs McGowan transfers from the car to the plane.

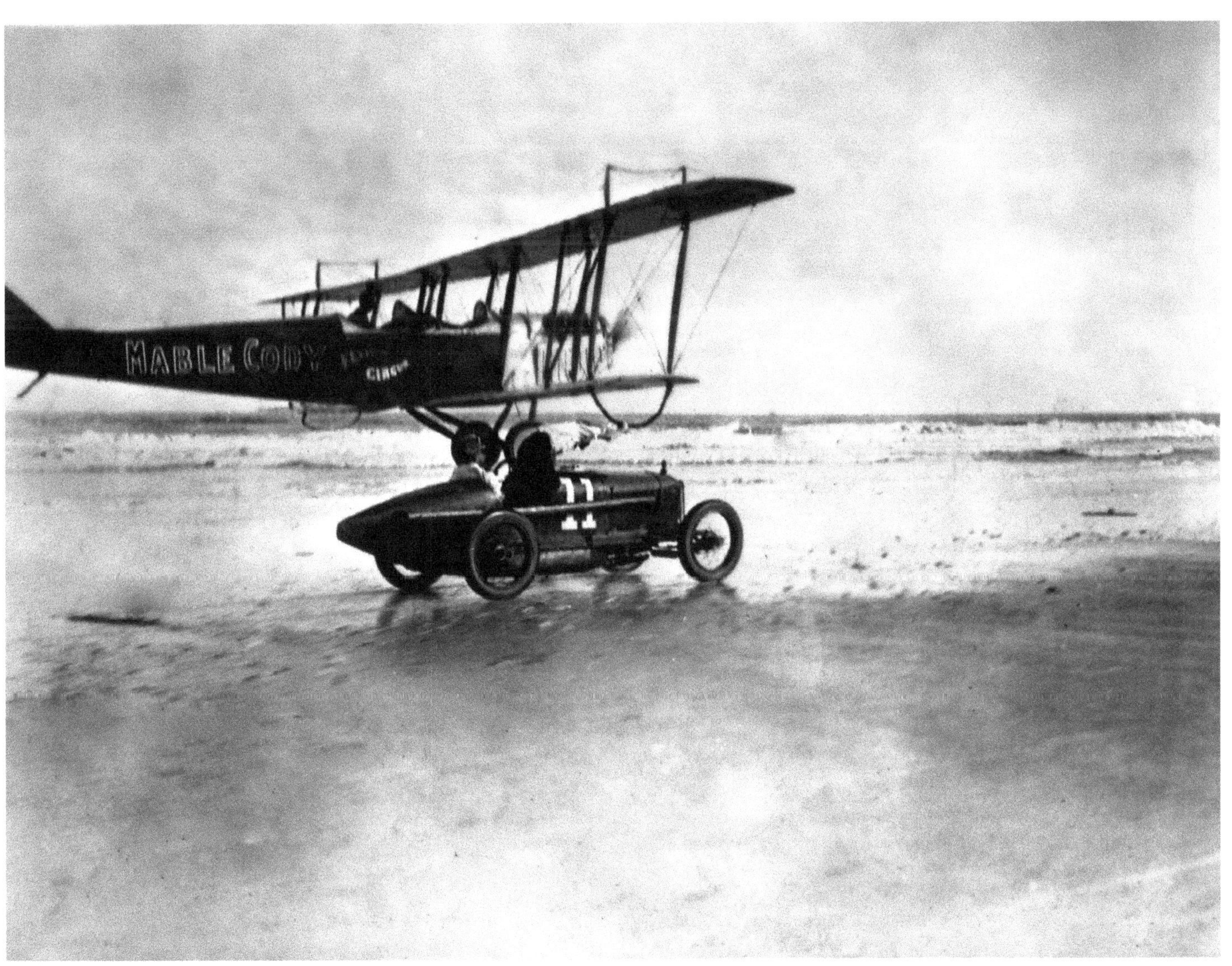

Mable Cody's daredevils thrill the crowds. While Bugs McGowan pulls himself up to hover on the lower wing of the plane, Sig Haugdahl, an experienced race car driver, paces alongside.

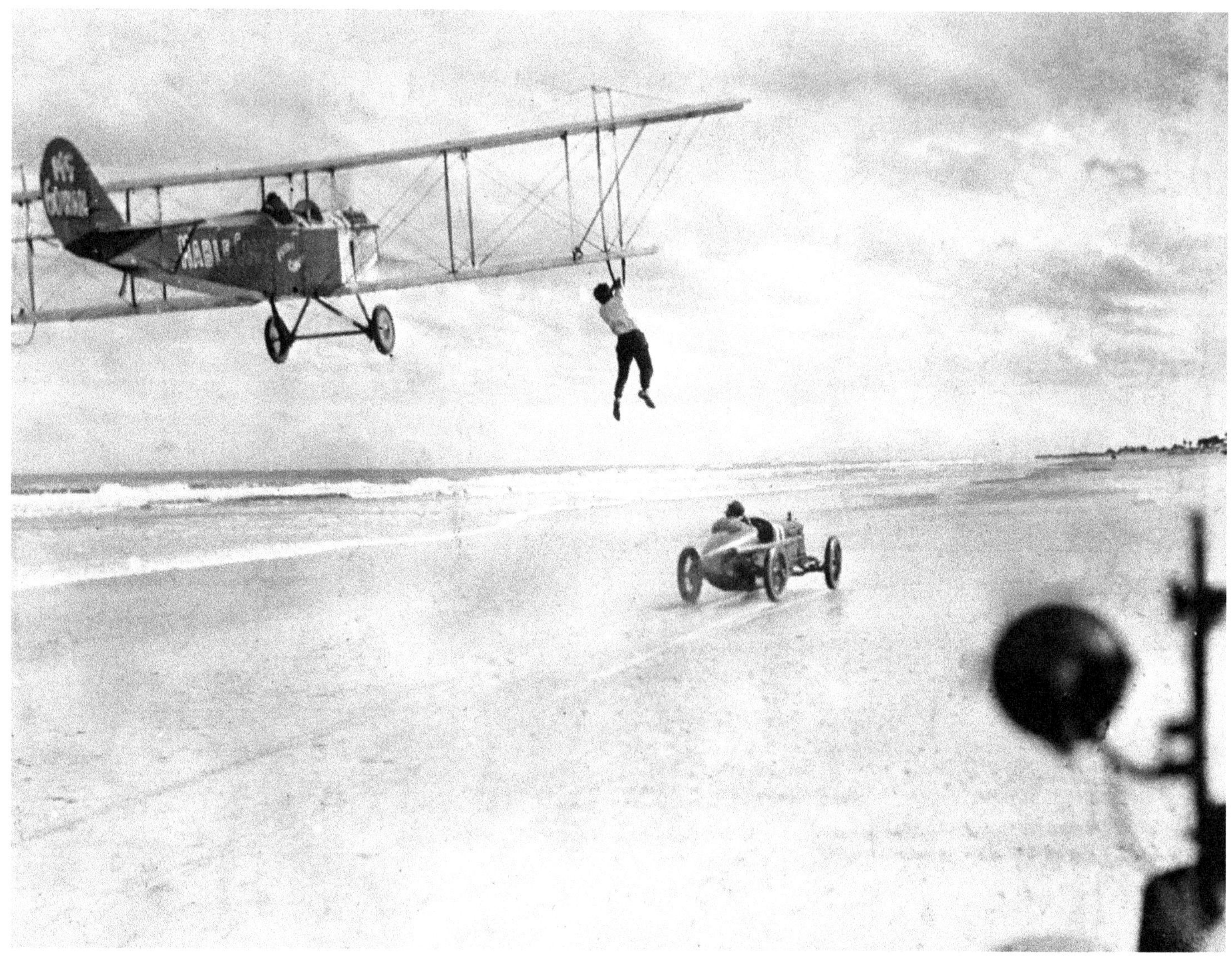

With mash barrels visible in the foreground, law officers confiscate illicit whiskey from a moonshine still.

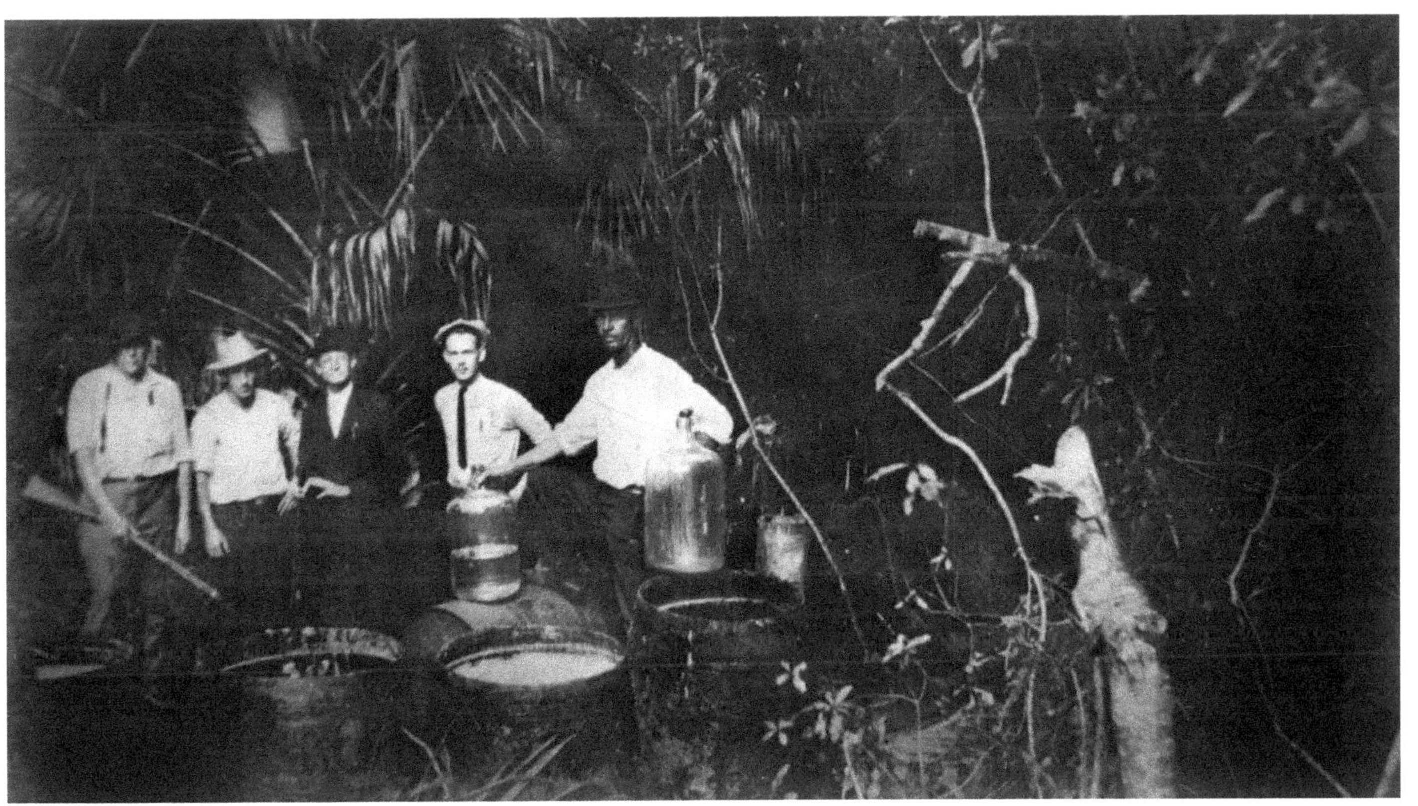

Men use land-clearing equipment to prepare streets and create building sites for future houses. Mediterranean Revival, featuring stucco walls and red tile roofs, was a style typical of the day for building houses.

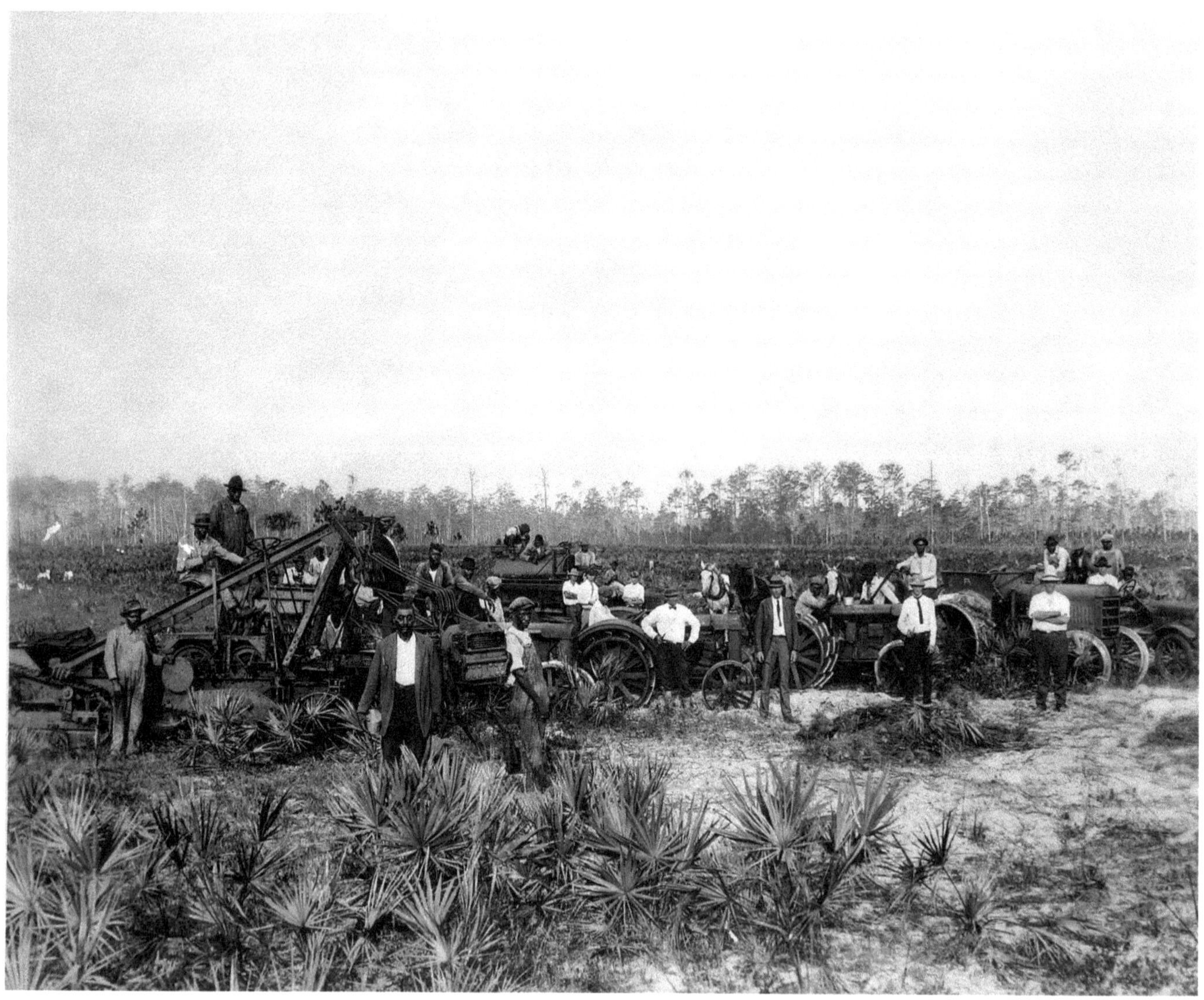

Pictured is Sig Haugdahl's Wisconsin Special. Haugdahl, probably one of the most experienced race car drivers at that time, was the first man to reach 180 m.p.h., on the beach April 7, 1922.

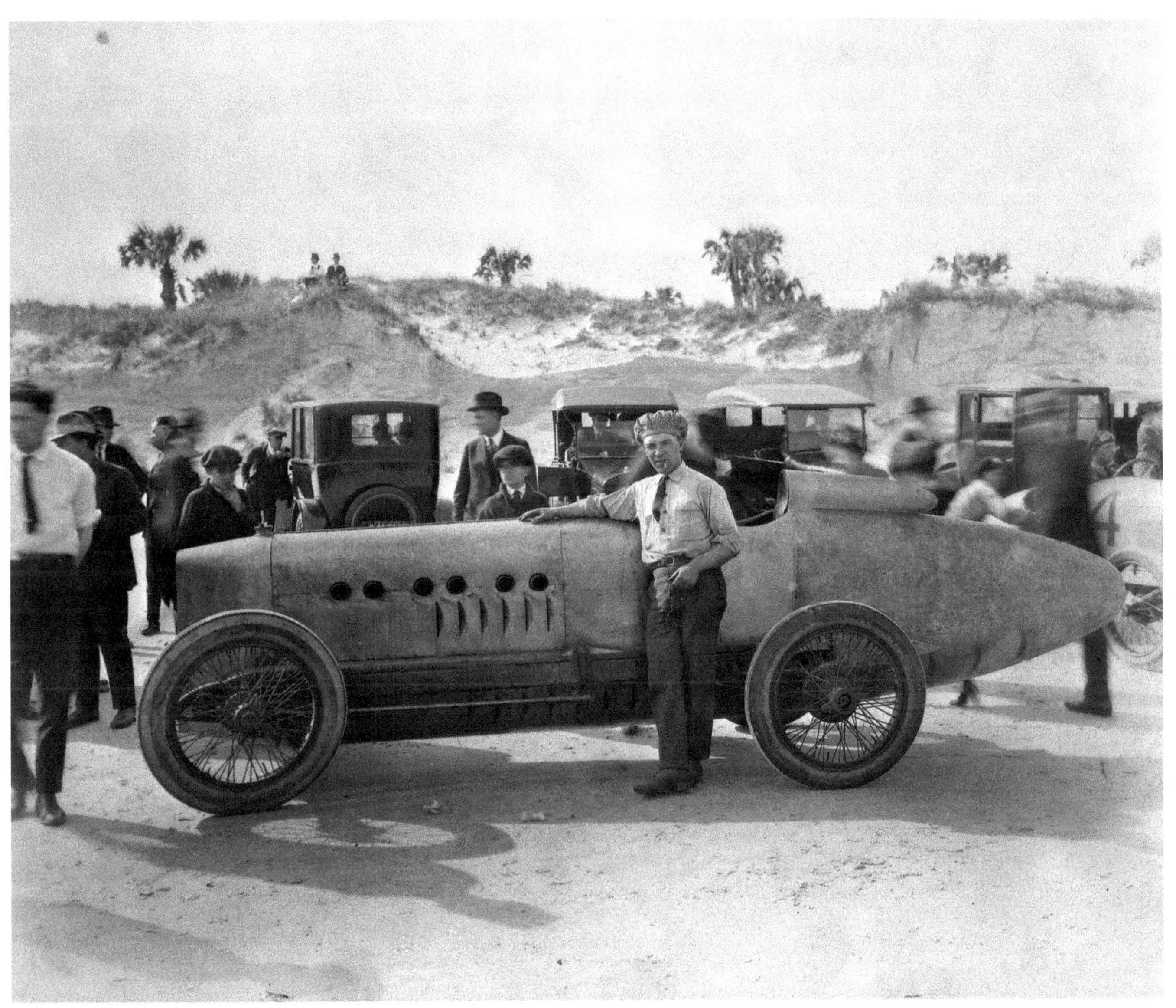

A warm winter day would bring out crowds at the beach. New-style bathing suits were being worn to see and to be seen. Wool was the predominant fabric.

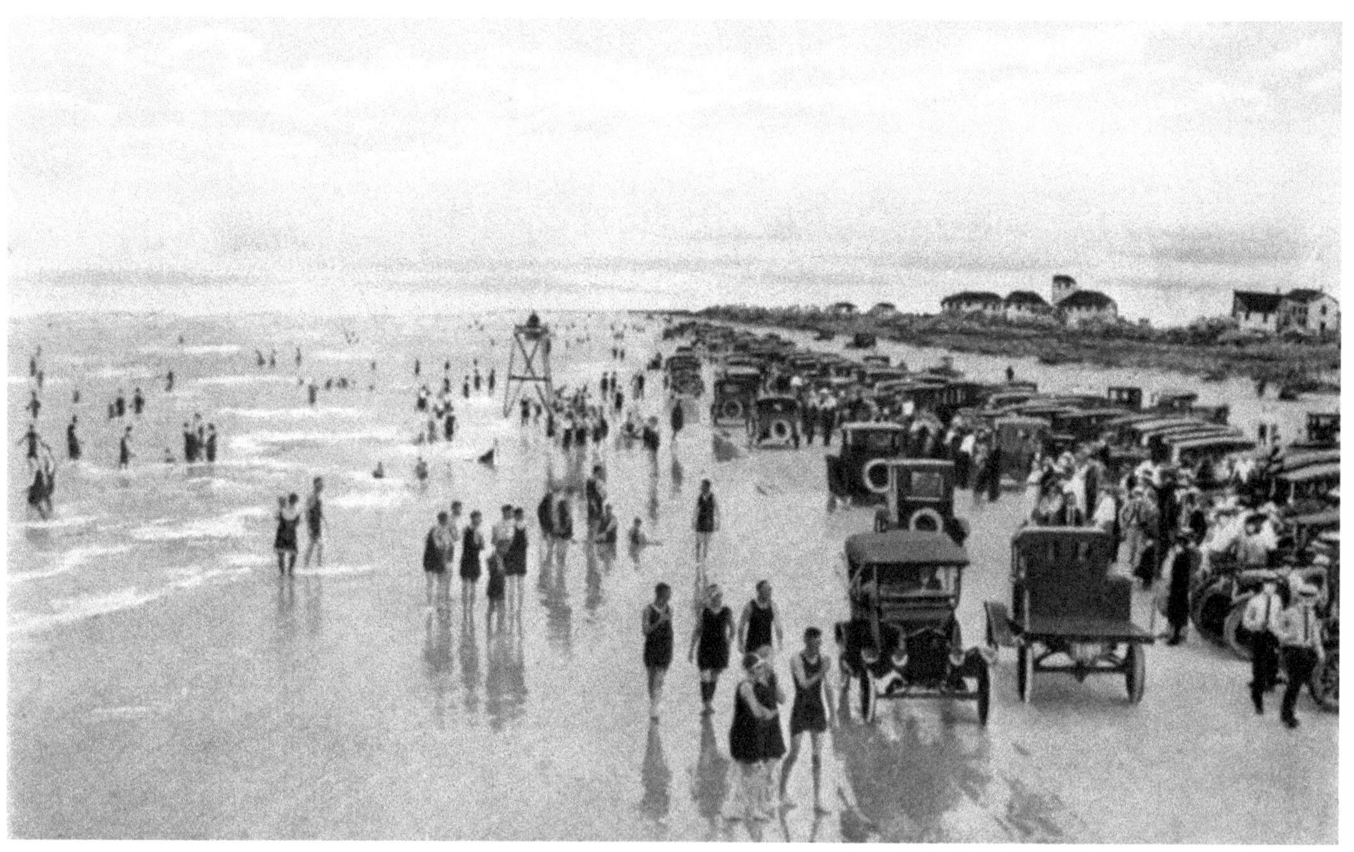

Leon Despland, an early hotel entrepreneur, built the beautiful wood and masonry Despland Hotel. Storefronts line the ground floor.

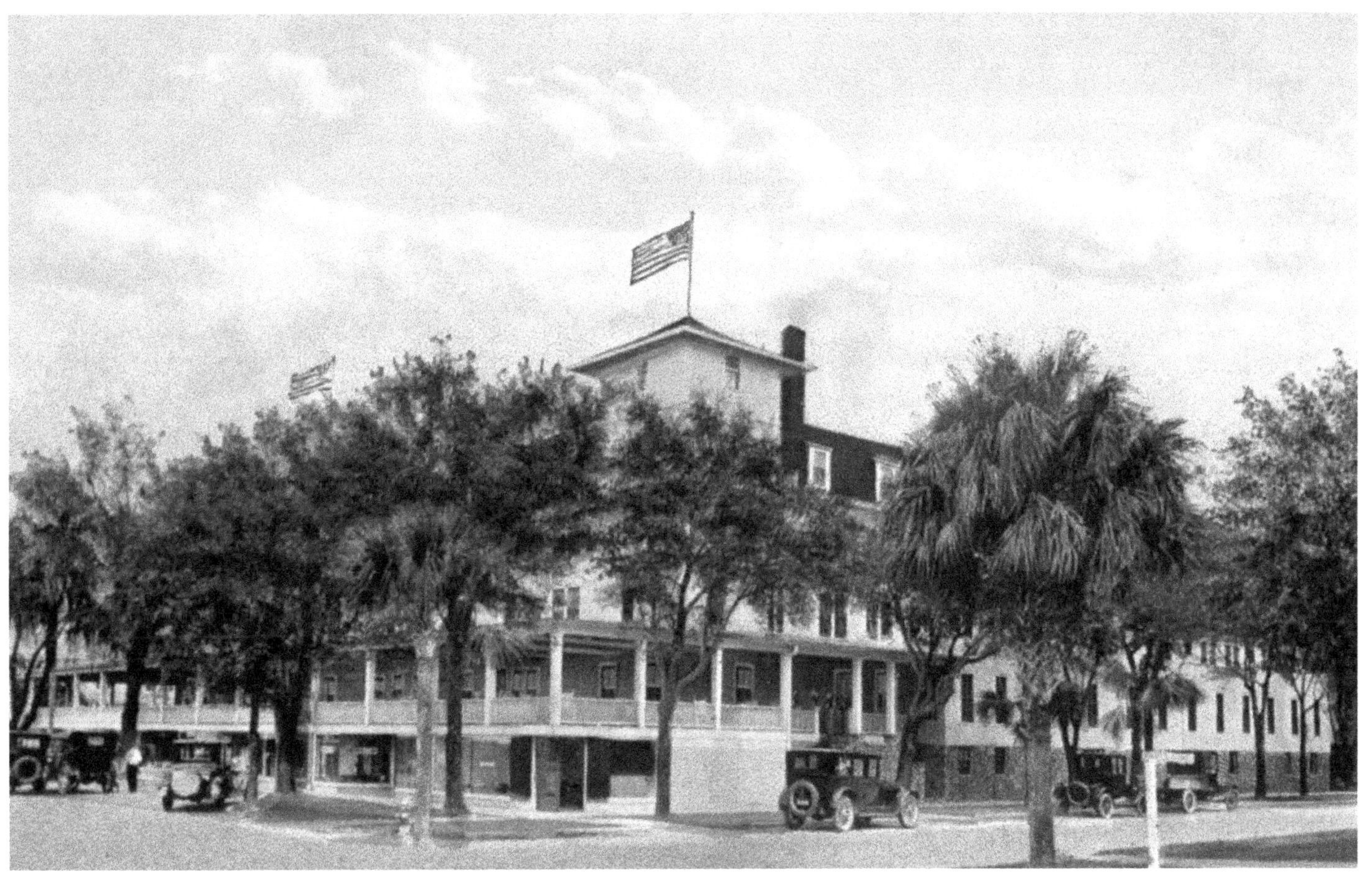

The Curtiss Oriole was a plane used in many daredevil maneuvers. In back are, left to right, stuntmen Bill Lindley, Glenn E. Messer, Steve Crane, and Gustav Slim Ekstrom. In front, left to right, Jimmy Johnson, Joe Wilson, and Joe Nichols. These men would gain fame for their risky exploits.

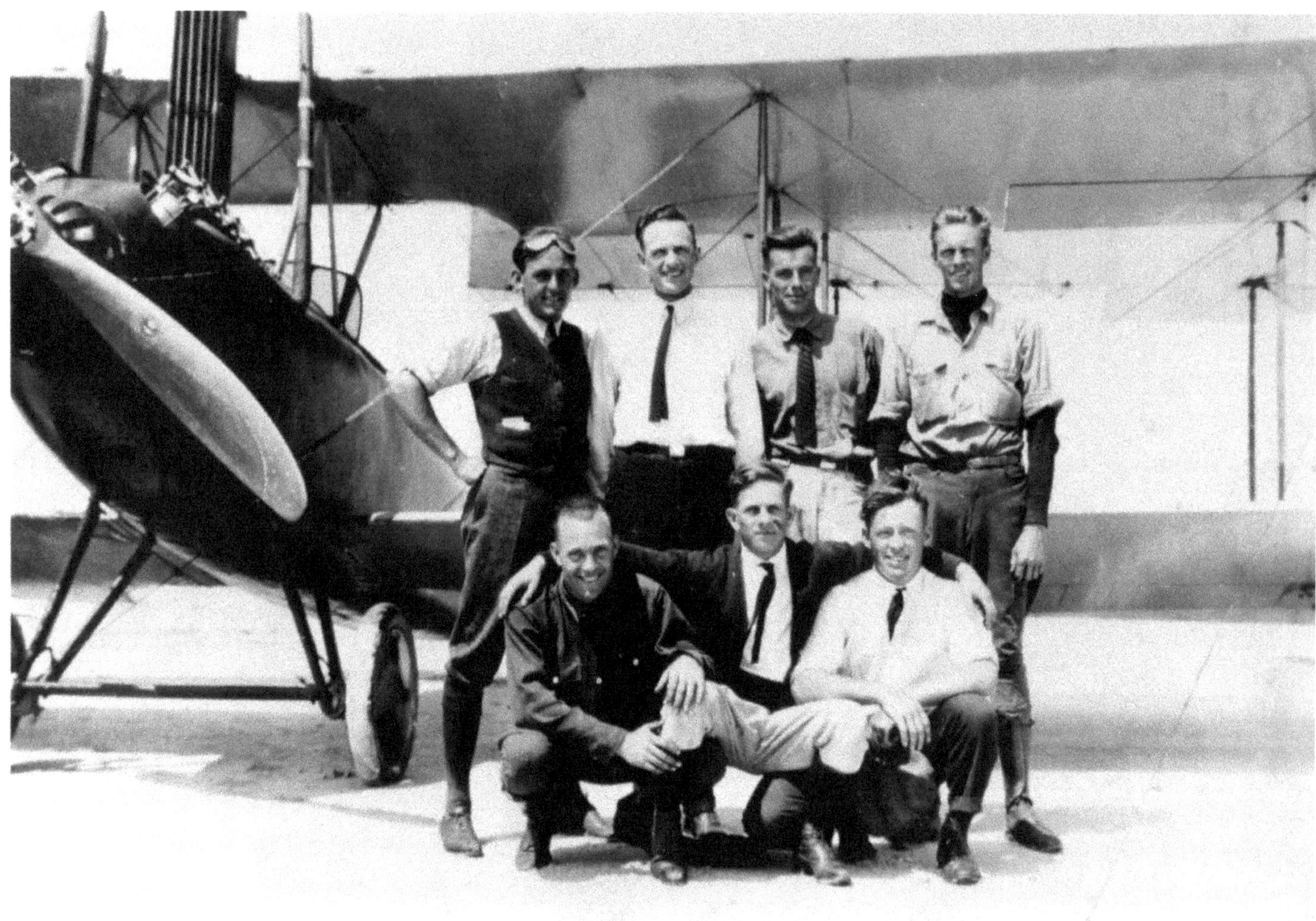

A Daytona Highland race car entry, promoted by the Highlands subdivision owners. Many racing events were held on the beach, some of them known as barrel and pillar racing. Smaller race cars were used for special events.

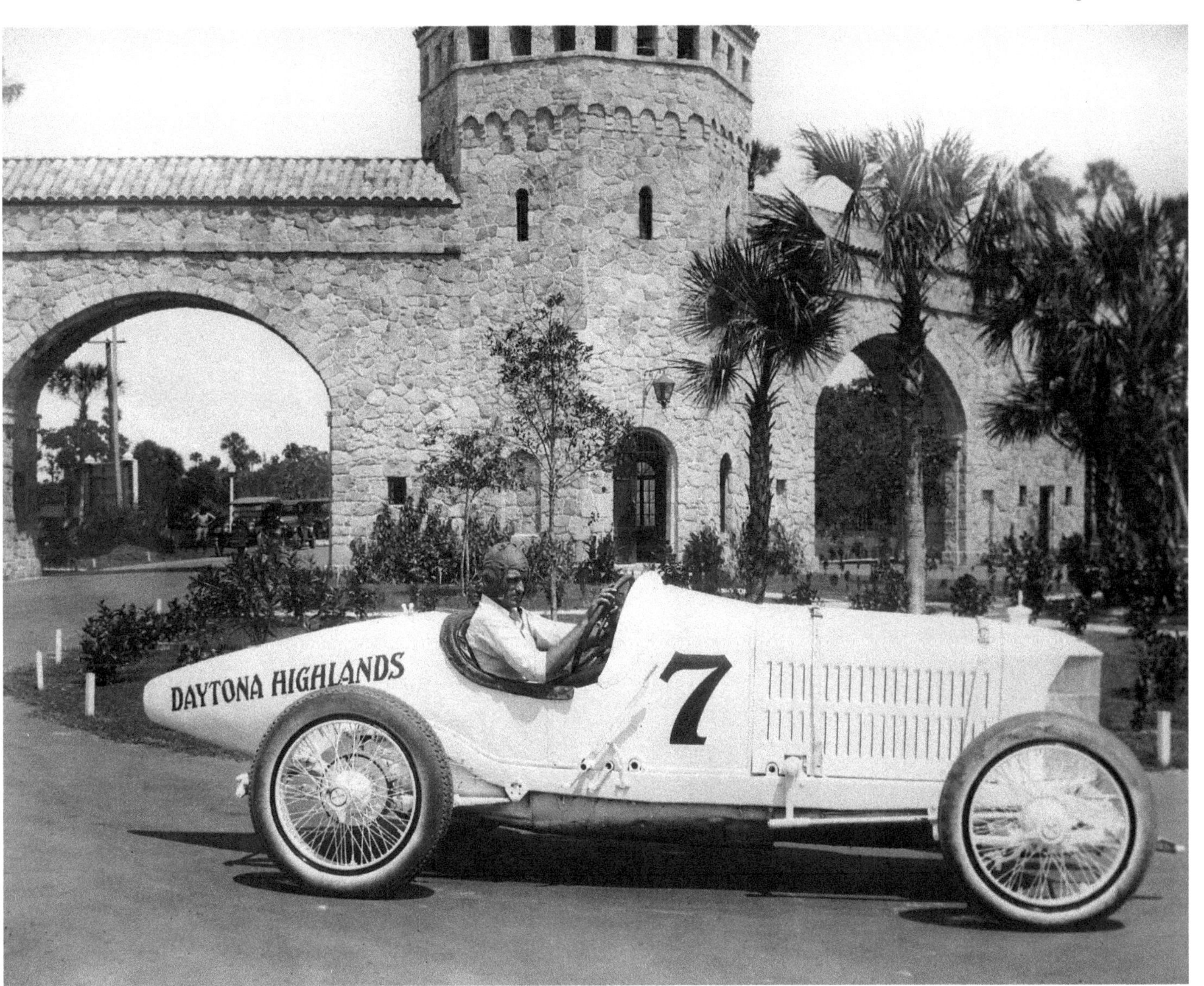

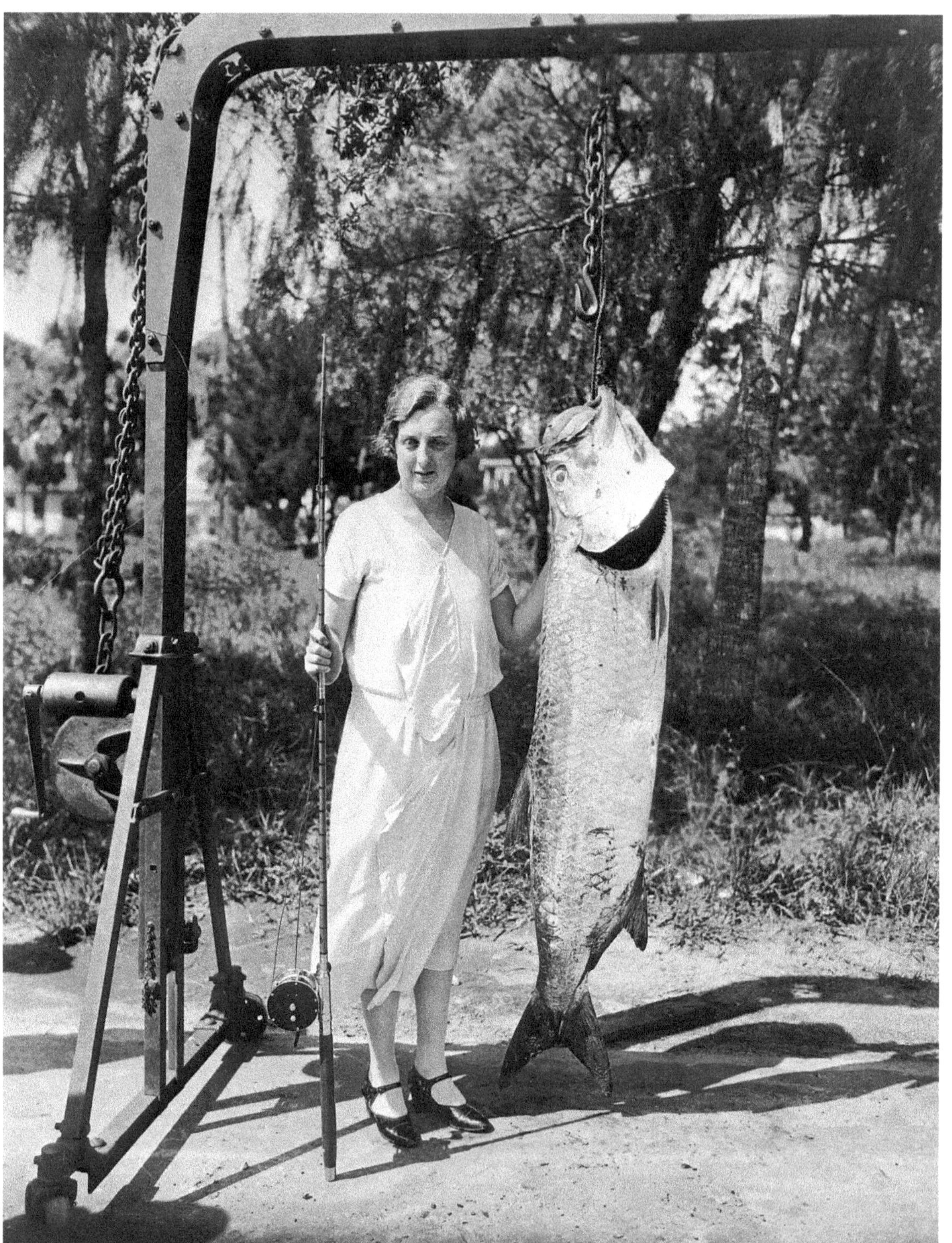

Margaret Biven Haugdahl was the wife of a Daytona sportsman and race car driver. Tarpon fishing was a popular sport and contests were often held for the largest fish. Whether she could have reeled in this big fish with the rod and tackle shown merits scrutiny.

This Mediterranean Revival–style home with its red barrel roof tile was a favorite among home designers. Sales people heavily promoted these new houses at the Highlands subdivision, a prestigious place to live adjacent Daytona.

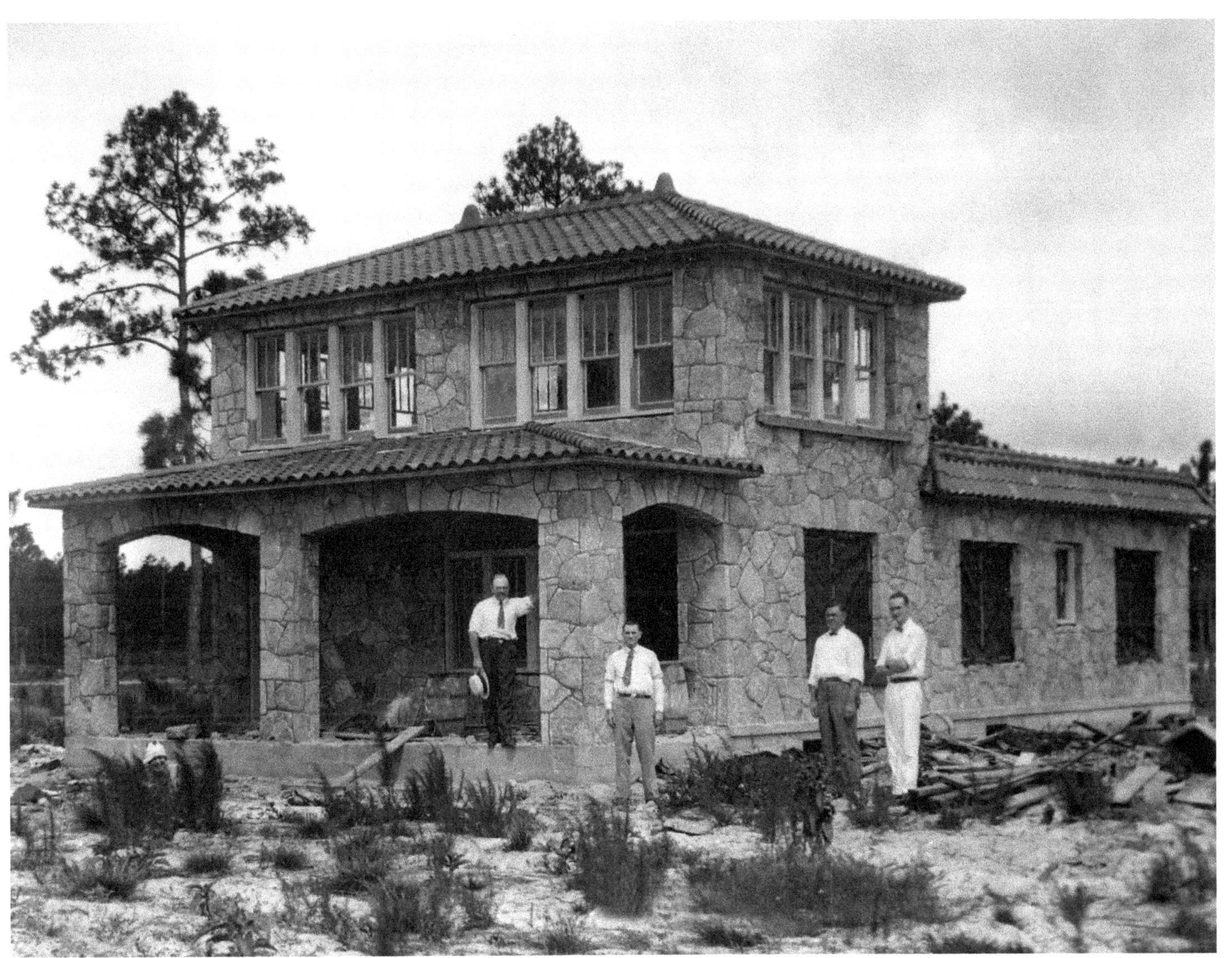

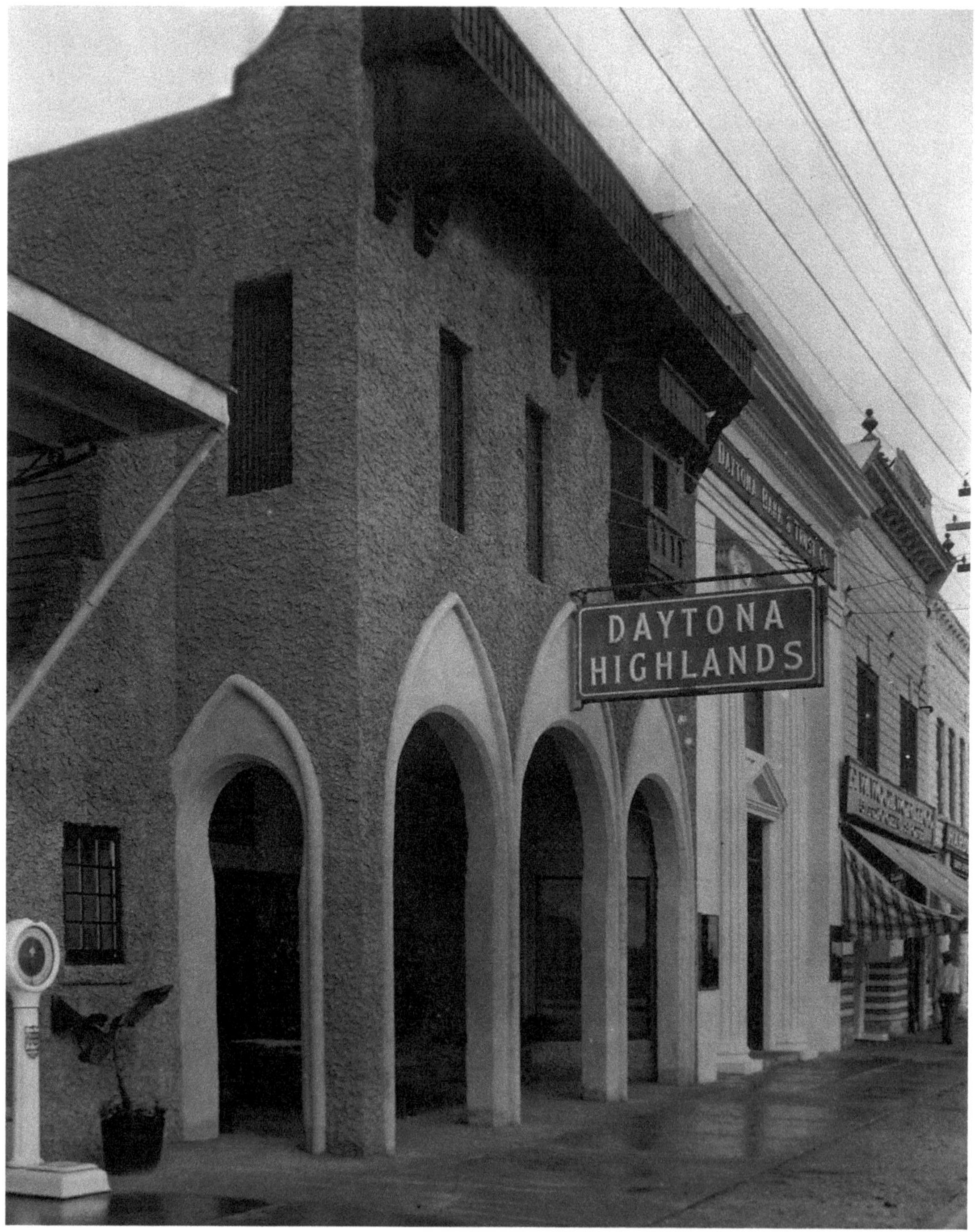

The scales at lower left were a gimmick to call attention to the new, modern subdivision with exceptional architectural home styles. The scales were placed near an early bank on Beach Street where tourists and prospective lot buyers would pass by.

Children in costume help promote the beautiful facades of Highlands houses during the peak of the real estate boom. Shown here is a replica of one of the facades, built by Daytona Highlands as part of a contest for which the prize was one of the new houses.

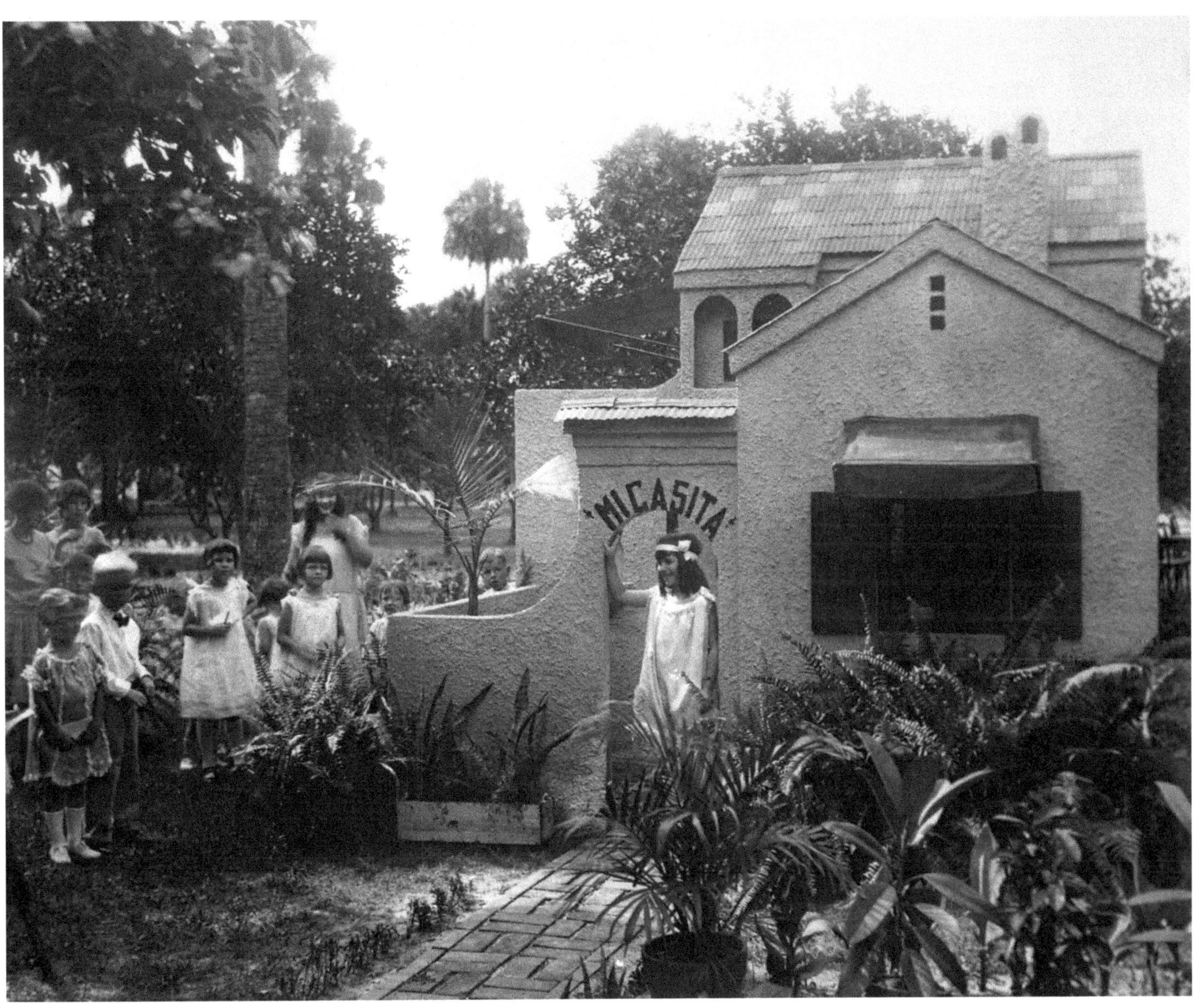

Winder Cowan built this shack on the beach south of the Main Street Pier as a refueling station for aircraft using the beach as a landing strip. Pilots could also purchase whiskey while their planes were being serviced. It was reported that Red, as Cowan was known, flew illicit whiskey from Bimini to Daytona during Prohibition. His first place was destroyed by a northeaster in 1932.

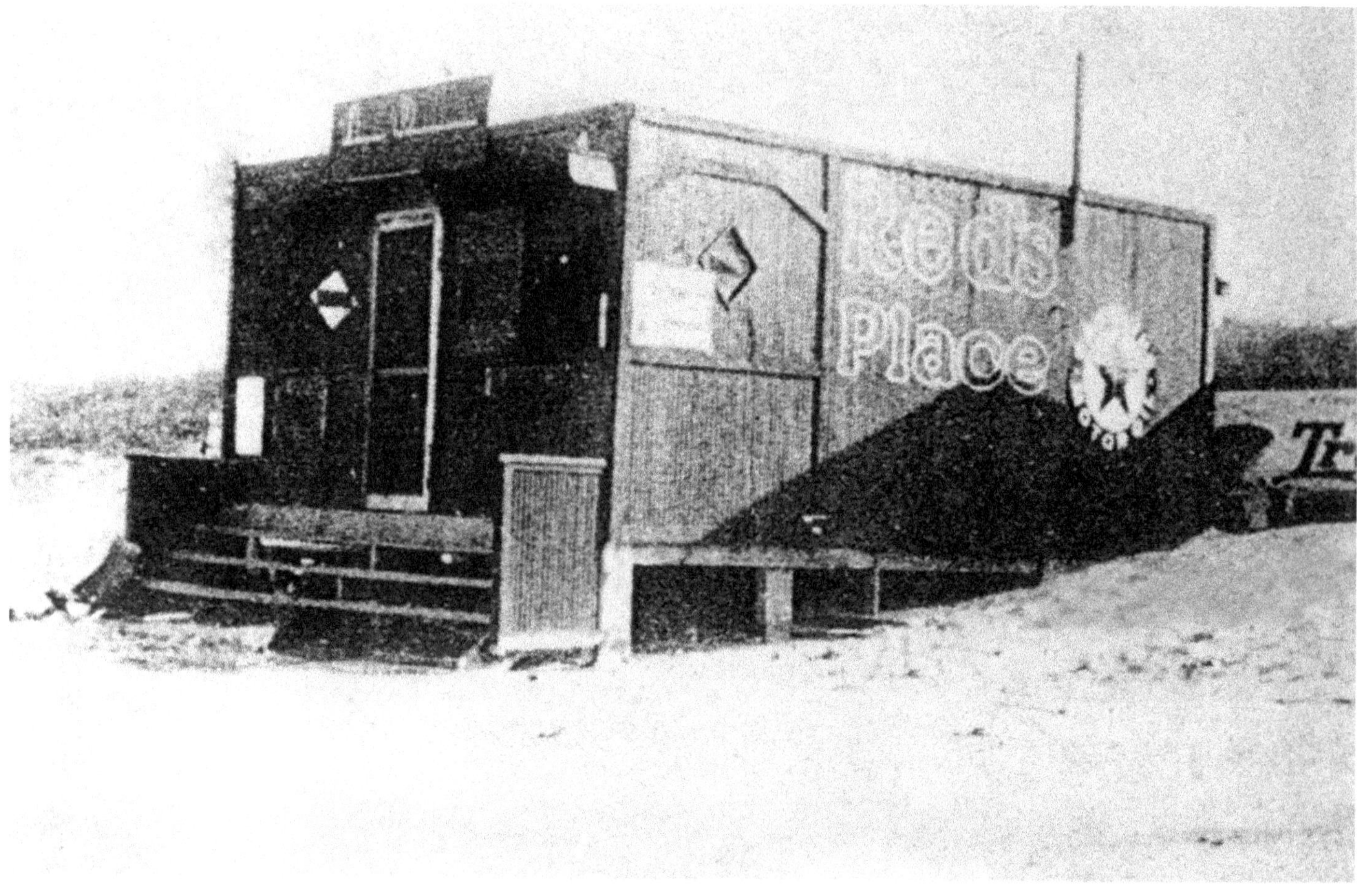

The Hotel Morgan, built in 1906, was a luxurious hotel. It was located on the southeast side of Palmetto and Volusia avenues. It had elevators, interspring mattresses, steam heat, and a family-style restaurant. The Greentree Inn and Gables Hotel were next door to the east.

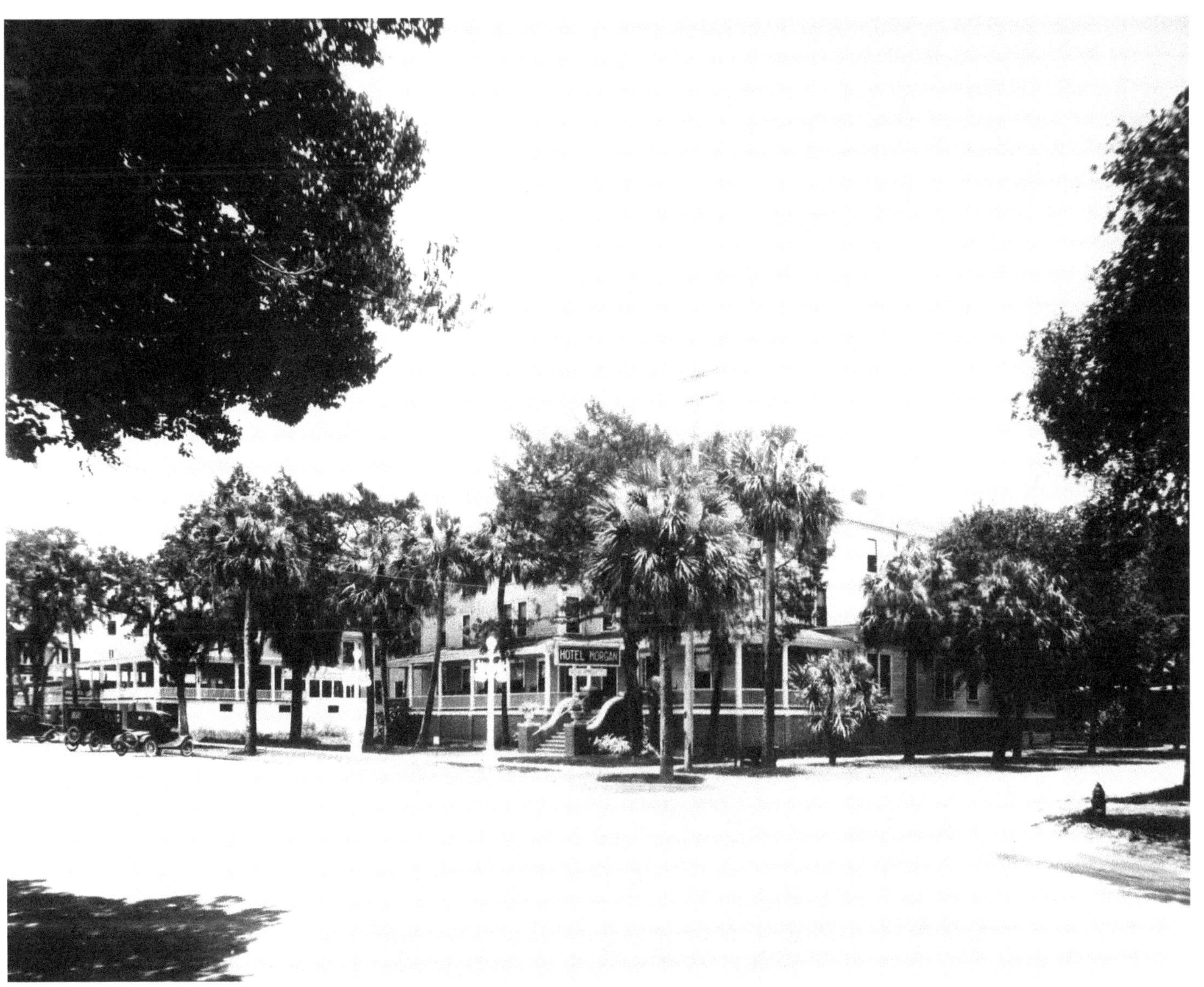

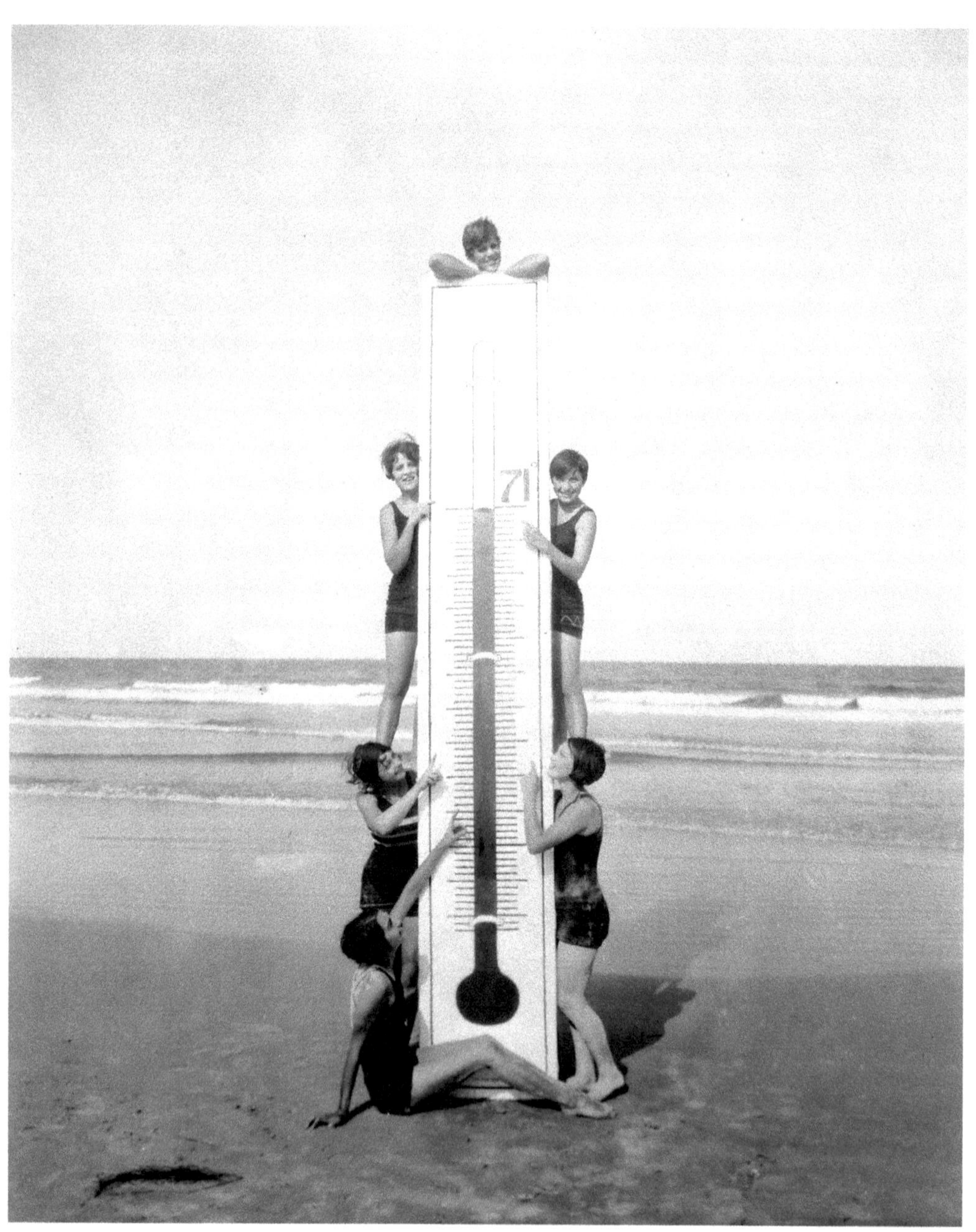

What better way to promote the climate and the beach at Daytona than with beautiful girls and a thermometer.

Hotels and businesses line Volusia Avenue. The Gables Hotel, the Greentree Inn, and Morgan Hotel were on the south side, known as Hotel Row. Several small businesses including a barber shop operated at street level under the Greentree Inn.

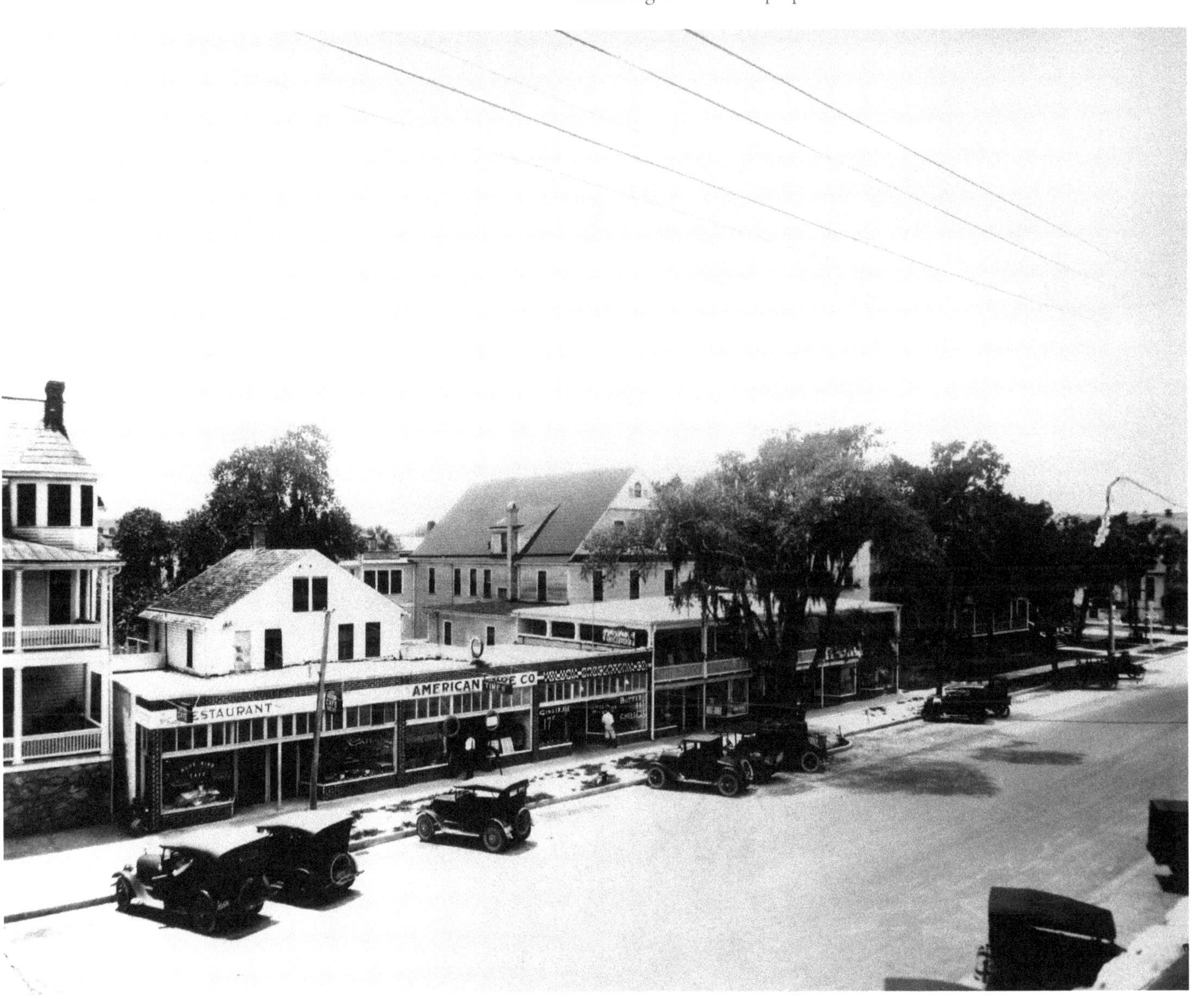

A policeman directs traffic on the beach as beachgoers gather for a gala occasion. The Clarendon Hotel can be seen to the north, with other smaller hotels nearby.

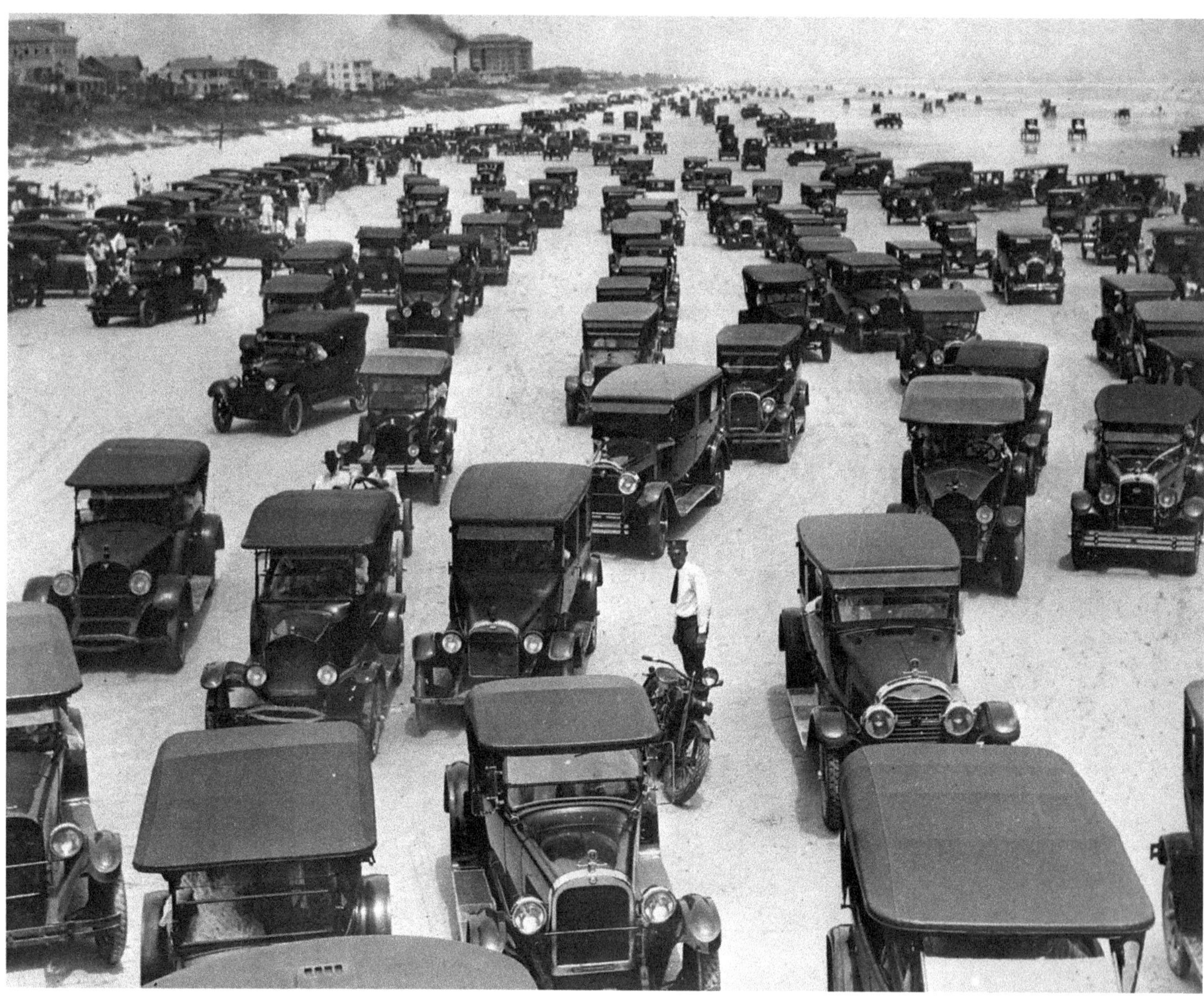

Yachts lie anchored on the south side of the Halifax Yacht Club. From time to time these pleasure craft moored in the basin.

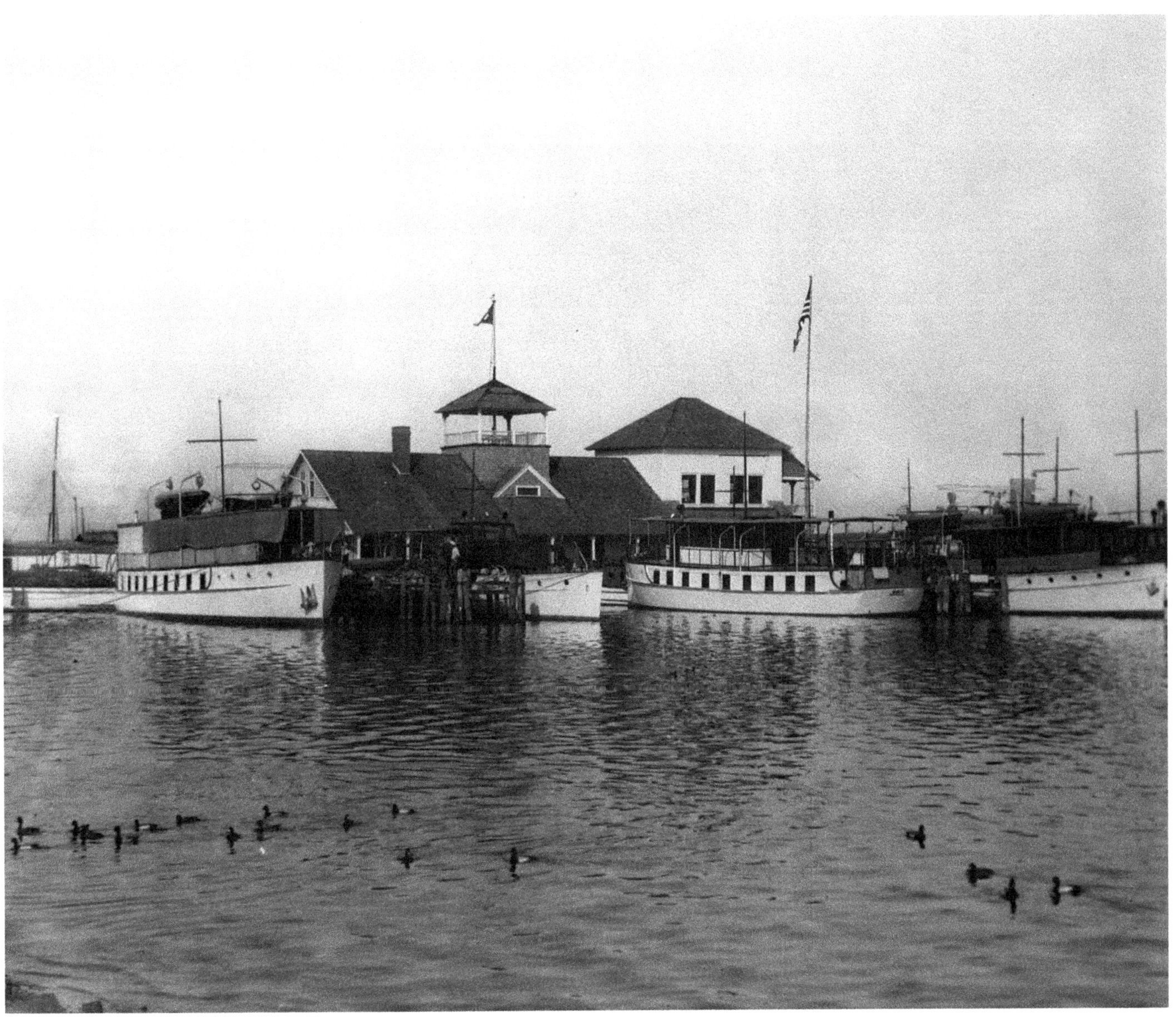

Beauty contests were an attraction advertising the businesses of the Halifax area. These seven contestants are hoping to take first place. The Daytona Beach Pier was a landmark recognized throughout the country.

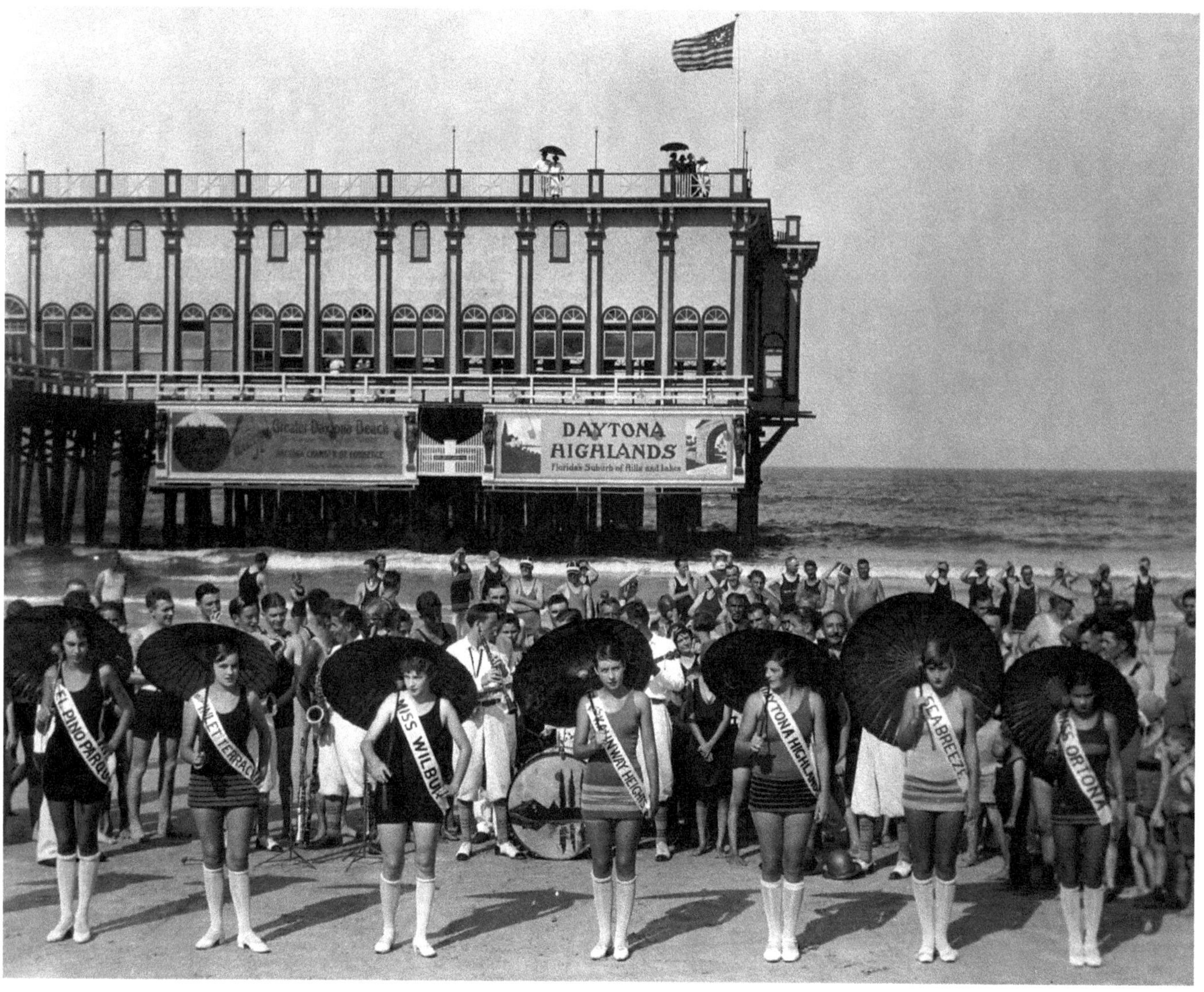

This multi-purpose building was located on Beach Street between First Avenue and Bay Street, where the U.S. Post Office stands today. The bottom floor housed a number of small businesses. This was a popular block for tourists and local citizens to meet and shop.

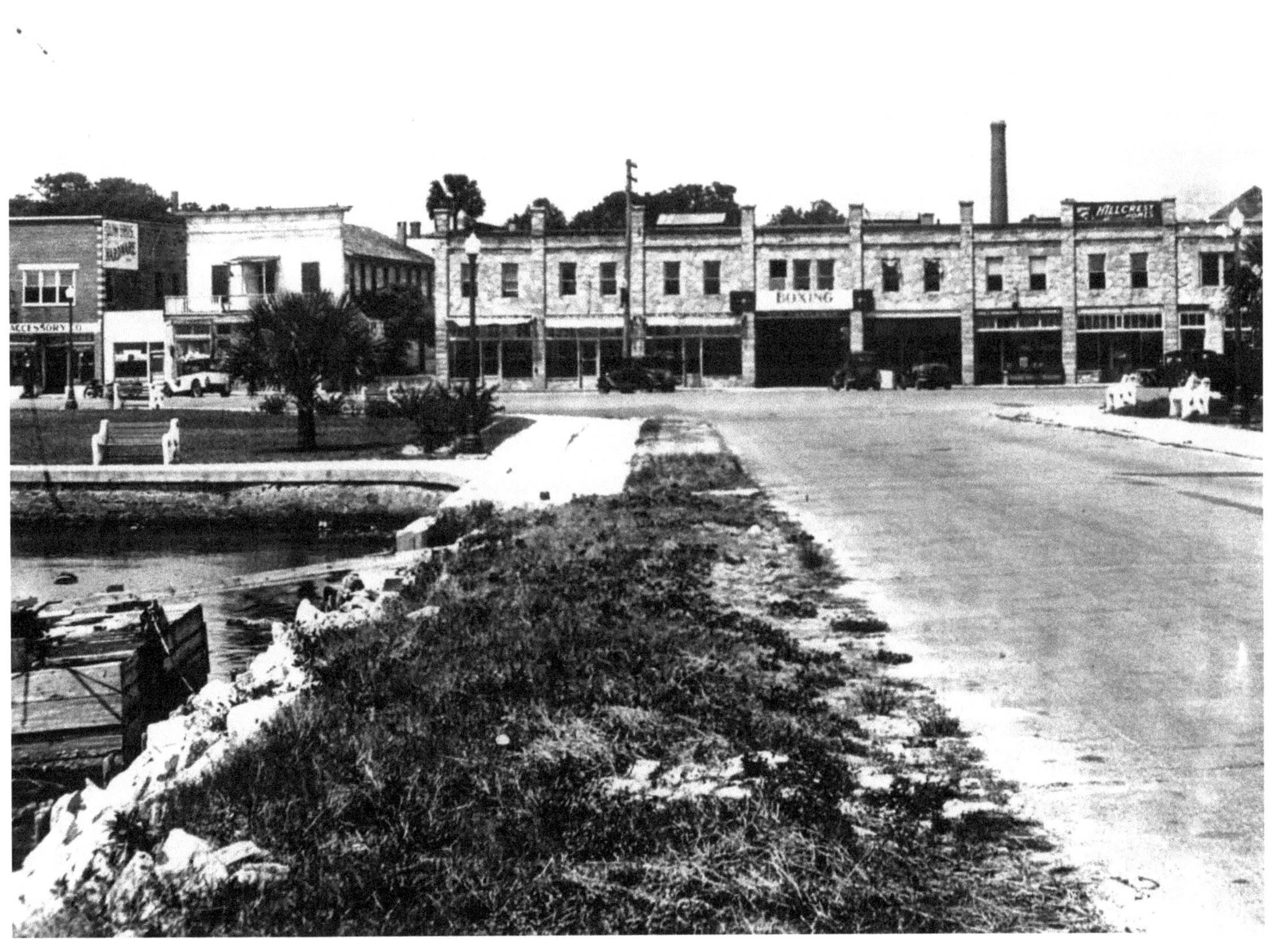

Seaside Inn was a popular hotel for beachgoers. It was located on the northeast corner of Main Street and Ocean Avenue. The year this image was captured, 1926, the three towns of Daytona, Seabreeze, and Daytona Beach were incorporated into one city—Daytona Beach.

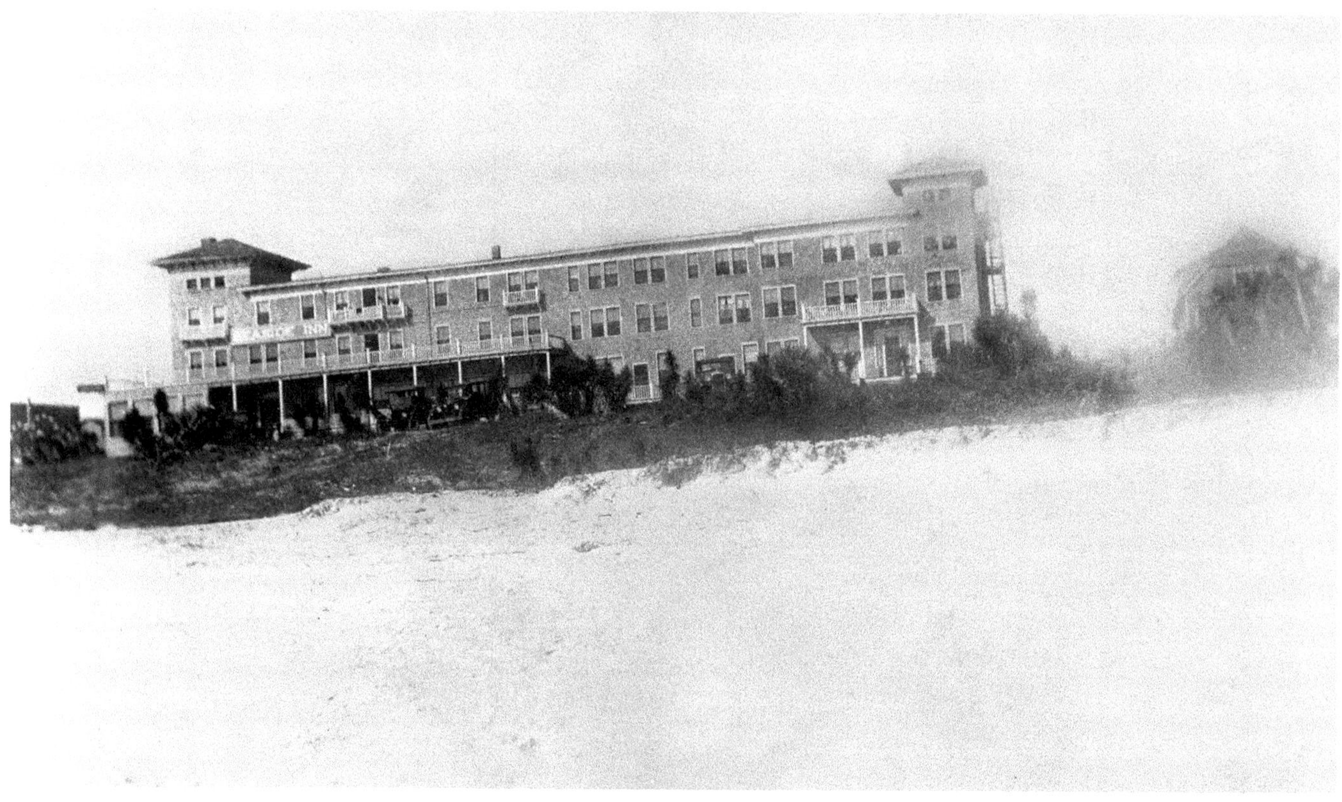

Pepp's Pool was a saltwater pool. Water was pumped in from the ocean. It was located south of Main Street near the Pier. Hotels nearby included the Breakers and several others.

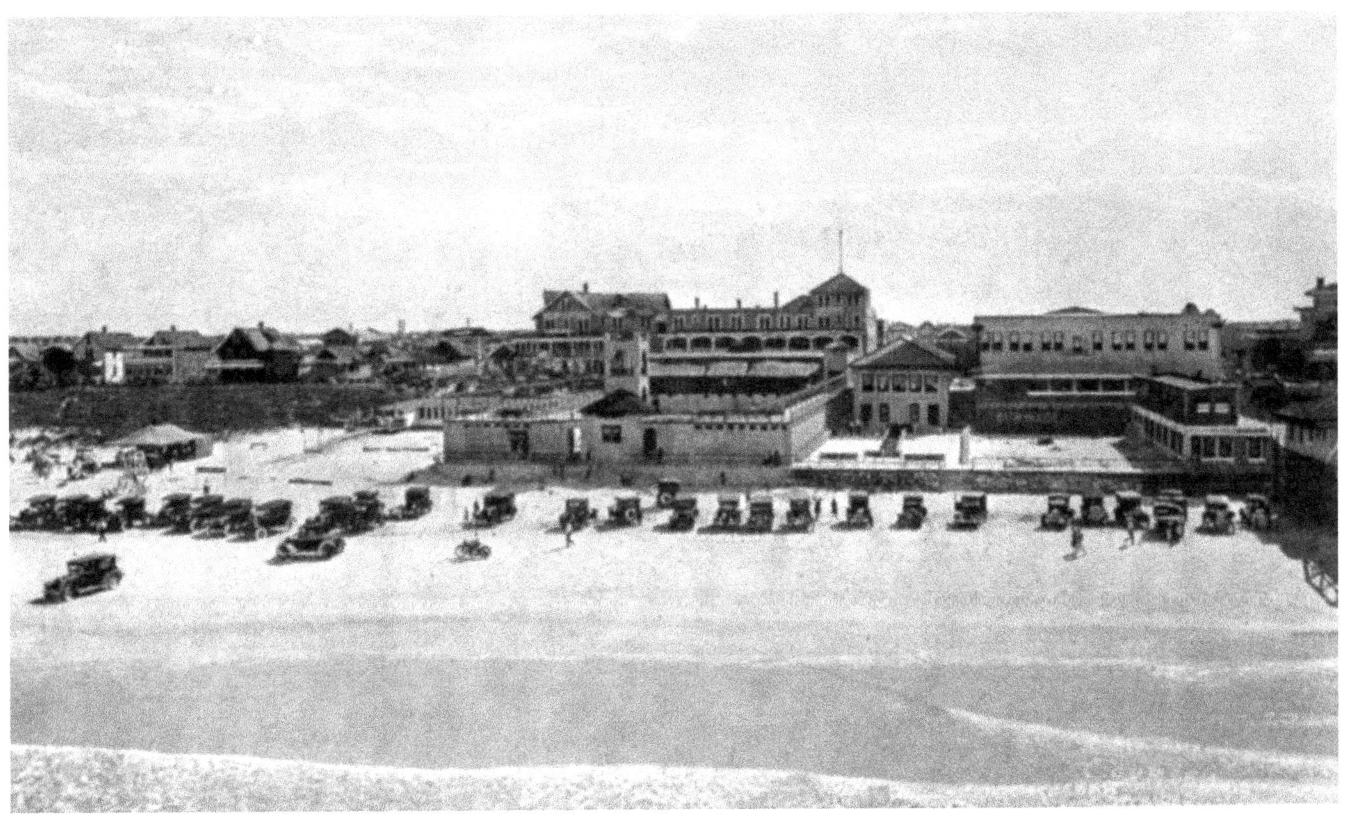

The old News-Journal building was where the *News-Journal* paper started. The roof line was trimmed in red barrel tile giving it an architectural style matching the style promoted in the real estate boom. The News-Journal, the leading newspaper publisher for east Volusia County, published a morning journal and evening news.

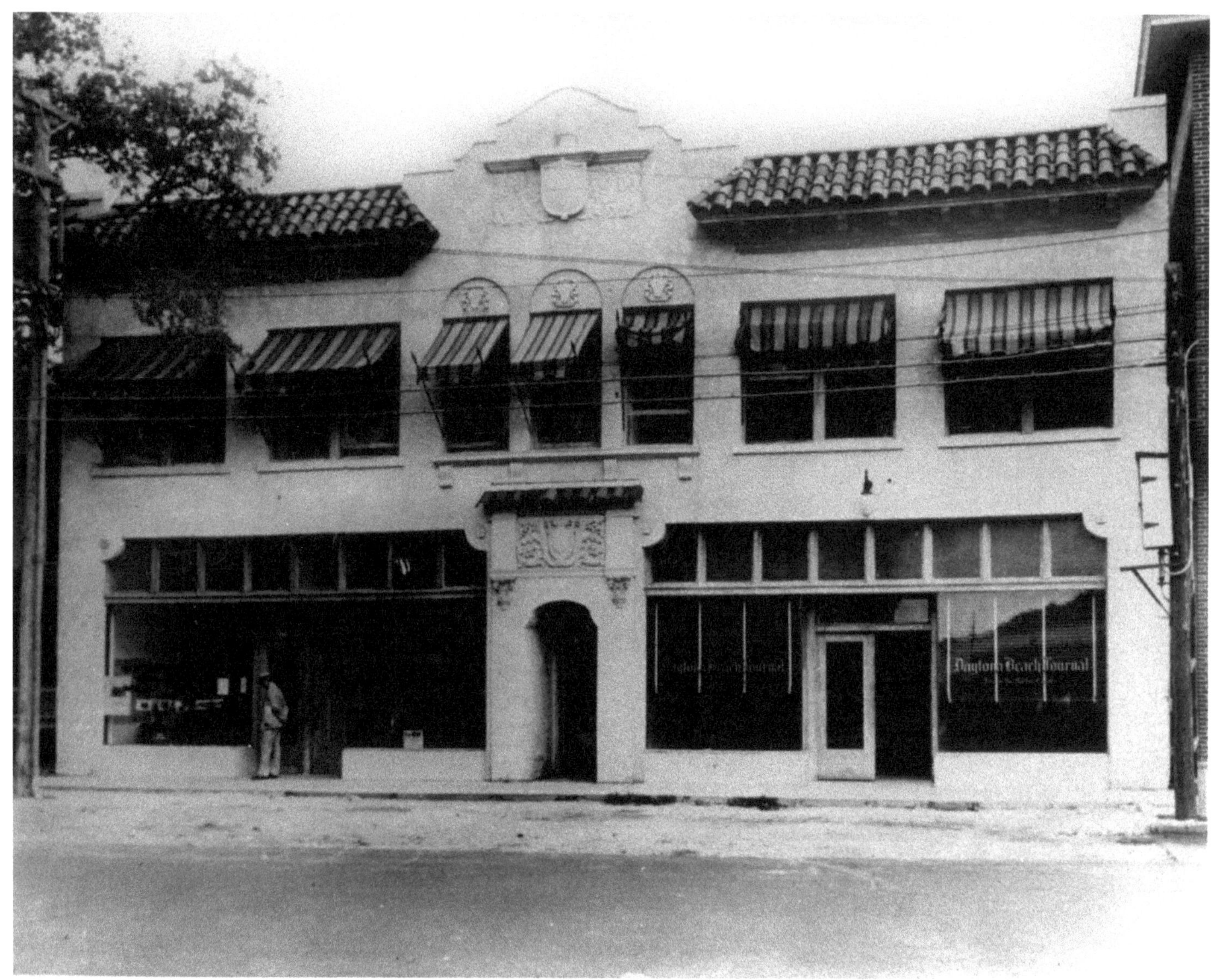

These tourists from the north—(father, mother, and daughter) Rudolph Posner, Marie Posner, and Florence Posner, with a friend—enjoy beverages on an outdoor patio. Their attire considered, the weather must have been cool that day.

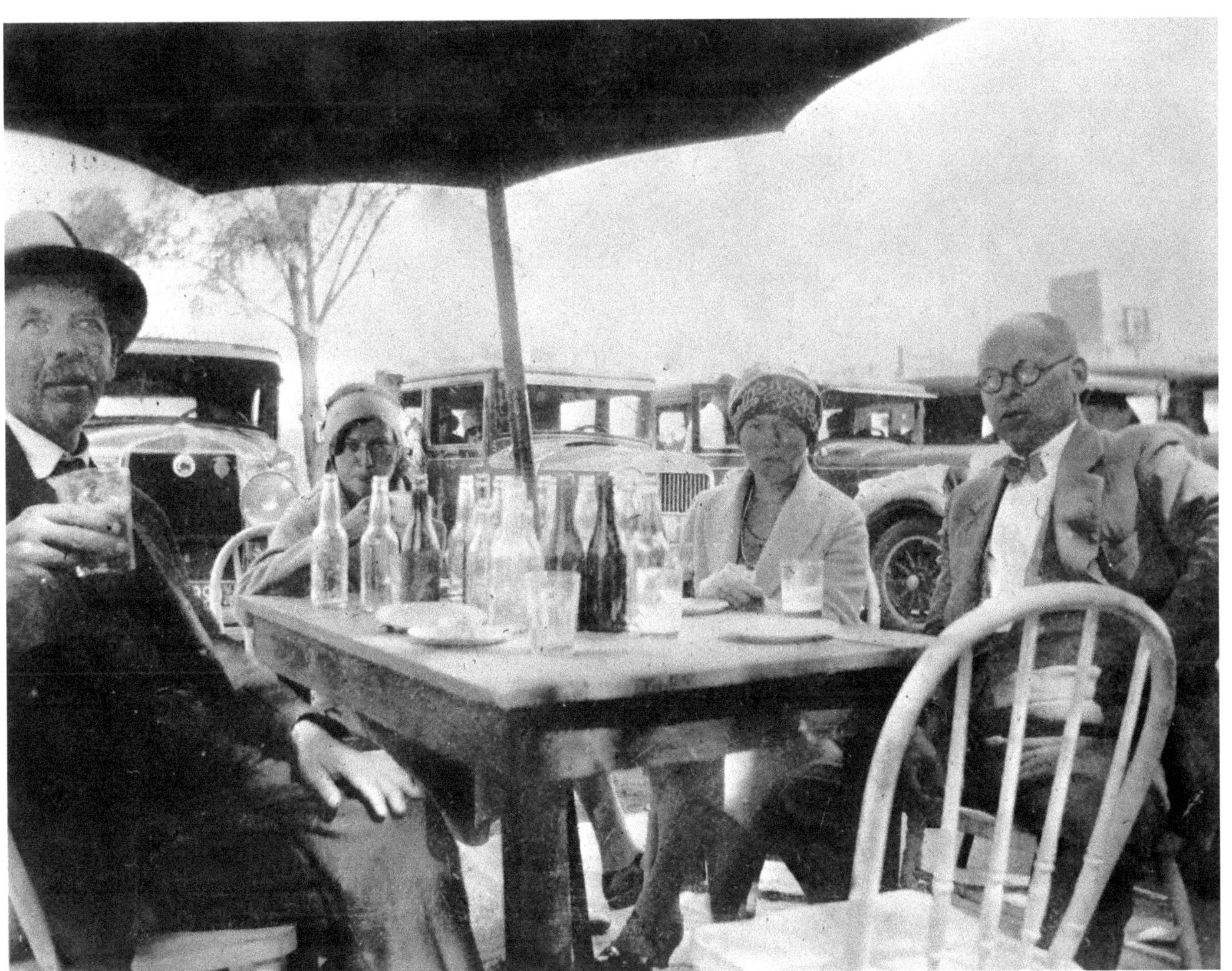

Three days after Kaye Don tried to break the speed record traveling over 190 miles an hour through the measured mile, crowds gather again to see the competition of cars. This early concrete walk, which later became the WPA boardwalk, was a favorite place to view the start of the time trials. This photograph was taken from the Ocean Pier.

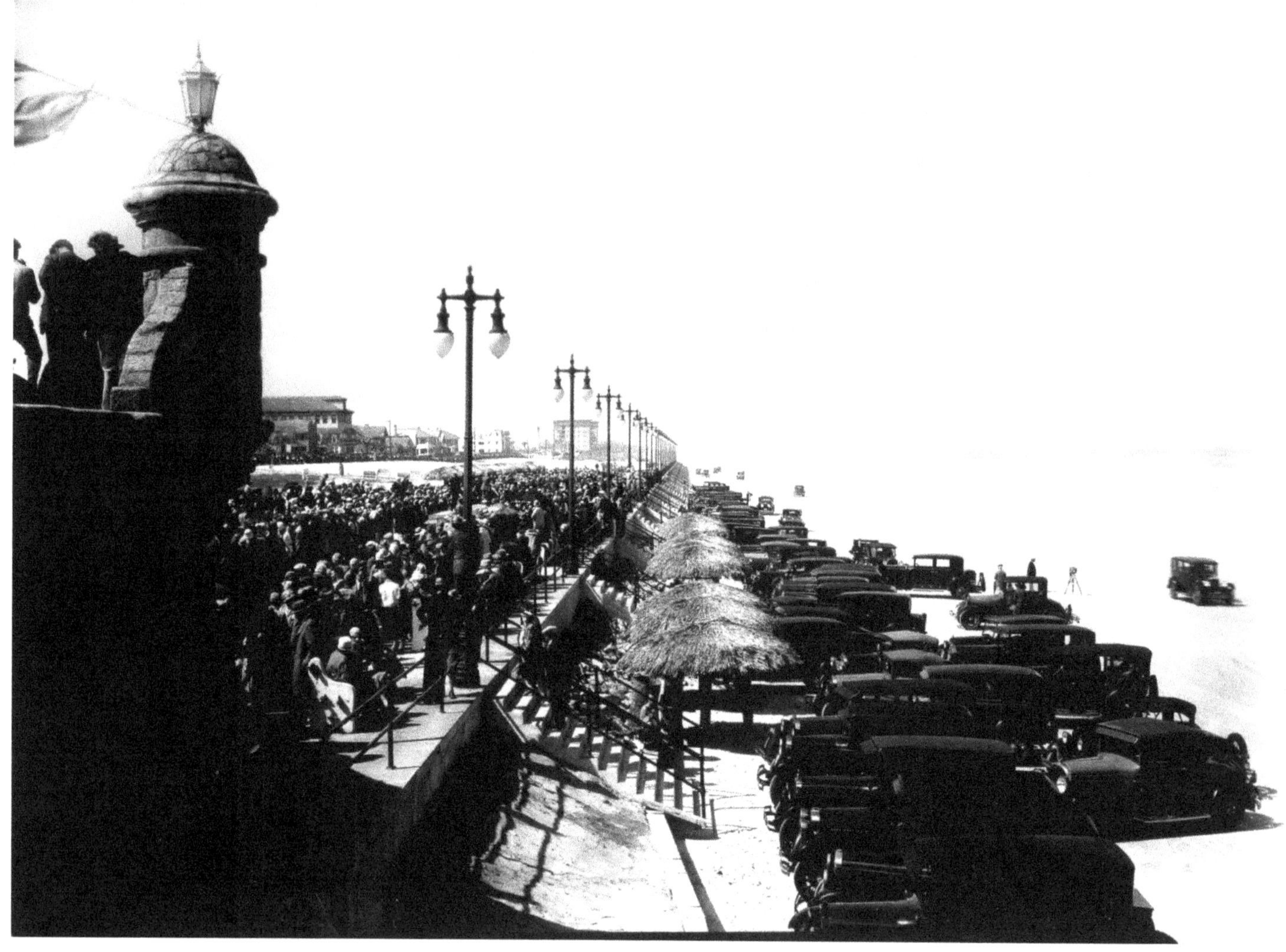

Kaye Don and his Sunbeam Silver Bullet Race Car. This was the longest race car to appear on the beach to run through the measured mile. At 31 feet long, it had rear stabilizing fins, two supercharged V-12 Sunbeam engines, and the driving compartment sat over the rear wheels. Don failed to reach the projected speed.

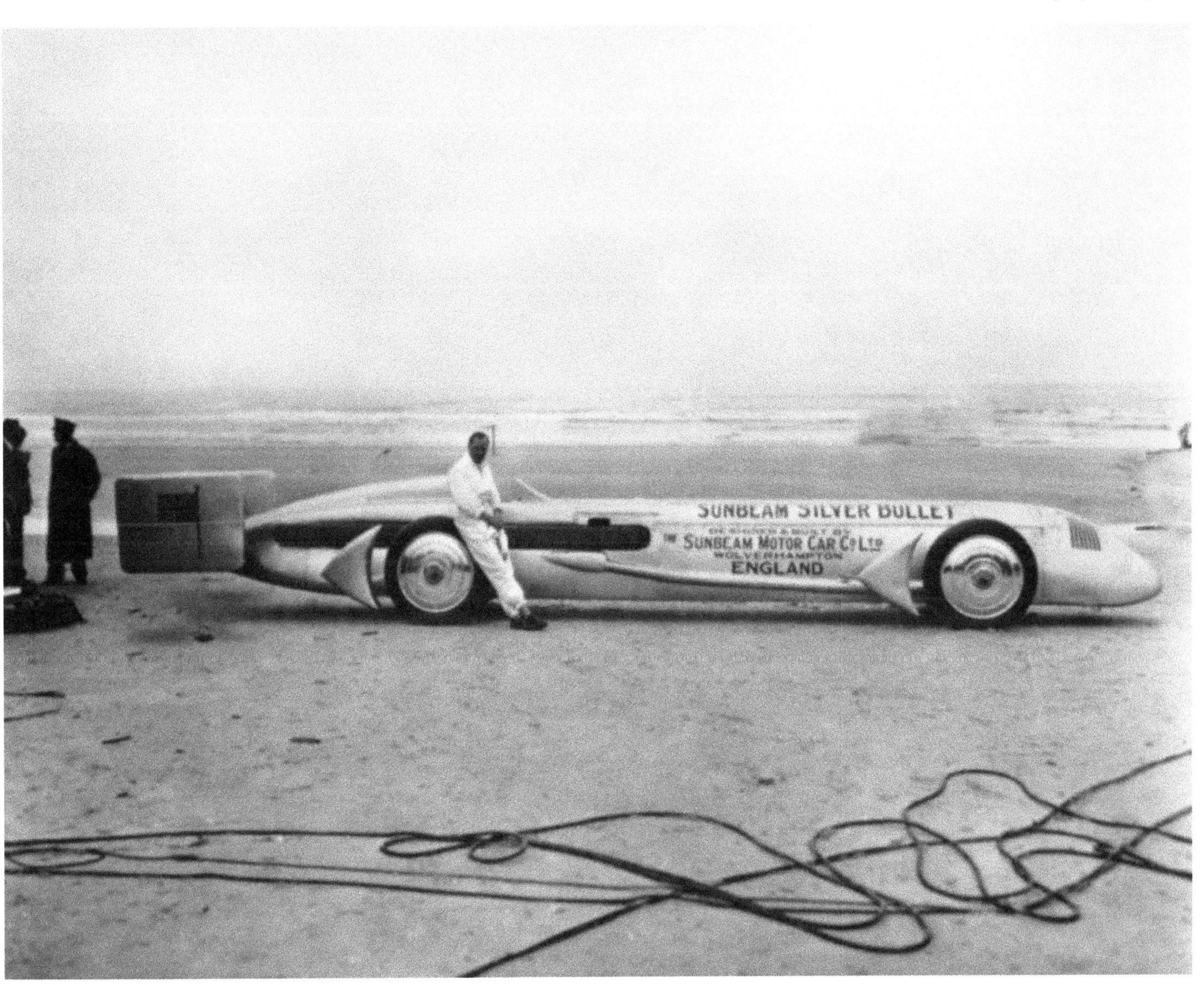

Charles G. Burgoyne died in 1916, but he left a legacy of tourist diversions, including the Burgoyne Shuffleboard Club pictured here. Competition took place on the mainland and the peninsula. Other recreational games, such as lawn bowling, were played near the Beach Street Burgoyne Casino.

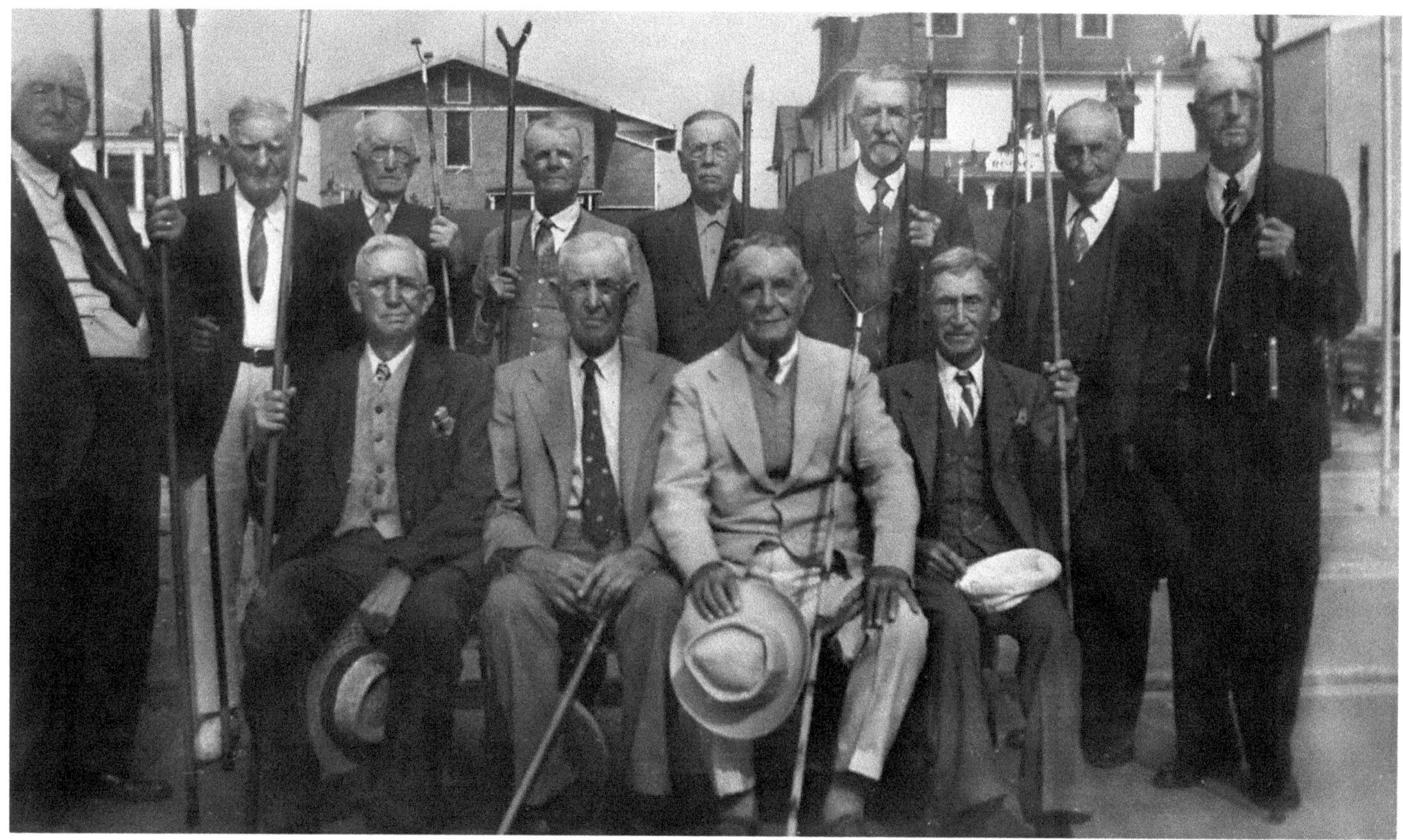

Dave Sholtz campaigns in the summer of 1932 for governor of the state of Florida. Beach Street was always crowded for political rallies. Sholtz's law office was on Beach Street, and he was well known throughout the city.

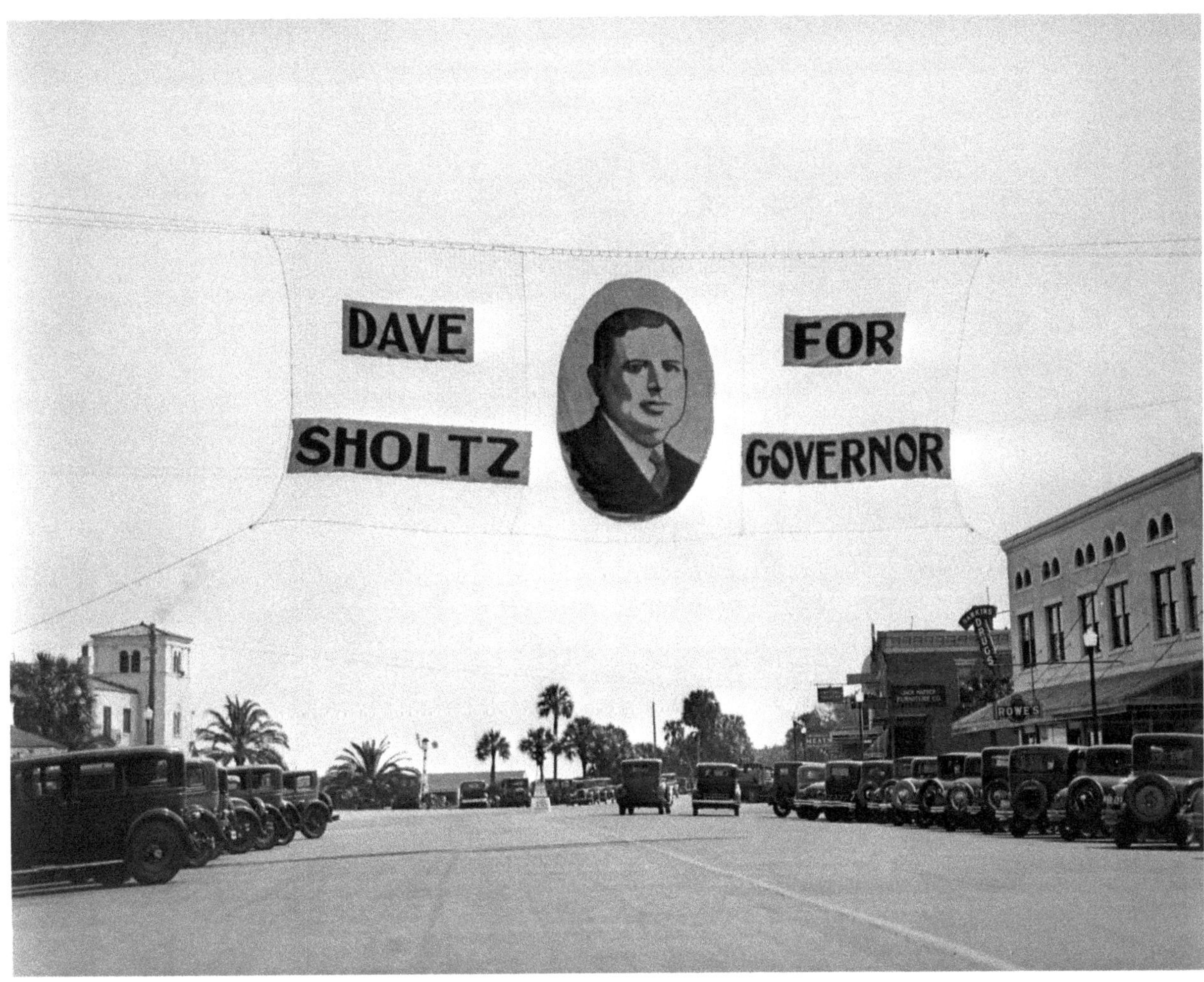

David Sholtz and his wife, Alice May. This couple worked very hard campaigning for the governorship of Florida. Always well dressed with his familiar Palm Beach strawhat, Sholtz traveled throughout Central Florida as the democratic candidate for this office.

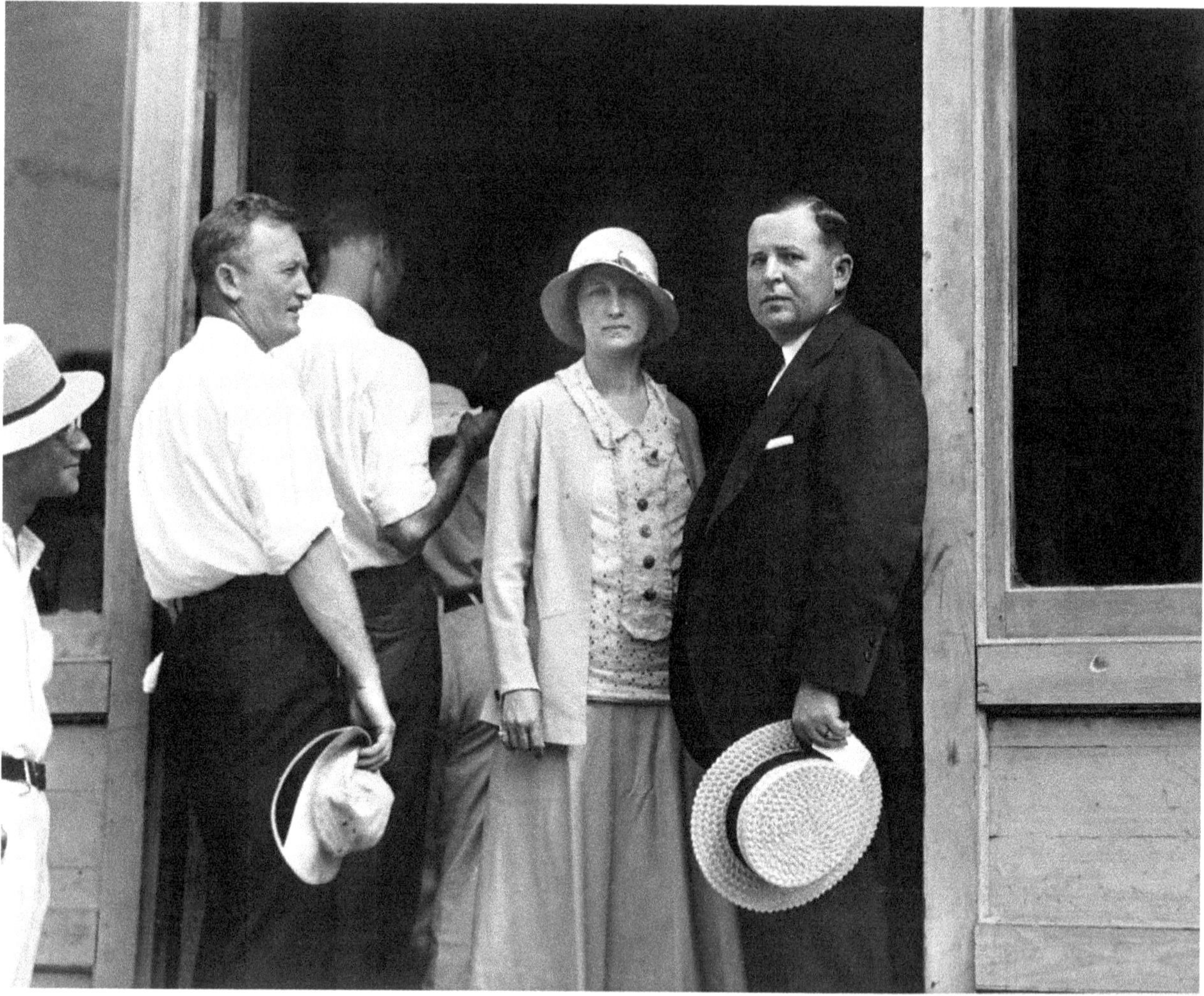

Mr. Strapp worked two clandestine years in Paris, France, to build this race car. He claimed 300 miles per hour on the Daytona sands were possible. The car appears to be designed for speed, but he was unable to substantiate his claims.

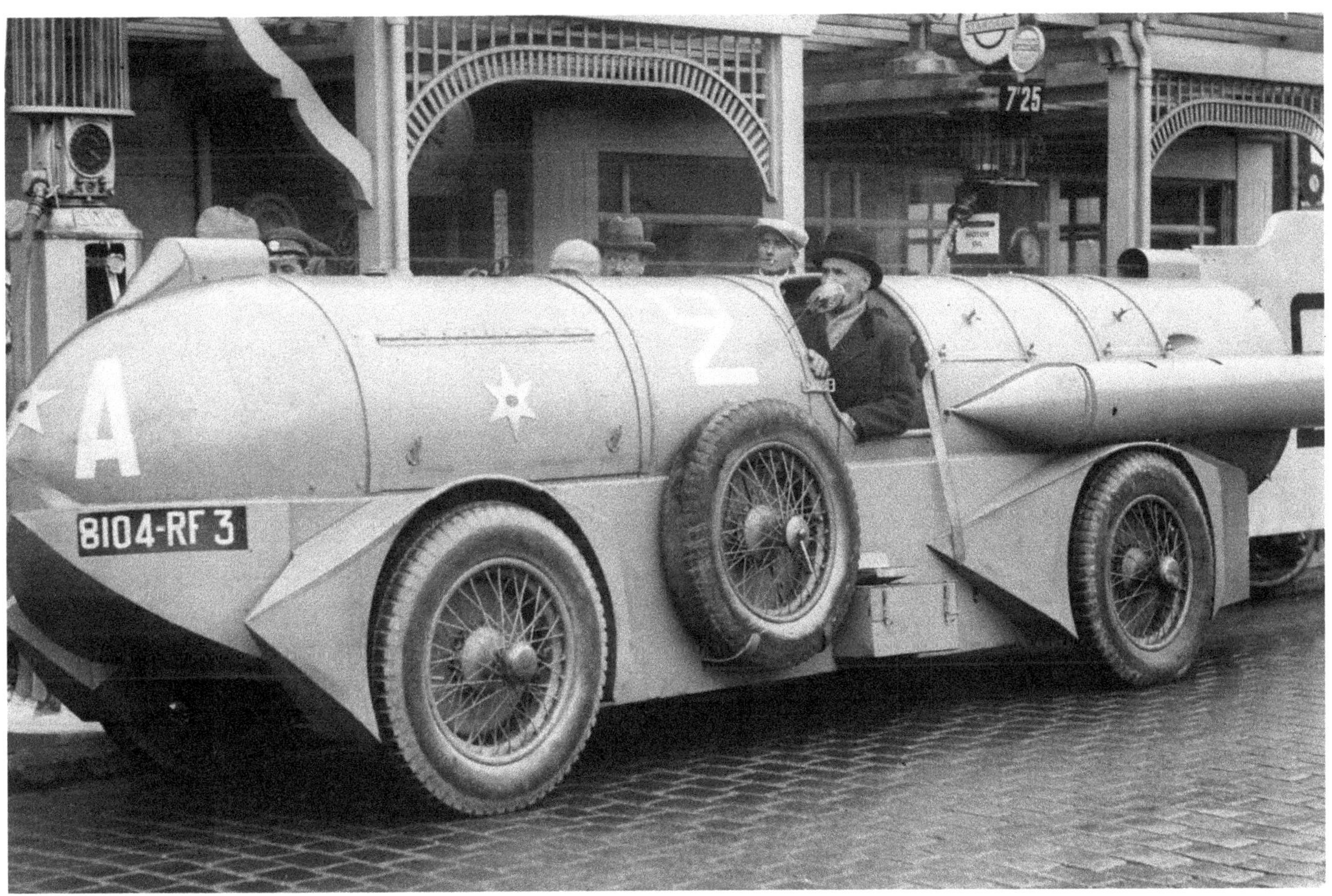

Fun and sun were reason enough for an outing on the beach. These young people, in bathing suits more like those of today than of earlier times, are ready for a brace of ocean air and bravery in the surf.

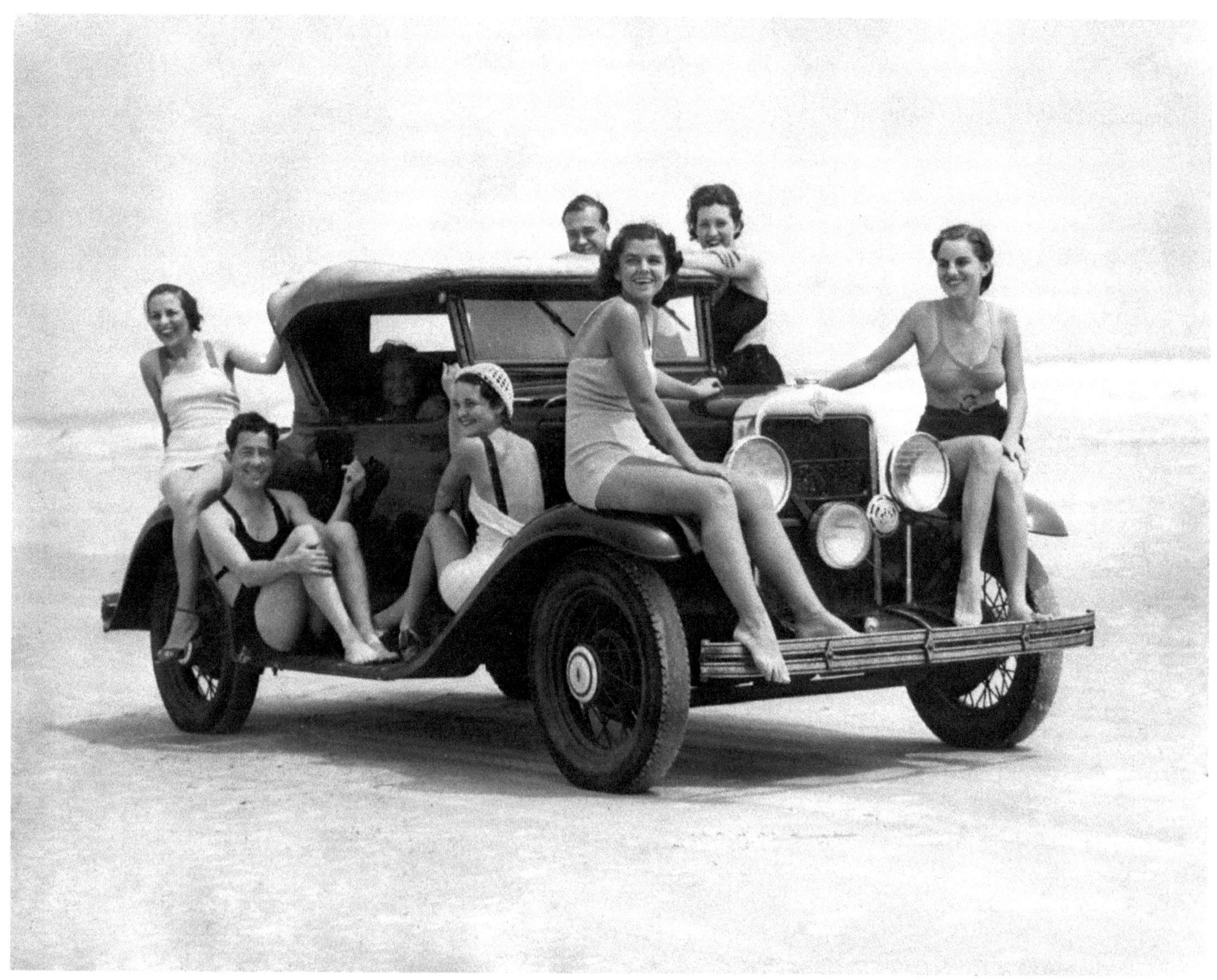

The Shooters Gun Club under construction as a Federal Emergency Relief Administration project. During the Great Depression, jobs and money were scarce. Government aid projects helped provide men the jobs they needed to pay the bills and feed their families.

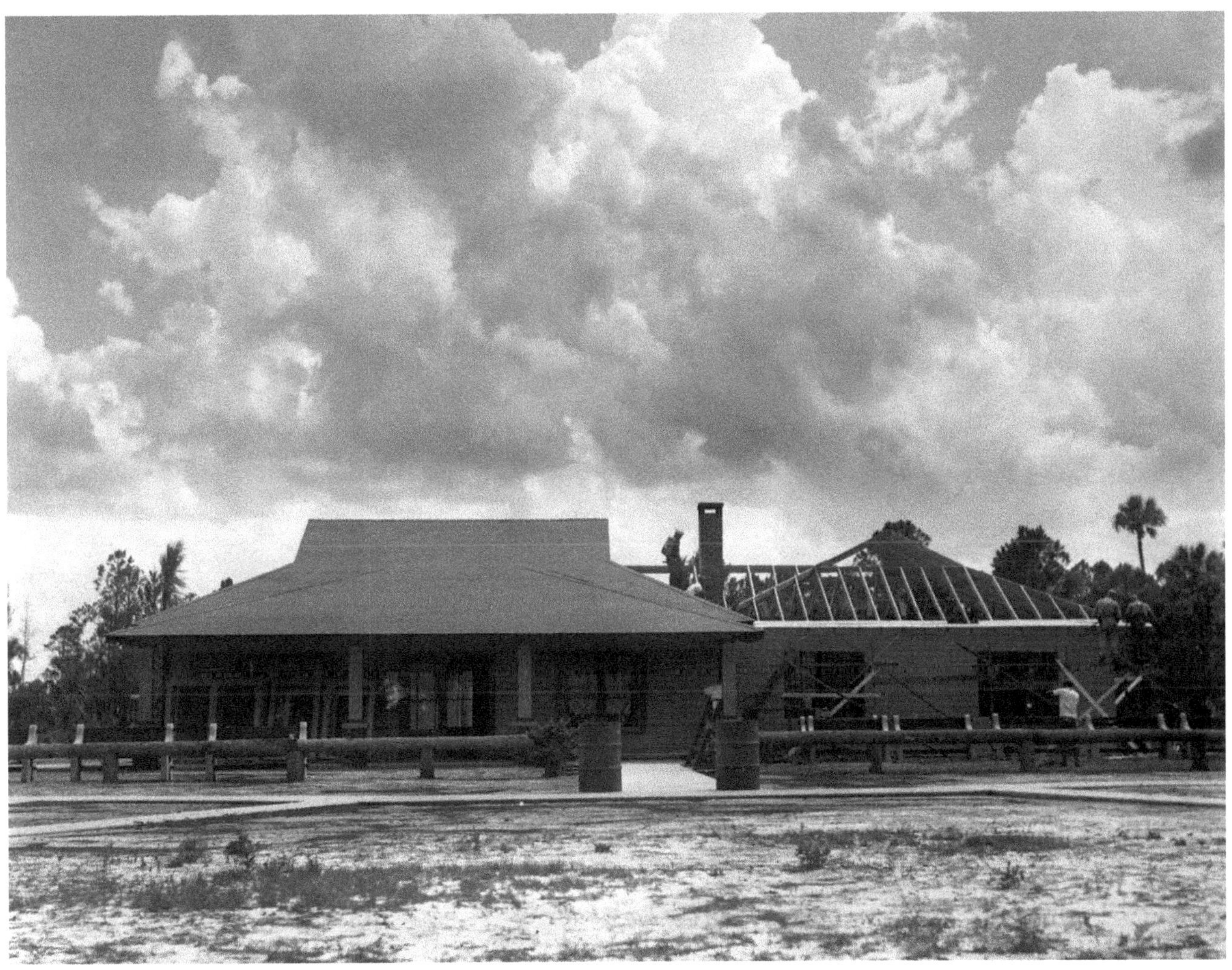

Captain J. Kershaw flew a National Airlines plane—a single engine Ryan. He made the first flight from Daytona Beach to St. Petersburg on October 15, 1934. Like many pilots, he also carried U.S. mail.

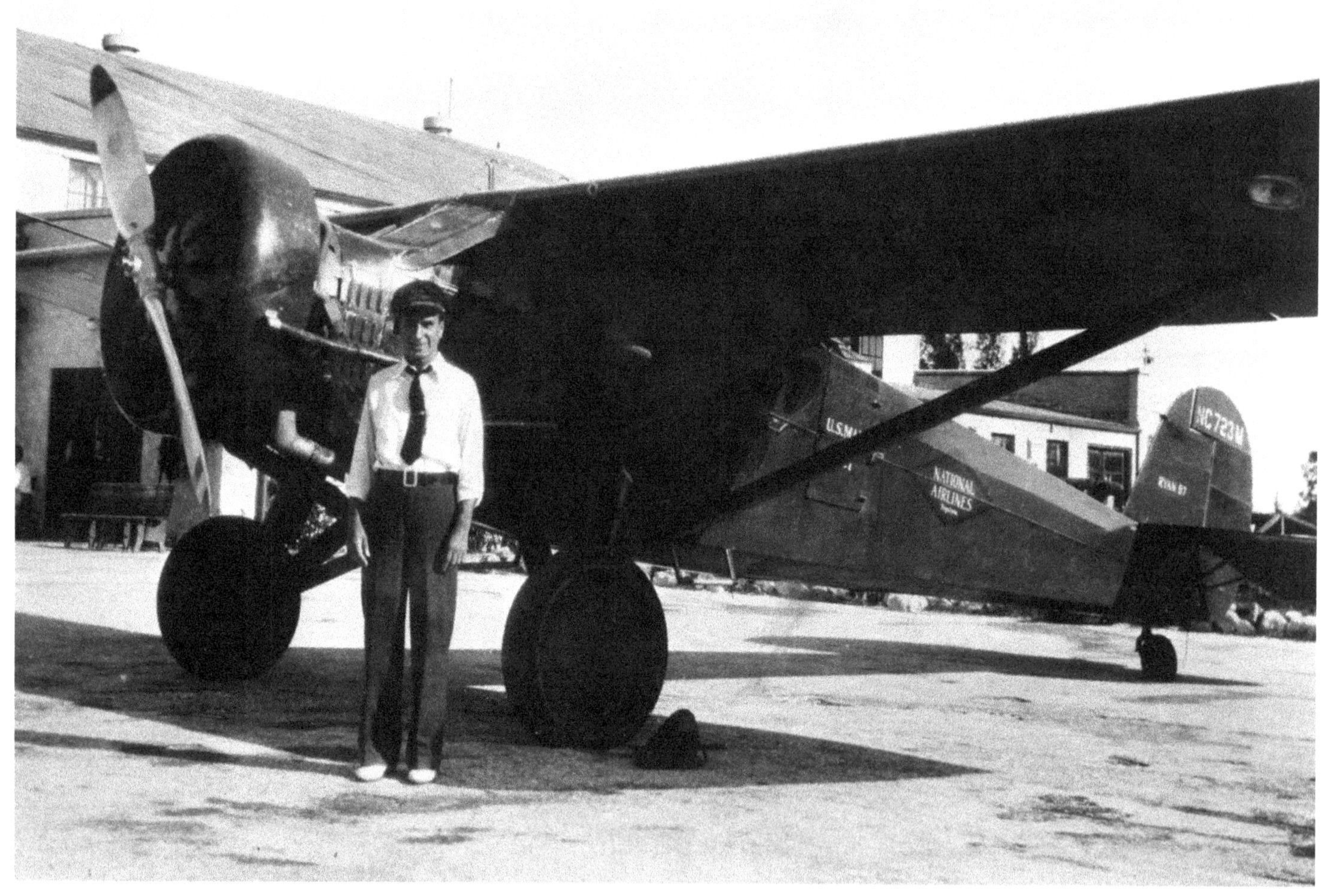

The Federal Emergency Relief Administration assisted with funds to build this shuffleboard court near the baseball field. In the distance the new fire station can be seen. To the left the Halifax River Yacht Club and boat shelter are visible.

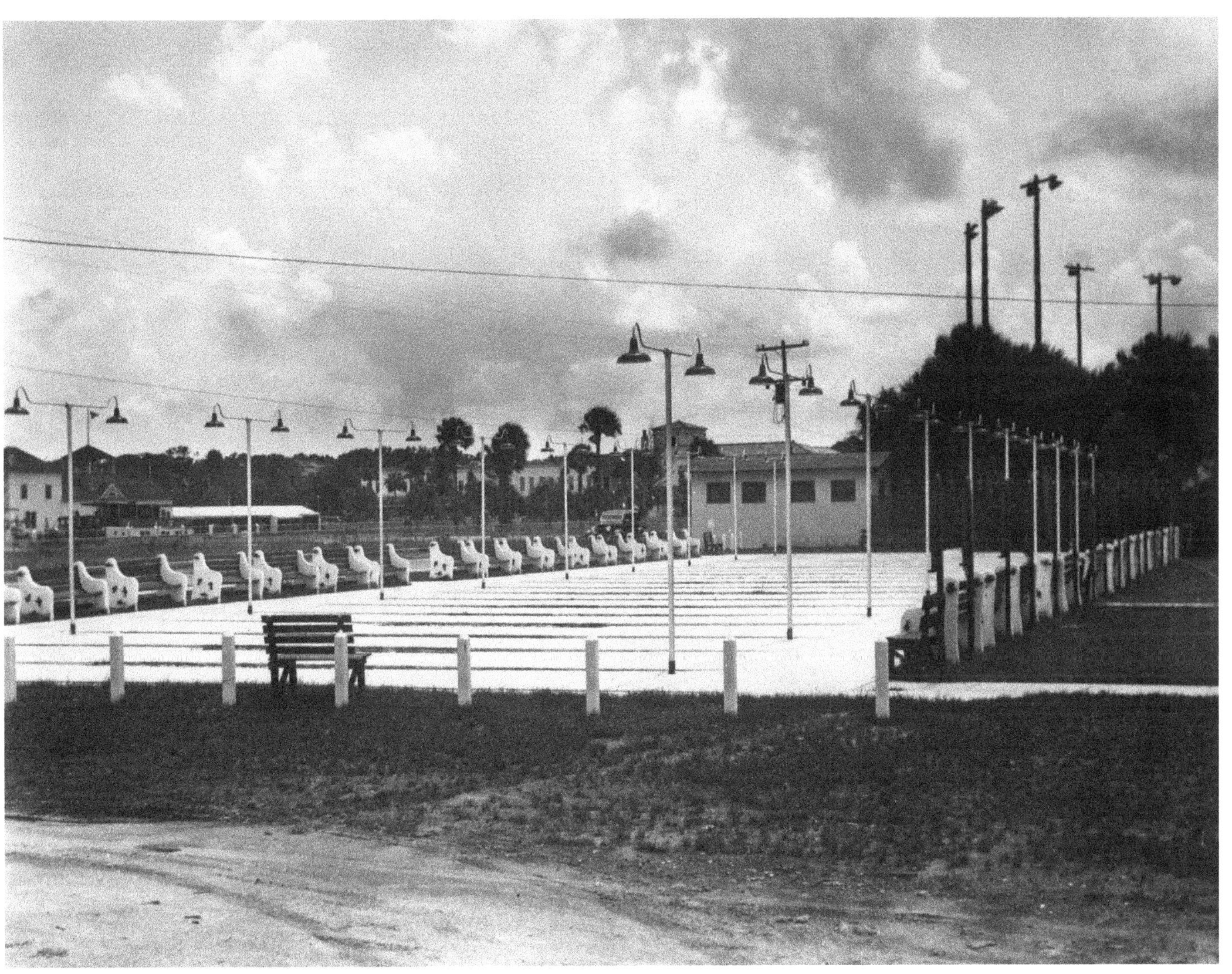

The fashionable three-story Hotel Gilbert on the corner of Main Street and Atlantic Avenue was a destination for winter tourists. The lobby and interiors were up to datewith the latest furnishings. The hotel was known for its wicker chairs and recliners.

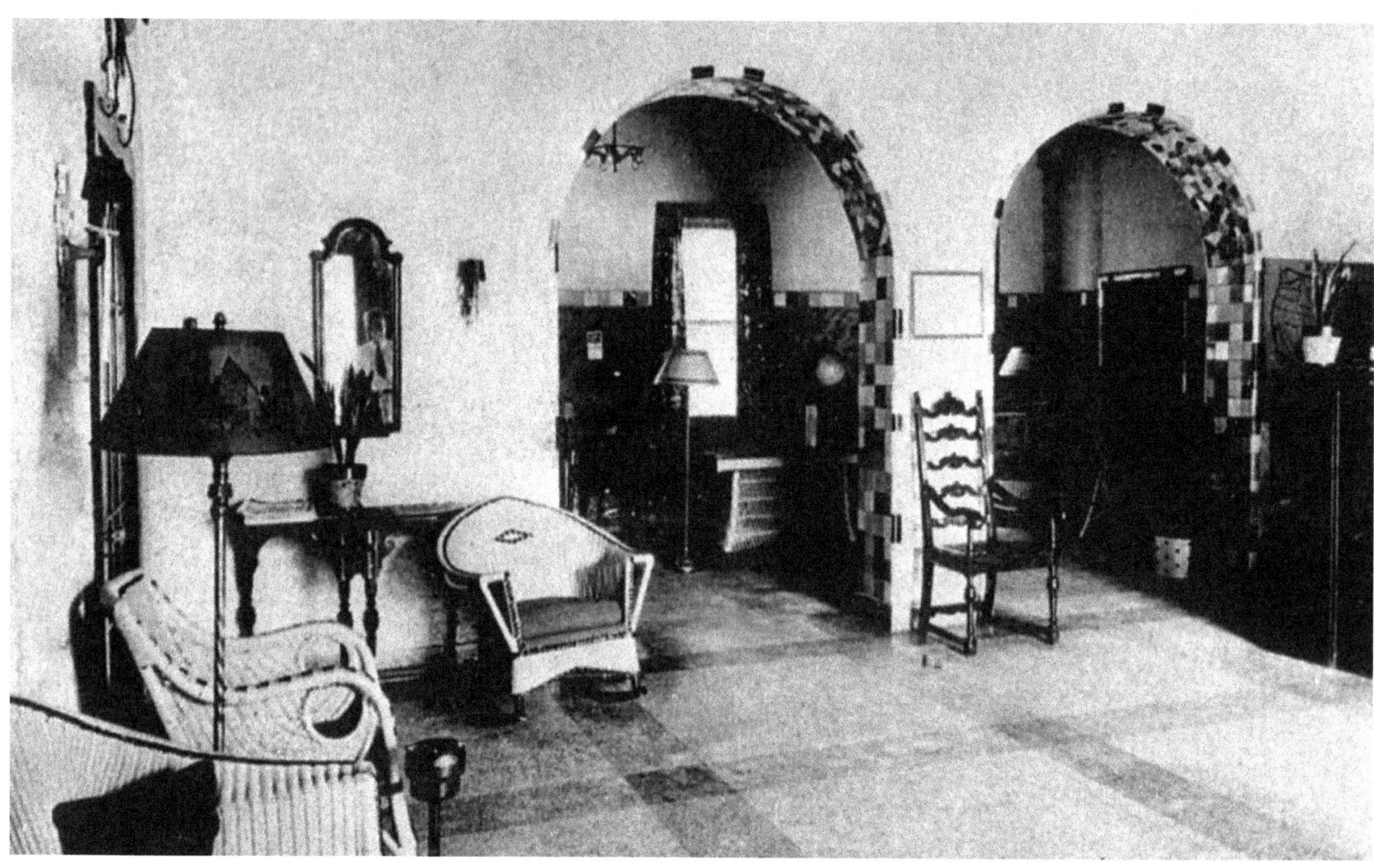

In a view south on Daytona Beach, motels had not yet been built on the sand dunes but there were a few tourist cabins with homes facing Atlantic Avenue. The portable lifeguard tower visible here could be moved during high or low tide.

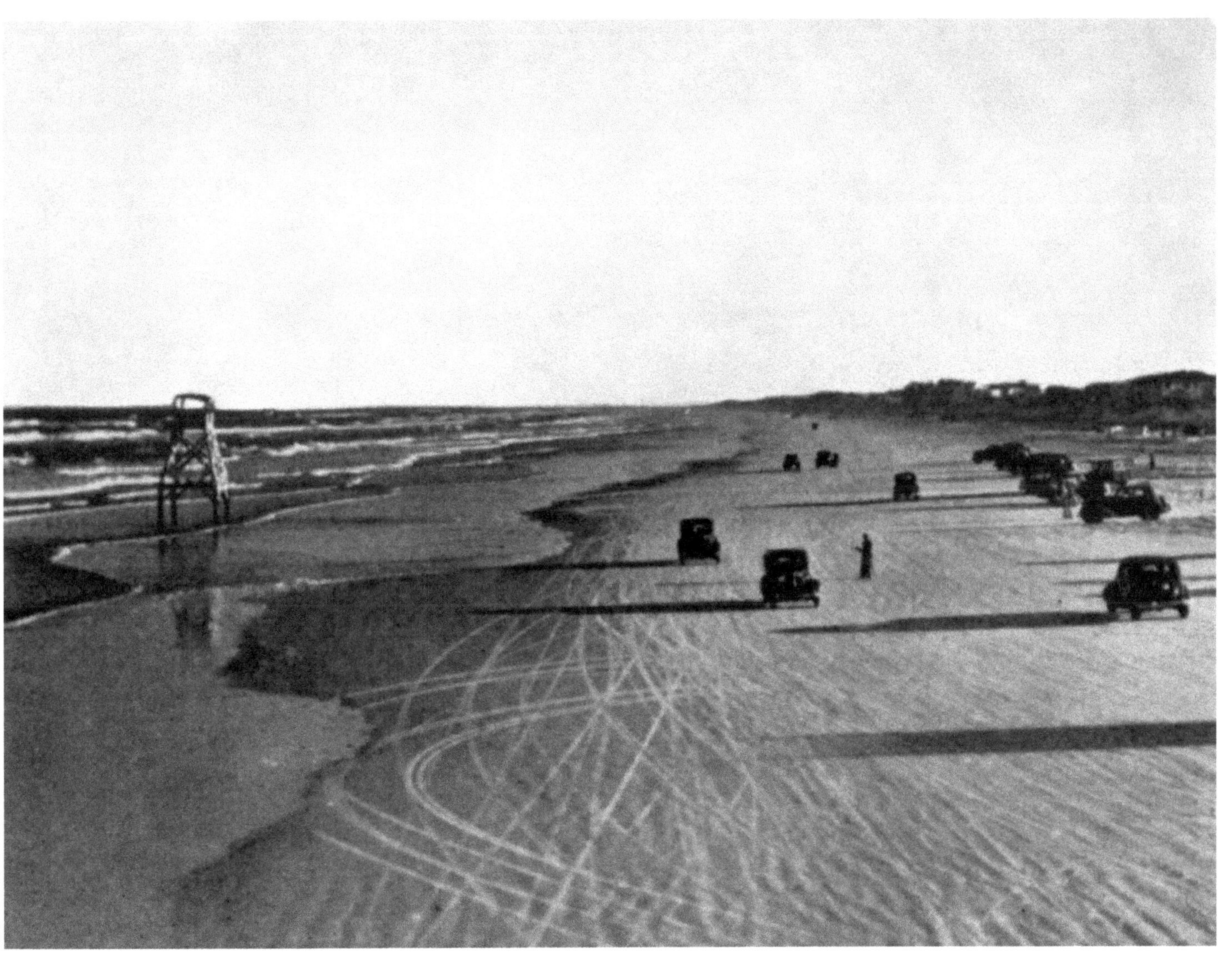

A Florida East Coast passenger train, headed up by a Flagler diesel locomotive, pulls streamlined coaches and Pullman cars. Each winter in this era tourists from the north traveled on these trains to sunny Florida.

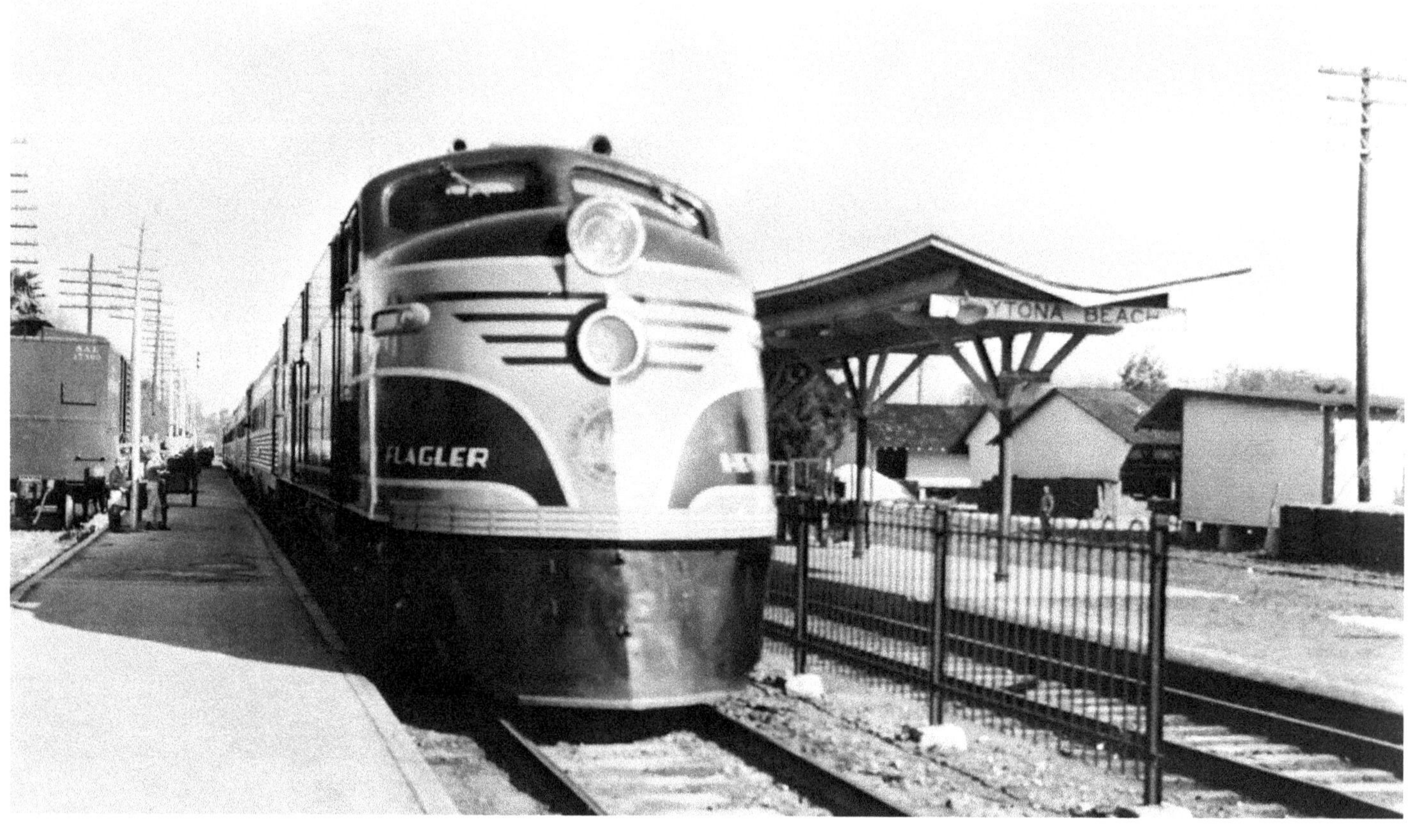

The Boardwalk Clock Tower was a beautiful coquina stone tower that stood as a sentry for the beach area. At boardwalk level was a sculptured fish pool. In the background an underground walkway with stairs led to the street.

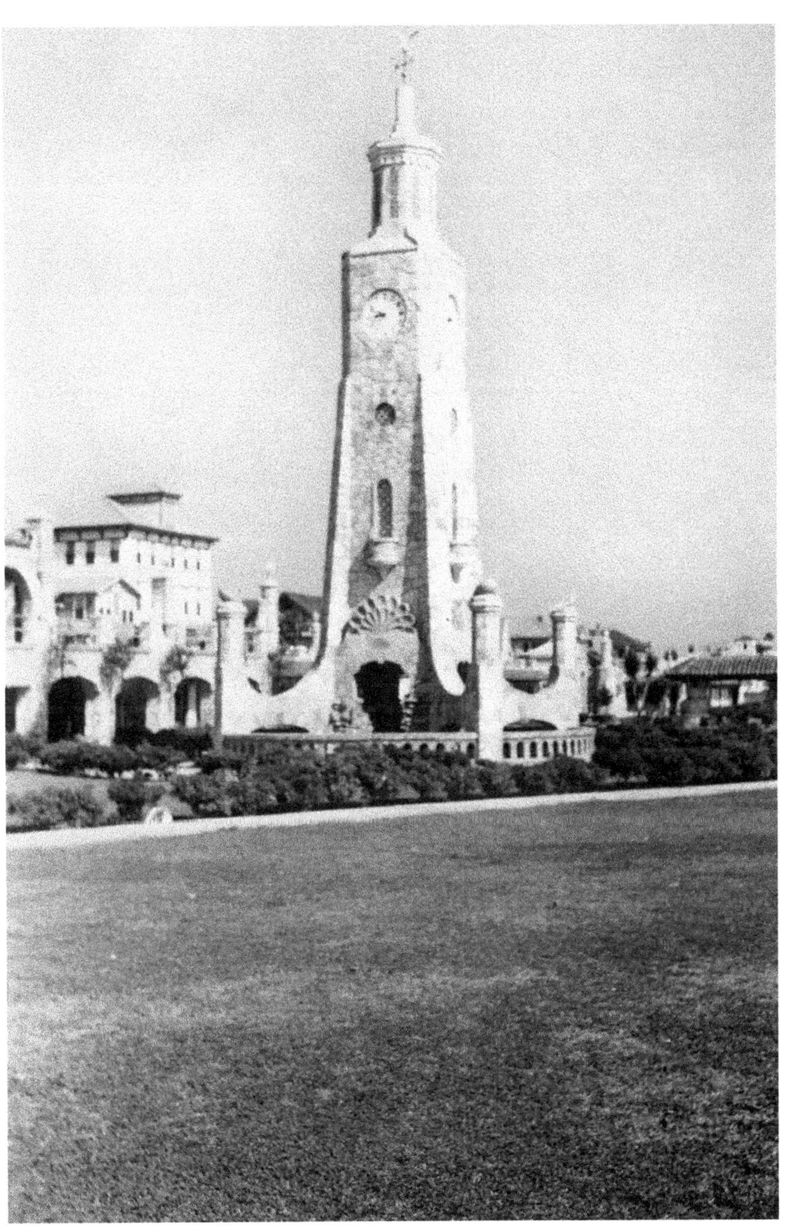

The Daytona Beach Bandshell was a Work Projects Administration (WPA) funded project. With benches of concrete and wood, this large outdoor theater featured coquina rock walls enclosing the seating area.

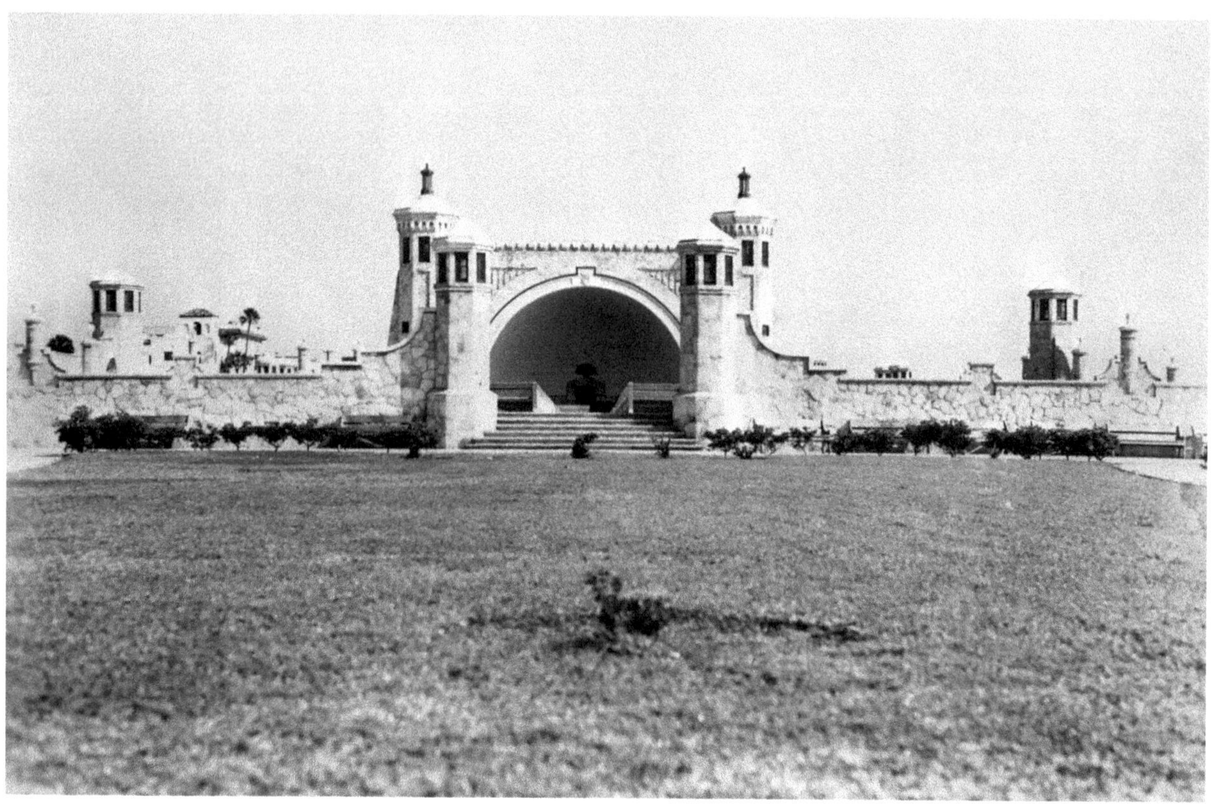

This casino, a landmark along Beach Street, was built by Charles G. Burgoyne, who died in 1916. The photo was taken from City Island depicting the back view of the casino. Shown are the veranda and gazebo, which were used by tourists and local citizens.

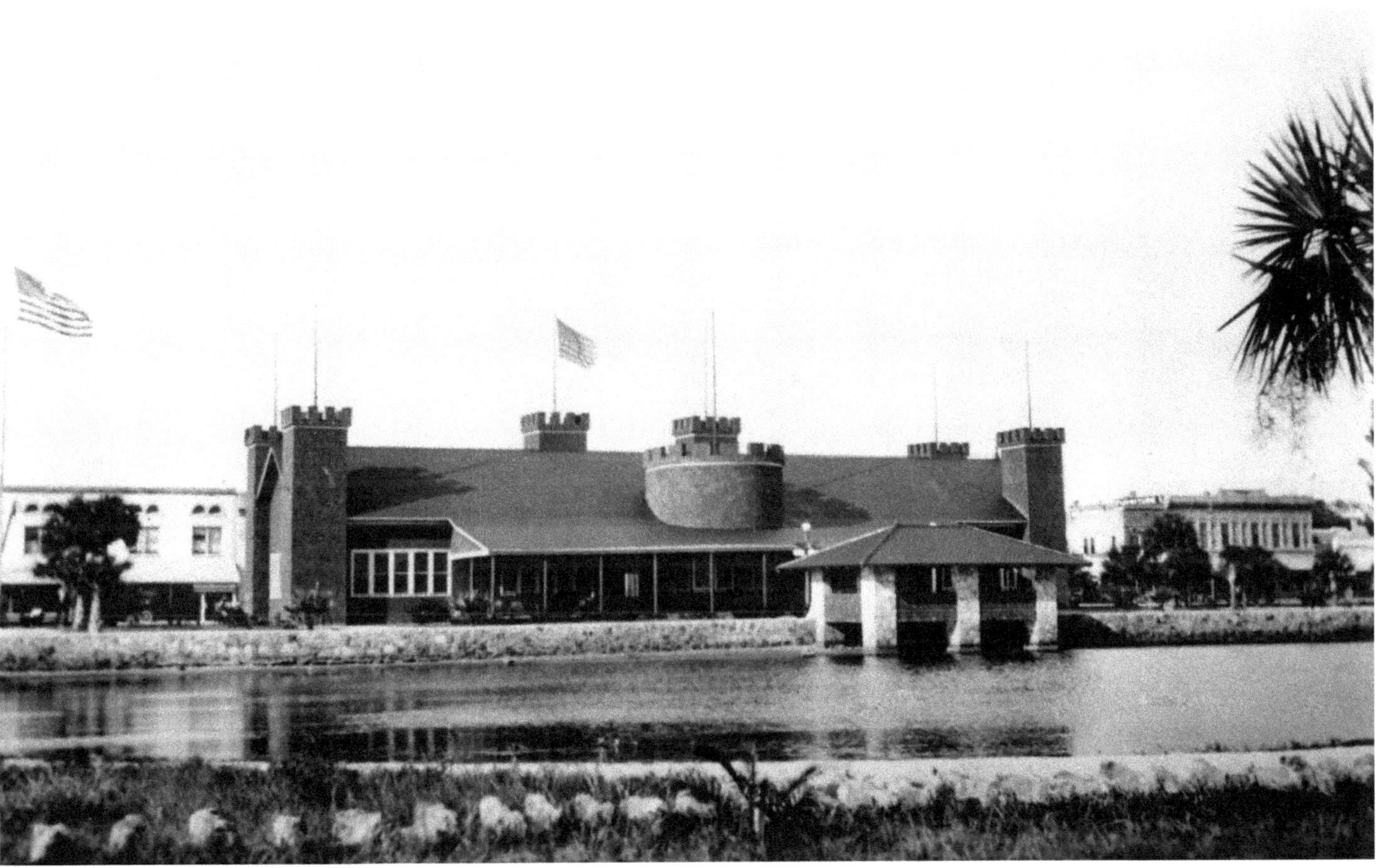

These cars bear the school colors during the Bethune-Cookman College 41st Anniversary celebration. Mary McLeod Bethune was very proud of the accomplishments that had been made.

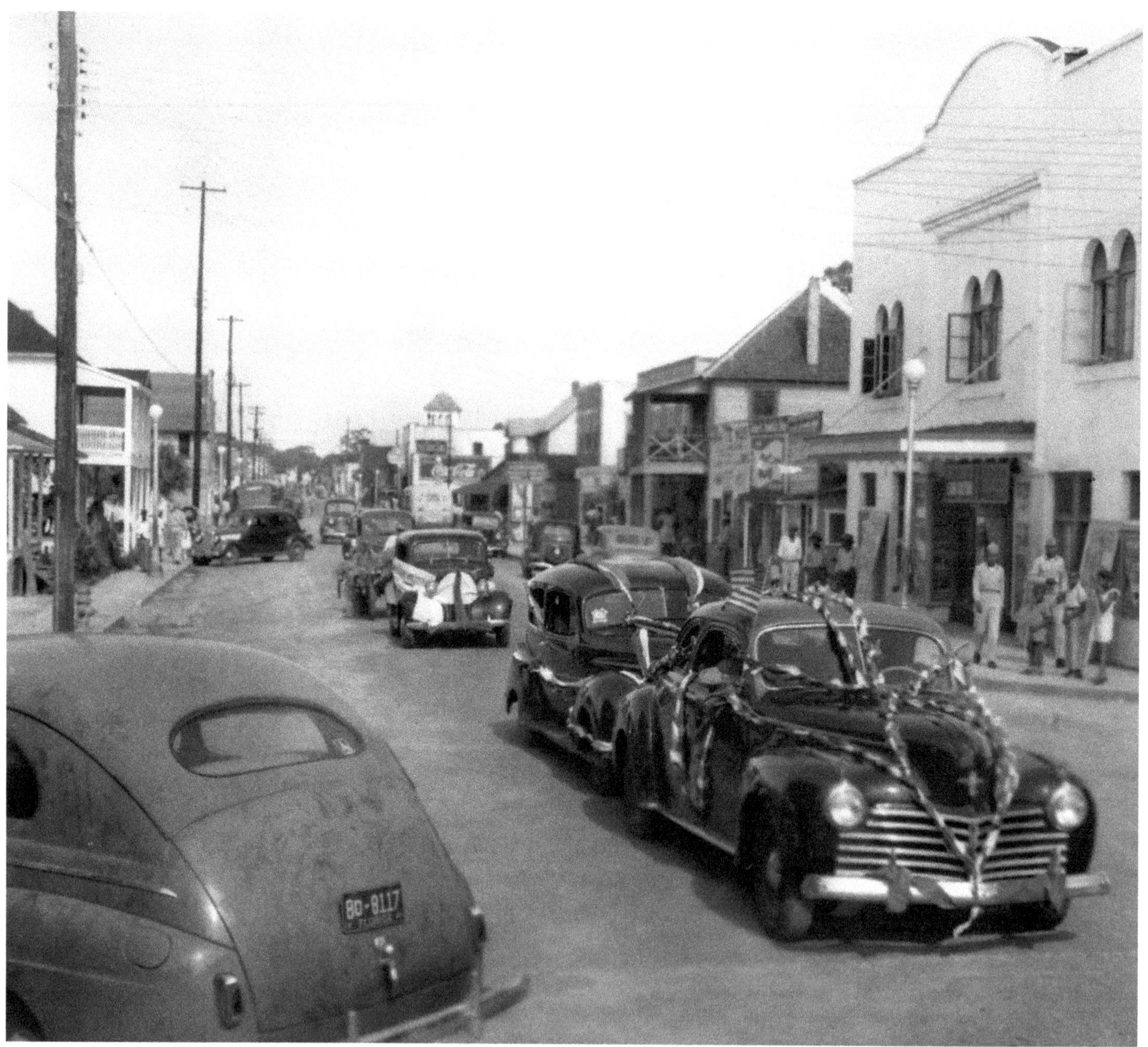

In this view north from the Bandshell tower, picnic shelters and umbrella trees are visible. This area was maintained as a park, and at high tide locals and tourists could park their cars on the street behind the bandshell.

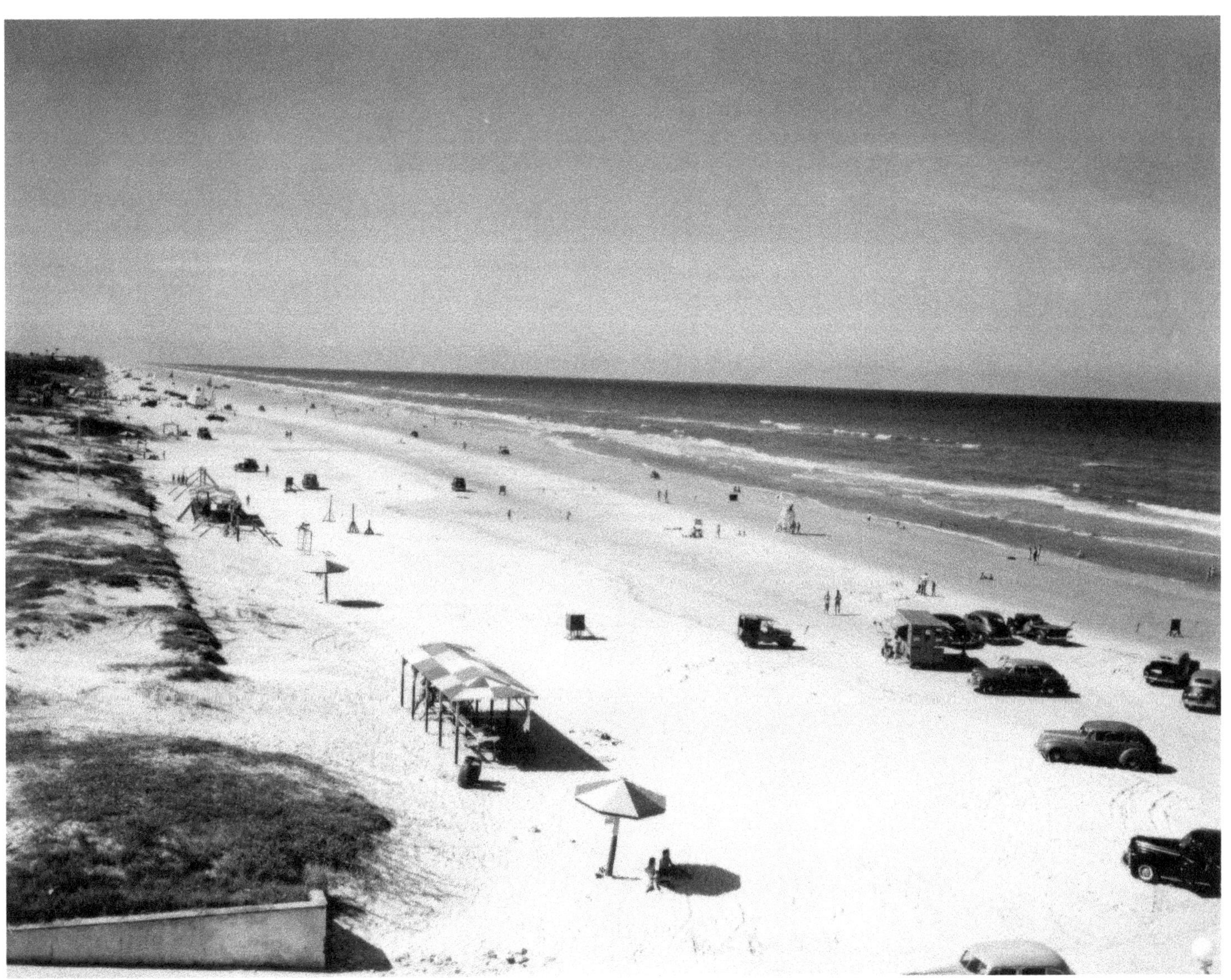

World War II was over and once again the beach was a playground for tourists. Left to right, Shirley Ostroff of Boston and Peggy Devers of Norfolk are enjoying a drive on the beach. These electric cars were a profitable rental service.

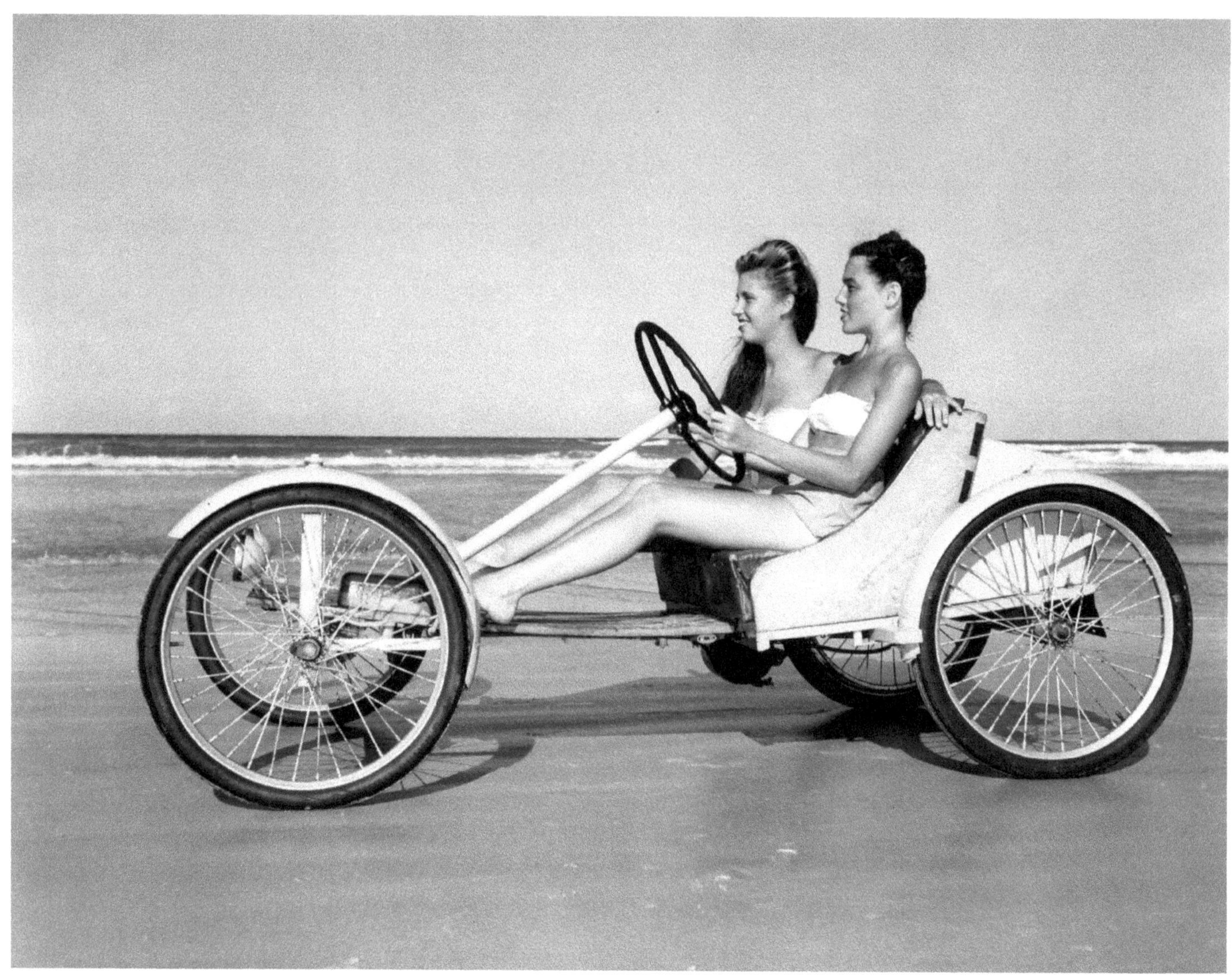

Growth, the Beach, Tourism, and Racing (1946–1965)

Soldiers returning home from the war helped to create a new land boom, and new construction soon followed. New housing and a new era of hotels and motels replaced the old tourist cabins and courts. The first motels to appear were mom-and-pop establishments, but corporations moved in later to erect larger inns and hotels.

After a hiatus during World War II, motorcycle and stock car racing resumed. NASCAR was established in 1947 becoming a draw for tourists and visitors. The 3.5-mile race course was used through 1948 on the beach known as Daytona Shores today. In 1948 a new road-beach course was established at Ponce Inlet. It operated through the 1958 season. Finally Bill France saw the need for a larger international speedway, a dream that became reality in January 1959. Racing on the beach itself came to an end because of the spread of beach houses, motels, and ever-increasing numbers of tourists and race fans, and the challenges of traffic control. Today, the International Speedway is the most outstanding speedway in the world.

The Boardwalk and Bandshell became a popular attraction. Visitors could come to Daytona Beach, visit the boardwalk and bandshell with its Mediterranean-style architecture, and return home feeling they had been in a faraway place. In the evenings, at a time when many homes and automobiles did not have air conditioning, the boardwalk offered relief from the summer heat. Visitors and local citizens, then as today, also enjoyed the cooling ocean breezes. Families gathered to enjoy band concerts and beauty contests, and to participate in the midway and other recreational attractions.

Mary McLeod Bethune died in May 1955, but her spirit and inspiration lived on in a college, and the college grew. Bethune Cookman College was established primarily for African American students, but all races are represented at the school today. Embry Riddle Aeronautical University moved from Miami to Daytona Beach, and Daytona Beach Junior College (later Community College) and the University of Central Florida were established on the old U.S. Army Convalescence Center grounds. Halifax Hospital was also improved.

As the 1960s approached, Daytona Beach could look forward to a future of prosperity as an important destination for Americans seeking warmer climes and an array of diversions.

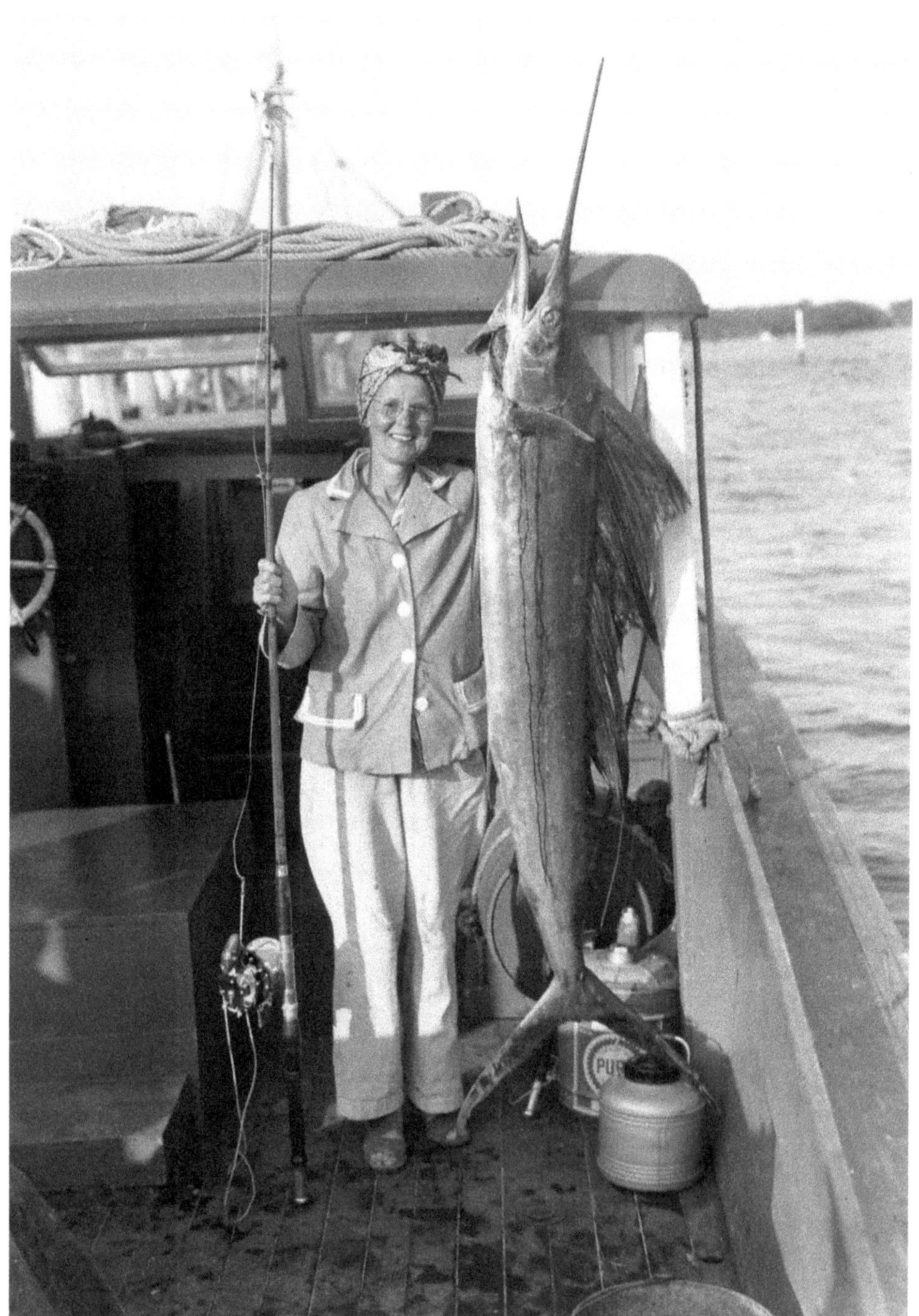

Some tourists, then as now, came to Daytona Beach to enjoy the beach and some came to enjoy the fishing. Nannie Boaz of Nashville, Tennessee, catches a 40-pound sailfish over 6 feet long, several miles out on a party boat. Fishing tournaments were held each year in the Daytona Beach area.

Beach trams have always been popular on day and night tours. Often tram drivers would pick up the passengers at the hotels, motels, and near the boardwalk. The price of the tour pictured here was 25 cents a person.

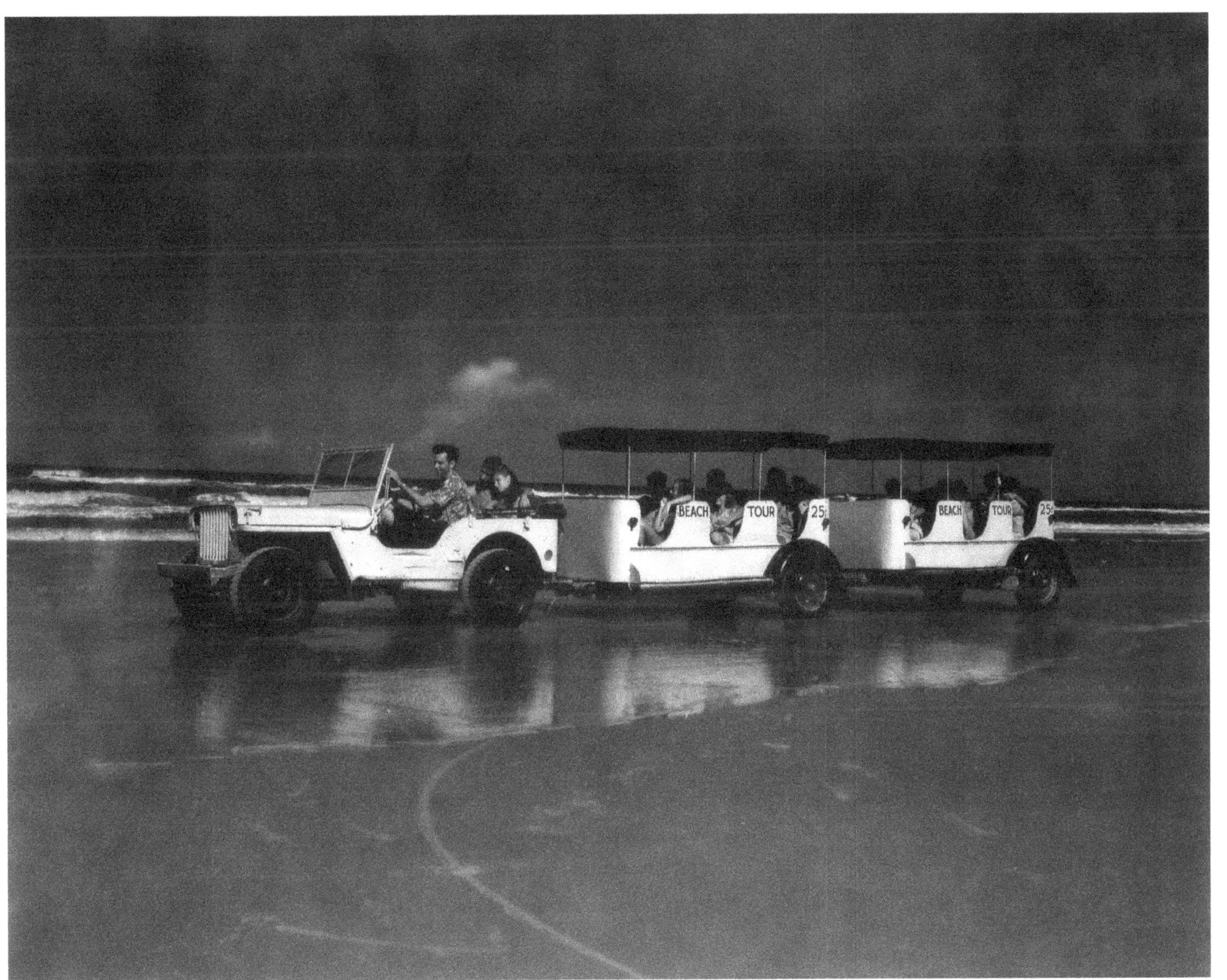

Looking south from the bandshell, the south wall of the outdoor theater can be seen. Farther south are concessions and to the right the clock tower. On the left in the distance is the ocean pier.

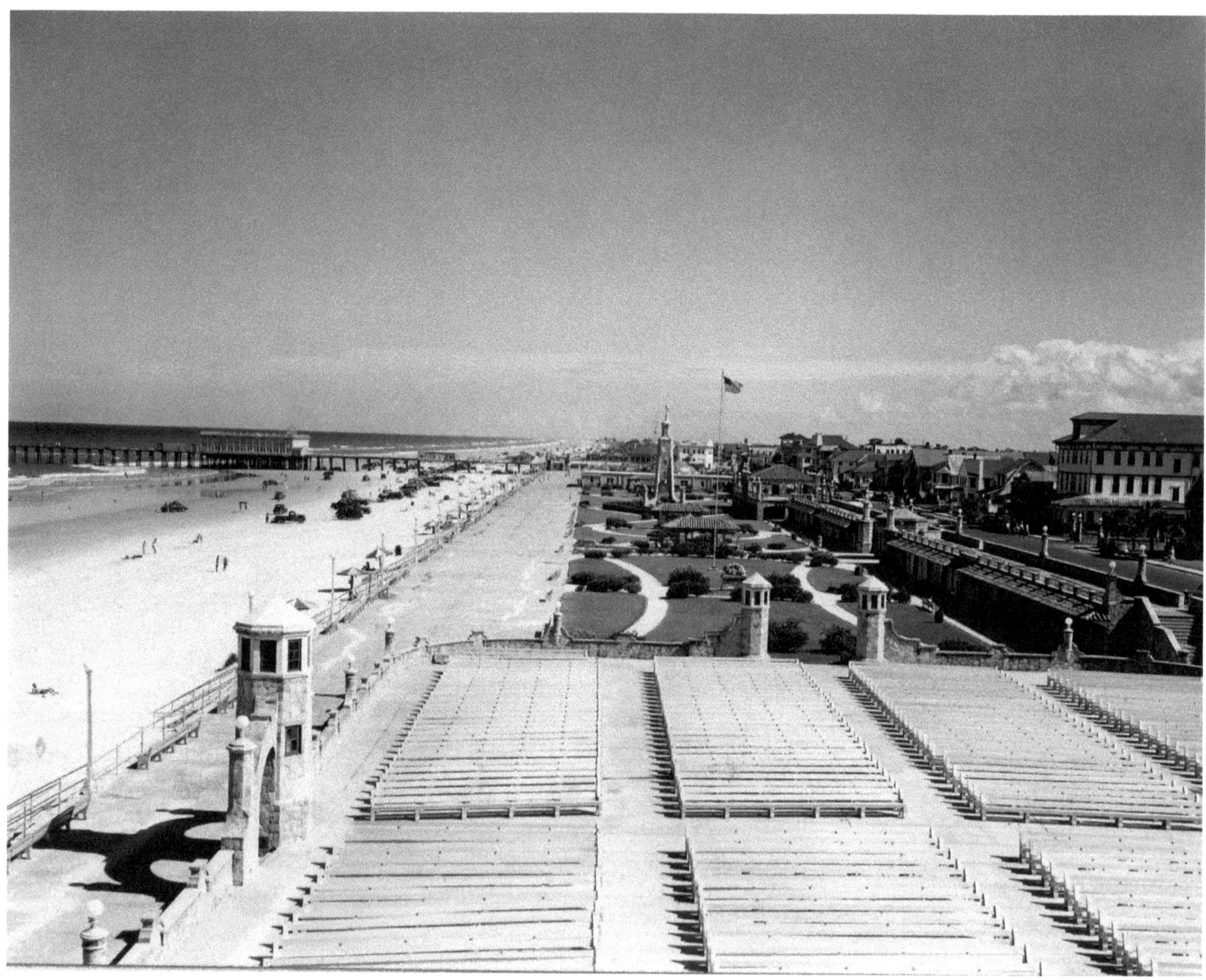

These odd, three-wheeled cycles featuring canvas sunshades were seen for several years on the beach. These two girls enjoy themselves pedaling on the hard-packed sand.

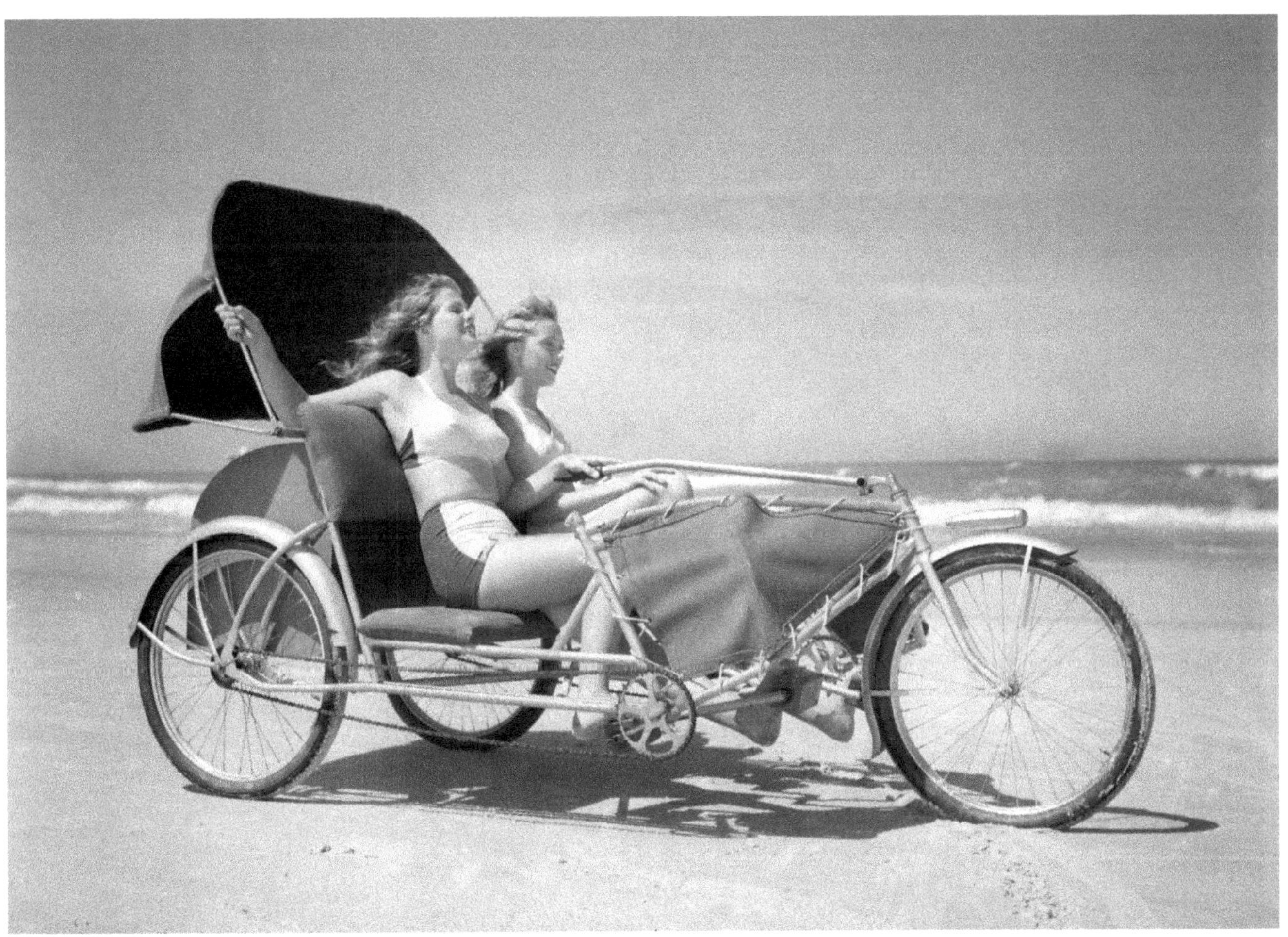

Robert Byron was one of the most colorful drivers after World War II. Fans gave him the name Boss of the Beach. Passing other cars in the turns, he would come into the north turn so fast his vehicle was turned sideways. He won four races.

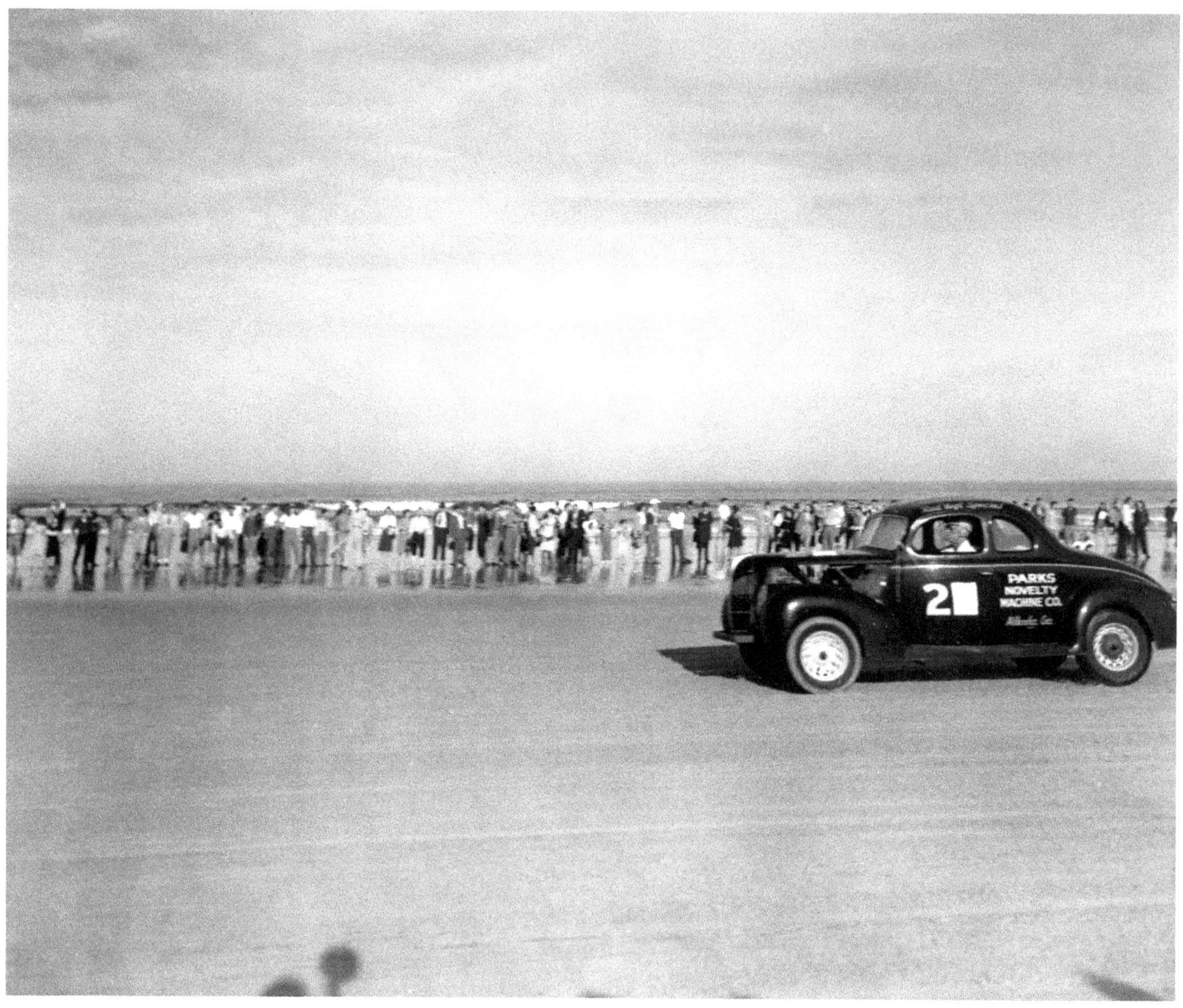

Gil Ferrell serves as flag man to open stock car races on the beach. With roaring engines, the cars headed for the north turn. Photographers were eager to see who would take the lead.

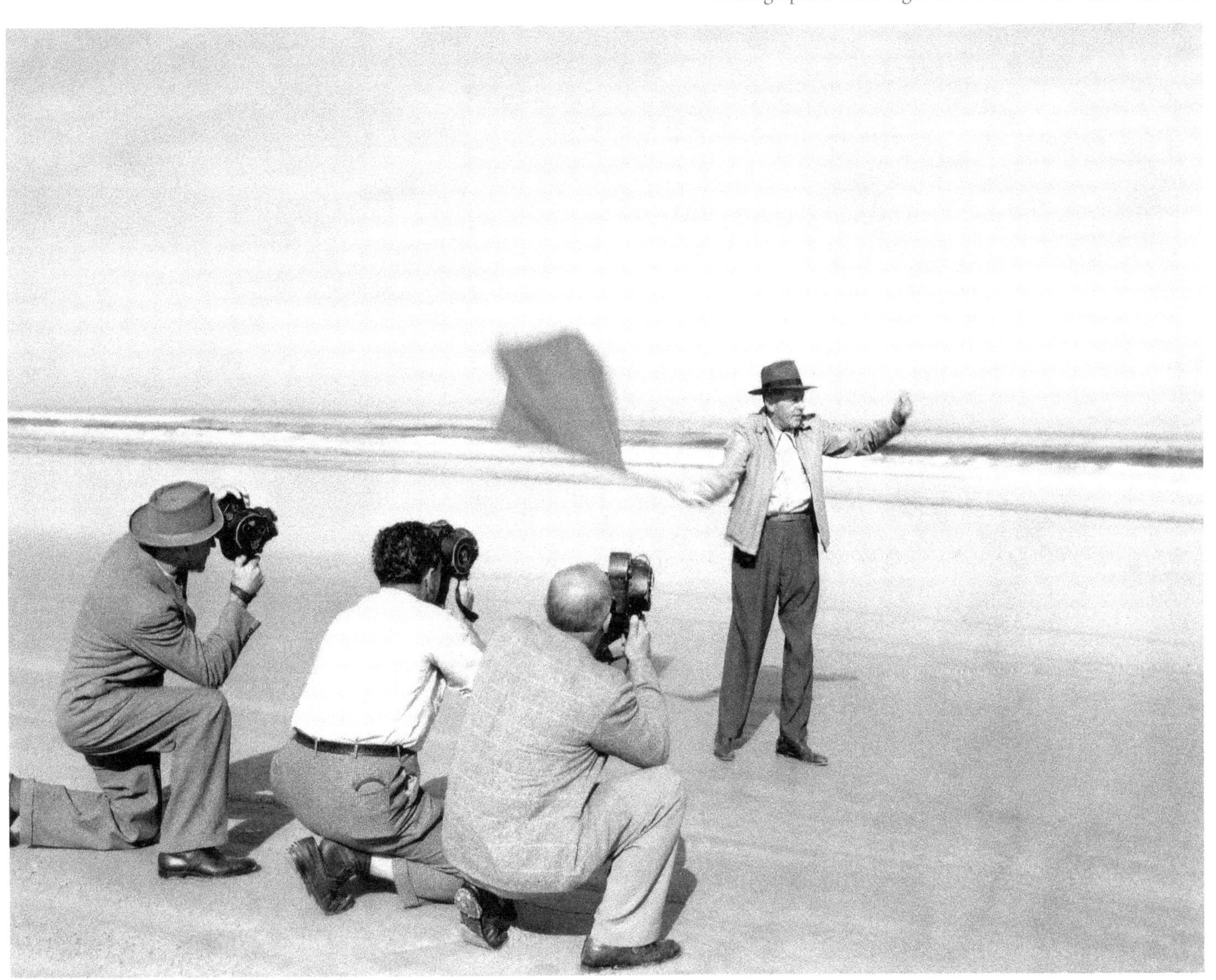

Bob Flock—in race car #14—leaves the north turn as another racer pursues. Race drivers put on a show for the fans at this turn, with spinning tires throwing marl and sand. The Flock brothers were favorites at the 3.5-mile road-beach course.

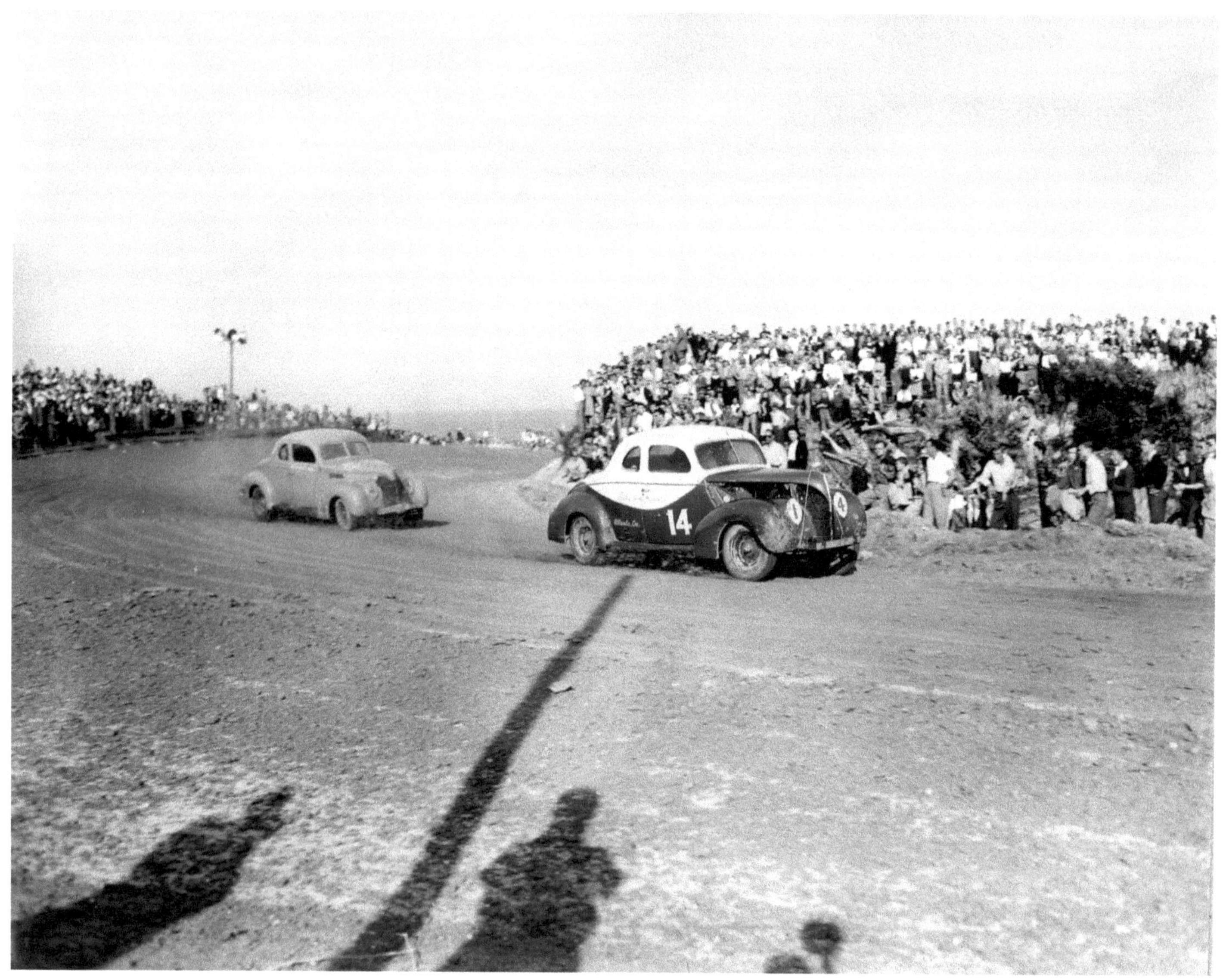

Left to right are Bill France, Sr., race director, and Robert Byron, race driver. Byron accepted the Edward Knowles Rayson Memorial Trophy (cup) for winning the January 26, 1947, race. Red Vogt built the 39 Ford race car in 48 hours.

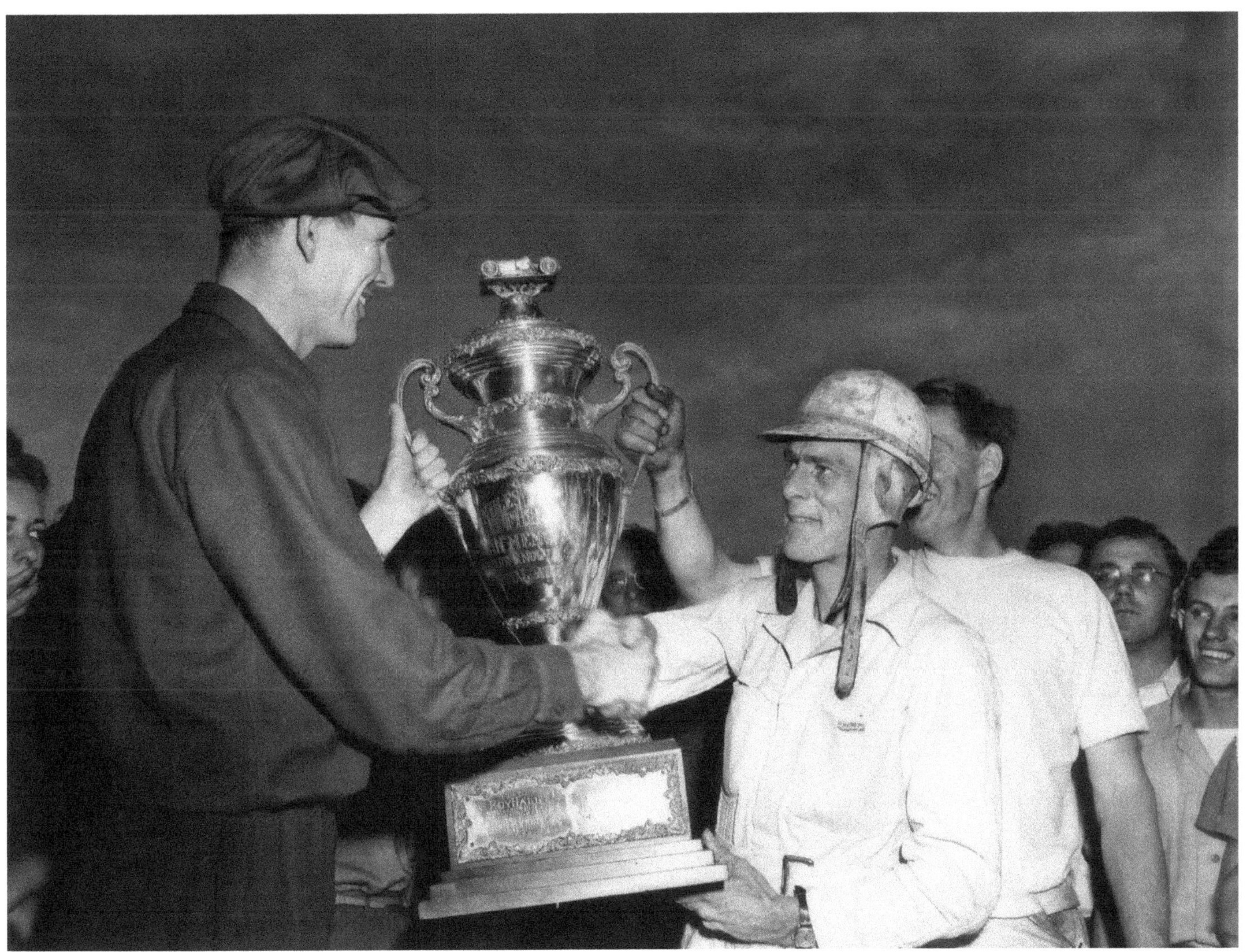

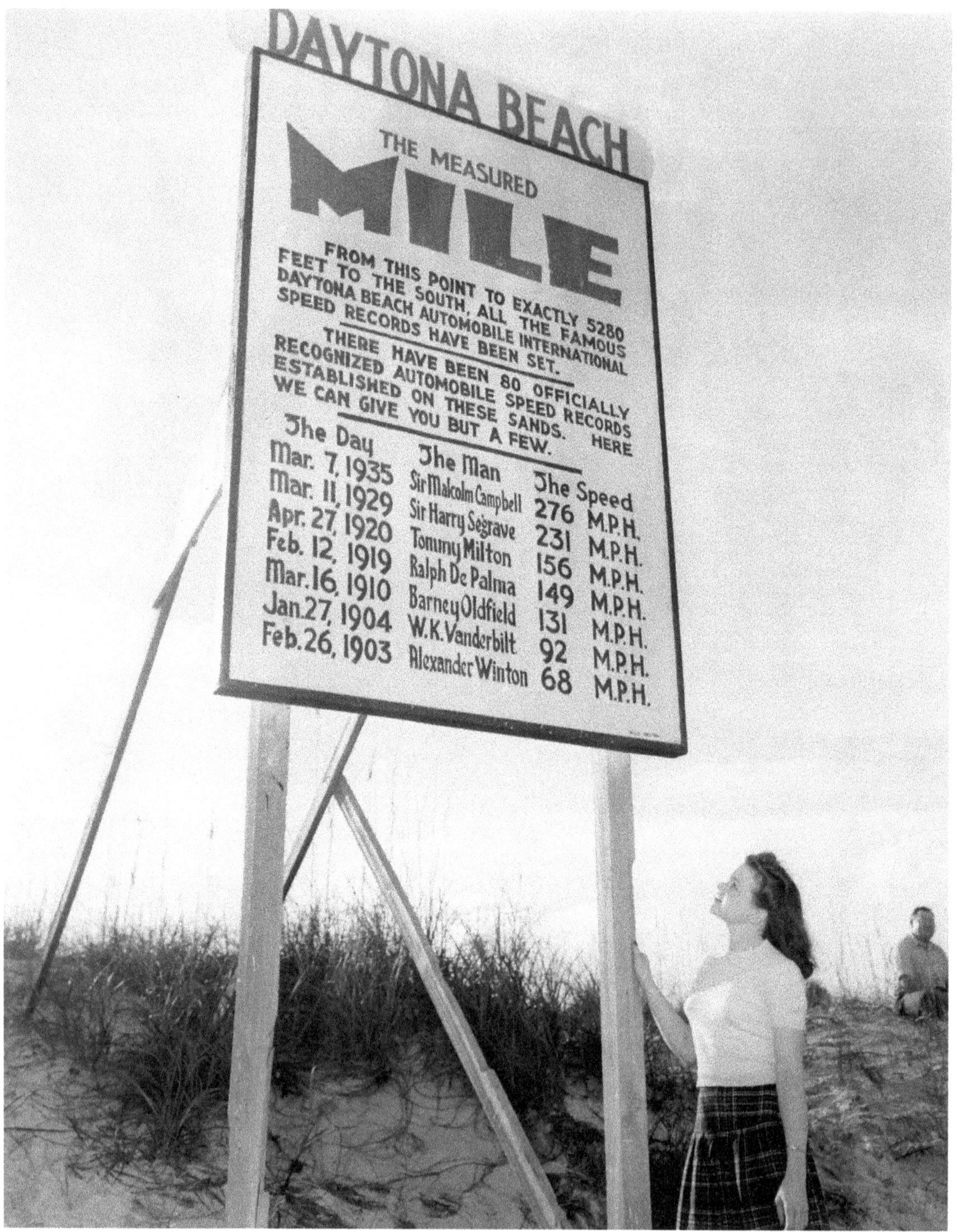

The marker pretty well speaks for itself: On this beach, along the Measured Mile, over the course of time, racers set 80 world automobile speed records. The sign stood on the beach near the Dunlawton Beach approach. Sir Malcolm Campbell was the last racer to break the world's land speed record, setting a new record of 276.82 m.p.h.

After World War II, Daytona Beach was growing. The beach races attracted winter tourists, and tourist courts and cabins were built along the beach. These accommodations were the forerunner of hotels and motels built later along Atlantic Avenue.

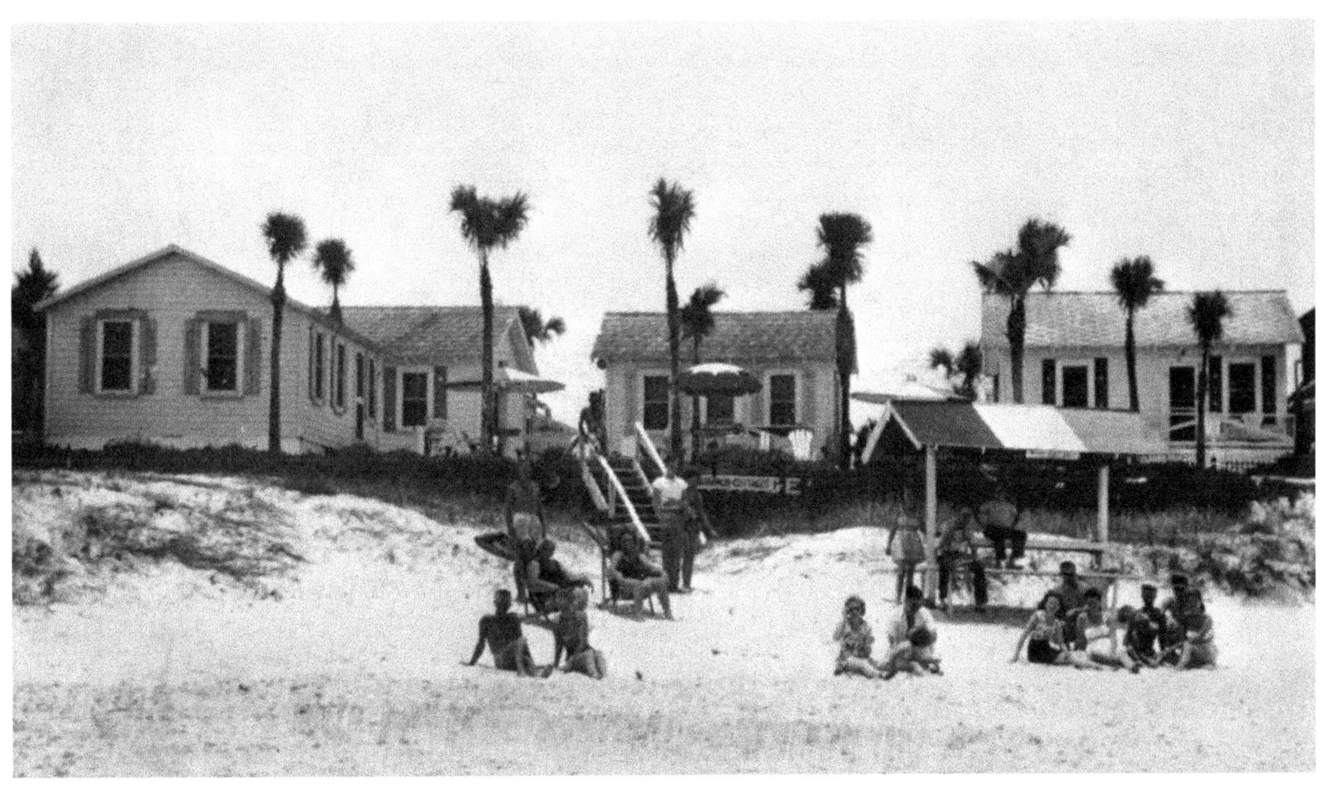

Young people are creative with their beach games. Here playing leapfrog are four youngsters, photographed on Armistice Day, November 11, 1948.

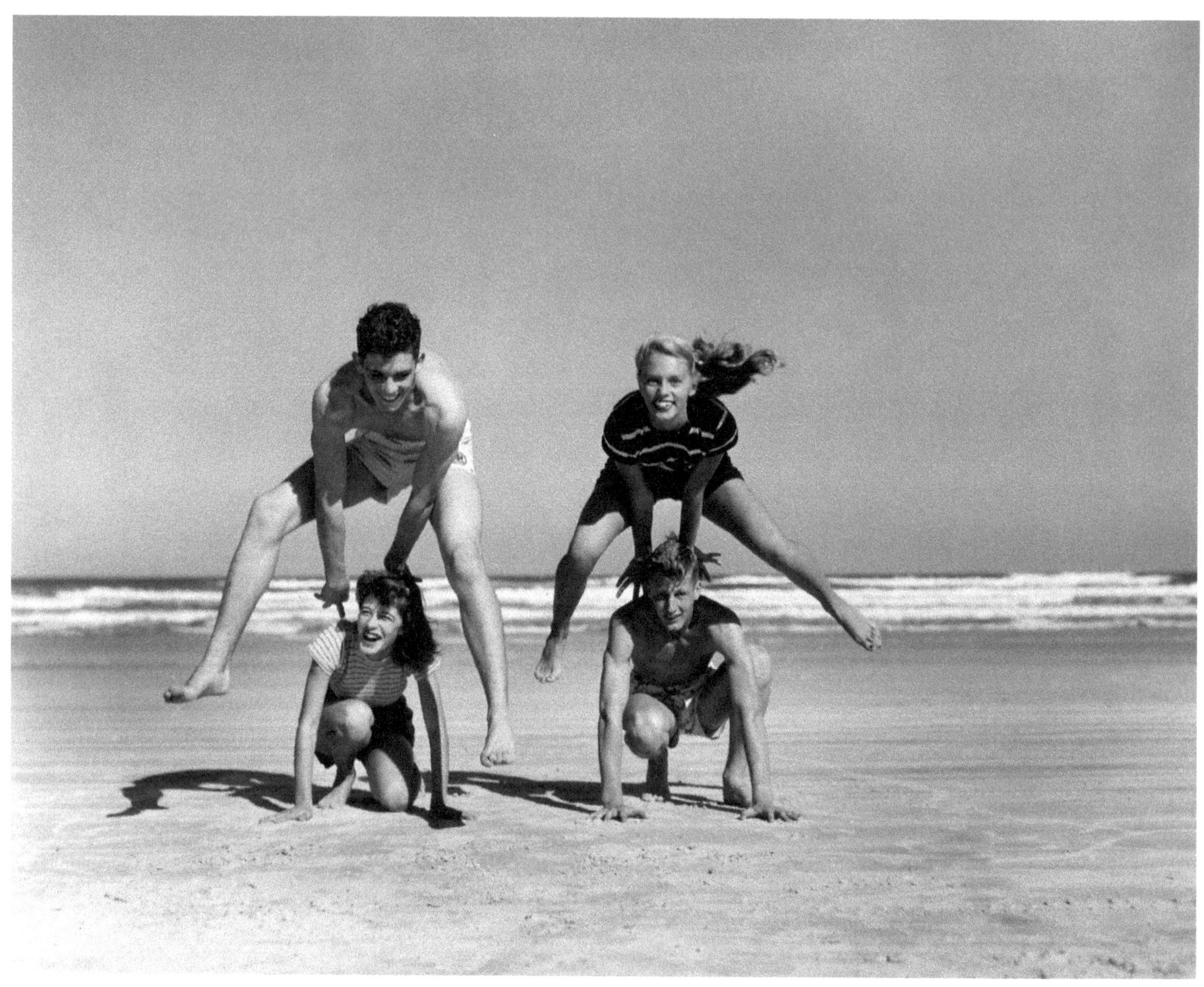

This boat works had a dry dock and large machine shop area. Here boats could be overhauled with new planking, siding, and other needed repairs. New gasoline or diesel engines could be replaced inside the craft on new engine beds.

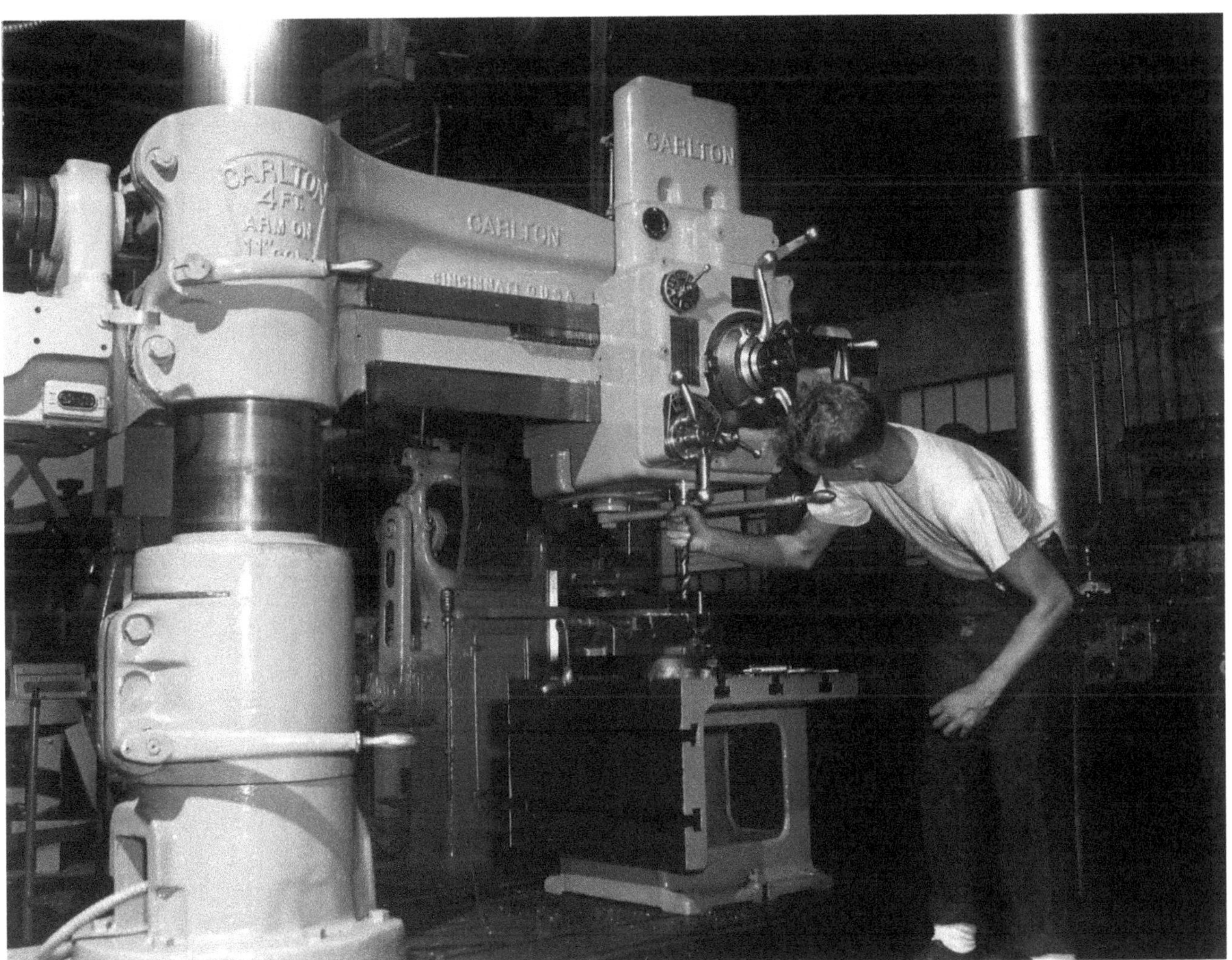

Over time, tourist facilities on the beach were growing larger. The names of tourist houses, courts, and cabins were changing. This new facility called its resort a Colony. Entertainment (recreation) on the beachfront was added.

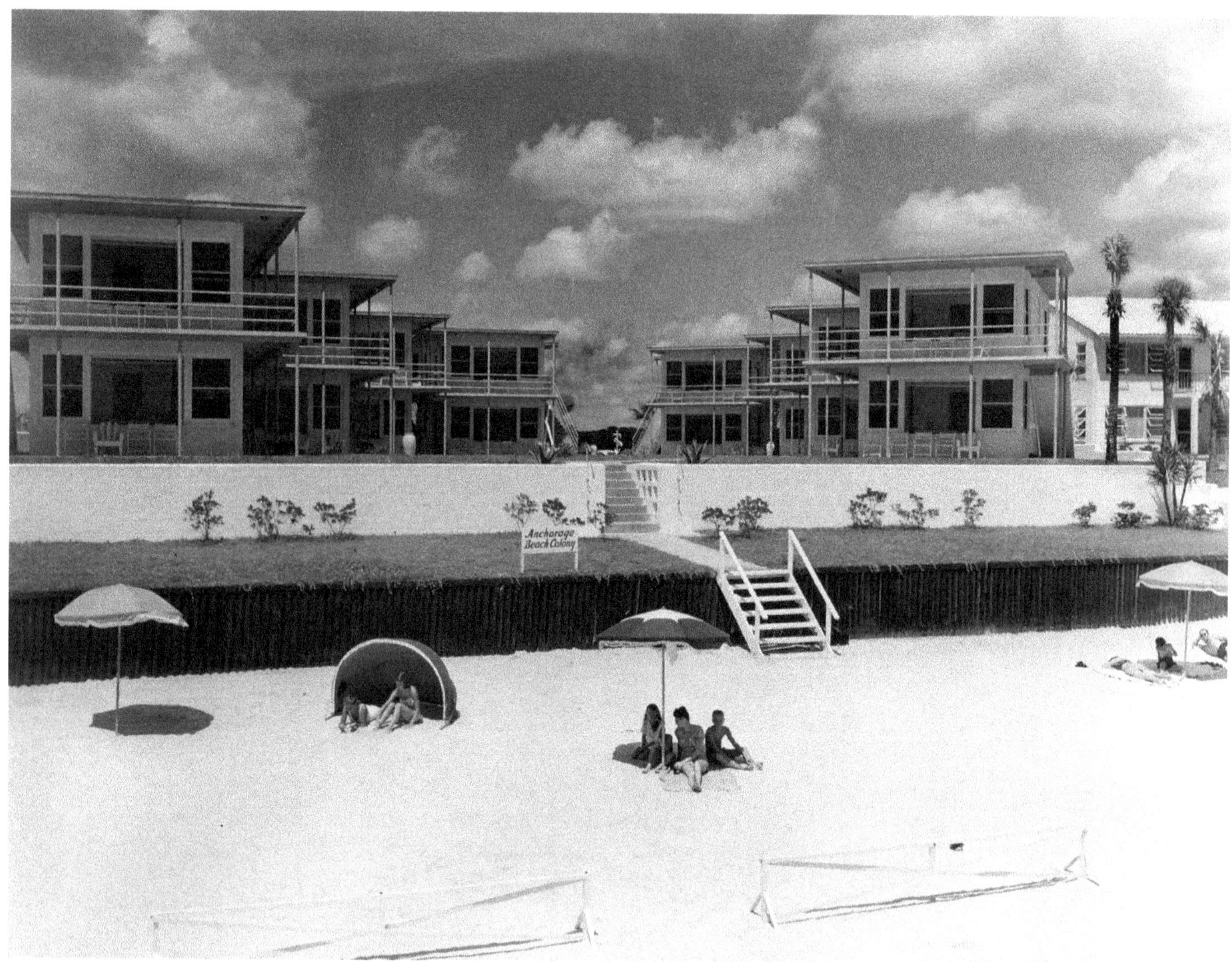

At one time shoppers could call at McCrory, Kress, Dunn Brothers, Three Sisters, and Yowell-Drew stores, which served customers across from the beautiful Riverfront Park on Beach Street. The park was well maintained and boasted a botanical garden with lily pools, subtropical plants, and flowing water. It was a welcome rest stop for weary shoppers.

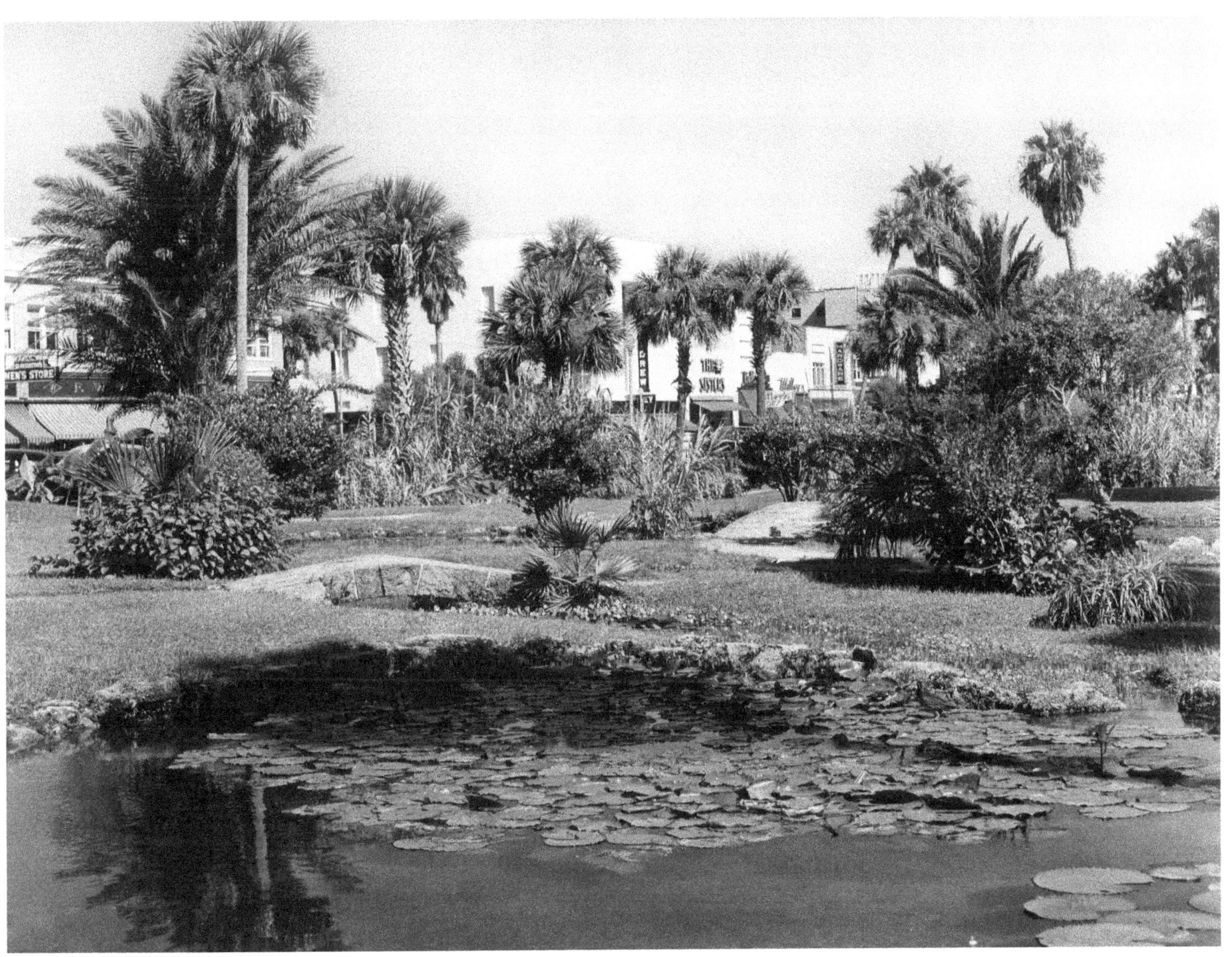

The Flamingo Shoe Company plant was located in a former Navy building. At the time this photograph was taken, very few buildings offered air conditioning for their employees. Workers are shown here with short sleeves or no shirts at their work tables.

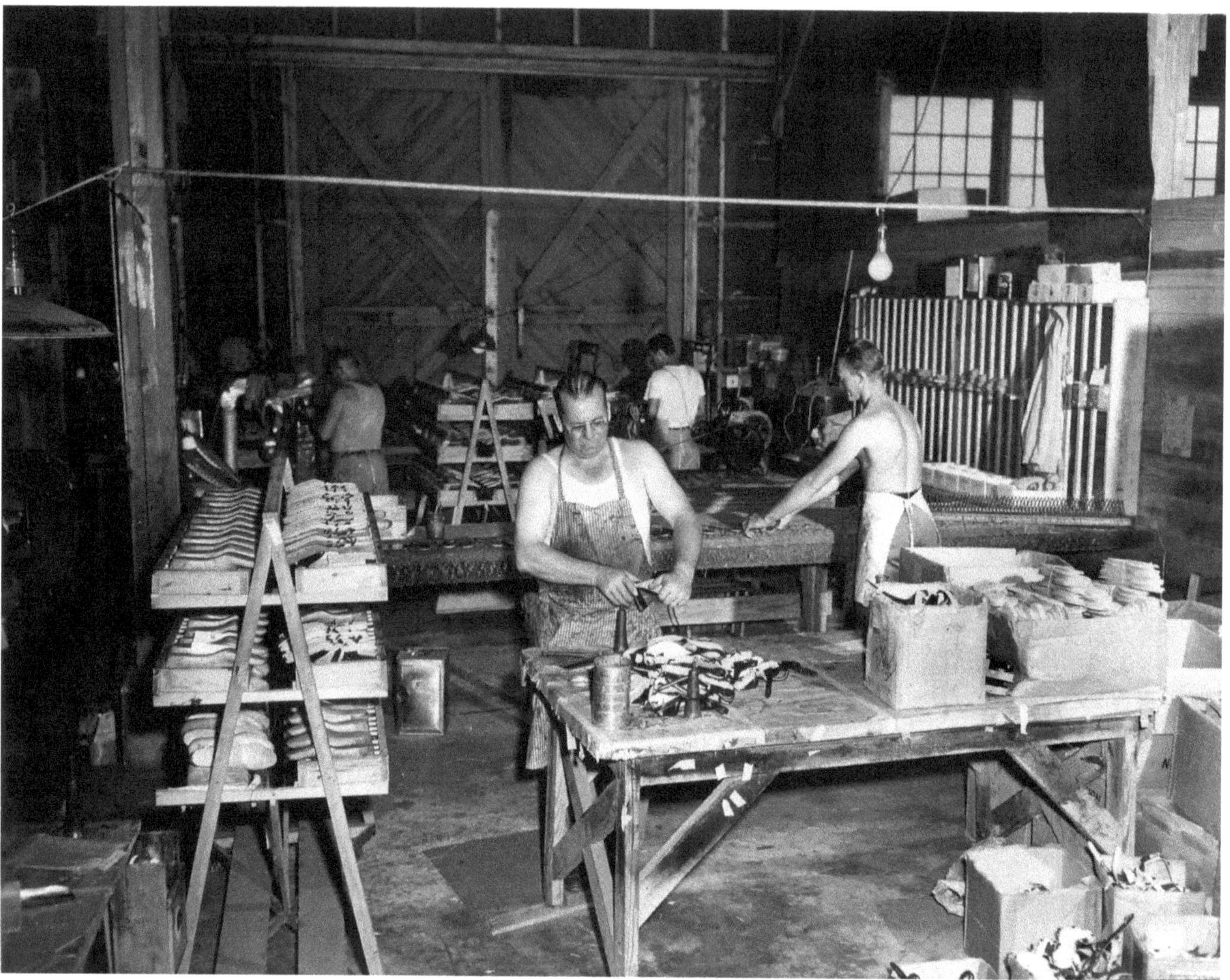

Henry Pierce teaches six young visitors on the beach the skills of sand sailing. This three-wheeled sailing craft could be dangerous in strong winds; without a breeze, it sat motionless. Tacking was the name of the game to operate the land-sailor successfully.

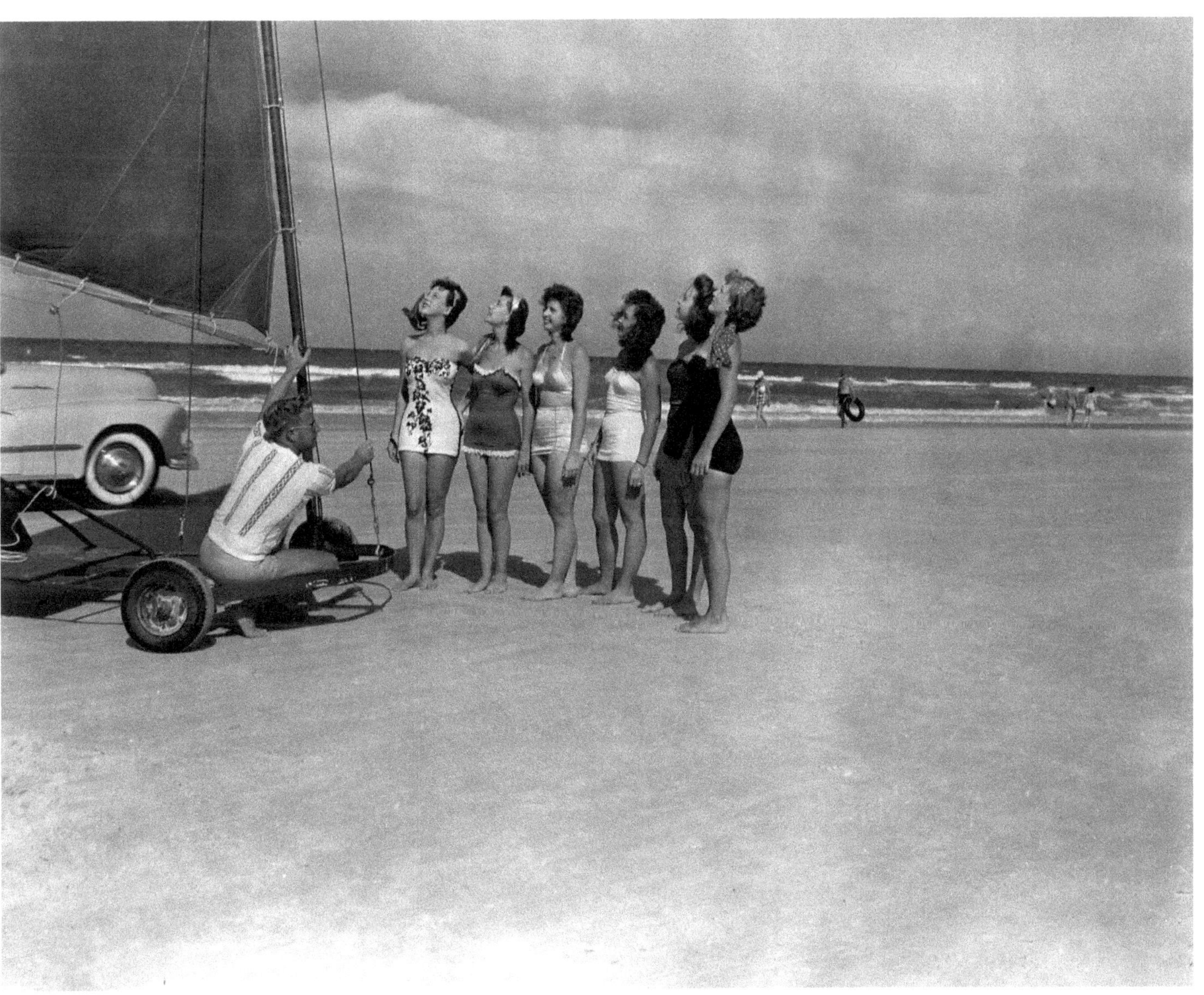

A huge crowd convenes at the bandshell for a special program and beauty contest. Participants came from nearby cities. There were age limits and strict rules for those who entered the contest.

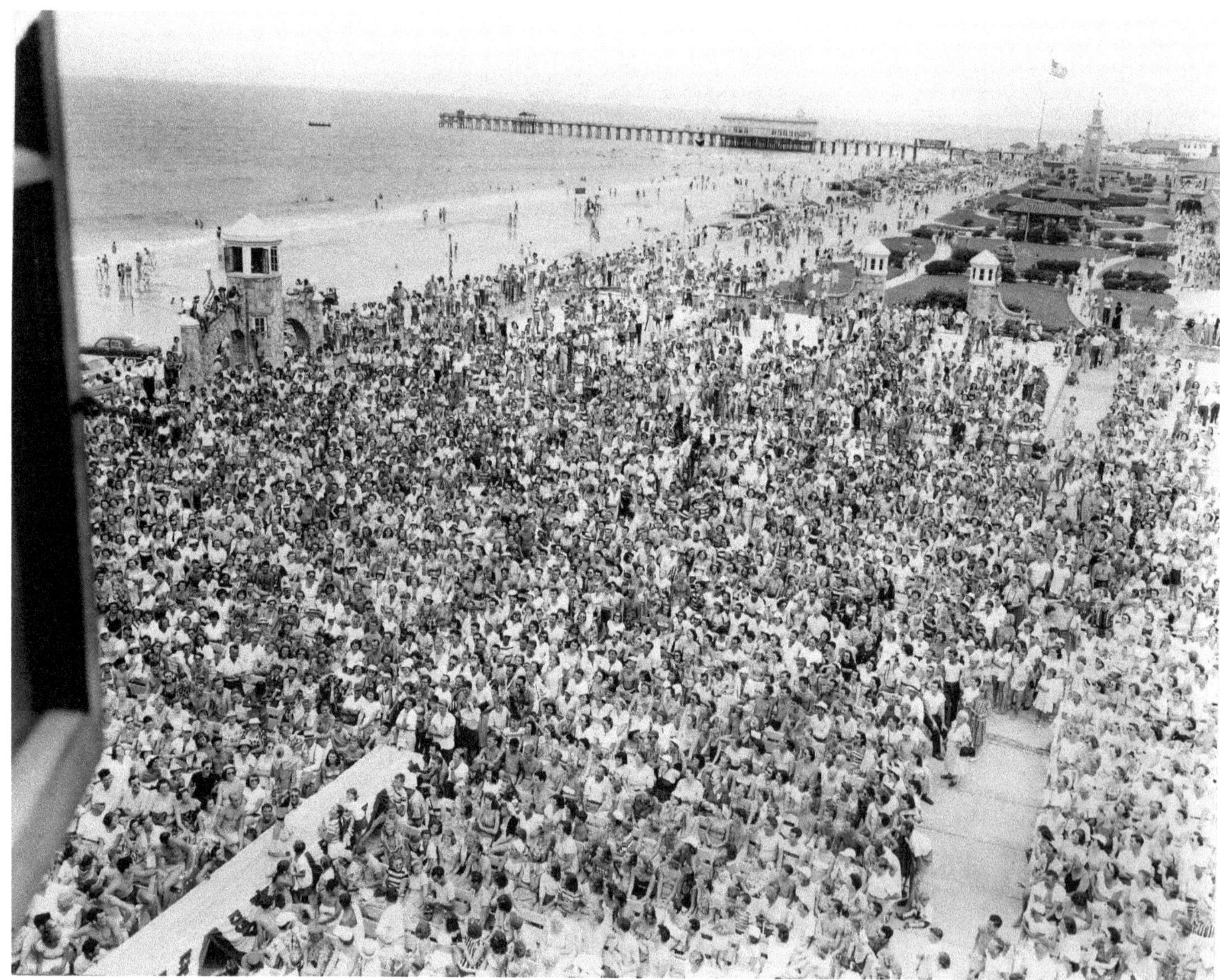

This land-water craft called the Duck was at one time used for tours along the beach and in the surf. An added attraction for beachgoers, these World War II craft had played a significant role in the beach invasions in the Europe and Pacific theaters.

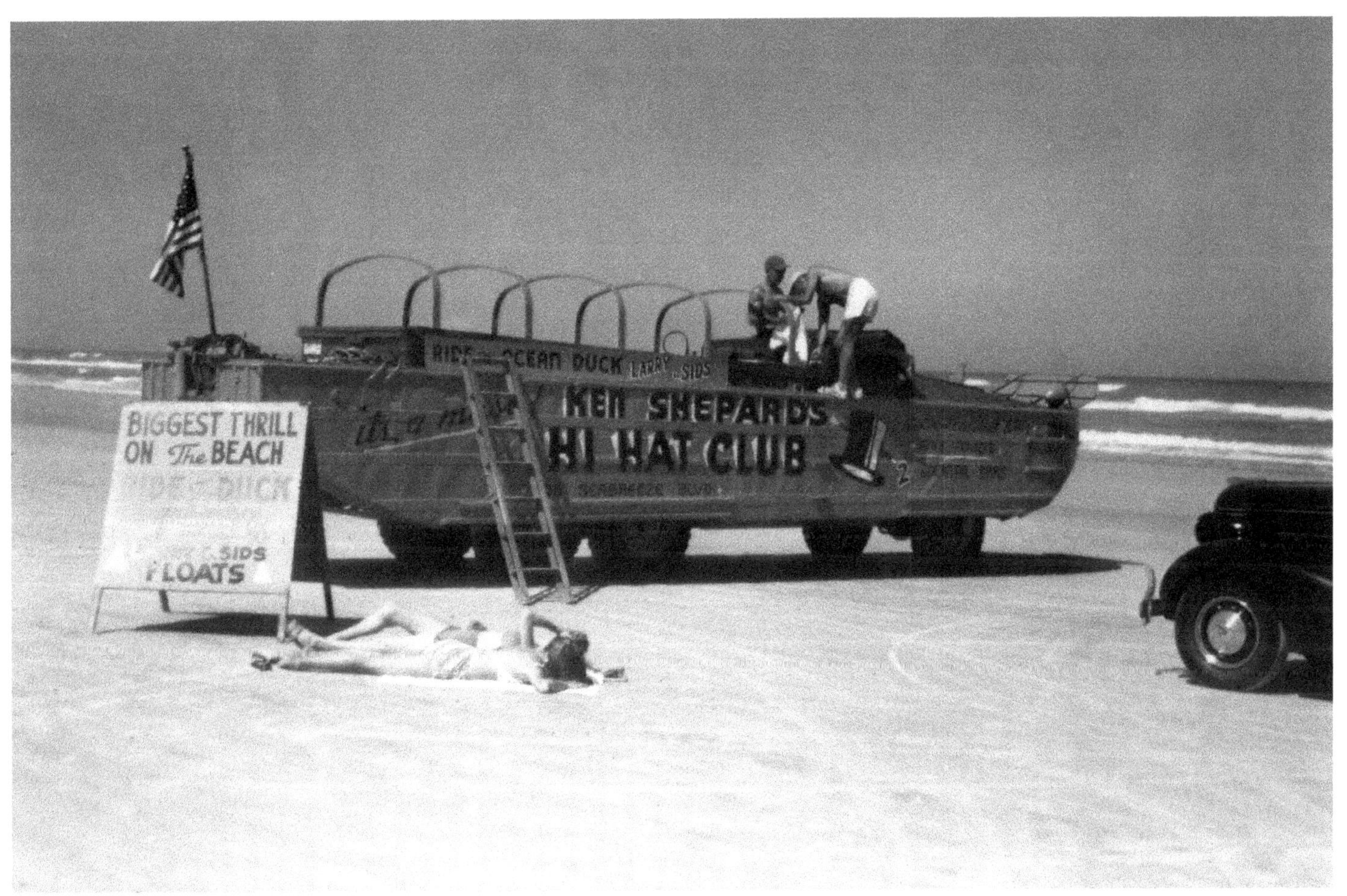

July 4th has always been a special day on the beach. This photo was taken from the pier. Visible are peanut shelters in front of the boardwalk, a huge crowd, Ferris wheel, the clock tower, and the bandshell. Sun bathers enjoy the beach sand and surf.

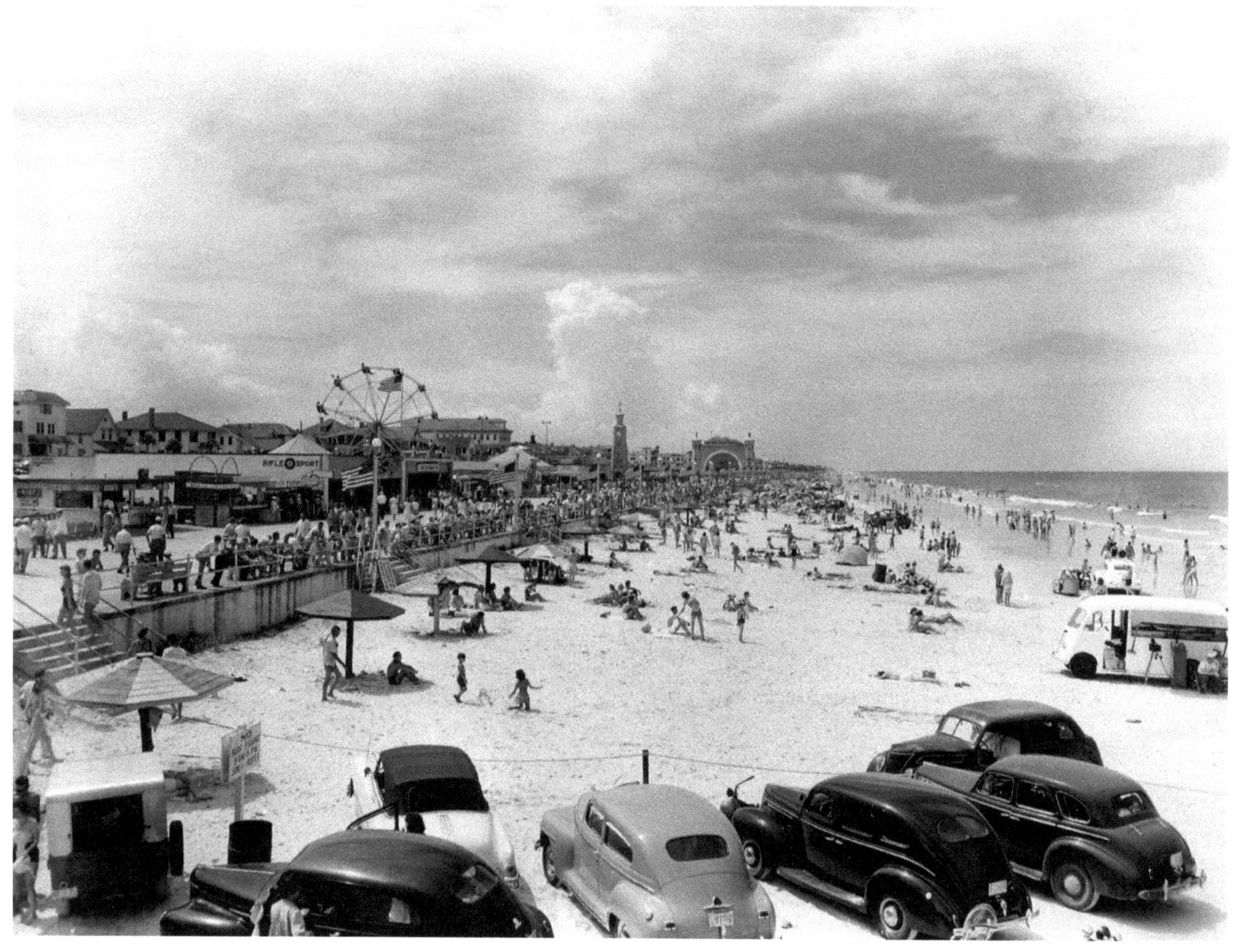

Pictured here on the sands of Daytona are seven young ladies and a lifeguard. In the background are a number of motels and apartment buildings.

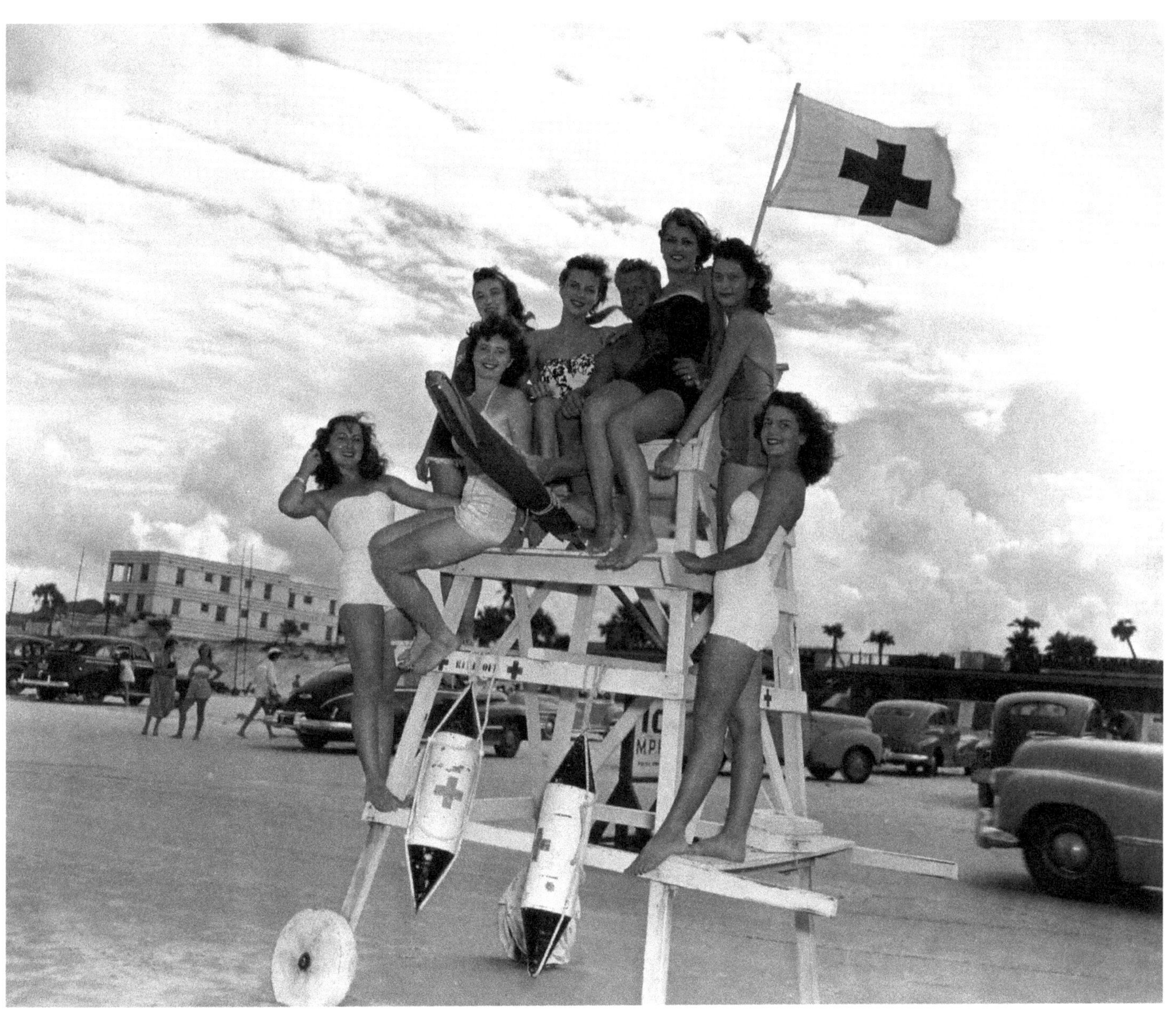

In this view from times gone by, beachgoers enjoy the boardwalk, beach, and ocean pier. At night, fireworks were set off at the end of the pier. Visitors with cars on the beach have always been alert to an incoming tide; when parking was permitted on the beach, the risk of saltwater seeping into one's car was ever-present.

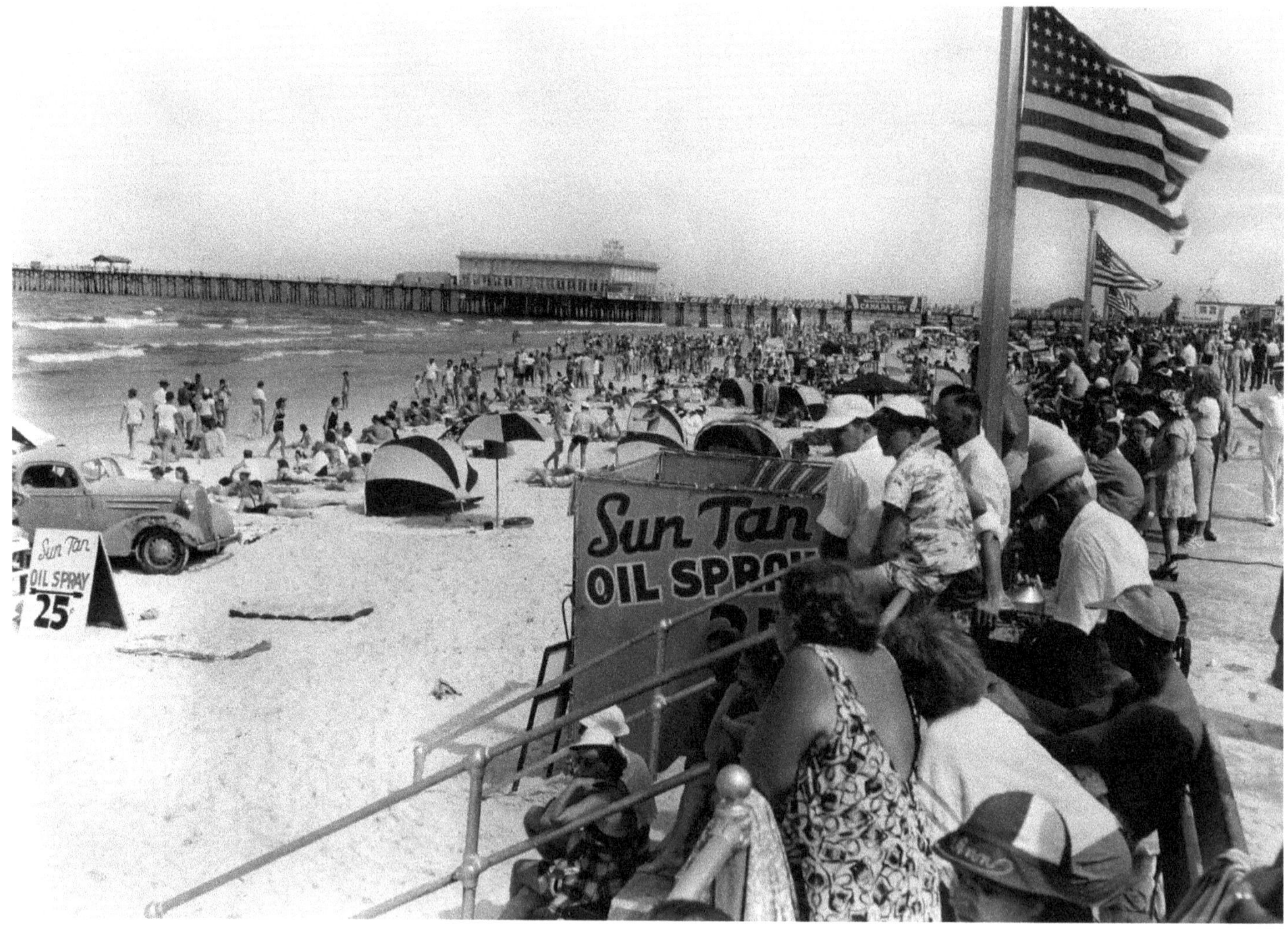

In this view, girls involved in the beauty pageant are being instructed in their role in the contest while the musical director plans his part of the program.

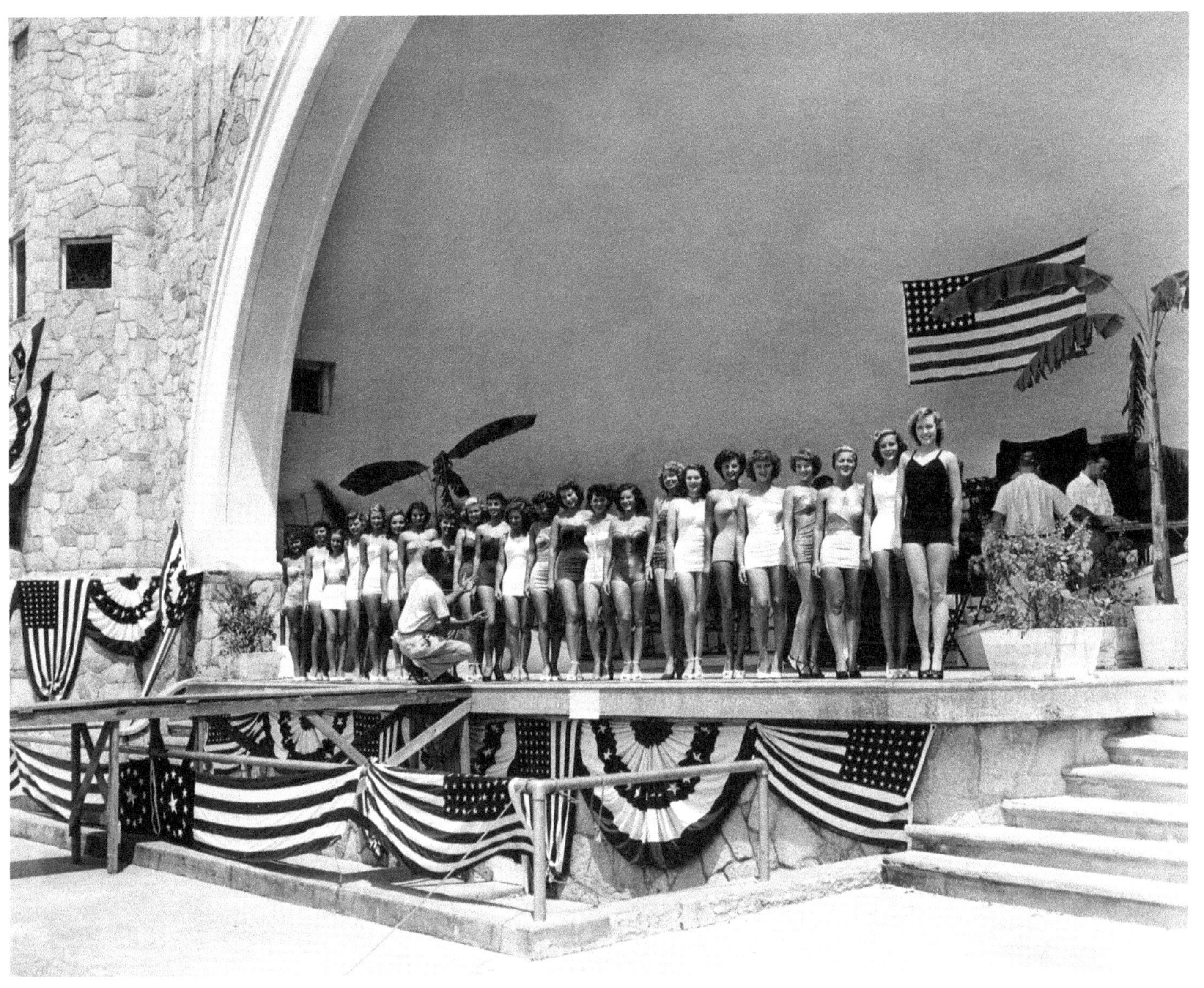

Travelers once frequented this well-known local tourist court, Sun and Sand Motel Court. Located near the famous Dutch Pantry restaurant, it offered golf accommodations and was not far from the World's Most Famous Beach.

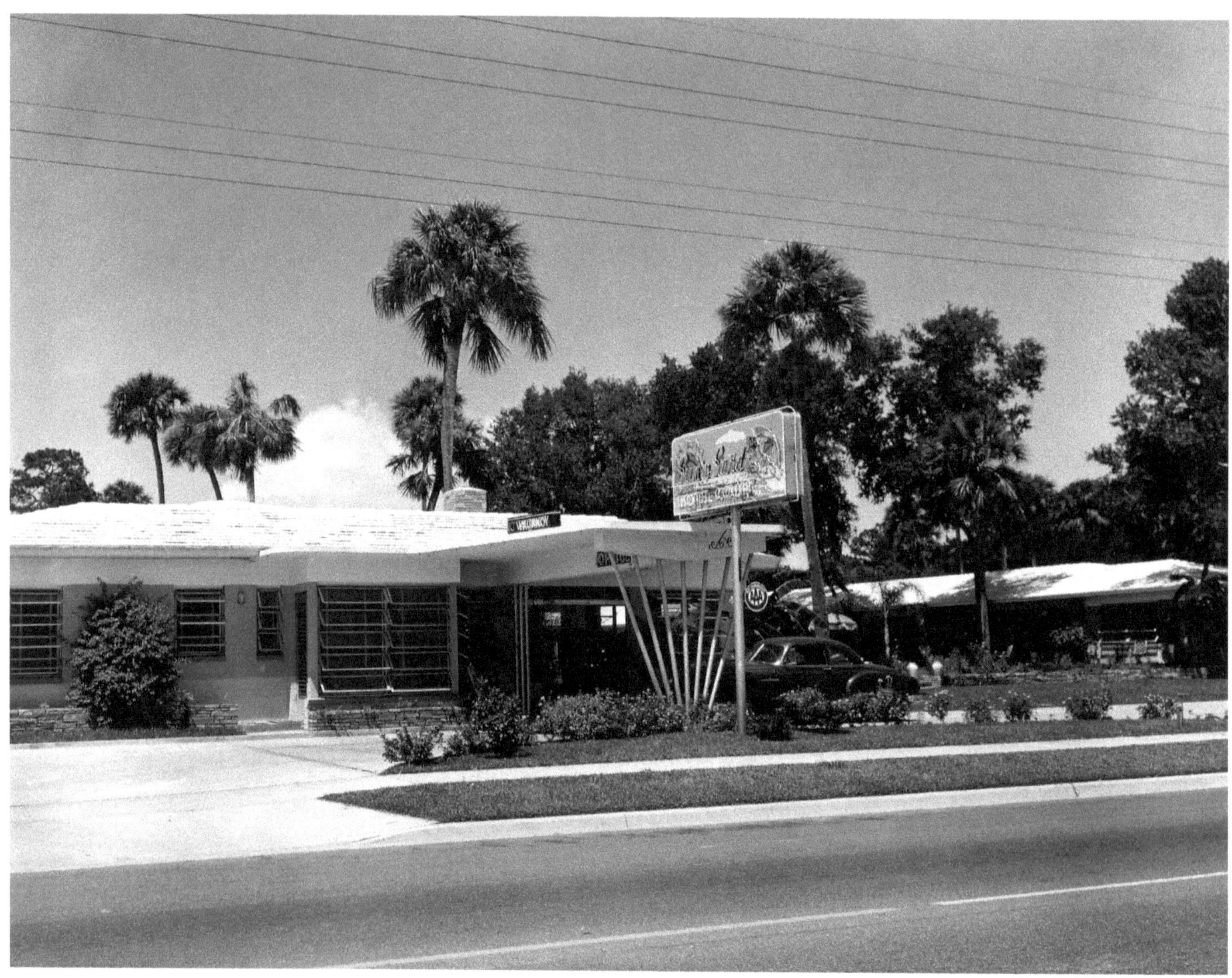

Former First Lady Eleanor Roosevelt, Mrs. Richard Moore, wife of Bethune-Cookman College's president, and Mary McLeod Bethune, founder of Bethune-Cookman College, and others pose for the camera in front of Bethune's home. The local dignitaries were accompanying Mrs. Roosevelt on her visit to the campus in 1952. When this image was captured, segregated conditions still separated African Americans from the white community.

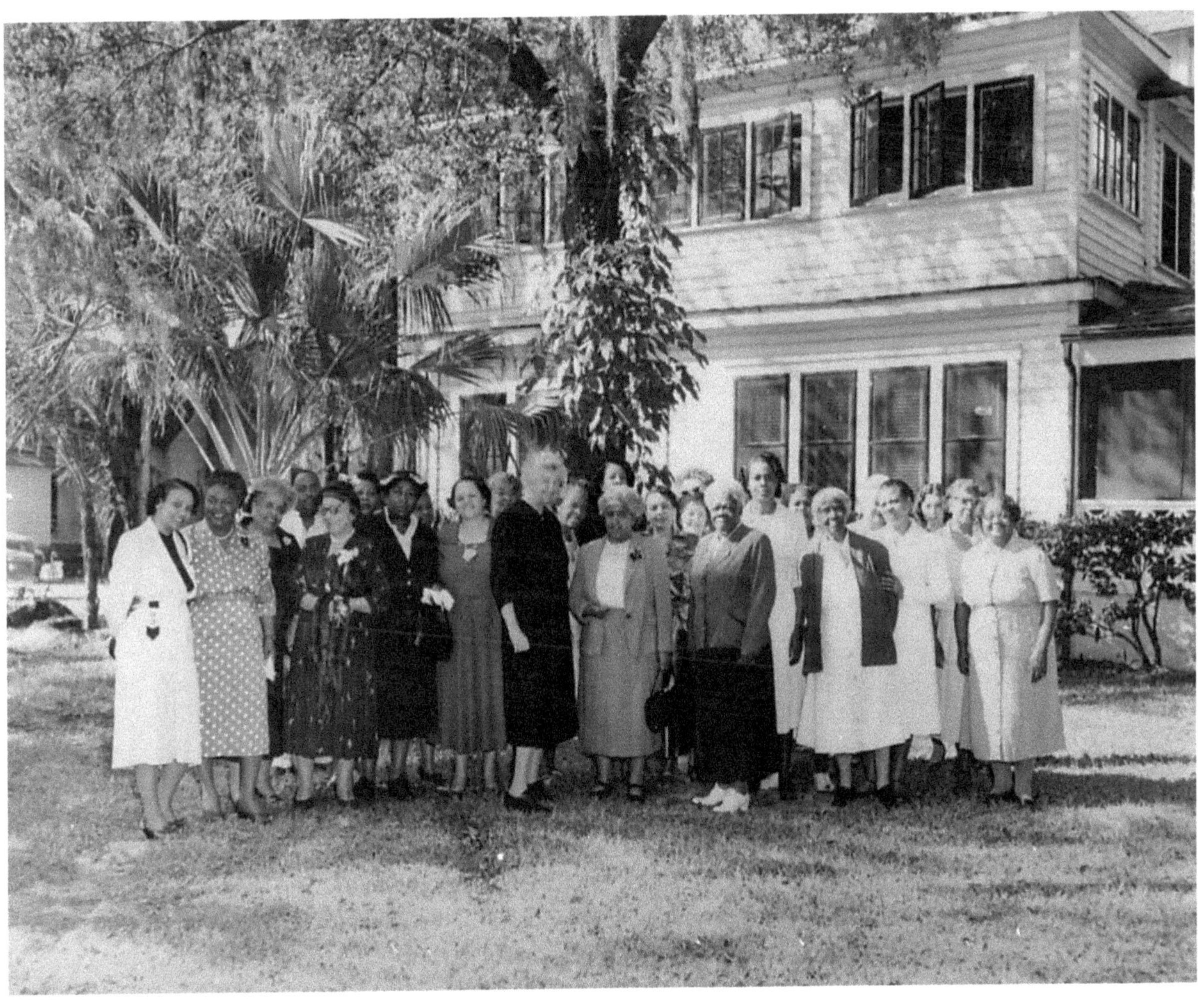

The Daytona Beach morning's news and evening's news were published in this building when this photograph was taken. The radio station WNDB studio was on the top floor. Next to this building (east) was the Bayview Hotel on Orange Avenue.

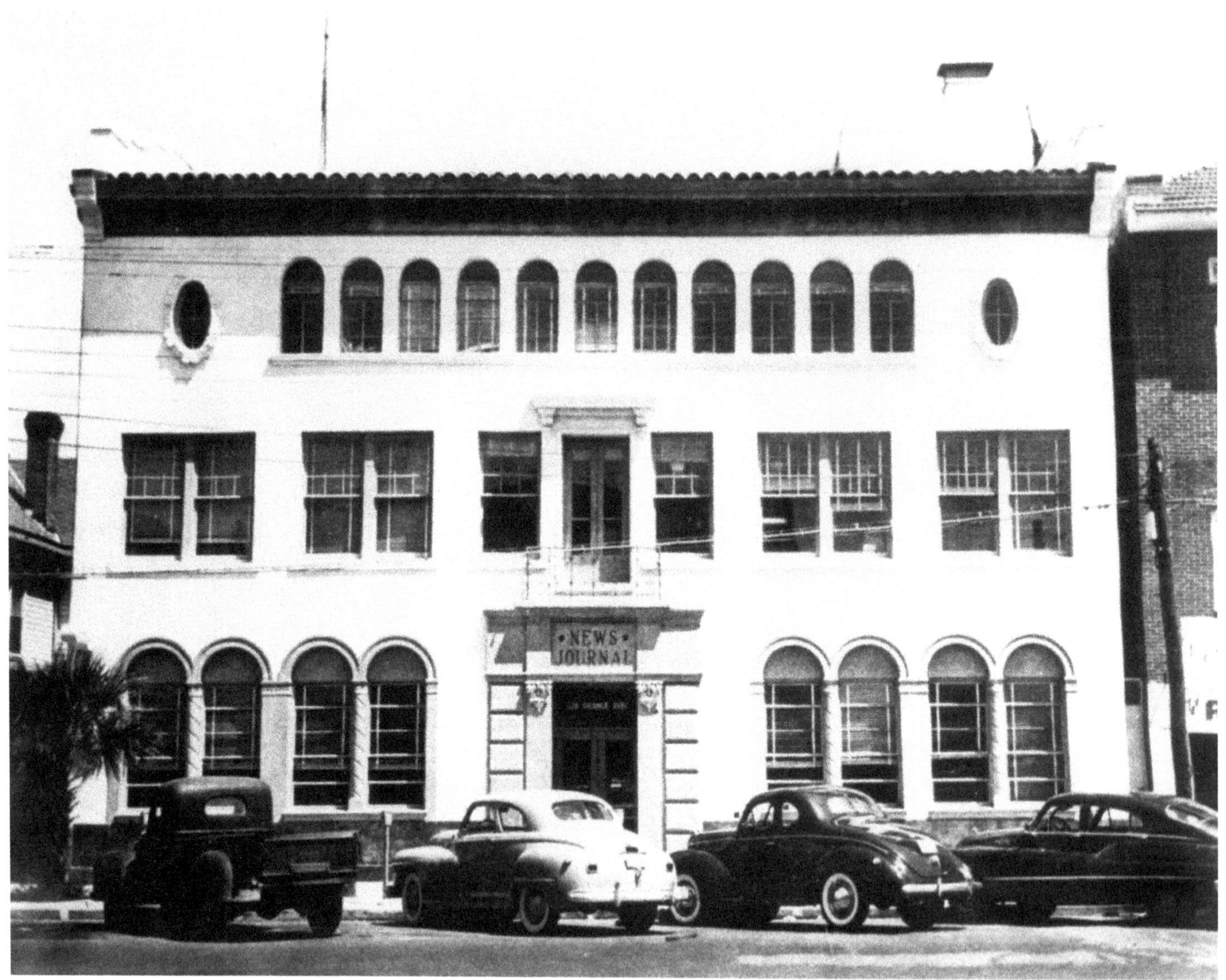

Here mechanics are checking this racing car in the pit area on the beach. The Ponce Inlet track, located south of Daytona Beach, was a 4.1-mile race course with 2.1 miles of track on the beach and 2 miles on the paved road.

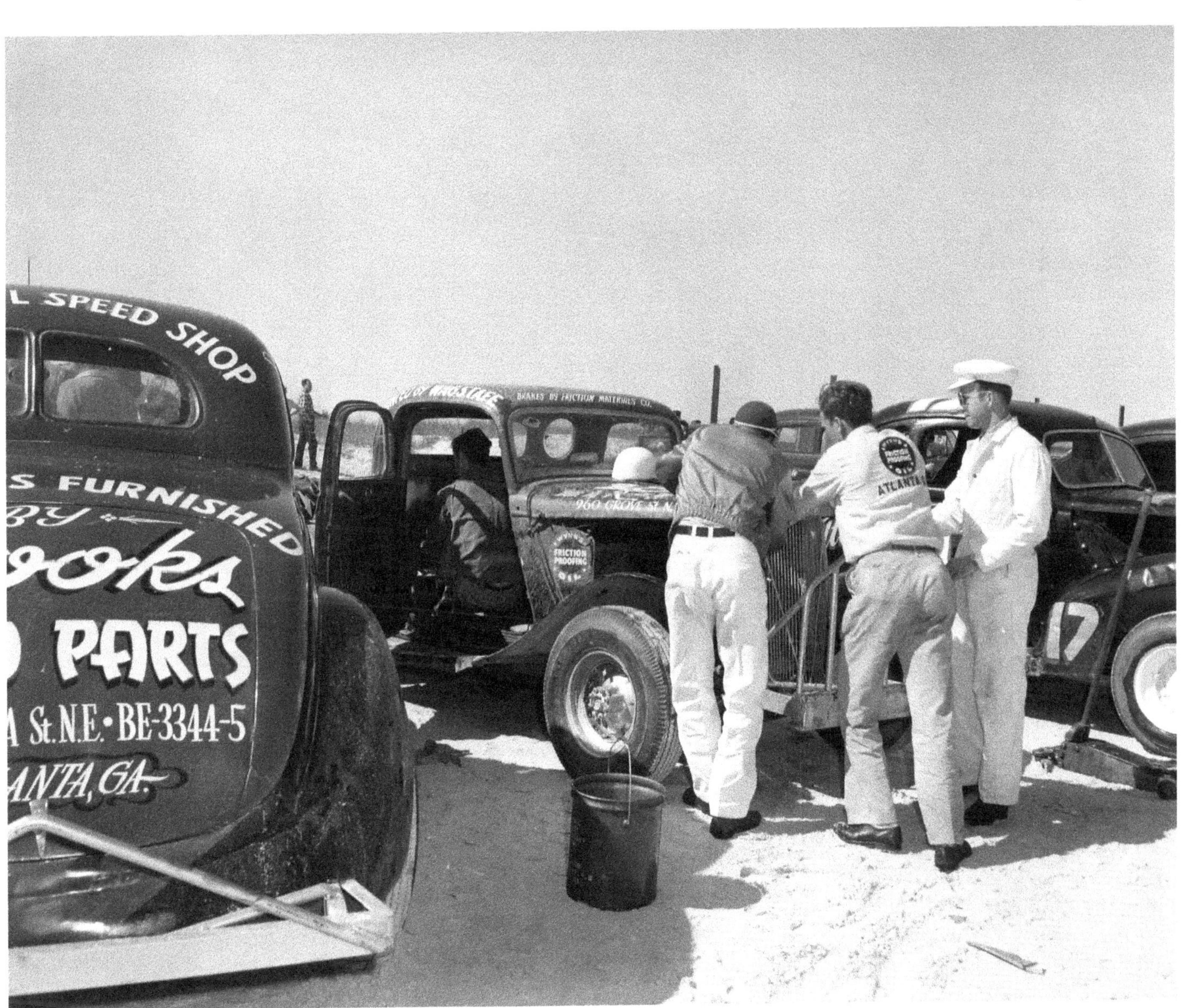

On February 10, 1952, racers enter the north turn in the Grand National Race. Marshall Teague, #6, won this race in his Hudson Hornet. Herb Thomas, #92, came in second place in a Hudson.

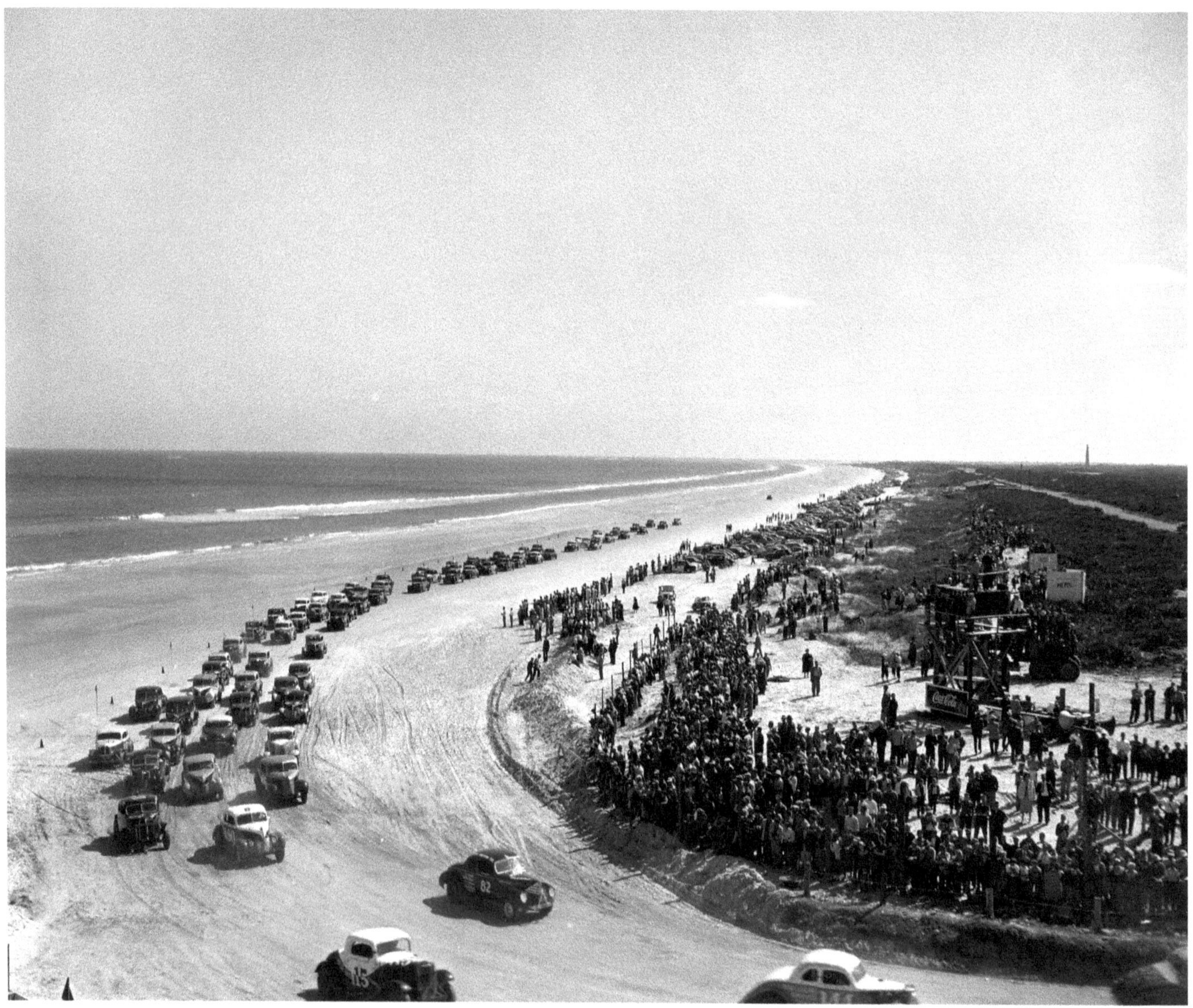

Race car drivers here rely on the edge of a sand dune for their pit stops, where they keep fuel, tools, batteries, and tires. Families often helped with the fueling and tire changes to keep their car in the competition. Standing are onlookers and mechanics.

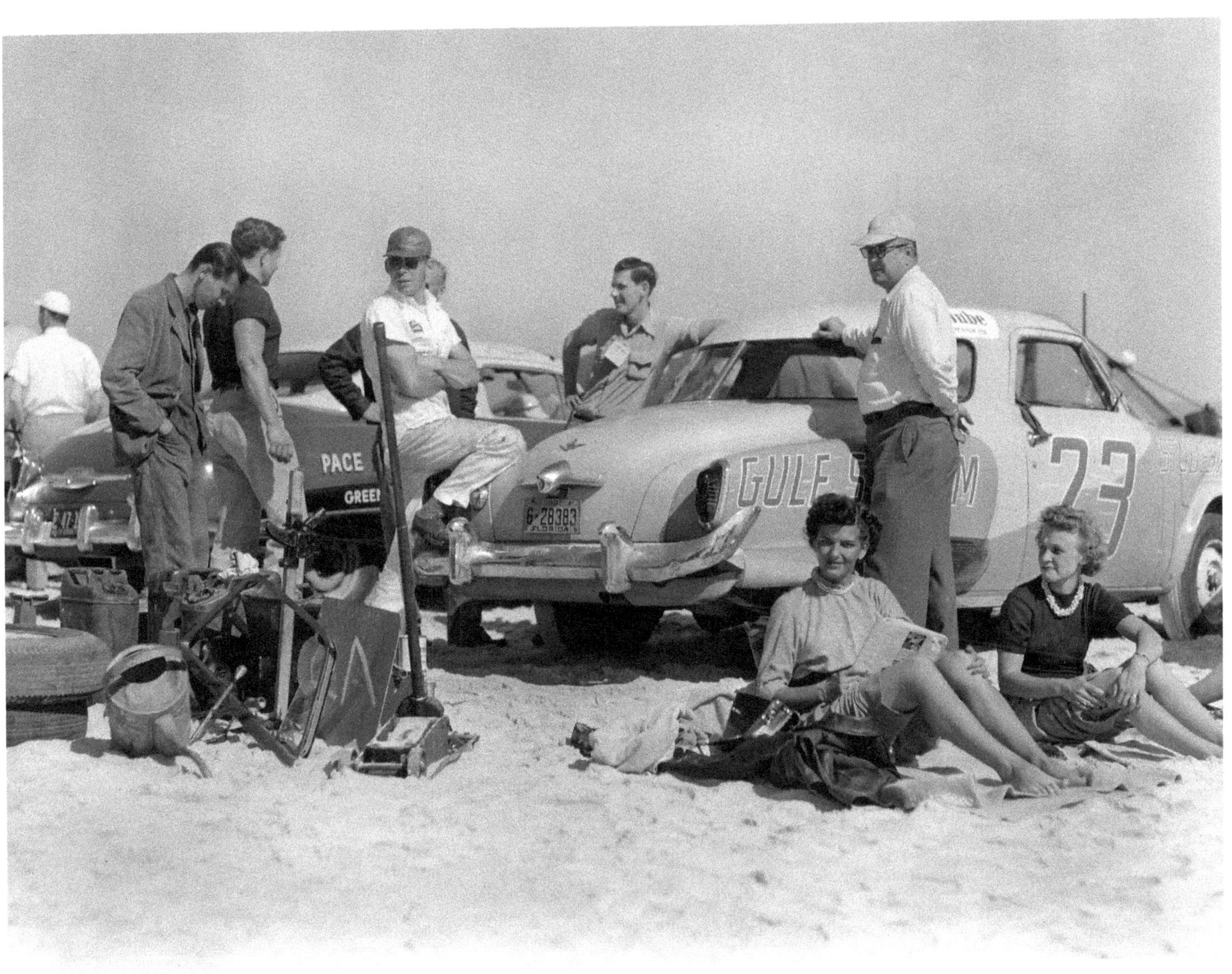

Sunrise services were once held each Easter at the bandshell. Special programs were open to all local residents and tourists. The ocean pier with its dance hall and casino was near the entrance to Main Street.

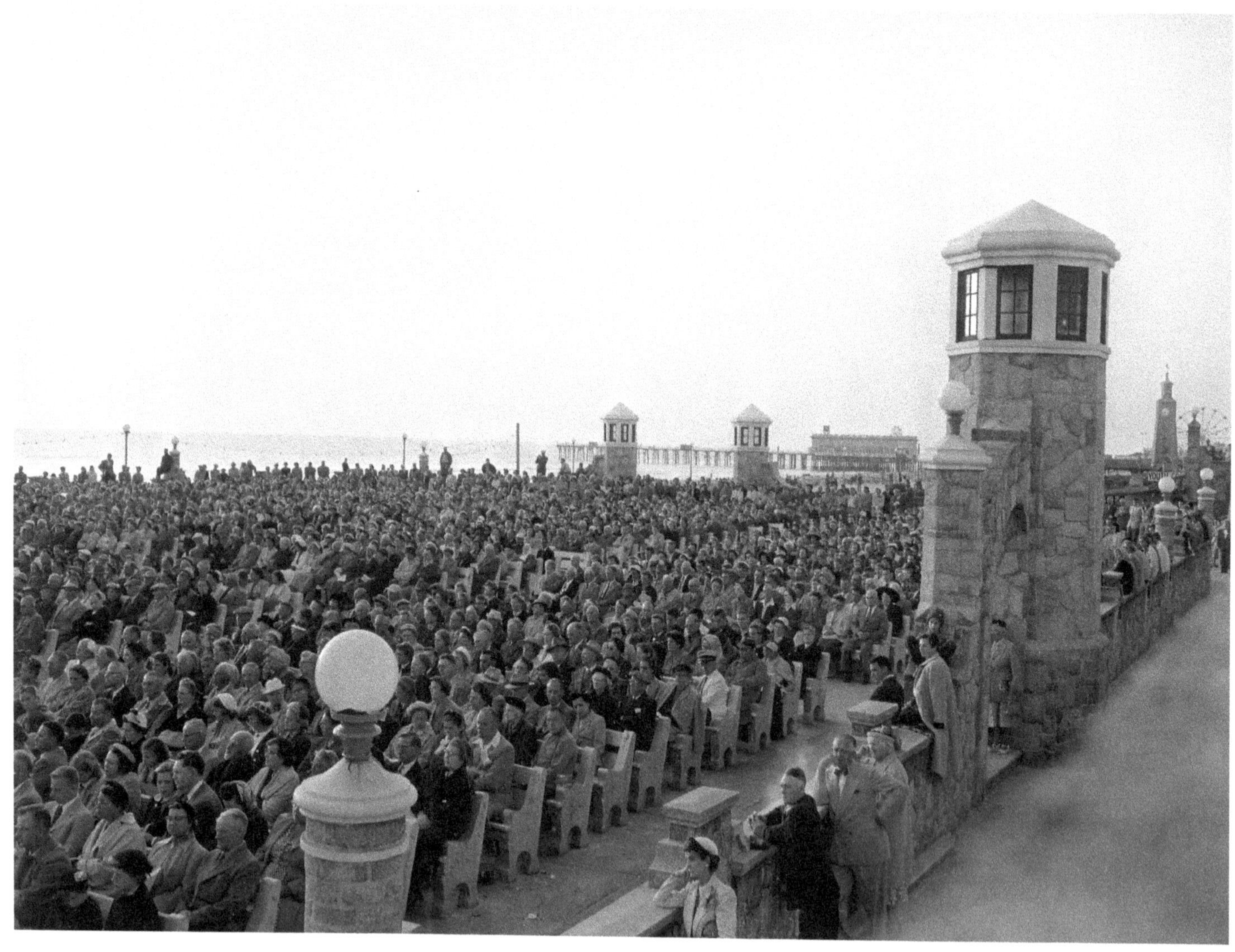

Chaperones and children in this view participate in the yearly Easter Egg Hunt held in the riverfront park. Children were always excited to find the special, colored eggs. The City Island can be seen in the background.

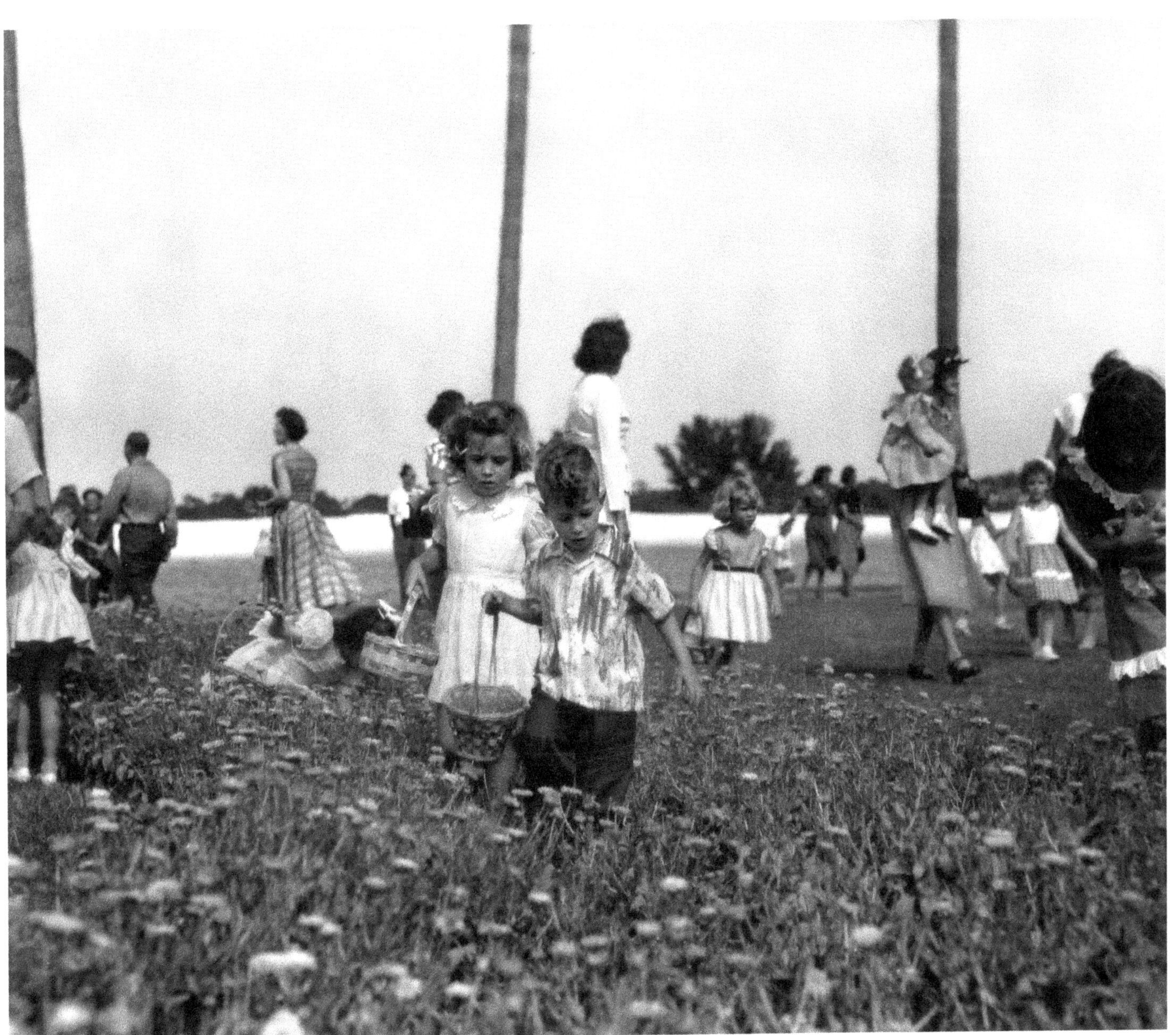

Dakar Motel owners decide to be innovative to catch the eye of tourists coming into town. This motel displayed a life-sized concrete zebra and advertised a swimming pool to welcome its guests.

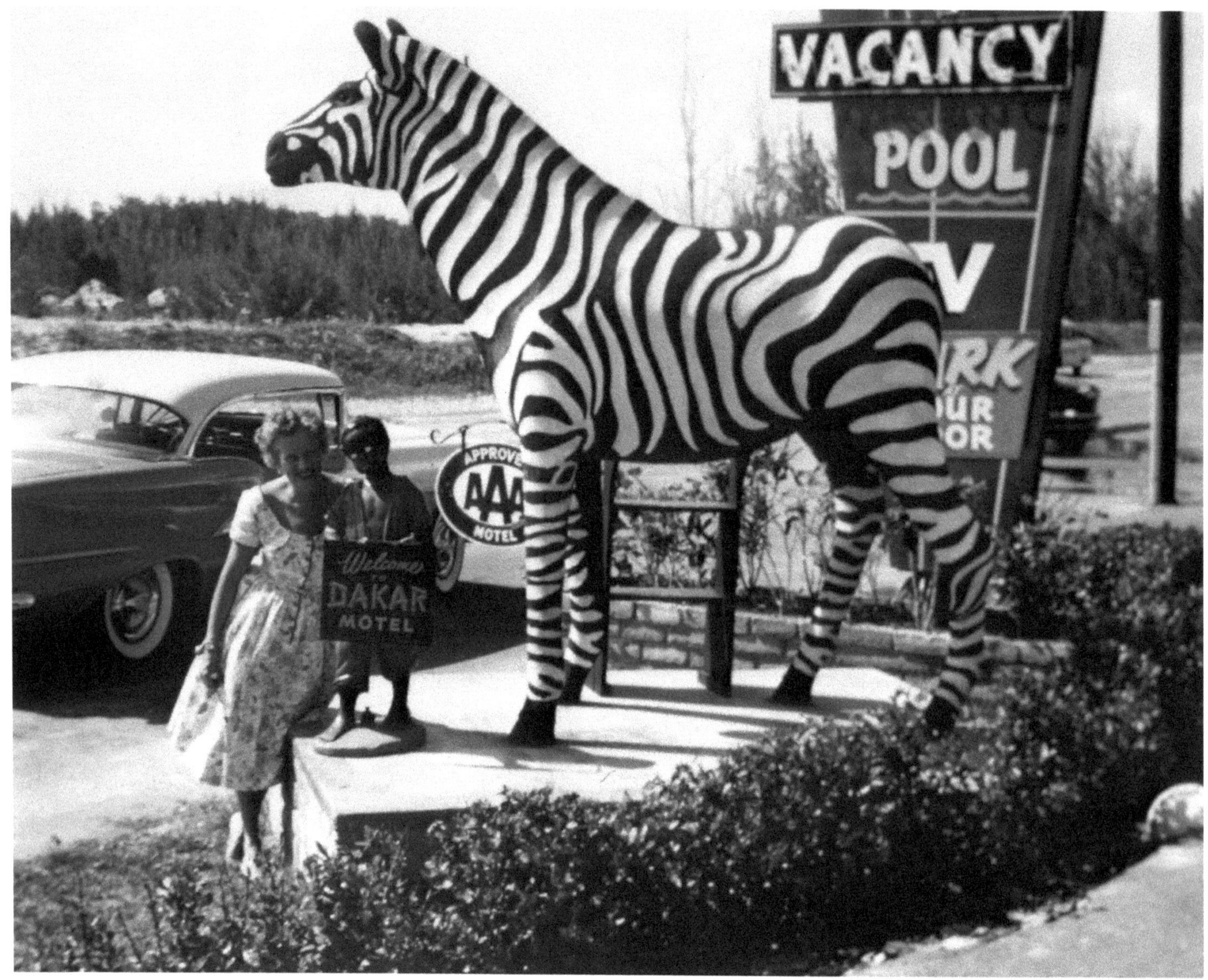

Race cars exit the north turn onto the back road course during the Grand National Race of February 26, 1956. Making the turn from the sandy beach to the hard pavement caused cars to slide sideways. Tim Flock was the winner and Billy Meyers took second place.

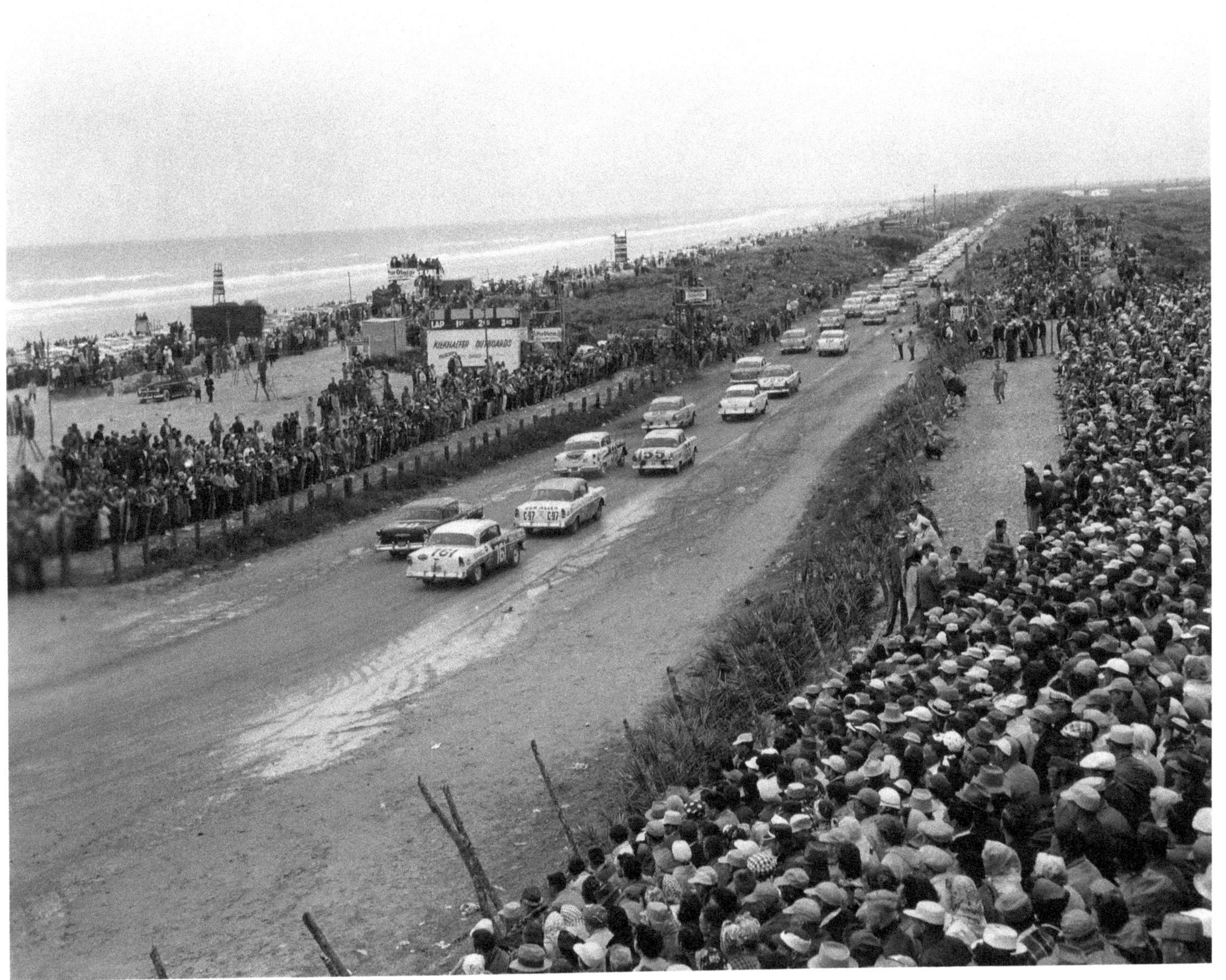

All race car entries had to conform to the rules of NASCAR. Cars were inspected at a drive-in theater north of Dunlawton Boulevard on Highway A1A. Overlooking the inspection here are Commissioner Cannonball Baker, Johnny Bruner, and Norris Friel. Race cars that did not meet the requirements were disqualified.

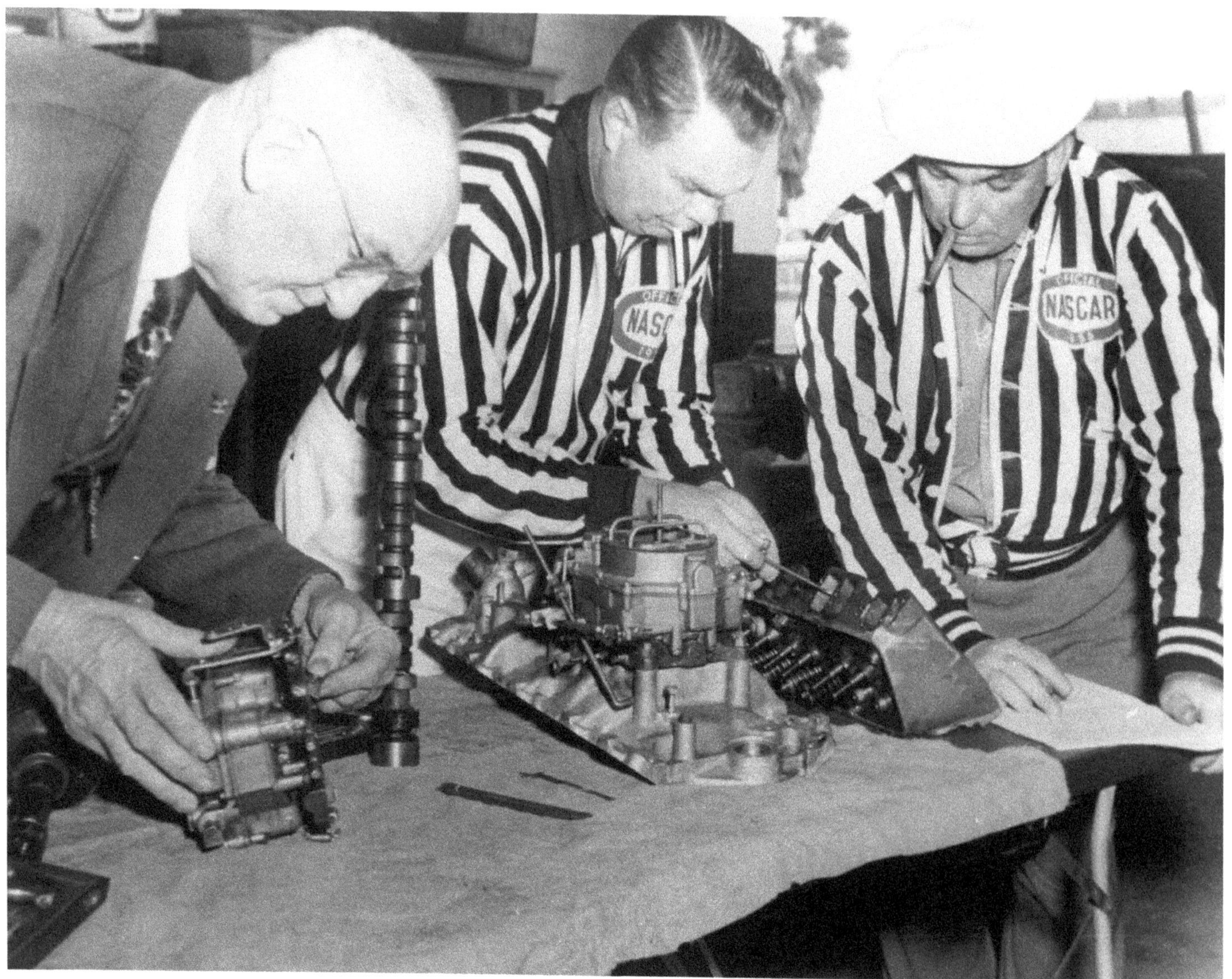

When this image was captured, pedestrians could cross from the boardwalk to a stairway on Main Street to the pier casino. The pier offered accommodations for ocean fishing in the daytime and entertainment at night at the pier casino dance hall. The pier was a place to observe the full length of the beach.

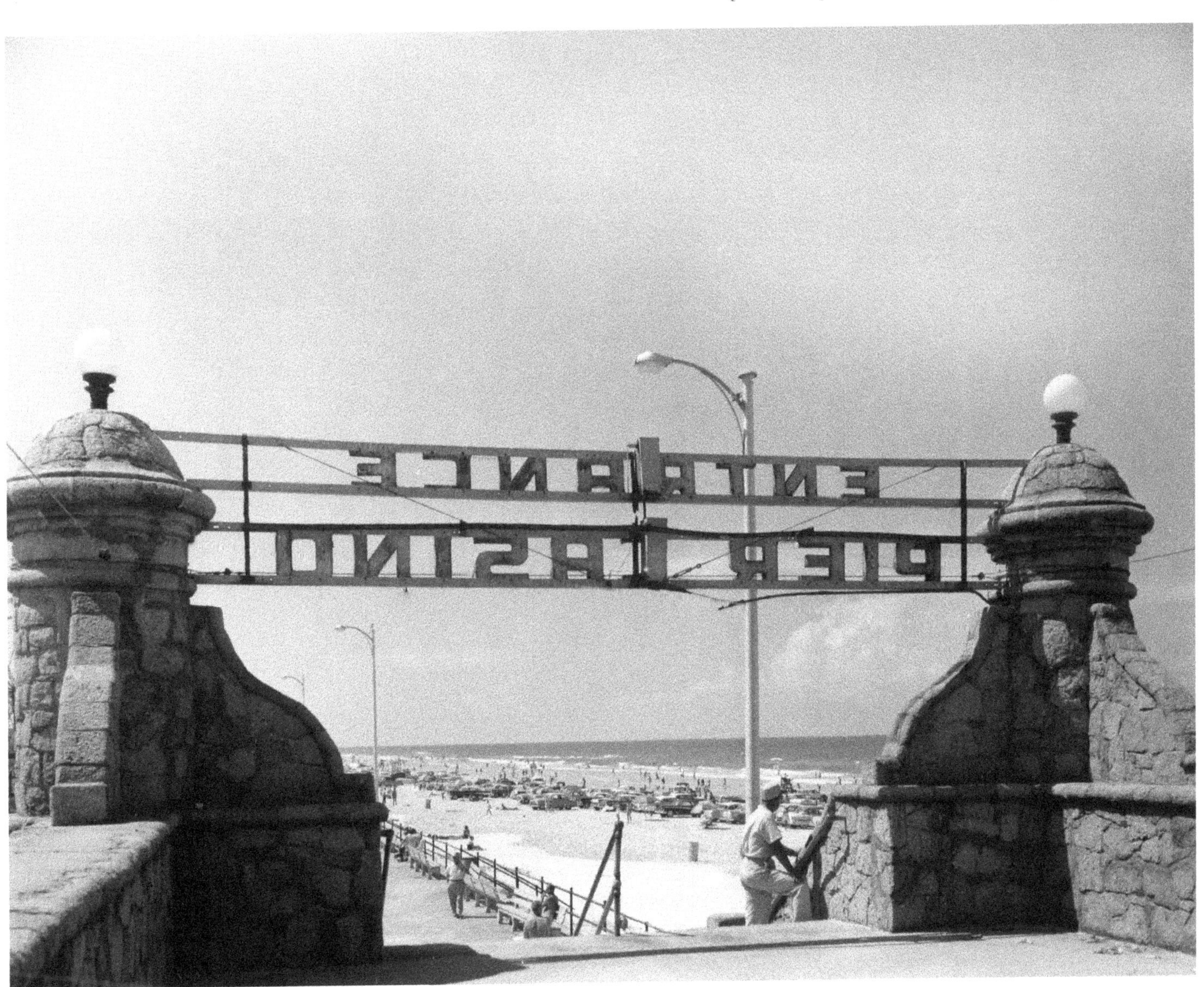

Tex Madsen, over 7 feet tall and from Texas, at one time ran a photography concession on the beach. For a small fee, beachgoers could sit astride a saddle on the back of Ferdinand the Bull and have their picture taken. His wife, Verna, continued the enterprise after her husband's death.

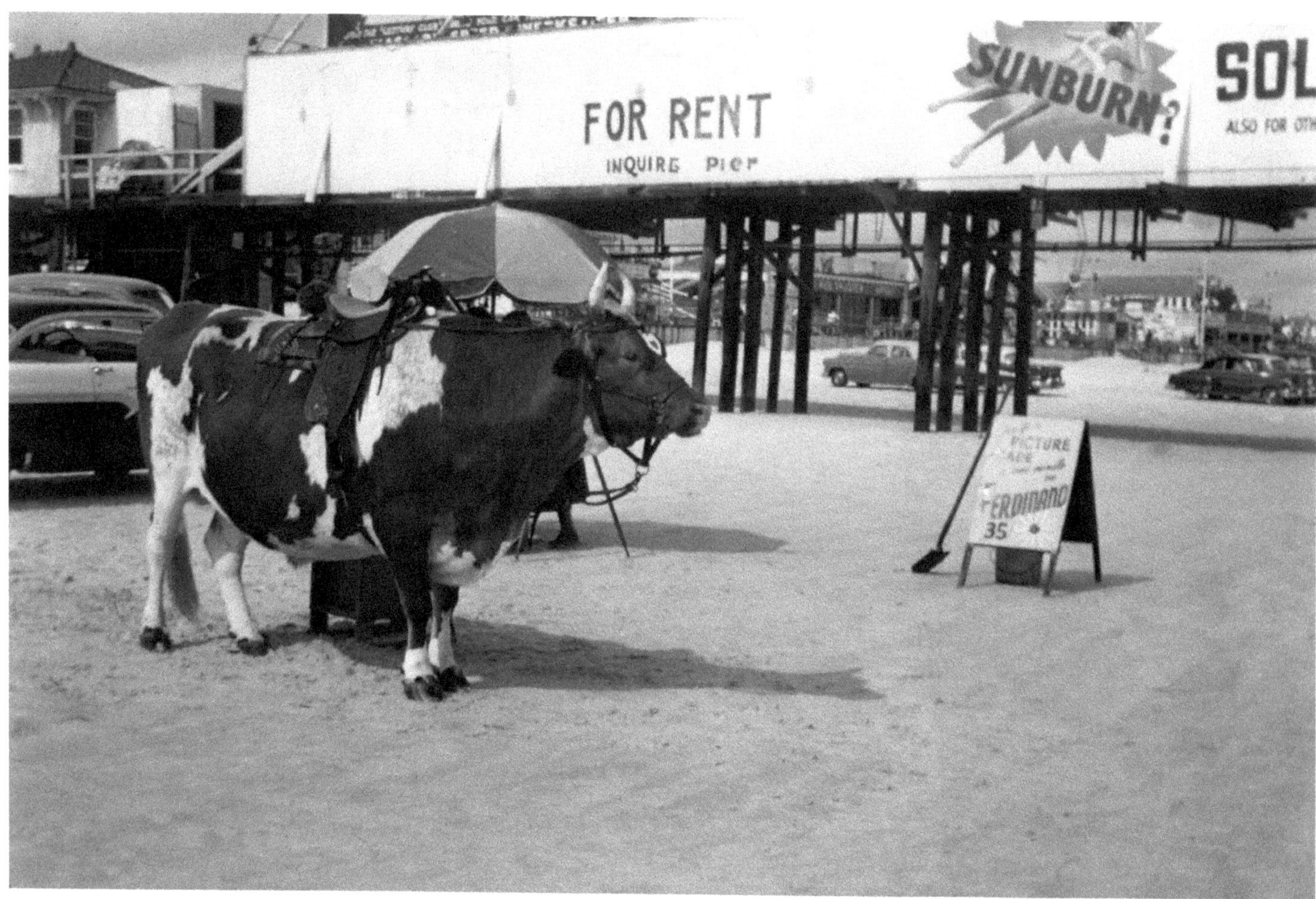

High school students receive the prestigious Gautier Good Government Award. These twelve students were from Volusia County, two of them from Mainland High School. Governor Collins and his cabinet members are seated at a table made by a Daytona Beach cabinet maker.

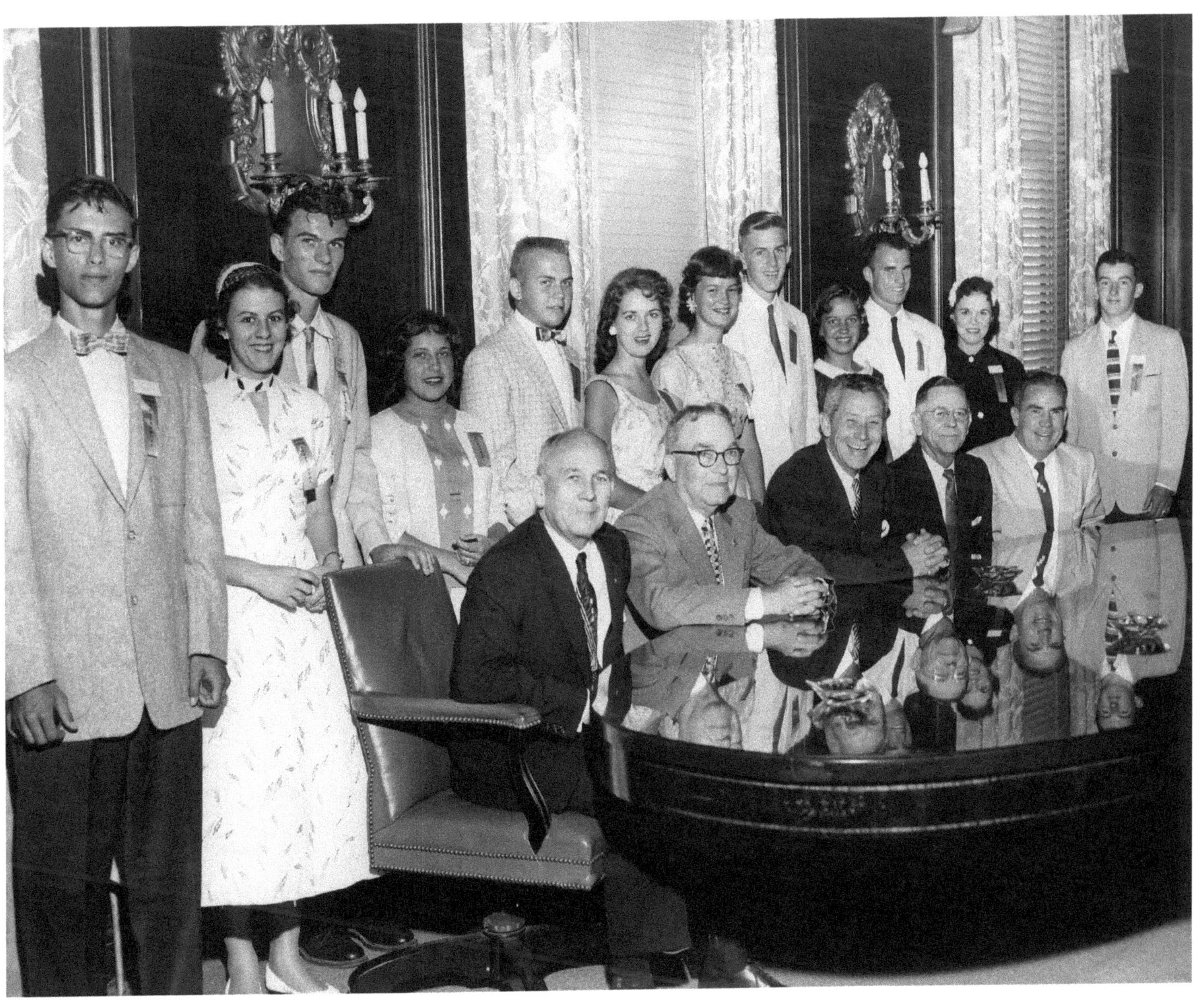

Notes on the Photographs

These notes, listed by page number, attempt to include all aspects known of the photographs. Each of the photographs is identified by the page number, photograph's title or description, photographer and collection, archive, and call or box number when applicable. Although every attempt was made to collect all available data, in some cases complete data was unavailable due to the age and condition of some of the photographs and records.

II **Beach Racing**
Florida State Archives
rc13545

VI **Firecracker 400**
Florida State Archives
c630055

X **145 South Beach Street**
Florida State Archives
rc08576

2 **Steam Sawmill**
Florida State Archives
rc16394

3 **Boat Construction**
Florida State Archives
rc16383

4 **Manley's Sawmill**
Florida State Archives
rc16392

5 **Steam Locomotive**
Florida State Archives
rc6067

6 **Colony House**
Florida State Archives
rc16381

7 **Thompson House**
Florida State Archives
rc12464

8 **Ocean Boulevard**
Florida State Archives
rc06727

9 **Ridgewood Avenune**
Florida State Archives
no34716

10 **Developing Beachside**
Florida State Archives
rc9728

11 **Yacht Club**
Florida State Archives
rc16391

12 **Kearing Pier**
Florida State Archives
rc9170

13 **Yacht Club and Pier**
Florida State Archives
rc16409

14 **First Car In Daytona**
Florida State Archives
rc16410

15 **South Bridge**
Florida State Archives
rc7626

16 **Waterside Hotel**
Florida State Archives
rc13165

17 **Beach Riding**
Florida State Archives
rc7068

18 **Post Office**
Florida State Archives
rc16387

19 **Beach Street**
Florida State Archives
no31175

20 **Jitney**
Florida State Archives
rc05157

21 **DuBois' Wife on Beach**
Florida State Archives
no38250

22 **South Beach Street**
Florida State Archives
no31177

23 **Engineering Convention**
Florida State Archives
no29824

24 **Wooden Pier**
Florida State Archives
cc297

25 **Rail Station**
Florida State Archives
rc04352

26 **Opera House**
Florida State Archives
rc16371

27 **Ocean Boulevard**
Florida State Archives
rc9056

28 **Ormond Beach**
Florida State Archives
rc10954

29 **Tree Lined Avenue**
Florida State Archives
pr02323

30 **The "Dixie"**
Florida State Archives
rc6943

31 **Burdine's Pharmacy**
Florida State Archives
rc6949

32 **Ormond Beach**
Florida State Archives
no41926

33 **The "Cherokee"**
Florida State Archives
rc16390

34 **The "Uncle Sam"**
Florida State Archives
rc4761

35 **Mary McCleod Bethune**
Florida State Archives
pr0788

36 **City Island**
Florida State Archives
rc9057

37 **Beach Visitors**
Florida State Archives
rc02758

38 **Sport Spectators**
Florida State Archives
rc-063

39 **Queen Anne Mansion**
Florida State Archives
rc12466

40 **Public Library**
Florida State Archives
rc13167

41 **To The Sawmill**
Florida State Archives
rc02742

42 **Beach Race**
Florida State Archives
rc7071

43 **Croker Wreck**
Florida State Archives
no41923

44 **Bethune's Students**
Florida State Archives
no41432

45 **Beach Street**
Florida State Archives
rc16361

46 **McDonald's Racecar**
Florida State Archives
rc5327

47 **Hotel Despland**
Florida State Archives
rc4705

48 **Turpentine**
Florida State Archives
cc897

51 **Fred Marriot**
Florida State Archives
no41920

52 **Main Street Bridge**
Florida State Archives
rc7521

53 **Fashionable Home**
Florida State Archives
pr02340

54 **Generations On Beach**
Florida State Archives
rc13501

56 **Main Street**
Florida State Archives
rc02834

57 **Organ Grinder**
Florida State Archives
rc13652

58 **Putnam House**
Florida State Archives
rc1743

59 **New Generator**
Florida State Archives
rc7651

60 **Beached Whales**
Florida State Archives
rc12083

61 **Winter Inn**
Florida State Archives
no29837

62 **Library And Jail**
Florida State Archives
no29859

63 **Dayona's Midway**
Florida State Archives
no31171

64 **Roxana**
Florida State Archives
no40786

65 **Ridgewood Avenue**
Florida State Archives
pr02326

66 **Future Main Street Pier**
Florida State Archives
rc16367

67 **Crowded Depot**
Florida State Archives
pr02328

68 **Haberdashery**
Florida State Archives
rc16403

69 **Hotchkiss Racer**
Florida State Archives
rc10417

70 **Fire Disaster**
Florida State Archives
no31169

71 **Wool Suit Bathers**
Florida State Archives
pr02333

72 **Carl Bates**
Florida State Archives
rc12773

73 **Despland Hotel**
Florida State Archives
rc07522

74 **Ladies On The Beach**
Florida State Archives
pr0233

75 **Future Loomis Street**
Florida State Archives
no29878

76 **Halifax Yacht Club**
Florida State Archives
rc16373

77 **Band Entertainment**
Florida State Archives
rc13174

78 **Curtiss' Aircraft**
Florida State Archives
rc11256

79 **Bethune Students**
Florida State Archives
no28175

80 **Oldfield At Ormond**
Florida State Archives
no041914

81 **Halifax River Ferry**
Florida State Archives
rc16389

82 Future Main Street
Florida State Archives
rc16366

83 Hotel Austin
Florida State Archives
no29813

84 Young Girls on Daytona
Florida State Archives
pr14025

85 First Halifax Bridge
Florida State Archives
no28462

86 Elks Clubhouse
Florida State Archives
no29500

87 Bethune In Faith Hall
Florida State Archives
pr000796

88 Bay Street School
Florida State Archives
pr023339

89 Daytona Trolley
Florida State Archives
rc07701

90 Race Car Clubhouse
Florida State Archives
rc16372

91 Miss Law's Flight
Florida State Archives
rc7964

92 Jenny Plane Crash
Florida State Archives
rc12767

93 Gables Hotel
Florida State Archives
rc07526

94 Johnson's Bicycle
Florida State Archives
rc13498

95 Beachgoers
Florida State Archives
no29468

96 Two Cars On Beach
Florida State Archives
no29478

97 Mr. Norwood
Florida State Archives
no29853

98 Norwood's Office
Florida State Archives
no29860

99 Burgoyne's Seaside
Florida State Archives
no29818

100 Gable Home
Florida State Archives
no29864

101 Pepper Family
Florida State Archives
ms25322

102 Group In The Surf
Florida State Archives
no29482

103 Seaplanes
Florida State Archives
pr00480

104 Indian Motorcycles
Florida State Archives
pr13972

105 Daytona Flying Club
Florida State Archives
rc15198

106 DePalma
Florida State Archives
no41916

108 Planes On Beach
Florida State Archives
no27962

109 Plane Crash
Florida State Archives
rc12772

110 Slot Machines
Florida State Archives
pr03969

111 Trip To Daytona
Florida State Archives
no27964

112 Halifax River
Florida State Archives
rc12467

113 People By The Pier
Florida State Archives
ms25317

114 Daytona Airport
Florida State Archives
no27976

115 Saint Mary's
Florida State Archives
pr02321

116 Beach Racers
Florida State Archives
no41974

117 Florida State Guard
Florida State Archives
no313198

118 Norwood's Family
Florida State Archives
no42734

119 Flying Circus
Florida State Archives
pr00465

120 Cody's Daredevils
Florida State Archives
rc12187

121 Confiscating Mash
Florida State Archives
rc13902

122 Clearing The Land
Florida State Archives
no29844

123 Wisconsin Special
Florida State Archives
no41959

124 Warm Winter Day
Florida State Archives
no029488

125 Despland Hotel
Florida State Archives
no29822

126 The Curtis Oriole
Florida State Archives
rc15183

127 Highlands Racecar
Florida State Archives
no41940

128 Tarpon Fishing
Florida State Archives
no29854

129 Highlands Subdivision
Florida State Archives
no29871

130 Scale Gimmick
Florida State Archives
no29874

131 **Highlands Promotion**
Florida State Archives
no9850

132 **Red's Place**
Florida State Archives
rc16369

133 **Hotel Morgan**
Florida State Archives
rc16396

134 **Beach Climate**
Florida State Archives
no28823

135 **Volusia Avenue**
Florida State Archives
rc16397

136 **Beach Traffic**
Florida State Archives
no29480

137 **Halifax Yacht Club**
Florida State Archives
no29872

138 **Beauty Contest**
Florida State Archives
no28821

139 **Beach Street**
Florida State Archives
rc16395

140 **Seaside Inn**
Florida State Archives
no29816

141 **Pepp's Pool**
Florida State Archives
no29474

142 **News Journal Building**
Florida State Archives
pr02316

143 **Northern Tourists**
Florida State Archives
no29852

144 **Kaye Don's Attempy**
Florida State Archives
rc00270

145 **Silver Bullet**
Florida State Archives
rc10436

146 **Shuffleboard Club**
Florida State Archives
no29496

147 **Sholtz Campaign**
Florida State Archives
no27176

148 **Sholtz And His Wife**
Florida State Archives
no27158

149 **Mr. Strapp**
Florida State Archives
pr14099

150 **Young People on Beach**
Florida State Archives
pr02310

151 **Shooter's Gun Club**
Florida State Archives
no29812

152 **National Airlines**
Florida State Archives
rc4827

153 **Shuffleboard Club**
Florida State Archives
pr02341

154 **Hotel Gilbertson**
Florida State Archives
no29838

155 **Daytona Beach**
Florida State Archives
rc7518

156 **Passenger Train**
Florida State Archives
rc29858

157 **Boardwalk Clock Tower**
Florida State Archives
ge1825a

158 **Daytona Beach Bandshed**
Florida State Archives
ge1827

159 **Casino On Beach Street**
Florida State Archives
rc16386

160 **Parade Of Cars**
Florida State Archives
pr0774

161 **Beach Park**
Florida State Archives
c005379

162 **Electric Beach Cars**
Florida State Archives
c005377

164 **Sailfish**
Florida State Archives
c06313

165 **Beach Trams**
Florida State Archives
c005346

166 **South Wall**
Florida State Archives
c005381

167 **Three Wheeled Cycles**
Florida State Archives
c002626

168 **Boss Of The Beach**
Florida State Archives
c002640

169 **Gil Ferrell**
Florida State Archives
c002655

170 **Bob Flock**
Florida State Archives
c002647

171 **Rayson Memorial Trophy**
Florida State Archives
c002641

172 **Measured Mile Board**
Florida State Archives
c002677

173 **Winter Tourists**
Florida State Archives
no29842

174 **Armistice Day**
Florida State Archives
c006680

175 **Machine Shop Area**
Florida State Archives
c10710

176 **Colony Resorts**
Florida State Archives
c10425

177 **Riverfront Park**
Florida State Archives
c10593

178 **Flamingo Shoe Co.**
Florida State Archives
c10704

179 **Henry Pierce**
Florida State Archives
c11338

180 **Beauty Contest**
Florida State Archives
c007898

181 **The "Duck"**
Florida State Archives
pr02346

182 **July Fourth**
Florida State Archives
c11277

183 **Lifeguard Stand**
Florida State Archives
c11328

184 **Beachgoers**
Florida State Archives
c11238

185 **Beauty Pageant**
Florida State Archives
c11301

186 **Sun And Sand Motel**
Florida State Archives
c13710

187 **Eleanro Roosevelt**
Florida State Archives
pr00791

188 **News Building**
Florida State Archives
pr02318

189 **Ponce Inlet Track**
Florida State Archives
c015959

190 **Grand National Race**
Florida State Archives
c015971

191 **Pit Area**
Florida State Archives
c015991

192 **Easter Services**
Florida State Archives
c17775

193 **Easter Egg Hunt**
Florida State Archives
c17907

194 **Dakar Motel**
Florida State Archives
pr02303

195 **Grand National Race**
Florida State Archives
c022795

196 **Car Inspections**
Florida State Archives
pr09095

197 **Pier Island**
Florida State Archives
c25522

198 **Ferdinand The Bull**
Florida State Archives
pr02298

199 **Governor Collins**
Florida State Archives
cv036007

HISTORIC PHOTOS OF DAYTONA BEACH

Daytona Beach is an American city quintessentially founded upon change. From its birth to the present, Daytona Beach has consistently built and reshaped its appearance, ideals, and industry. Through changing fortunes, Daytona Beach has continued to grow and prosper by overcoming adversity and maintaining the strong, independent culture of its citizens.

Historic Photos of Daytona Beach captures this journey through still photography selected from the finest archives. From Daytona Beach as a tourist destination to its role in motorcycle and car racing, *Historic Photos of Daytona Beach* follows life, government, education, and events throughout the city's history.

This volume captures unique and rare scenes through the lens of hundreds of historic photographs. Published in striking black and white, these images communicate historic events and everyday life of two centuries of people building a unique and prosperous city.

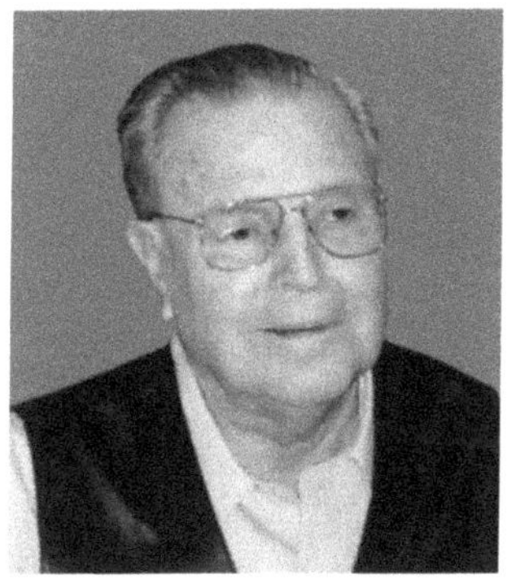

Harold D. Cardwell, Sr., is a retired Senior Rehabilitation Specialist with the Florida Department of Labor and Employment Security, Division of Blind Services. He is a lifelong resident of Volusia County and a graduate of Florida Technological University. During World War II he was assigned to the Atomic Bomb Project at Oak Ridge, Tennessee, and Los Alamos, New Mexico.

Mr. Cardwell is currently president of the Port Orange Historical Trust. He is a board member of the Florida Historical Society, the Halifax Historical Society, the Daytona Beach Historic Preservation Board, and the Volusia Anthropological Society. He is past president of the Florida Anthropological Society, and the Halifax Historical Society, and is active in many other state historical and anthropological organizations. Mr. Cardwell is the author of many journal articles on local history and has written a number of books on the history of Port Orange and Daytona Beach, Florida.

WWW.TURNERPUBLISHING.COM

www.ingramcontent.com/pod-product-compliance
Lightning Source LLC
LaVergne TN
LVHW060604110826
845154LV00003B/33